County and Nobility
in Norman Italy

County and Nobility in Norman Italy

Aristocratic Agency in the Kingdom of Sicily, 1130–1189

Hervin Fernández-Aceves

BLOOMSBURY ACADEMIC
LONDON • NEW YORK • OXFORD • NEW DELHI • SYDNEY

BLOOMSBURY ACADEMIC
Bloomsbury Publishing Plc
50 Bedford Square, London, WC1B 3DP, UK
1385 Broadway, New York, NY 10018, USA
29 Earlsfort Terrace, Dublin 2, Ireland

BLOOMSBURY, BLOOMSBURY ACADEMIC and the Diana logo are trademarks of
Bloomsbury Publishing Plc

First published in Great Britain 2020
This paperback edition published in 2022

Copyright © Hervin Fernández-Aceves 2020

Hervin Fernández-Aceves has asserted his right under the Copyright, Designs and Patents
Act, 1988, to be identified as Author of this work.

Cover design: Charlotte James
Cover image: "*Burgerbibliothek Bern, Cod. 120.II, f. 99r*". Image supplied
by Codices Electronici AG, www.ecodices.ch

All rights reserved. No part of this publication may be reproduced or transmitted
in any form or by any means, electronic or mechanical, including photocopying,
recording, or any information storage or retrieval system, without prior
permission in writing from the publishers.

Bloomsbury Publishing Plc does not have any control over, or responsibility for, any third-
party websites referred to or in this book. All internet addresses given in this book were
correct at the time of going to press. The author and publisher regret any inconvenience
caused if addresses have changed or sites have ceased to exist, but can accept no
responsibility for any such changes.

Every effort has been made to trace copyright holders and to obtain their permissions
for the use of copyright material. The publisher apologizes for any errors or omissions
and would be grateful if notified of any corrections that should be incorporated
in future reprints or editions of this book.

A catalogue record for this book is available from the British Library.

A catalog record for this book is available from the Library of Congress.

Library of Congress Control Number: 2020940857

ISBN: HB: 978-1-3501-3322-8
PB: 978-1-3502-0165-1
ePDF: 978-1-3501-3831-5
eBook: 978-1-3501-3833-9

Typeset by Deanta Global Publishing Services, Chennai, India

To find out more about our authors and books visit www.bloomsbury.com and
sign up for our newsletters.

*A mis padres,
Zaida y Rubén*

Contents

List of illustrations	viii
Preface	ix
Acknowledgements	x
List of abbreviations	xi
Introduction: Documenting Italo-Norman agency	1
1 The counts of Norman Italy before Roger II	13
2 The new kingdom's nobility and the creation of the south Italian counties	27
3 Leadership and opposition under the count of Loritello	59
4 Coalition and survival of the nobility	79
5 New spheres of comital action under Margaret's regency	105
6 Consolidated counties during the reign of William II	133
7 Beyond the county: The counts' new military and political role	167
Conclusions	179
Appendix 1: A note on the *Duana Baronum*	183
Appendix 2: Figures	185
Appendix 3: Maps	192
Appendix 4: Tables and diagrams	196
Notes	201
Bibliography	242
Index	259

Illustrations

Figures

1 Funerary inscription of Matilda, daughter of Count Sylvester of Marsico 185
2 Tancred's triumphant entry into Palermo 186
3 Address of Count Richard of Acerra and the archbishop of Salerno to the Neapolitans 187
4 Count Richard of Acerra and a band of *milites* 188
5 Lead seal of Count Roger of Andria 189
6 Count Roger of Andria 190

Maps

1 The Norman kingdom of Sicily (1130–89) 192
2 Abbeys and churches involved in comital activities and transactions 194

Tables and diagrams

Chronological Table. The Counties of Apulia, Capua and Calabria (1130–89) 196
Genealogical Network. Comital Kinship in the Norman Kingdom of Sicily (1137–89) 198

Preface

This monograph offers a rounded account of the local ruling elite in mainland south Italy during the first dynasty of the Sicilian kingdom. It does so through a chronological, wide-ranging exploration of the counts' activities, and an in-depth analysis of both the role the counts played during the development of the kingdom's aristocracy and the function the county acquired in the establishment of social control on the mainland. This is supported by an extensive and detailed prosopographical survey of the vast relevant diplomatic material, both edited and unedited, combined with a comparison of the diverse available narrative sources, both local and external.

The study has two central objectives: The first is to uncover the composition of the peninsular upper nobility and its continuities and discontinuities, by revealing how lordships were reorganized through the appointment and confirmation of counts, the total number of counties after this reorganization, and the transactions and major events in which the counts were involved throughout the kingdom's Norman period. The second is to interpret the extent of the upper aristocracy's capacity to act self-reliantly, by explaining how the counts operated and exercised their own authority between other economic and political agents, such as lesser barons, royal officials and ecclesiastical institutions.

I argue that the creation of the kingdom of Sicily did not hinder the development of the nobility's leadership in southern Italy, but, in fact, the Sicilian monarchy relied on the county as both a military cluster and an economic unit, and, eventually, on the counts' agency, in order to keep the realm united and exercise effective control over the mainland provinces – especially in Apulia and the Terra di Lavoro. Such a finding should encourage further revision of the traditional interpretation of the kingdom's social mechanisms for military mobilization, administration of justice and political stability. By emphasizing the importance of the comital rank and the changeability and endurance of the members or the peninsular nobility, this study underlines the complexity of medieval, south Italian societies and the intersecting agencies which allowed the kingdom of Sicily to be a viable polity.

Acknowledgements

The completion of this book would not have been possible without the support and assistance of many colleagues, friends and family members. A few of these have made such a contribution that it is my duty and pleasure to recognize them in particular.

It has been a privilege to be a part of the cadre of students that came together under the supervision of Graham A. Loud; his knowledge, direction and resources have been an invaluable pillar upon which I was able to conduct my research. I am very grateful also to Isabelle Bolognese, Francesca Petrizzo, Daniele Morossi and James Hill for their advice, exchange of opinions and debate. Also, I regularly benefited from the efficacy, kindness and patience of the staff of the Brotherton Library, and especially that of the Documentary Supply Service – all of whom provided invaluable support. Among the esteemed and dear company that I found in Leeds I must recognize Otávio Luiz Vieira Pinto, Ioannis Papadopoulos, Mike Burrows, Cătălin Țăranu, Christian Aragón Briceño, Lourdes Parra and Martín Lima for their companionship; I especially thank Otávio and Mike for kindly commenting on drafts of this thesis. Great colleagues, but even greater friends. I will miss your sincere support and our enjoyable tertulias.

This entire research would not have been possible without the very generous funding of the University of Leeds's research scholarship, and the overseas programme of the National Council for Science and Technology (CONACYT – Mexico). I am keenly aware of how fortunate and privileged I was to be given their support. Preparation for this book was also carried over a number of months at the British School at Rome, as an award-holder. To them, all my gratitude.

Beyond the confines of the University of Leeds, I must also attribute special thanks to my friends Antonella Furno and Paola Massa who provided me with very valuable material and advice. I am likewise indebted to Piero Scatizzi and Elia Mariano, archivists of the Biblioteca S. Scolastica in Subiaco, for their assistance. Also, I am greatly thankful to Hiroshi Takayama, Paul Oldfield, Markus Krumm, Alan Murray and Antonio Macchione, for sharing their work and opinions with me and providing useful suggestions. I also thank my friend and paisana Isell Chavarin, who facilitated my access to resources from the University of S. Barbara, California. I am especially grateful to Alex Metcalfe, for his encouragement, guidance, generosity and kindness. Finally, I must devote special thanks to Kate Solomon, who not only helped me correcting my English but also was a fountain of patience and support.

My most personal thanks are for my family and friends from 'back home'. Both my parents and my sister Chantal, all of whom I deeply love, have been greatly supportive and caring. They know how important they all are.

Abbreviations

Actes de Gargano	*Les actes de l'Abbaye de Cava concernant le Gargano (1086–1370)*, ed. Jean M. Martin, Cod. Dipl. Pugliese, 32 (Bari: Società di storia patria per la Puglia, 1994)
Al. Tel.	*Alexandri Telesini abbatis Ystoria Rogerii regis Sicilie, Calabrie atque Apulie*, ed. by Ludovico De Nava, FSI, 112 (Rome: Istituto storico italiano per il Medio Evo, 1991)
Annales Casinensis	*Annales Casinenses*, ed. by Georg H. Pertz, MGH SS, 19 (Hanover: Hahn, 1866)
Annales Ceccanenses	*Annales Ceccanenses*, ed. by Georg H. Pertz, MGH SS, 19 (Hanover: Hahn, 1866)
Annalista Saxo	*Die Reichschronik des Annalista Saxo*, ed by Klaus Nass, MGH SS, 37 (Hanover: Hahn, 2006)
ASPN	Archivio Storico per le Province Napoletane
Benevento	Archivio Storico Pronviciale di Benevento, Museo del Sannio
Catalogus Baronum	*Catalogus Baronum*, ed. by Evelyn M. Jamison, FSI, 11 (Rome: Istituto storico italiano per il Medio Evo, 1972)
Carte di Molfetta	*Le carte di Molfetta (1076–1309)*, ed. by Francesco Carabellese, Cod. Dipl. Barese, 7 (Bari: Levante, 1912)
Cartulaire de Sculgola	*Le cartulaire de S. Matteo di Sculgola en Capitanate (Registro d'instrumenti di S. Maria del Gualdo 1177–1239)*, ed. by Jean M. Martin, 2 vols, Cod. Dipl. Pugliese, 30 (Bari: Società di storia patria per la Puglia, 1987)
Cava	Archivio della badia della Santissima Trinità, Cava dei Tirreni
Chartes de Troia	*Les chartes de Troia. Édition et étude critique des plus anciens documents conservés à l'Archivio Capitolare. I (1024–1266)*, ed. by Jean M. Martin, Cod. Dipl. Pugliese, 21 (Bari: Società di storia patria per la Puglia, 1976)

Choniates	*Nicetae Choniatae Historia*, ed. by Jan L. Dieten, 2 vols, Corpus fontium historiae Byzantinae, 11 (Berlin: Walter de Gruyter, 1975), I
Chron. Cas.	*Chronica Monasterii Casinensis*, ed. by Hartmut Hoffmann, MGH SS, 34 (Hanover: Hahn, 1980)
Chron. Casauriense	*Chronicon Casauriense, auctore Iohanne Berardi [Liber instrumentorum seu chronicorum monasterii Casauriensis]*, ed. by Ludovico A. Muratori, RIS, 2 (Milan: Societas Palatina, 1726)
Chron. de Carpineto	*Alexandri Monachi Chronicorum liber Monasterii Sancti Bartholomei de Carpineto*, ed. by Berardo Pio (Rome: Istituto storico italiano per il Medio Evo, 2001)
Chron. de Ferraria	*Ignoti Monachi Cisterciensis S. Mariae de Ferraria Chronica et Ryccardi de Sancto Germano Chronica Priora*, ed. by Georg H. Pertz and A. Gaudenzi (Naples: F. Giannini, 1888)
Chron. S. Sophiae	*Chronicon Sanctae Sophiae: cod. Vat. Lat. 4939*, ed. by Jean M. Martin, 2 vols (Rome: Istituto storico italiano per il Medio Evo, 2000), II
Cod. Dipl. Aversa	*Codice diplomatico normanno di Aversa*, ed. by Alfonso Gallo (Naples: Luigi Lubrano, 1926)
Cod. Dipl. Barese	*Codice diplomatico barese*, 19 vols
Cod. Dipl. Cajetanus	*Codex Diplomaticus Cajetanus*, 2 vols (Montecassino: Abbey of Montecassino, 1890), II
Cod. Dipl. Molisano	*Codice diplomatico molisano (964–1349)*, ed. by Bruno Figliuolo and Rosaria Pilone (Campobasso: Palladino, 2013)
Cod. Dipl. Pugliese	*Codice diplomatico pugliese* (Continuation of *Cod. Dipl. Barese*)
Cod. Dipl. Tremiti	*Codice diplomatico del Monastero Benedettino di S. Maria di Tremiti: 1005–1237*, ed. by Armando Petrucci, 3 vols. FSI, 98 (Rome: Istituto storico italiano per il Medio Evo, 1960), III
Cod. Dipl. Verginiano	*Cod. Dipl. Verginiano*, ed. by Placido M. Tropeano, 13 vols (Montevergine: Edizioni Padri Benedettini, 1977–2001)
Falcandus	*De rebus circa regni Siciliae curiam gestis Epistola ad Petrum de desolatione Siciliae*, ed. by Edoardo D'Angelo (Florence: Sismel, 2014)

Falco	*Falcone di Benevento. Chronicon Beneventanum: città e feudi nell'Italia dei normanni*, ed. by Edoardo D'Angelo (Florence: Edizioni del Galluzzo, 1998)
FSI	Fonti per la storia d'Italia
Italia Sacra	*Italia sacra sive de Episcopis Italiae*, ed. by Ferdinando Ughelli and Nicolò Coleti, 2nd edn, 10 vols (Venice: S. Coleti, 1717–1721)
Kinnamos	*Ioannis Cinnami [Kinnamoi] epitome rerum ab Ioanne et Alexio Comnenis gestarum*, ed. by Augustus Meineke, Corpus Scriptorum Historiae Byzantinae, 26 (Bonn: Weber, 1836)
Malaterra	*De rebus gestis Rogerii Calabriae et Siciliae comitis et Roberti Guiscardi ducis fratris eius, auctore Gaufredo Malaterra*, ed. by Ernesto Pontieri, RIS, 5.1 (Bologna: N. Zanichelli, 1928)
MGH	Monumenta Germaniae Historica, following the usual conventions, e.g. SS = Scriptores
Necrologio Cas.	*I Necrologi Cassinesi. I Il Necrologio del Cod. Cassinese 47*, ed. by Mauro Inguanez, FSI, 83 (Roma: Istituto storico italiano per il Medio Evo, 1941)
Necrologio di S. Matteo	*Necrologio del Liber confratrum di S. Matteo di Salerno*, ed. by Carlo A. Garufi, FSI, 56 (Rome: Istituto storico italiano per il Medio Evo, 1922)
PBSR	*Papers of the British School at Rome*
Pergamene del Duomo di Bari	*Le pergamene del Duomo di Bari (952–1264)*, ed. by Francesco Nitti di Vito, Cod. Dipl. Barese, 1 (Trani: V. Vecchi, 1897)
Pergamene di Barletta	*Le pergamene di Barletta, archivio capitolare (897–1285)*, ed. by Francesco Nitti di Vito, Cod. Dipl. Barese, 8 (Trani: V. Vecchi, 1914)
Pergamene di Capua	*Le pergamene di Capua*, ed. by Jole Mazzoleni, 3 vols (Naples: Università degli Studi di Napoli, 1957), I
Pergamene di Conversano	*Le pergamene di Conversano (901–1265)*, ed. by Giuseppe Coniglio, Cod. Dipl. Pugliese, 20 (Bari: Società di storia patria per la Puglia, 1975)
Pergamene di S. Nicola di Bari	*Le pergamene di S. Nicola di Bari. Periodo normanno (1075–1194)*, ed. by Francesco Nitti di Vito, Cod. Dipl. Barese, 5 (Bari: V. Vecchi, 1900)

Pergamene di Salerno	*Le pergamene dell'archivio diocesano di Salerno (841–1193)*, ed. by Anna Giordano (Salerno: Laveglia & Carlone, 2015)
Pergamene di Terlizzi	*Le pergamene della Cattedrale di Terlizzi (971–1300)*, ed. by Francesco Carabellese, Cod. Dipl. Barese, 3 (Bari: Commisione provinciale di archeologia e storia patria, 1899)
QFIAB	*Quellen und Forschungen aus italienischen Archiven und Bibliotheken*
Reg. Neap. Arch. Mon.	*Regii Neapolitam Archivii Monumenta*, 6 vols (Naples: Equitis G. Nobile, 1854–1861)
RIS	Rerum Italicarum Scriptores
Roger II Diplomata	*Rogerii II. Regis Diplomata Latina*, ed. by Carlrichard Brühl, Codex Diplomaticus Regni Siciliae, 2 (Cologne: Böhlau, 1987)
Romuald	*Romualdi Salernitani Chronicon*, ed. by Carlo A. Garufi, 2nd edn, RIS, 7 (Città di Castello: S. Lapi, 1935)
Sicilia Sacra	*Sicilia sacra disquisitionibus, et notitiis illustrata*, ed. by Rocco Pirri, 3rd ed, 2 vols (Palermo: Haeredes Petri Coppulae, 173)
Tyrants	*The History of the Tyrants of Sicily by 'Hugo Falcandus', 1154–69*, trans. by Graham A. Loud and Thomas Wiedemann (Manchester: Manchester University Press, 1998)
William I Diplomata	*Guillelmi I. Regis Diplomata*, ed. by Horst Enzensberger, Codex Diplomaticus Regni Siciliae, 3 (Cologne: Böhlau, 1996)
William II Diplomata	'Guillelmi II. Regis Siciliae Diplomata 1166–1189', ed. by Horst Enzensberger, 31 March 2016, <http://www.hist-hh.uni-bamberg.de/WilhelmII/index.html>
William of Apulia	*Guillaume de Pouille. La Geste de Robert Guiscard*, ed. and trans. by Marguerite Mathieu (Palermo: Istituto Siciliano di Studi Bizantini e Neoellenici, 1961)
William of Tyre	*Willelmi Tyrensis Archiepiscopi Chronicon*, ed. by Robert B. Huygens, 2 vols, Corpus christianorum, 63 (Turnhout: Brepols, 1986), II

Introduction

Documenting Italo-Norman agency

Although Norman Italy has caught the attention of many English-speaking scholars in the last decades, they have so far failed to adequately cover a crucial component of its history: the composition and role of its nobility. Trapped between the agency of characters, such as Robert Guiscard and Roger II, and a structuralist tradition that has forced research into certain avenues of study, such as long-duration processes of civic identity and rural life, modern scholarship has left the upper aristocracy of southern Italy a somewhat marginalized group.

Errico Cuozzo, one of the most renowned scholars in the field, had by 1985 already identified one of the most important challenges facing current scholarship. In his exploration of the origin and development of the county of Montescaglioso, Cuozzo claimed that the county of the Norman Kingdom in Italy had not been subject to systematic research, and that the few researchers occupied with the matter – himself included – had done so in an indirect and episodic manner, limited to piecing together the biographical and prosopographical data of some specific counts and baronial families.[1] Despite Cuozzo's extensive work, this challenge remains to this day. His attempts to disentangle the fragmented and intricate diplomatic evidence have resulted in an invaluable collection of material, yet a wide-ranging study of all the *exempla* of counts and counties under the Norman monarchy is still missing.

It is only with a systematic examination of the comital class and the documented activities of its members that an accurate identification of the original south Italian counties and a synchronic analysis of the nobility's social capacity can be conducted. We are yet to fully understand these important lords, and the sources lend themselves better to this than to understanding the lesser aristocracy, which included landholding knights and barons, and other lower social strata. At that time, public-record-keeping was not yet a generalized and systematized practice, so the vast majority of the surviving documents relate to the estates of ecclesiastical foundations or prominent aristocratic families whose political importance was maintained in the following centuries. It is therefore impossible to reconstruct the entire edifice of the aristocracy from its individual building blocks, and the structures of society are wrapped in a fog almost impossible to clear. Nevertheless, the available data on the upper nobility allows us to overcome this by reaching a better understanding of the social interactions of this group and identifying the capacity for action of its components. To do so, I propose neither a top-down examination of political hierarchies nor a bottom-up study of social structures; instead, I will perform a comprehensive and detailed dissection of the activities and capabilities of a group apparently subdued by a new monarchy but positioned high enough for their members to be identifiable and consistently documented. To reach this aim, the study stands on one key pillar: a prosopographical exploration of the counts who were made, confirmed and displaced under the first dynasty of the kingdom of Sicily.

I now present the epistemological reflection and methodological definitions upon which this work is based.

A contribution to current Italo-Norman historiography

To build a sound social interpretation it is necessary to first set the foundations. For Norman Italy, a great deal of prosopographical work was necessary before beginning to analyse the whole region's social strata, or even to discuss modern historiography. In recent decades, historians have started to explore the less hierarchical relationships through which collectives, active in medieval communities, were embodied: for example, and to mention just a few, Skinner, Drell, Metcalfe and Oldfield.[2] These approaches have relied on both a more careful understanding of the sociological implications of the object of study and a reconsideration of classic socio-economic structuralism.

Historians have traditionally called this period 'anarchical' or 'feudal', but recently scholars have begun to look at the various ways in which people in this decentralized society transacted their social interactions. Indeed, the predominant theory which still informs the thought of both historians and archaeologists – unconsciously or not – is French structuralism. An example of this trend has been the fixation with 'feudalism'. From the foundational works of Bloch and Cahen to the recent monograph by Carocci, researchers have continued to focus on the systematization of the 'feudal relationship', with its critiques of landholding, lordship and settlement patterns.[3] Structuralist thinking has proved a useful tool, but it has also had an important conditioning and distorting effect on our assumptions, preconceptions and interpretations. This is not least because the supposed structures of lordship and settlement nucleation have become the model of choice for explaining historical representations of core–periphery systems: society and power, urbanization and urban communities, the rural economy and the diverse arrangements of the countryside. However, structuralism in general still provides a bottom-up model for societal formation which seeks to explain economic transformation, acculturation and, ultimately, broader processes of social change as derived from a putative *incastellamento* and 'feudal' movement of localized lordship. While this can be helpful, the diplomatic evidence for southern Italy, at least in the twelfth century, does not portray a uniform or defined process of land acquisition and 'ownership'.[4]

The unclear pre-modern definition of ownership, nevertheless, does not mean that grants of lands or other transactions were meaningless. Every donation conveyed a significance that was not only economic but also enhanced by an array of ideological and political mechanisms. The territorial holdings and economic privileges that these transactions concerned appear to remain tied to their original tenants, granted away and then taken back, exchanged, redefined to then be claimed or relinquished again.[5] This fluid back and forth could last for several generations of barons, and the changes in the upper social echelon do not appear to have obstructed it; the higher aristocracy seem to have consolidated their roles as territorial leaders by mediating the complexity caused by a mutable understanding of land ownership. It is clear therefore that it is wrong to impose our own notions of property on earlier periods. A more careful reading, not bound by the traditional legal notions common in continental historiography, can help shatter the chains of our modern mental constructs, and allow the sources to take their own shape. I present here an alternative to assuming the modern, Western preconception of property that has forced scholarship to see land tenure either as allodial – owned outright or as a freehold – or as 'feudal'. I offer a more balanced view of so-called feudal ties in southern Italy in the twelfth century, advocating that medieval communities and local authorities were grounded in this case on a grid of autochthonous notions, where fluidity and multiplicity of usage was the rule rather than the exception.[6]

The emphasis placed on state, state-formation, kingship and structures of authority, as well as administrative 'systems' in the kingdom of Sicily, for instance by Jamison, Marongiu, Takayama and Johns, is no less problematic.[7] The so-called royal assembly of Silva Marca has become, for example, an almost undeniable fact adopted by many scholars. As suggested by Jamison and advocated by Cuozzo, this assumes the existence of a constitutional assembly at which King Roger gathered all the men of the realm in 1142 at Silva Marca to introduce a new central administrative system for the entire kingdom, which allegedly included the establishment of a regular military service, the creation and reorganization of counties and the introduction of 'feudalism'.[8] This premise, however, raises fundamental questions on the chronology of the south Italian counties and the documented political and military role played by the counts.

Who made up the ruling class of the new kingdom in southern Italy? The reduced group of royal appointees and commanders or an aristocracy integrated by a coherent, albeit diverse and complex, group of powerful landholders and local overlords? After the kingdom's creation and almost ten years of civil war, there was no actual discernible, fixed form of central authority that would embed the higher nobility within an established administration. The diverse royal functionaries attested in the surviving documentation appear to keep mutating, and the control exercised by the royal regime would only start to consolidate and be widely documented on the basis of the actual role played by the peninsular nobility and local lords. The dominant social force at the local level was represented by the group of major landholders and overlords. The 'royal state', as it existed at least in the peninsular provinces, consisted of the image of a recurrently absent monarch, a scattered staff of justiciars, constables and chamberlains, and a mobile court of the king's justice (which the king and his entourage could attend, if he was on the mainland) that appeared at itinerant provincial assemblies. However, one of the most important studies on this topic repeatedly speaks of 'administrative systems' at work in the 'central government' in capital cities – Palermo in Sicily and Salerno on the mainland.[9] Furthermore, a recent 800-page monograph that deals with such state-and-society history has been conceived in exactly the same tradition;[10] one reviewer politely concluded that 'this great history book lacks further reflection in anthropology and sociology'.[11] The importance of such state-driven views of structures and systems has been exaggerated, inviting thus both a historical and historiographical reconsideration of the available evidence and, other, dismissed social actors. The Italo-Norman counts of the Sicilian kingdom provide a precise example of a societal group whose importance has been disregarded in modern scholarship, commonly placed at the margins of a central political structure preconceived as highly administrative and subordinating. I argue instead that in the historical study of society and power, it is necessary to engage in a discussion of the documented interactions and interconnectivity that make up social phenomena, therefore providing a nuanced account of the composition and capacity of a predominant societal group to act autonomously.

The snapshots in time and connections presented here do not necessarily imply the total hierarchy or property of the Italo-Norman nobility. Instead of modelling hierarchies of lords and vassals, my exploration focuses on the morphing positions and community groups that formed the upper layers of society under the Sicilian kingdom. The survey and hypotheses constructed by my research map the intersections of social agents of political, ideological, economic and military control, and the upper aristocracy in the south Italian mainland.[12] Among other things, the studied relationships were revealed, created, confirmed and supported through charters. The legal proceedings and the guarantees included in the charters acted as a bond between the territorial leaders and the lords of the land. The charters in which the counts are attested reflect the bonding through which social control was exercised in the peninsular domains.

The recorded economic and legal interactions functioned to define and validate the individual's role and enforce social cohesion. The secular use of monastic donations and judicial records, the military and monetary fees demanded, and the flux of property and wealth created a grid of interactions and relationships. I label this grid 'social', and not merely 'secular', 'political' or 'economic', because of the importance of the relationship that affirmed or created transactions, a bond that functioned as the actual channel through which social control – political, ideological, economic or military – could be exercised and implemented. The mechanisms of control expressed by charters and other documental records go beyond their transactional function due to the presence of extra-economic and legal factors: specific frameworks, active enough that political activity maintains its ability to preserve social order. In other words, social relations are maintained within a political shell, a wrap of sorts that gave coherence to the count's transactions and allowed them to exercise their own activities and role, connecting thus a society often seen as centrally oppressed and locally divided. In this way, my exploration of the counts' agency revolves around how power was distributed among the upper Italo-Norman aristocracy and how this distribution developed.

I should also clarify the extent of this study's contribution. Although at times it invites comparison with different realities, be that the contemporary societies of Normandy, England and the Latin East, or the socio-institutional vestiges of the Carolingian and Byzantine empires, this raises problems of interpretation beyond the scope of this book. Some discussion and contextualization are provided when particular common areas are identified, but this is neither a work that aims to argue assumptions of a 'pan-Norman' culture nor a comparative exploration of other medieval and European aristocracies. I expect, however, that the findings and arguments presented here will serve as a basis for further, more nuanced comparative studies, so that the Italo-Norman nobility is considered in its own terms, more integrally and carefully.

The observatory: Timescale, sources and diplomatic evidence

The vast and relatively accessible quantity of material available forced certain limitations on the study, for obvious reasons of space. Its chronological scope has been chosen for a number of reasons; it gives a broad enough timescale to discern relevant continuities and disruptions, while not being so broad as to prevent in-depth analysis. Also, a considerably rich corpus of charters survives for twelfth-century southern Italy, along with a series of chronicles and accounts composed by foreign and native contemporary witnesses. Last but not least is the fact that the creation of the Sicilian monarchy and its first dynasty was a watershed in southern Italy's history, after which the local social and political arrangements were developed and defined. However, this book goes beyond the kingdom's creation and Roger II's reign and connects these episodes to the entire period of the Norman dynasty.

A diverse range of chronicles, histories and other narrative accounts have been employed. The chronicles composed by Alexander of Telese and Falco, a notary of Benevento, in the first half of the twelfth century contribute vital material on the early decades before and after the creation of the kingdom of Sicily, a transformative period when the peninsular nobility changed greatly. Alexander's work stops in 1135, while Falco's chronicle in its present, incomplete, form ends in 1140, although it seems to have been continued until 1144; a rudimentary version of the last section has survived in the anonymous chronicle of Santa Maria of Ferraria in Vairano Patenora.[13] This chronicle, together with the also anonymous annals of the abbeys of Montecassino (*Annales Casinenses*) and Fossanova in Ceccano (*Annales Ceccanenses*), were written in the late twelfth and early thirteenth centuries, and provide a useful view of key events and activities in the northwestern border of the realm, which confirm both the changes in the nobility of the Terra di Lavoro and some of the military operations the kingdom was involved in.

One of the most important narrative sources is the history attributed to the so-called Hugo Falcandus (henceforth Pseudo-Falcandus), which provides a vivid and detailed account of the political machinations and rebellions under William I and the first years of William II (1154–69). Although the identity of this author remains a mystery, Pseudo-Falcandus's testimony has become, for better or worse, key to understanding the kingdom of Sicily's nobility and *curia regis* in the second half of the twelfth century – this *curia*, sometimes translated as 'court' or council, was the political body comprised of the king and his ministers and offices. Likewise, the Salernitan chronicle, attributed to Romuald Guarna, archbishop of Salerno, offers a rich and crucial testimony for both the external events that surrounded southern Italy from a pan-European scope, and the kingdom's internal politics, a useful tool for checking and comparing with Pseudo-Falcandus's account. It is possible that Romuald Guarna himself wrote the entries in the Salernitan chronicle starting in c. 1153–6, after he became archbishop of Salerno and subsequently a crucial eyewitness, given the archbishop's role as a Sicilian diplomat and occasional member of the royal *curia*. The authorship of the chronicle is expressly declared at the end of the description of the peace conference at Venice in 1176–7, which he himself attended as a chief Sicilian negotiator.[14] However, Donald Matthew has suggested that, due to the inconsistencies in the older part of the chronicle, Romuald wrote only the account of the conference of Venice. Matthew doubts that Romuald penned the entries after 1127, but his argument is not conclusive.[15]

External testimonies also offer useful, brief information about the Italo-Norman nobility and the key events in the development of the Sicilian monarchy. The histories of John Kinnamos and Niketas Choniates recorded the presence of several Apulian noblemen, both rebels and royal generals, in the Constantinopolitan court and the military campaigns between the kingdom and the Eastern Empire. William of Tyre also recorded relevant episodes which attested members of the Italo-Norman nobility. Likewise, complementary information can be drawn from German testimonies such as the *Annalista Saxo*, Otto of Freising and the letters of Wibald of Corvey, who cover the conflicts in the 1130s and the subsequent contact between the German Empire, the south Italian nobility and the Sicilian monarchy.

Other types of textual material were also helpful. A collection of ordinances that contain the legislation of Roger II – better known, albeit inaccurately, as his assizes or constitutions of Ariano – shed some light on the relationship between the nobility and the kingdom's government. The work of Arabic cartographer Al-Idrisi, often called 'The Book of King Roger', provides a topological description of the mainland territories which proved useful in the identification of the northern Adriatic borders of the kingdom; Al-Idrisi used many sources, including route descriptions and portable maps. The critical edition and translation prepared by Amari and Schiaparelli, although focused solely on a geographical description of Italy, was more than sufficient for this study.

Other useful documentary sources include the Abruzzese cartulary-chronicles from Casauria, Carpineto and Maiella, which offer both diplomatic and narrative evidence, at times otherwise unattested, for the activities in northern Apulia in the twelfth century. These codices were more than a cartulary – a hybrid but integral textual instrument used to attest and corroborate the abbey's estates – which not only provided a collection of documents but also gathered many other texts and testimonies. The chronicle of John Berard, monk of Casauria, was written c. 1175–80, in the margins of the chartulary of the abbey of St Clement in Casauria, whose bulk is composed of 2,150 documents, dating back to the foundation of the monastery (c. 872).[16] Alexander the monk, the author of the chronicle of the abbey of St Bartholomew of Carpineto, composed his work in the last decade of the twelfth century, appended to a collection of 161 documents from the same monastery.[17] Similarly, the *Liber instrumentorum monasterii Sancti Salvatoris de Maiella* is an unedited codex composed by the monks of the Holy Saviour at M. Maiella between the twelfth and the thirteenth centuries that compiles both transcribed charters and narrative testimonies.[18]

In addition to textual material, the available diplomatic evidence formed an integral part of the sources for this study. Donations, exchanges, disputes and any other legal transactions that illustrate the links established by the counts place us at the very heart of this aristocratic society. The documentary heritage for the study of the Norman kingdom of Sicily comes mostly from archives with an overwhelmingly ecclesiastical provenance; the relative wealth of monastic archives compared with the small number of surviving episcopal ones is noteworthy. The archbishoprics of Salerno and Bari, and the bishoprics of Aversa, are the only substantial such survivals – other episcopal archives that preserve twelfth-century evidence (e.g. Benevento, Brindisi, Caiazzo, Capua, Chieti, Taranto and Troia) are smaller, and preserve only a fraction of what once existed. Some also have more from the thirteenth century than the twelfth century, for example Benevento. There is also a geographical imbalance; there are far more from Campania and Adriatic Apulia than the Basilicata and Molise.

This surviving *corpus* of charters has been mostly assembled from cartulary collections, which provide thousands of private and public documents. Important collections include the *Codice diplomatico barese* and *pugliese*, *Le pergamene dell'archivio diocesano di Salerno*, *Codice diplomatico normanno di Aversa*, *Le pergamene di Capua*, *Le pergamene normanne della Mater Ecclesia Capuana*, *Regesto di S. Angelo in Formis*, *Codice diplomatico molisano*, *Syllabus Graecarum membranarum*, *Codex Diplomaticus Cajetanus* and the *Codice diplomatico verginiano*, which considerably facilitated the diplomatic exploration of this study. Compilations of charters that are not specific to a particular city or region were also employed; the *Codex Diplomaticus Regni Siciliae* contains a variety of royal charters from the twelfth century, and Ughelli and Coleti's eighteenth-century *Italia Sacra*, a historical survey of Italy's bishoprics, offers copies of certain documents that are otherwise unedited or unidentified. The royal charters that survive now form a small fraction of what was once written, and their edition is still incomplete.[19] Neither the charters of William II nor the Greek documents of Roger II are available in print yet; Enzensberger is still working on *Guillelmi II Diplomata*, although many of his edited charters are available online. The study of the surviving production of the Sicilian royal chancery reveals, nevertheless, a great deal about the *regnum*'s government.[20] Moreover, a seventeenth-century manuscript supplied material that was fundamental for this study: the *Historia delle famiglie di Salerno normande*, by Giovan Battista Prignano (Rome, Biblioteca Angelica, cod. 277–76). Prignano was one of the first scholars to systematically survey archival repositories for the study of the genealogy of the Norman aristocracy, visiting numerous archives and producing summaries and excerpts from the sources. Many of these documents have since been lost, making Prignano's *Historia* the only known surviving source for many of these transactions. Additionally, this study has relied on editions appended to academic articles and a handful of local prosopographies. All the published charters have been used extensively for histories of southern Italy and peninsular communities, having been heavily mined by scholars including Jamison, Ménager, Martin, Takayama, Cuozzo, Loud and Houben.

Unpublished charters found in repositories in Rome, Benevento (specifically in the *Museo del Sannio*), Naples and Cava de' Tirreni were equally fundamental. Of special importance is the abbey of the Most Holy Trinity of Cava, which contains one of the largest and most relevant archives for the study of the medieval Mezzogiorno – most of its twelfth-century charters remain unedited. The charters from Cava not only attest the economic and legal interactions among the local aristocracy and the abbey itself but also shed light on the genealogies of southern Italy and the activities of local functionaries, including judges, justiciars, constables and comital officials.

Given the range of available diplomatic material, it was necessary to define a theoretical framework and data gathering method that would allow for a systematic survey of the relevant charters and the preparation of a prosopographical database. The first decision involved defining the medieval charter. In the last decades, charters have experienced a sort of historiographical resurgence: Rosenwein's and Barton's research and the collected works edited by Davis and Fouracre are a good illustration of this.[21] The transactions attested in charters are not as straightforward as they might appear. Donations, for example, might actually conceal a sale. As is the case with many south Italian charters, a document that initially records a grant may subsequently present another clause in which 'compensation' is given to the donor. Additionally, although classical charter elements are present, the surviving diplomatic material for twelfth-century southern Italy is relatively heterogeneous, and there is little standardization between charters from either different regions or different social strata (royal vs. baronial). Moreover, many documents only survive in later copies that follow different formats, or in summaries compiled in a non-charter layout.

Two persistent challenges of compiling data from diplomatic material are recurring names and vague geographical definitions. One way to tackle the former is to manage and correlate the names of the social actors attested in the charters together with the other names recorded in the same context and organize them under a single 'key' spelling. The vague geographical definitions can be organized under the recurring geographical terms found in the charters themselves. For the south Italian documents of the twelfth century, these include *casale, castrum, villa, campus* and *mons*. The boundaries of the *campus* were not as certain as many researchers may think, and those of the *mons* are broader than those of the *villa* and the *casale*. A subsequent issue of geographical definitions is place-name identification. Any modern equivalent of a place-name in the south Italian charters is bound to be approximate. The very organization of the land upon which the charters are drawn was changing into a layout that most likely remains the underlying pattern of the south Italian communes and countryside. Overall, these are identified on a case-by-case basis.

My methodological proposal is indebted to multiple lines of social interpretation and diplomatic research. If new questions are formulated and new answers suggested, it is because many of the old issues have already been resolved. Nevertheless, my efforts are bound to the axiomatic limitation of the available diplomatic material; the fragmented corpus of surviving charters is in many ways unsatisfactory, many documents have been lost and others only survive as interpolated or even forged documents. Although charters do not necessarily attest what actually happened, they do reflect how people wanted themselves and their social spaces to be recorded. The documents offer thus a public impression of a social system lost in time. The recorded interactions might not tell us the whole story, but they are the closest approximations we may have to the social environment in which they were constructed. The charters present valuable insights into at least four aspects of the period in question: (1) the flux of land and wealth between individuals, families and communities; (2) the exercise of authority between the aristocracy and people of lesser rank; (3) the public display of prestige and authority; and (4) the practical implementation of laws and customs.

Alongside charters, another key document employed is the *Quaternus magne expeditonis*, which is a contemporary record present in the compendium known as the *Catalogus Baronum*. This administrative document has been identified as a general register of the military service owed to the royal *curia* for the *auxilium magne expeditionis*: the 'aid of the great military campaign' – an *expeditio* in this context is a military operation.[22] I have discussed before the terminology, structure and use of this source in 'Royal comestabuli and Military Control in the Sicilian Kingdom', whose proposal stands behind the historical exploration of this book.[23] I argued that the *Quaternus magne expeditionis* reveals two overlapping structures: a military layer drawn above an economic one. Accordingly, the *feudum* provided a basic reference to the royal *curia* for the computing and demand of the military aid levy from the land-holding aristocracy.

Where in Southern Italy?

The study focuses on mainland territories of the kingdom of Sicily, especially the contemporary provinces of Apulia and the Terra di Lavoro. Although the regions of Abruzzo and Calabria are not discounted, they are not fully covered because their regional and cultural differences set them apart from the constituent peninsular provinces of the kingdom, and these variations require further and careful consideration. Not all the regions are represented equally by the surviving documentary evidence; the available documentation for the peninsular territories of Apulia and the Terra di Lavoro is far more extensive and accessible than the surviving material for Calabria. Likewise, the Calabrian territories are not covered in the *Catalogus Baronum*. In addition, and as is argued throughout this work, Sicily was essentially different from the mainland because there were no actual counties on the island during this period, and the counts who conducted transactions in Sicily were tied to a mainland lordship.

The *Quaternus magne expeditionis* is divided between the two constituent provinces of the kingdom: the duchy of Apulia and the principality of Capua. These once separated polities became united *aeque principaliter* under the Sicilian crown. The full royal title normally concerned the duchy and the principality, as well as the highest royal offices on the mainland (e.g. *magister iustitiarius totius Apulie et Terre Laboris*). The former principality of Capua, however, was more commonly identified as the 'Terra di Lavoro' in most of the surviving charters and chronicles of the second half of the twelfth century, except when enunciating the king's full titles. Consequently, this study uses the principality of Capua and the Terra di Lavoro as interchangeable terms for the same territory, from the county of Fondi to the former principality of Salerno. The former duchy of Apulia was far more extensive than the modern region of Apulia; the province included the former principality of Salerno, the mountainous district of Irpina and the region of modern Basilicata. For clarity, although the principality of Salerno ceased to exist formally, and this princely title was no longer used, I employ it as a geographical identifier. When it is helpful to emphasize the coastal area of modern Apulia, I refer to Adriatic Apulia.

Structure of the argument

This book focuses on the counts as the members of the highest levels of the aristocracy, because it has been possible to situate them historically with a considerable degree of certainty. In this way, the activities of the upper nobility and the configuration of the counties provide a sound platform upon which to start looking at the operation of social control on the mainland and analyse how these people were embedded in the new social order as nodes of regional authority.

To achieve these aims, the opening chapter explores the immediate origins of the peninsular counts in the decade before the instauration of the Sicilian monarchy. Chapter 1 surveys thus the political background, social context and kinship of the south Italian upper aristocracy on the eve of the kingdom's creation, in order to understand the original features of the peninsular nobility.

Chapter 2 discusses the implications of the related findings and the calendar of activities of the peninsular nobility during the reign of Roger II. The kingdom's social arrangement cannot be discussed without knowing the composition of the upper aristocracy and their roles as agents of war and order. I present hence a complete picture of the peninsular nobility's new configuration. Here, the social meaning of the aristocracy's documented activities is examined around the concept of the comital rank and the county.

The following two chapters present a more detailed analysis of the altered roles and new relationships the counts acquired during periods of intense political and military turmoil. Chapter 3 and 4 explores William I's reign and the presence and role of the nobility when the endurance and relevance of the social arrangement achieved in the previous period was tested. Through a discussion of the episodes of conflict and rebellion surrounding, first, the leadership of the count of Loritello (Chapter 3) and then the position acquired by the count of Gravina in the midst of the counts' rebellion (Chapter 4), these chapters present a detailed description of the comital activities and acquired competences. These two chapters also offer an analysis of the aristocracy's development with, without and against the Palermitan authority.

After having analysed in Chapter 4 the transformative role played by the count of Gravina and its effect in the power balance in the peninsular provinces, Chapter 5 will then survey the political and military control exercised by the counts during the regency of Queen Margaret. I present a reconstructed picture of the mutated continental nobility, a result of both counts and relatives of the queen becoming central agents in affairs of the royal *curia*, and the re-assignment of vacant counties. This serves to identify spheres of action which delimit the extent of the counts' agency during this pivotal stage.

Chapter 6 offers a complete account of the new and consolidated ruling elite in the peninsular provinces, covering each county separately from 1169 to 1189. Although the argument progresses chronologically up to this point, here I provide a sequential account of all the documented activities of the kingdom's counts and an analysis of the development and consolidation of each county until the end of the Norman period, on the eve of the succession wars and the Hohenstaufen takeover.

The final chapter encompasses a long-deferred discussion of the kingdom's social mechanism for military mobilization and administration of justice during the last stage of the development of the Italo-Norman counts. This deferral is necessary to avoid falling into the circular argument which expects to see an effective model of centralization and royal state-building in the Norman kingdom of Sicily. Chapter 6 therefore discusses the enhanced role played by some counts as active agents of the king's justice and army, and contextualizes their position within the peninsular nobility.

This book is supplemented by a reflection on the Sicilian *duana baronum*; a chronological chart which illustrates the number of counts and the existence of specific counties at any given time throughout the kingdom's Norman period; a genealogical chart in which the ancestry of those counts and the kinship connections between their families can be traced and visualized; and two maps of which show all the locations relevant to comital activities and transactions.

1

The counts of Norman Italy before Roger II

Sicily, though nominally attached to the duchy of Apulia, was practically ruled autonomously by Count Roger II during the 1120s. The Sicilian count was also the undisputed ruler of the whole of Calabria, after his cousin Duke William ceded him the shares he and his father had retained in Palermo, Messina and Calabria. By autumn 1124, Roger II had moved into Apulian territory, as he attempted to establish control over the lordship of Montescaglioso, which had been held by his sister Emma in the right of his son Roger, after her husband Rudolph Machabeus had died.[1] While the Sicilian count claimed Montescaglioso, he was accompanied by Christodoulos, his chief minister, and George of Antioch, the Arab-speaking Greek official who, a couple of years later, succeeded Christodoulos and became the first Sicilian 'Emir of Emirs'.[2] These two administrators are an iconic example of the sort of Greek officials Count Roger II could rely on to exploit and manage his extensive resources in Sicily.

The expertise of such functionaries allowed Roger II to organize his income and develop an army and a fleet that enabled him to impose his authority over the peninsular lands. However, their social arrangement differed greatly from that of the county of Sicily, and the authority of the Norman overlords acted as one of the central sources of this arrangement. The counts and princes of southern Italy were the vanguard of a society accustomed not only to its political autonomy but also to the absence of a uniform system of government and social recognition.

The overlords' power basis

After Roger II's cousin died in 1127, the count of Sicily claimed the mainland territories as the rightful heir of the duke of Apulia. Duke William, as the last surviving direct heir of Robert Guiscard, was not only the nominal leader of the Normans who settled in Apulia following its conquest from the Greeks after 1042 but also the heir to the Lombard princes of Salerno – the Tyrrhenian city had become the dukes' chief city after Guiscard took it in 1076. It took Roger II three years to bring all his insular and peninsular dominions together under a kingdom; after having subjected the most prominent lords in southern Italy by force, Count Roger of Sicily became the king of Sicily in 1130, ruling over all the Norman dominions in Italy. These lands, however, had not previously seen a widespread and univocal notion of nobility and government. What was once a constantly warring setting became the breeding ground for descendants of the original Norman mercenaries who had arrived in the Mediterranean 100 years earlier. The leaders of these northern mercenaries flourished and established their own rule, eventually becoming the princes of Capua and the dukes of Apulia.

Bringing all these units together into one single polity, under the same crown, might have heightened the expectation for autonomy of the territorial leaderships. The Sicilian king's new subjects could have been prepared to acknowledge him as their nominal overlord, but they certainly did not expect to lose power in their own lands. Many of the counts in both Capua and Apulia were in practice independent of princely or ducal authority. In their documents, they did not formally acknowledge the authority of either the prince of Capua or the duke of Apulia. They appeared instead as counts, not by the grace of their overlord but by grace of God alone, with those in Apulia referring to the emperor in Constantinople. Robert of Loritello (modern Rotello) and his son, furthermore, styled themselves in the 1090s and 1110s with the title *comes comitum*, 'count of counts', and they also appear to have used their own cruciform monograph as the comital signature.[3] The portions that were nominally subject to the duke of Apulia, like the *Terra Beneventana* and the dominions of the count of Loritello and his kin, threw off all obedience to any constituted authority, not to mention the actual independent lordships such as the Salento peninsula and the county of Sicily itself.[4] Let us not forget that King Roger II had once been a count himself, a sovereign over his own dominions and without any effective lordship or authority exercised over him. The comital title was, hence, used to identify specific, prominent lords as leaders – or even potential leaders – among a community of other lords. In the eleventh century, as Cuozzo highlighted, the Norman leaders' power was based on two components: their economic power as landholders and their local authority as military warrantors of order and justice.[5] In this sense, the 'county' that could have emerged from these eleventh century *comites* in Norman Italy should have referred more to the original and ancient voice of *comitatus* as a company or band of soldiers than to the political and territorial unit found in successive centuries.

The search for the original south Italian counties has led to an overflow of misguided and anachronistic readings across history and historiography. From forged charters to modern Italian scholarship, it has been assumed that the south Italian county existed continuously since the Norman conquest. A revealing example of this is the case of Richard the Seneschal, a Norman lord in the Terra d'Otranto at the end of the eleventh and beginning of the twelfth century. Since Prignano's seventeenth-century *Historia*, Richard had been identified as count of Mottola. Until Cuozzo argued against his identification as a count, it was assumed that a county of Mottola existed. After careful examination of the documents on which Richard's comital title had been attested, Cuozzo came to the conclusion that this dignity was ascribed to the lord of Mottola and Castellaneta around the thirteenth and fourteenth centuries, to provide diplomatic evidence for the litigations concerning the Castellaneta properties of the monasteries of the Most Holy Trinity of Cava dei Tirreni, St Mary of Pisticci, St Anastasius of Carbone and the Most Holy Trinity of Venosa.[6] What was thought to be an early Norman county turned out to be a treacherous fiction, created by both monastic forgery and institutional preconceptions.

The social typology of territorial lordships adopted by the Normans in the eleventh century appears to have been oriented towards distinguishing the ultimate coercive role exercised by the leaders of military units of knights, acknowledging also their condition as prominent and prosperous lords, in that they held most of the land.[7] The material resources that must have resulted from exploiting the land, and the miscellaneous local customs – which could have included *plateaticum*, *porticum* or *incultum* – exacted from the populations under their control, suggest that the early Norman counts could have amassed a substantial sum. Nevertheless, the counts' revenues as overlords cannot be measured due to the lack of surviving evidence.

The scarcity of surviving documents at the beginning of the twelfth century makes it impossible to present a systematic treatment of comital prerogatives and competences; moreover, there is no clear or categorical usage of the title of *comes* before the creation of the Sicilian kingdom. At that time, the comital title did not carry any specific definitions of rights or responsibilities, which may reflect the absence of an effective central authority or a generalized notion of government. The authority these early Norman counts exercised over the local population must have been given by the fact that they were the only ultimate coercive force in the region.

The title of *comes* was also an honorific title employed during the Norman conquest to express social prestige – an ideological source of power – by alluding to either old noble Lombard families or the descendants of the 'new nobility' of conquerors. The latter group comprised of the handful of Norman kin-groups that provided both the upper aristocracy in southern Italy and the most influential lineages: the extended family of the princes of Capua; the Buonalbergo of Ariano; the Molise of Boiano; the descendants of Guiscard's brother William of Principato; and the 'sons of Amicus' of Andria, Lesina and Molfetta.[8] This expression of prestige, nonetheless, did not bear any special faculties that were not already enjoyed in the capacity of overlords. Some lords (*domini*) might have held their lands from some of these counts, such as the counts of Loritello. However, other lords did not acknowledge any overlordship at all.[9] It was the actual coercive capacity of the *dominus*, and not necessarily the title, that granted additional judicial and financial rights over other lords.[10]

Once these territorial military leaders, the *comites*, were securely established, the hereditary claims of their own kin prevailed in successive generations. The vanishing central authority left after Guiscard's death, together with the steady displacement of the older upper authorities, rendered the nominal endorsements superfluous. Hence, the power of these first Norman counts could go as far as their political abilities and military successes would allow. The northern regions, both in the principality of Capua and in the Adriatic lands north of the Capitanata, granted the greatest opportunity for these counts to extend their authority beyond their own chief cities. In the east, the counts in the north of Bari and in the east of Benevento occupied lands and considerably expanded their dominions in the previously unconquered northern Adriatic, thus enlarging their territorial and military resources. Contrastingly, in Capua, the older Lombard comital dignities provided the new 'counts' with a useful model of social prestige and political distinction that they could use to consolidate their authority over other lords and local communities, both urban and of tenant-farmers.

Regardless of their location, be that Apulia, Calabria or Terra di Lavoro, the counts' lordships do not appear to have constituted a delimited territorial unit, and the toponyms ascribed to some of the comital titles indicated either an autochthonous dignity attached to a specific city or urban population (such as the count of the 'Caiazzans' or the count of Catanzaro) or the location of the count's residence or main lordship (such as the count of Loritello). Since the title by itself did not define the border of the count's holdings, these must have varied significantly because of territorial expansion and political quarrelling. Although the comital dignity provided an enhanced and recognized social status for its bearer, the actual geographical area of authority and influence depended on the count's activities and operations, and not solely on the title.

In summary, the military and political ability of each Norman lord were the means through which they could acquire a place of prestige and enhanced social status, regardless of their origins and family, or however distinct their respected areas of influence.[11] That prestigious position was confirmed by the usage of the title of *comes*, which was ambiguous enough to allow a varied array of prominent barons to confirm their superior status over other lesser lords, although it marked their inferiority to the duke of Apulia and the prince of Capua. This ambiguity echoes the usage that the comital dignity had in the Carolingian era. The title of *comes* was employed by Charles Martel and his son Pippin not only to appoint commanders who undertook special military and paramilitary missions but also to designate officers who commanded garrison units at forts and in cities.[12] The *comites* then developed into the archetypal secular officials on which Charlemagne and Louis the Pious relied to carry out their will in the provinces. These Carolingian *comites*' responsibilities included not only military duties – such as gathering those eligible to serve in the army – but also the collection of various types of imposts, presiding over cadres of other functionaries, and enforcing justice through a system of local courts. However, the power enjoyed by these *comites* varied significantly, mostly considering that there were probably around 400 counties north of the Alps which were not cleanly defined. Despite the new Carolingian administrative framework, local conditions ended up determining the actual duties carried out by these *comites* as agents of a distant imperial rule.[13] The role of the first Norman counts in Italy also differed, and the individual's status and prerogatives depended not on the comital title itself but on the web of ties with their inferiors, superiors and peers, and the specific relationship between the *comites* and their communities.

The usage of the comital title at this stage created thus a broad buffer zone of social recognition which simply distinguished the *comites* from less powerful barons. Unsurprisingly, this created asymmetric relationships between counts, as is illustrated in the following section. Furthermore, although the title was different and inferior to the dukedom in Apulia and the princedom in Capua, the social status of the early twelfth-century Norman counts seems not to have differed practically from those who bore autochthonous titles attached to prestigious maritime cities, including the duke and *magister militum* of Naples and the duke and consul of Gaeta in the principality of Capua, and the patrician princes of Bari in Apulia.

Kingless counts

The organized resistance against the imminent takeover of the mainland by Roger II is a good starting point to reconstruct the composition of the peninsular aristocracy during the decade preceding the kingdom's creation. Alexander of Telese recorded that Pope Honorius II publicly threatened the count of Sicily with anathema if he should make any further effort to obtain the duchy of Apulia, and that Count Rainulf was the first local noble to follow the papal call to arms to oppose Roger II. Rainulf was the brother-in-law of Roger II, married to the latter's sister Matilda.[14] Neither Alexander of Telese nor Falco of Benevento refer to a specific toponym to Rainulf's comital title, and in Romuald's *Chronicon* he is only regarded as Count Rainulf of Airola, although he was most certainly known contemporarily as count of the *Caiazzans* and Airola. Although many modern scholars follow Chalandon in calling Rainulf count of Alife, perhaps as an extrapolation of the later county of Alife which covered just a fragment of Rainulf's dominions in the principality of Capua, this title is not attested in any surviving contemporary source.[15] Count Rainulf and his father are generally recorded in their charters using the formula 'count of the Caiazzans and many others'.[16] Pope Honorius's stand against Roger II was also attested by Falco of Benevento, who described a purported harangue preached in Capua to bishops and a multitude of distinguished men, including the archbishop of Capua, Prince Robert of Capua and Count Rainulf. The pontiff appealed to the assembled warriors to rally behind 'the cause of St Peter' and to take up arms against the enemy of the Roman See, Count Roger of Sicily, who was already under anathema. Falco subsequently described how Prince Robert and Count Rainulf, among other nobles and bishops, promised to commit to the papal call to arms.[17]

Many prominent barons joined the pope and Count Rainulf in an alliance against the Sicilian count after they openly opposed Roger II. The leaders of this party provide a useful picture of the peninsular upper aristocracy of the time; according to Alexander of Telese, these were Count Geoffrey of Andria, Tancred of Conversano, Count Roger of Ariano and 'Prince' Grimoald of Bari. The latter was an urban patrician who had claimed the title of 'prince' for himself; he was recorded in October 1121 as the 'very excellent lord, ruler of Bariots', and by 1123 he presented himself as 'prince of Bari by the grace of God and St Nicholas'.[18] Tancred of Conversano was the lord of the Adriatic cities of Brindisi and Barletta, and of other lands in central Apulia, including Acquabella, Corato, Minervino and Grottole.[19] He was the son of Geoffrey, the erstwhile count of Conversano, and thus brother of Alexander, count of Conversano, during the early decades of the twelfth century.[20] Grimoald and Tancred are also recorded by Falco of Benevento as part of the resistance against Roger II, because they seem to have been summoned by the pope and marched into Apulia with the Capuan barons.[21] Count Geoffrey of Andria is the only attested count in Adriatic Apulia to have joined the opposing party, since the other count, Roger of Ariano, was based in the Irpina mountainous region, in the east of the Terra di Lavoro. Ariano, a town east of Benevento, was on the border between the duchy of Apulia and the Terra di Lavoro, and thus a strategic location. This location might partially explain why Count Rainulf pushed Roger II, as soon as he arrived in Salerno and before the papal call to arms, to make the count of Ariano a subordinate of Rainulf. According to Alexander of Telese, despite Roger II's unwillingness to allow that 'one equal should make submission to another', the Sicilian count ultimately made the count of Ariano a 'subject' of the count of the Caiazzans.[22] This passage holds additional significance, in that it displays the contemporary presumption that the bearers of the comital title were different not only from other lords but also from political equals.

Alexander, count of Conversano and brother of the aforementioned Tancred, joined the opposition later. Although the count of Conversano is not recorded as an original member of the alliance, he is attested by Alexander of Telese as part of the group of magnates that surrendered to Roger II, finally acknowledged as the duke of Apulia in 1129.[23] According to Falco of Benevento, Pope Honorius confirmed the ducal dignity to Roger II earlier, in 1128; after allegedly discovering the deceitfulness of the prince of Capua and other barons, he came to an agreement.[24] Consequently, in Alexander of Telese's account, only four counts are accounted for during the years before the kingdom's creation: Rainulf of Caiazzo, Roger of Ariano, Geoffrey of Andria and Alexander of Conversano. The royal apologist focused mostly on the aristocracy that opposed Roger II, leaving any possible local supporters unaccounted for before 1129.

On the other hand, Falco of Benevento provides a more detailed record. He noted that an earlier count of Ariano, Jordan, had risen against Duke William and was finally defeated and disinherited in 1122.[25] This Jordan of Ariano was surely the father of the aforementioned Count Roger of Ariano. Falco also indicated that after young Duke William's death, Count Jordan rose again and seized all the cities and towns that were under his 'countship' (*comitatus*).[26]

Aside from the testimonies of Alexander and Falco, other counts can be attested on the peninsula in the 1120s: Count Nicholas of Principato, Count Henry of Sarno, Count Richard of Carinola and Count Pandulf of Aquino. The latter is attested in the *Chronica Mon. Casinensis*, which registered a donation made in 1127 by Pandulf, son of Count Lando of Aquino, at Tyrilla.[27] This Count Pandulf also built a castle (*castrum*) '*in silva monasterii Casinensis Tirilla*', ordered by Emperor Lothar to be destroyed by September 1137.[28] These counts of Aquino did not, however, descend from the Norman conquerors; instead they came from a Lombard family that had held Aquino since the mid-tenth century.

Still in the principality of Capua, Richard is recorded as 'count of Carinola' (*Calinesium comes*) when in December 1109 made a donation to his mother Anna.[29] The same Count Richard of Carinola (*Calinensium comes*) is attested in February 1115 as a donor to the church of St Mary outside Carinola, which had been built by the same Anne, mother of Richard of Carinola and former wife of Bartholomew.[30] This charter is the last documented surviving instance in which Richard is explicitly regarded as count of Carinola. Additionally, he is recorded in two subsequent charters issued by Prince Robert II of Capua. First, a charter of 1117 reveals that a Capuan court was attended by Richard son of Bartholomew as one of Prince Robert's esteemed barons.[31] Richard is later recorded as taking part in another Capuan court, this time as 'Richard of Carinola, our [Prince Robert's] relative', when Prince Robert II made a donation in favour of Montecassino, in March 1128.[32] After this, no count of Carinola makes another documented appearance, to my knowledge, until Jonathan is recorded in both an 1152 charter and the *Quaternus magne expeditionis*. However, Richard of Carinola was still operating in the Capua area during the decade of the kingdom's creation, as he was last attested as duke of Gaeta in a May 1135 charter, issued in the thirteenth year of Duke Richard's rule.[33] Richard, the son of Bartholomew, may have thereafter been in the second decade of the twelfth century both count of Carinola and duke of Gaeta, as his father was before him.[34] Nonetheless, although he was still recognized as duke of Gaeta, one cannot automatically assume Richard of Carinola kept the comital distinction throughout the 1120s.

Henry, the count of Sarno, is attested in May 1125, in the monastery of Holy Trinity at Metiliano (i.e. Cava), as a witness to the grant of a mill to the monastery.[35] In this document, Henry is recorded as son and heir of Count Richard of Sarno. Two other men from Sarno testified that while Count Richard was ill, but sound of mind and clear of speech, in the presence of them and others including his wife Agnes, he made disposition for his property after his death. The late Count Richard seems hence to have died in 1125, after leaving a testament.

In the region of the former principality of Salerno, the only notable overlord, besides the duke, was Count Nicholas of Principato, son and heir of Count William II of Principato. There is, nevertheless, a gap of more than sixteen years in the surviving evidence. The latest documented appearance of a count of Principato before 1128 is found in a February 1112 charter under which William, count of Principato, and his wife Countess Cassandra donated the church of St Nazarius *de la Mocava* to the abbey of Venosa.[36] The following source is a December 1128 charter, which records Count Nicholas, as 'count of Principato, son of the late William', confirming a deathbed donation to Cava by his father, consisting of a half share in lands between the Rivers Tusciano and Sele, with all the men at Tusciano.[37] It is therefore safe to argue that Nicholas of Principato was an acting count in the years preceding Roger II's accession as a duke.

Additional members of the upper Norman aristocracy can be positively identified despite the lack of surviving evidence. First, one can expect that the same count of Boiano (Hugh II of Molise) who is recorded by Alexander of Telese and the *Annales Casinenses*, c. 1134/5, was already an acting count when Duke William died.[38] Hugh's father, Simon of Molise, count of Boiano, had died during the 1117 earthquake in Isernia.[39] Hugh II of Molise was seemingly too young to become count of Boiano immediately after this, and hence his uncle Robert was Count Simon's direct successor.[40] Robert is recorded a year later, in November, as count of Boiano, and son of the late Count Hugh, suggesting that Robert might have indeed acted as a count during Hugh's minority.[41] The register of Peter the Deacon contains a June 1128 donation, by which Hugh, as count of Molise, granted half of the *castrum Serre* to Montecassino, 'just as late Count Robert, my uncle, left on his deathbed to the same abbey [Montecassino] for the salvation of his soul'.[42] This conflicts with what is recorded in the Montecassino chronicle, which reports that the charter in favour of the monastery was in fact issued only by Robert, 'count of Molise' (*comes de Molisio*), through which the latter donated the same half of the *castrum Serre*.[43] However, Peter the Deacon and the Montecassino chronicle are by no means sources free of the charge of omission or of deliberate alteration, and either could have mistakenly recorded the original donor. Besides, the former charter recorded that Count Hugh made the donation in favour of the abbey according to what his late uncle had decided. Nonetheless, it is clear that Hugh of Molise ultimately succeeded his uncle and was a count before 1130. The counts of Boiano ruled an extensive lordship in a strategic watershed area in the east of the principality of Capua. It stretched across the Matese mountain range into Adriatic Apulia, connecting thus the regions of the Terra di Lavoro, Capitanata and central Italy.

In the Capitanata region, two other counts can be suggested to have existed before 1127: Count Rao of Lesina and whoever succeeded Count Robert II of Loritello. The latter might not have been alive when Roger II invaded the peninsula, but his lordship was probably passed on to a relative.[44] Count Robert of Loritello's last documented appearance takes place in 1122, when he is recorded as the overlord of his brother William of Hauteville, lord of Biccari, in a charter by which said William granted '*ad montem Erbemale*' – which his brother had handed over to Prior John and the monastery of St Leonard before – to the church of St Pamfilus.[45] This William appears to have been the same count of Loritello who, at the request of Bishop Rusticus of Chieti, confirmed in 1137 what his grandfather Count Robert (I) and his father Count Robert (II) gave to the church of Chieti: various churches and the *castella* of Forca, Genestrella, and, on the far side of the River Pescara, Sculcula, Lastignano and St Casideus.[46] Interestingly enough, Count William is recorded here as 'count of counts' (*comes comitum*). Two other undated documents record a Count William of Loritello granting the abbey of S Maria a Mare in Tremiti a tribute of twenty *solidi* a year and the church of St Paul of Petazati.[47] This may have been the same William of Loritello who was regarded as a 'palatine [count]' who swore allegiance to Lothar II in 1137.[48] Count Rao of Lesina, on the other hand, is attested as count of Lesina (*comes Lisine*) and heir and son of count Petron in a February 1119 charter.[49] Therefore, Rao might still have been alive before Roger II was invested duke, although it is as likely that he died without an heir, because there is no evidence of either Rao or any successor after 1119.

In the principality of Capua, it seems that the old Lombard comital titles for Avellino and Fondi were vacant at that time, although a 'consul' of Fondi, Leo and his son Peter appear to have been active in the 1120s. According to the chronicle of Montecassino, *c.* 1123–4, Consul Leo of Fondi and his son were betrayed by Richard Pygnardus who handed them over as prisoners to Richard, 'lord' of Carinola.[50] Following this, *c.* 1125, the same Leo and his son were finally freed from Richard of Carinola's captivity, and then received by the Abbot of Montecassino who offered his support and 50 pounds of gold in exchange for immunity for his monastery in Fondi.[51] The chronicle here does not employ the title of 'count' to refer to either Leo of Fondi, the consul, or Richard of Carinola. This not only shows that the consulship of this Leo of Fondi was the immediate precedent for the counts of Fondi but also reflects the flexible usage of these titles at this stage – dignities such as *consul* or *comes* were seemingly equivalent.

The use of *cosul* as an interchangeable title to *comes* was not restricted to southern Italy. In England and northern France, the old Roman title of *consul* was employed, for example, by the comital dynasty of Anjou in the early eleventh century and by two English 'counts' in the twelfth century: Robert, earl of Gloucester, and Ranulf II, earl of Chester.[52] Similarly, a superficial survey of charters of the dukes of Normandy suggests that the usage of the term *consul* for *comes* increased dramatically in the mid-eleventh century, only to then decrease after the first quarter of the twelfth century.[53] Nicholas Paul, who noted this pattern, understood it as an indication of the so-called twelfth-century Renaissance, in that it suggests changes in forms of reading and education among the scribes responsible for framing charters in northern France.[54] Although it could be tempting to see here a common mark of a supposed pan-Norman tradition, this suggestion would be much more problematic for Norman Italy. These scribal patterns cannot be identified in the available south Italian evidence, and the usage of *consul* is both infrequent and limited to specific regional realities predating the creation of the kingdom of Sicily – only in Fondi is *consul* connected to a comital title. This did not mean that south Italian rulers or scribes used the old Roman term carelessly. Instead, the specific instances in which *consul* is attested suggest a flexible practice where the highest dignity for the local ruling class was still tied to a pre-Norman past, and the title was not a fixed category for the top tier of the peninsular nobility.

In the area around the gulf of Taranto, Montescaglioso was the seat of another count. A June 1130 charter from the abbey of Cava records that William, a son of the count of Montescaglioso, made a donation to Cava. The comital title is employed here exclusively for William's father, Count Robert, and not for William himself (*W[illelmus] Montis Caveosi filius comitis Rob[erti]*).[55] The document attests him as lord of the fortified village (*castellum*) of Brienza, located far from Montescaglioso, in the Melandro valley, on the eastern fringe of the Cilento region.[56] Additionally, the *subscriptio* signature of William of Montescaglioso does not employ any title. However, Roger II himself moved to establish his control over the lordship of Montescaglioso in 1124, which had been held by his sister Emma in the right of his son Roger Machabeus, after her husband Rudolph Machabeus died; in that year, at Montescaglioso, Count Roger II confirmed to the abbey of St Michael the Archangel which had been donated before by his sister Emma, without reference to his nephew Roger Machabeus.[57] If all these documents are correctly depicting two different facets, then the recorded lords of Montescaglioso must have been somehow connected. Count Robert and the counts of Montescaglioso before him were descendants of Umfridus and his first wife Beatrix, sister of Robert Guiscard; her marriage is suggested by the *Gesta Roberti Wiscardi*, which names 'Count Robert of Montescaglioso (*Scabioso Monte*), [...] Geoffrey's brother, both born from the duke's sister'.[58] Garufi and Antonucci have offered a documented genealogy of this family, in which Count Robert of Montescaglioso is placed as one of the sons of Umfridus, brother thus of Rudolph Machabeus.[59] Cuozzo has expanded on this, putting together two distinct pictures by contrasting the evidence from Cava with that from the abbeys of St Mary of Pisticci and St Michael the Archangel of Montescaglioso.[60] After untangling the documentation and analysing the different types of forgeries, Cuozzo concluded that Rudolph Machabeus was already holding Montescaglioso in 1099, after his father Umfridus died after 1093.[61] Robert son of Umfridus must have then taken Montescaglioso at some point after the death of Rudolph's son, Roger Machabeus, *c.* 1120–4, and styled himself with the comital title. Neither Rudolph Machabeus nor his son Roger were regarded as counts in the surviving diplomatic evidence, only Rudolph's wife Emma held the title of 'countess', because she was the daughter of Count Roger I of Sicily; the last documented appearance of

Roger Machabeus is found in two July 1119 charters.[62] This might explain why Roger II marched over to Montescaglioso and claimed the lordship himself on the grounds that it belonged to his sister Emma.

The aforementioned William of Montescaglioso, hence, did not inherit Montescaglioso or hold the comital title. However, the descendants of Count Robert of Montescaglioso were allowed to keep their tenure near the Cilento region. A subsequent document dated September 1138 records a donation of land made by Robert of Montescaglioso (*Robbertus qui de Montescabioso vocor*) to the church of St Peter the Apostle, in Polla.[63] The charter registers the donor's signature as lord and 'ruler of the land of Polla'. According to Garufi, this Robert would have been William of Montescaglioso's son, although he could have actually been his brother. Whichever the case, Montescaglioso was employed by both William and Robert as a patronym that indicated the original focus of their lineage's dominions. Moreover, the proximity of Brienza and Polla serves to support the contention that Count Robert's descendants maintained their lordships for a time after 1124, albeit detached from Montescaglioso. However, c. 1150, the lordship of Polla was taken by Malgerius of Altavilla (Salentina), and in Brienza two *feuda* and some other tenancy units were held among five barons.[64]

If we also consider the separated province of Calabria, an additional count is found. In Calabria, Count Geoffrey of Catanzaro is recorded as 'Count Geoffrey, son of Count Rao of Loritello' (κόμητος Ιοσφρὶ υἱοῦ κόμητου Ράου του λωριτέλλου) in an 1131 document, in which he is attested as a donor in favour of the church of St Stephen del Bosco, still under the 'tutelage' of his mother Countess Bertha.[65] Count Geoffrey is further recorded as signatory of the treaty between Roger II and the city of Bari, dated 22 June 1132, in which he appears among other noblemen including Alexander and Tancred of Conversano.[66] The succession in the lordship of Catanzaro is hard to determine, mostly due to the relative paucity of surviving charters from Calabria, especially in Latin. It is, however, plausible to suggest that the Hauteville branch of Loritello kept the lordship throughout the beginning of the twelfth century (the Hauteville kin-group included the families of the dukes of Apulia and the counts of Sicily).[67] Geoffrey's mother Bertha is recorded in 1112 as 'countess of Loritello', indicating not her actual lordship but her position as a member of the Hauteville-Loritello kin-group – rather than a nuclear family, this was a case of an extended ancestral grouping with discrete branches.[68]

The Abruzzo: A different animal, part I

A Norman outpost in the vestiges of the duchy of Spoleto

The southeastern part of the duchy of Spoleto, a polity in Adriatic central Italy, had been divided into five counties towards the end of the Carolingian period, which were equivalent to the ecclesiastical dioceses: Marsia, Valva, *Aprutium*, Penne and Chieti. This region, later known as the Abruzzo, operated as a buffer zone on the northeastern border of Apulia. These territories originally formed 'a sort of a frontier march', whose border function was implicitly confirmed during the tenth century, as the scenario of the delimitation of both the duchy of Spoleto and the Lombard principality of Benevento.[69] The Franco-Lombard counties of Sangro, Marsia and Valva continued to dominate, but the old Carolingian counties in the region had disappeared by the end of the eleventh century, remaining only as formal geographical terms.[70] What is important here is that the old Franco-Lombard counties rarely coincided with the subsequent Norman lordships, used with great particularity as geographical specifications in the subsequent military register of the kingdom. The political weakness left by a dismantled and outdated duchy of Spoleto opened the door for new lords and families to claim their dominance in the area, both local (e.g. the 'sons of Borell') and external (e.g. the Normans).

By the end of the eleventh century, the followers of the old Norman counts of Loritello occupied part of the territory of the county of Chieti, up to the River Sangro. The old count of Loritello, Robert son of Geoffrey of Capitanata, originally launched a military campaign to seize the lands on the other side of the River Trigno (i.e. the county of Chieti and part of the county of Penne). Afterwards, Count Robert's brother Drogo 'the Badger' (*qui est* Tasso) and his followers were left in charge of the invasion. The Norman invaders from the Capitanata began thus to transform the political geography of these northern lands.[71] 'Marsia' was a contemporary term for the region comprising of the territories conquered by the Hauteville-Loritello kin-group, within what would be known in the following century as the jurisdiction of Bohemund of Manopello. This region was also gradually infiltrated and invaded by members of the 'sons of Amicus' and the Loritello kin-groups, and due to the lack of any central authority it remained unstable until its conquest by the royal forces in the 1140s.

In the decades preceding the creation of the kingdom of Sicily, three counts are found in the Abruzzo: Count Pandulf of Marsia, Count Theodinus of Sangro and Count Robert of Manopello. With regard to the first, Roger II confirmed a donation to Santa Maria della Noce, near Belmonte, made by Pandulf, son of Count Oderisius, on 5 October 1130, which suggests that Pandulf of Marsia was already a count by the 1120s.[72] Pandulf came from an old Frankish-Lombard family, descendants of the old Attonid counts who had once dominated the entire region.[73] Another notable family of indigenous aristocrats who retained their place in the twelfth century were the 'sons of Borell', a kin-group that dominated the Sangro valley and is well-attested in the eleventh century. The Borell kin-group was the creation of an *Oderisius dictus Burrellus* and his four or five sons, who descended from a Frankish family from the county of Valva. These sons held many lands in the Sangro valley and the southern part of the Marsia region, and profited at the expense of the monastery of St Vincent on Volturno. The usage of the comital title by the Borells dates to *c.* 1070, beginning with Oderisius II of Sangro.[74]

As for Robert of Manopello, the *Liber instrumentorum-Chronicon* of St Clement in Casauria records that, after his father Richard had died (after 1103), Count Robert was restrained from attacking the abbey for fear of his mother; however, after the latter had also died (*c.* 1136), this 'wicked son of a wicked father' (*a malo patre malus filius generatus*), began committing many hostile actions against the abbey of Casauria, seizing crop renders and harassing the abbey's men.[75] Count Robert's father, Count Richard, was a Norman lord who established the county of Manopello within the old Franco-Lombard lordship of Chieti, and the same count who, according to the chronicle of Casauria, was an enemy of said abbey.[76] It has been suggested that Robert of Manopello was related to either the 'sons of Amicus' or the Hauteville-Loritello kin-groups, because his father Richard might have been one of the sons of Count Peter II of Lesina, or perhaps a relative of the counts of Loritello.[77] As a Norman baron and a follower of either kin-group of the Apulian counts, the count of Manopello was the new ruler of the lands between the Rivers Trigno and Sangro; as such, his lordship became a physical and political bridge between Norman Italy and the Abruzzo. The influence of the old count of Loritello could have spread all the way up to the River Pescara and the town of Chieti, whose bishop Rainulf appears to have operated in collusion with Count Robert, but this would not have been possible without the extended Adriatic corridor that the Norman count of Manopello provided.[78] It was in this way that the town of Chieti, and the counts of Manopello and Loritello, became crucial components of the Norman presence on the Adriatic coast of central Italy.

Aristocratic lineages and family ties

There were a total of twelve counts on the south Italian peninsula before Roger II's takeover – five in Capua, one in Salerno, four in Apulia and one in Calabria. Additionally, the Norman count of Manopello was established in the Abruzzo. Before reviewing the changes the comital class underwent after the convulsions of the kingdom's first decade, the counts' parentage ought to be examined first.

The first important feature of the south Italian magnates and territorial leaders at this time is their shared genealogy. Most Norman counts were directly related to either the Drengot or Hauteville kin-groups; the former was the family of the Norman princes of Capua, known also as 'of Quarrel', while the latter were related to the dukes of Apulia. In the principality of Salerno, Count Nicholas of Principato descended from Robert Guiscard's younger brother William, who had married Maria, Prince Guaimar IV's niece.[79] The only Hauteville count in this area was thus the count of Principato. In the principality of Capua, Rainulf, count of the 'Caiazzans' (*Caiatianorum*), was a descendant of the Drengot kin-group. His grandfather, Rainulf I of Caiazzo (d. 1088), was the brother of Prince Robert I of Capua, and thus the son of Asclettin Drengot, the brother of Count Rainulf of Aversa.[80] The counts of Carinola were also related to the Drengots. The younger brothers of Prince Jordan I of Capua, Jonathan and then Bartholomew, had taken the title of '*comes Caleni*' – the Latin names for the town of Carinola were many: *Calenum*, *Calinulum* and *Carinula*. This title was perhaps taken by the princely family from the Lombard family of Landenolfus, who, before 1076, was 'count of Carinola' (*qui fuerat comes Caleni*).[81] Jonathan and Bartholomew are confirmed as brothers in a 1089 judgement (*iudicatum*) made by Prince Jordan of Capua 'in the presence of Jonathan and his brother Bartholomew'.[82] By 1092, Jonathan is recorded as having authorized a donation made by his tenant Umfridus, the 'count of Calvi'. As the overlord of Calvi, Jonathan would have been certainly the count of the region, namely Carinola, at the time.[83] Bartholomew would have then taken Carinola after 1092, based on the evidence that regards his son Richard as count of Carinola. The Gaetan charters that record Richard of Carinola as duke of Gaeta establish at least one certainty: a unifying link between the count of Carinola and the nominal authority over Gaeta.[84] As count of Carinola, Richard probably already had knew the Gaetan territories well, as the lands of Carinola neighboured the eastern borders of the maritime city.[85] The influence of this cadet branch of the Capuan princely kin-group seems therefore to have grown with the duchy of Gaeta.

In Adriatic Apulia, the counts of Conversano descended from a branch of the Hauteville kin-group, since Geoffrey of Conversano was the son of one of Tancred's daughters.[86] The count of Andria, conversely, had a different Norman lineage, because he was most likely a descendant of Count Peter of Andria, a member of the family of the 'sons of Amicus' – a kin-group that constantly competed against the Hautevilles in Apulia during the eleventh century.[87] Count Robert II of Loritello, whose last documented appearance takes place in 1122,[88] was the son of Robert I of Loritello, the eldest son of Count Geoffrey (of Capitanata).[89]

The same Hauteville lineage of Geoffrey of Capitanata produced the only count in Calabria at that time: Count Geoffrey of Catanzaro was the son of Rao/Rudolph of Catanzaro – Robert I of Loritello's brother – and his wife, Countess Bertha.[90] Geoffrey's ascendency is also confirmed in an 1131 document where he is recorded as 'Count Geoffrey, son of Count Rao of Loritello' (κόμητος Ιοσφρὶ υιου κόμητου Ρἀου του λωρ ιτέλλου).[91] Almost certainly, Rao of Loritello acquired the lordship over Catanzaro in 1088 because of his support for Duke Roger Borsa against Bohemund of Taranto.[92] Rao commanded the contingent of knights of the count of Sicily and defeated the rebel and erstwhile lord of Catanzaro and Rocca Fallucca, Adam,[93] whose lands Rao apparently received in return.[94] Rao of Loritello is also regarded as count of Catanzaro in 1096, acting as a witness of the foundation, by Count Roger of Sicily and his wife Adelaide, of the bishopric of Squillace, to which Rao subjected lands in Catanzaro, Badolato and Taverna.[95] Count Rao died by 1111, because a Greek charter, given in 'μονιοὺ τ(ῆς) μεγάλης ὡδηγατείας' (later known as the abbey of St Mary of Patire), records 'Countess Bertha of Loritello and her sons Count Geoffrey and Raymond' (Βέρτης κομητίσσης τοῦ Λοριτέλλου καὶ [...] υἱοῖς τοῖς ἐμοῖς [...] Γιοσφρὲ κόμητι κ(αι) Ραιμούνδῳ) as donors who appear to have donated the church of St Apollinarius Martyr in Conchile to the protonotary and admiral Christodoulos, to be given to the monastery *magnae Hodegetriae*.[96] This cadet branch of the Loritello-Hauteville kin-group survived Roger II's takeover and, unlike its northern relatives, kept its lordship and position of power.

Among the upper local leaders that were not tied directly either to the Hauteville or to Drengot kin-groups at this point, besides the count of Andria, were the counts of Aquino, Boiano and Sarno. Count Simon of Boiano, Hugh II of Molise's father, was the son of Hugh I of Molise, whose family originated from Moulins-la-Marche (dép. Orne, cant. Tourouvre), in the region of Mortagne-au-Perche in Normandy.[97] Count Henry of Sarno is recorded as the son and heir of Count Richard.[98] The same Richard appears in earlier charters from Cava, dated October 1114 and June 1115, as a count and son of the late Count Richard; the 1115 document records Count Richard as *ex genere nortmannorum*, without any specific toponymic reference.[99] Henry of Sarno was, nevertheless, related to another prestigious kin-group, although not Norman but Lombard: he was the great-grandson of a certain Norman count Alfred, whose wife,

Gaitelgrima, was a daughter of the Lombard prince of Salerno Guaimar IV.[100] Also of Lombard lineage were the counts of Aquino, whose family held this lordship before the Normans arrived.

Having surveyed the heritage and social context of the south Italian upper aristocracy on the eve of the creation of the kingdom of Sicily, it is now possible to understand the original features of the nobility created under Roger II. Despite the uncertainty surrounding the specific political and administrative responsibilities that these counts might have had, they operated as the most recognizable agents of social order in the peninsular territories. The absence of an effective central government over the southern Italian mainland did not cause chaos. Instead, overlapping spaces of local authority were established, where *comites* of different status, military ability and landed wealth exercised social control and competed for further power against other lords and, subsequently, opposing Sicilian rule.

In this way, the fate of this social group historically matches that of the institutions of both the previous Lombard polities and the incipient Sicilian monarchy. The political (understood in a broad sense, to include status and landed wealth), however weak it may have been, continued to make its mark on the social, by allowing social control to perpetuate. Therefore, the establishment of the successive royal regime would push this social layer into constant conflict, defending and redefining its own pre-eminent position in society. Some of its members would survive that phase and ensure that their lineage, finally settled, occupied a privileged place in a new social order, at the price of adaptation and mutation – installing thus the upper nobility of the Sicilian monarchy. Likewise, the power basis and the families of the original Italo-Norman counts became the foundations upon which the newly established monarchy rearranged the territory and attempted to provide peace and security on the mainland.

2

The new kingdom's nobility and the creation of the south Italian counties

As Alexander of Telese described in the preface to his story:

> Just as the great sin of the Lombards was once overcome by the violence of the Normans when they came, […] in the same way today it is also certain that it was given, or at least permitted, to Roger by Heaven to coerce the immense malice of these regions by means of his sword. […] those whom He [God] had long considered incorrigible should be frightened by fear of Roger and brought back to the path of justice.[1]

The ruling class and the nobility undoubtedly changed in almost a century since the Normans settled in the south; but, despite the existence of new formal polities, the territory that would later form the kingdom of Sicily was still submerged in a quarrelling polyarchy in 1127. It is in this complex political reality that the first step towards the counts' new organization took place: 'Some counties were therefore suppressed, others resized, and, in the new composition, redistributed.'[2] But, how did the counties at the middle of the twelfth century differ from the lordships held by the counts when the kingdom was founded? To what extent did the new monarchy employ the creation of counts and counties for either restructuring the organization of the mainland or rewarding loyal local leaders and major landholders? To answer these questions, we must first understand the developments and changes that shaped the kingdom's upper aristocracy, by presenting a systematic survey of the counts' documented activities throughout Roger's reign.

After Count Roger II had reached an agreement with the pope and was invested duke of Apulia, he was ready to be elevated to the position of king. However, relations with the Roman Church were still problematic when the death of Honorius II in February 1130 was followed by a divided election and a subsequent schism that produced two contending popes: Innocent II and Anacletus II. While the former secured extensive support north of the Alps, Anacletus II consolidated his position in Rome. Count Roger of Sicily supported Anacletus, who in exchange for military and political support, crowned Roger king of a new kingdom.[3] On 27 September 1130, Anacletus's papal bull made Roger the king of Sicily; he was crowned in Palermo on Christmas Day 1130.[4] As expected, some of the peninsular counts reacted against the foundation of the new kingdom, and in 1131 a baronial league was assembled against Roger II. Though defeated, the rebellion soon reignited in the winter of 1134 in the northwest, still headed by Robert II of Capua and Rainulf of Caiazzo. But the darkest moment of the newly established monarchy was still at hand. After being defeated in 1135, Robert of Capua and Rainulf of Caiazzo returned as invading forces in what was an imperial and papal coalition against Roger II.

Stubborn lords and a lenient king

From 1127 to 1139, Roger II faced an aristocracy reluctant to accept the consolidation of the Sicilian kingdom and the king's authority. Almost every spring during this turbulent decade (except in 1136), King Roger arrived on the peninsula with an army to wage war in the summer, and then to retire to the island in the autumn. At first, Roger II travelled there by crossing the Straits of Messina and marching through Calabria – a route that would allow him to look out over what had been a close and integral province annexed to his Sicilian dominions. Later, perhaps after 1133, he travelled to Apulia by sea, landing in Salerno, from where he customarily departed back to Palermo. The decade following the creation of the Sicilian monarchy was an intense period of armed conflict and gradual readjustment, both to Roger's attitude towards the aristocracy and to the kingdom's making of its own nobility.

In the beginning, the prominent peninsular magnates maintained their own lordships. Count Roger of Ariano, for instance, was allowed to keep his extensive and geographically strategic lordship in the Irpina, while the brothers from Conversano, Tancred and Count Alexander, got their lands back after surrendering in 1129. The extensive lordship of these brothers had two different foci: Conversano, to the southeast of Bari; and Gravina, in the west.[5] Although Gravina was not attached to a comital title at this time, that connection to Conversano partially explains why subsequent testimonies, and even Count Alexander himself, according to one of his surviving seals, employed the title 'count of Gravina'.[6] Even Grimoald of Bari and his sons were allowed to be consecrated princes, via a papal concession that Anacletus II gave to the archbishop of Bari, which in all probability was given under Roger's consent.[7] All these magnates led the first armed opposition against Roger II, and still they were treated with leniency. The new king invested at first in improving the legitimacy of his rule by appearing accessible to those who opposed his takeover in Apulia and Capua.

The flexible treatment of the kingdom's upper aristocracy proved a failure. By 1132, the baronial coalition was reassembled and raised against the new monarchy. This rebellion started as a quarrel between Roger II and his brother-in-law Count Rainulf of Caiazzo, over the former's sister and latter's wife Matilda. Although Alexander of Telese and Falco of Benevento present different versions of the causes for this (the former attributed it specifically to the count's seizure of Matilda's dower lands, whereas Falco referred to the '*convicia multa et afflictiones*' Rainulf had inflicted on the king's sister), both agree on Matilda being the source of the discord.[8] Alongside Rainulf's insurrection, his nominal overlord Prince Robert of Capua joined the opposition again. As Loud has pointed out, once the Capuan prince became involved in the rebellion, the war was not only a battle against the effective authority of the king but also a battle for the independence of the principality of Capua and its barons.[9]

The insurrection of the major barons in Adriatic Apulia is nevertheless much less clear. According to Alexander of Telese, as soon as Roger II started his summer campaign in 1132 and crossed the Straits of Messina into southern Apulia, in Taranto, he accused Count Geoffrey of Andria of certain inexcusable misdeeds, for which the latter had to hand over to the crown a great part of his lands.[10] According to Falco of Benevento, Tancred of Conversano rebelled and resisted Roger II initially, and was later exiled from Apulia after the king marched on Brindisi.[11] The Telesian apologist is however clearer when he reports that Prince Grimoald of the Bariots was captured and sent in chains to Sicily after the king besieged Bari, because the prince of Bari had broken the fealty owed to the king and agreed with Roger's enemies. As vaguely as it was with Count Geoffrey, Alexander's story omits the exact role played by Tancred of Conversano, limiting his report to the latter's fearful handover of Brindisi and other cities and towns of which he was lord to Roger II. Tancred ultimately renounced his lands to the king in exchange for 20,000 scyphate coins, with the intention of 'departing' to Jerusalem.[12] The Conversano brothers were, however, among the barons who swore in the king's name to respect the rights of the people of Bari after the city's surrender on 22 June 1132.[13] Tancred's capitulation may have occurred during this period, perhaps towards the final stages of Bari's siege. Count Alexander of Conversano, in contrast, seems to have then neither rebelled against the king nor renounced part of his lands. Meanwhile, Count Rainulf took advantage of the king's campaign in the Adriatic.

The rebellion in the Tyrrhenian front then changed in favour of Count Rainulf, who defeated Roger and his army in a pitched battle on the border between the principality of Capua and the Salernitan region, at Nocera, on 25 July 1132.[14] This turn of events reignited the latent opposition left in the Adriatic. Once the news of the royal defeat reached the Apulian barons, Tancred interrupted his plans to travel across the sea and captured the cities of Montepeloso and Acerenza in an attempt to recover his dominions. On this occasion, Alexander is clear in attesting that both Tancred's brother Count Alexander and Count Geoffrey of Andria followed Tancred's momentum and committed treason against the king, binding themselves in an alliance with the Capuan rebels. Roger crossed the Straits of Messina once more, taking over the lands of all the Apulian rebels, capturing the *castrum* of Matera which was left to be defended by Count Alexander's son Geoffrey. The remaining barons were defeated and sent in chains to Sicily; Count Geoffrey of Andria was banished, and Tancred was imprisoned. Whether it was a preferential treatment offered to the magnate who bore the comital title or simply a harsher punishment for allegedly inciting the counts into betrayal, the distinction Alexander of Telese makes between Geoffrey's exile and Tancred's imprisonment is noteworthy. The only Apulian magnate who was not captured was Count Alexander of Conversano, who fled first to Count Rainulf, and then to Dalmatia, after he discovered his son's surrender.[15]

Alternatively, Falco of Benevento reports that the king, after besieging Matera, captured Geoffrey, son of Count Alexander, and later imprisoned the 'illustrious' Tancred of Conversano. Falco, however, erred in recording that Count Alexander died soon after his son and his lands were captured.[16] The latter not only clashes with

Alexander's report of his exile flight to Dalmatia, but is also disproven by a multitude of evidence that attests Alexander of Conversano's activities as a political exile in both western and eastern imperial courts.[17] In any case, the barons' rebellion was not over yet; the Capuan rebels continued campaigning.

The count of Boiano, Hugh II of Molise, appears for the first time in Alexander of Telese's story as he joined the expedition of Count Rainulf, together with the *magister militum* of Naples, Duke Sergius.[18] After Roger II captured Troia and other rebel towns in central Apulia, he arrived in Salerno ready to face the remaining Capuan rebel coalition. Roger then marched into Count Rainulf's lands and captured Sarno and Nocera. Alexander of Telese makes no mention of any count or lord of Sarno, although Count Henry must have been around at this time. Count Henry is recorded granting a mill to the church of St Mary of Montevergine in 1134, as 'Henry, count of Sarno, son of the late Richard, count of the same Sarno'.[19] Just because Count Alexander of Conversano, his brother Tancred, Count Geoffrey of Andria, Count Hugh of Boiano and Count Rainulf openly rebelled against the crown, it does not necessarily mean that the remainder of the mainland's upper aristocracy did so too, at least at this stage. Both Count Henry of Sarno and Count Nicholas of Principato are omitted. Presumably, King Roger enjoyed almost complete support in the principality of Salerno, which operated as a safe base for his campaigns against the rebels on the Capuan border and in the Beneventan lands.

By 1134, Roger had finally defeated the leader of the rebellion, Count Rainulf, resulting in the latter's submission and homage, while Prince Robert of Capua stayed in exile. Count Hugh of Boiano begged for the king's pardon, which he only obtained after surrendering a considerable part of his extensive lordships: the land east of the River Biferno and the Castello Maris. In 1135, Sergius of Naples also surrendered and paid homage. After this, and following Alexander's testimony, the lord of the Borell family also paid homage to Roger II.[20] The heads of the Borell kin-group by the early twelfth century were Count Theodinus of Sangro and Borell IV, lord of Agnone.[21] The comital title of this Theodinus was only a dignity of Lombard origin, and so it does not necessarily imply possession of an authoritative, unified lordship. Jamison has suggested that Theodinus was a descendant of Count Oderisius II of Sangro, as well as the same count Todinus who, in 1140, accompanied Roger II to the abbey of the Holy Saviour at M. Maiella, the father of Count Simon of Sangro, later attested in the *Quaternus magne expeditionis*.[22] Although the lands of the Borell family – known as *Terra Burrellensis* – were altogether extensive, tenancy was fragmented among the family. Similar to that of the counts of Boiano, this *Terra* had an important frontier location, where the southern Adriatic plains of the Abruzzo meet the northern mountains that connected the principality of Capua and the duchy of Apulia.

After the 1133 campaign, the nature of Roger's tactics changed. The king was much less conciliatory, and his reprisals were severe. Falco of Benevento's tone also changes after 1133; his mild criticisms of Roger II are replaced by a severe critique of the king's cruelty. This new approach however was more successful; after this victory and until the German invasion of 1137, the peninsular provinces remained securely under Roger's authority. The king may not have campaigned on the peninsula in 1136, as this was a relatively stable year – with the exception of the blockade of Naples. Falco of Benevento does not mention a royal campaign in his brief record of 1136, and the surviving diplomatic evidence for that year made after the winter and before October was all issued to recipients in Sicily.[23] The general historiography concurs with this assumption.[24]

It is during this stage of changing tactics that the first effort to construct a nobility from the centre can be traced. Alexander of Telese states that, by 1134, after Roger II had captured Capua and Sergius VII of Naples rendered homage and swore fealty to the new king, Roger II granted to Robert son of Richard the lands that Hugh II of Molise, count of Boiano, had surrendered to him.[25] The Telesian abbot furthermore remarks that while Roger was at war with the count of Boiano and the others, he promised those lands to Robert son of Richard, providing that he remained loyal to the king.[26] These lands were east of the River Biferno, and the *Castellum Maris* (modern Castel Volturno), at the mouth of the River Volturno.[27] These cannot have constituted all of Hugh of Molise's possessions, but they could have very well made up half of his Apulian dominions. This provided Robert son of Richard with two strategic zones: one in the interior of central Apulia that bordered the Capitanata and the lordship of Loritello and another on the Tyrrhenian shore between Gaeta and Naples.

Robert son of Richard was a local baron before the arrival of Roger II in Apulia. Robert was recorded in a July 1121 charter, drafted by Falco of Benevento himself, as the lord of *castrum* Cerentia.[28] Falco also recorded Robert son of Richard's request that Count Jordan of Ariano join and help him take the city of Fiorentino in 1127.[29] Given Robert son of Richard's prominent role as an avid royalist, his conspicuous absence during the first royal campaigns in the chronicle of Falco of Benevento should not come as a surprise, since Falco was a clear antagonist to the royal party. Count Robert is, nevertheless, recorded by Bishop Henry of Sant'Agata, an anti-Rogerian partisan. In the letter that Bishop Henry wrote to Pope Innocent informing him of Count Rainulf's victory over Roger II in Nocera in 1132, he recorded that 'the names of the barons of the duke [Roger II] who were captured and held are these: Count R(oger) of Ariano, Count R[obert] of Civitate and almost thirty others'.[30] Robert son of Richard is acknowledged here as count of Civitate, which suggests two things: first, that he had already been honoured with the comital honour, even before he received the lands confiscated from Hugh of Molise; second, that his original lordship was located in Civitate.[31] Thanks to his performance as both a royalist commander and an outstandingly loyal baron, in 1134 Count Robert was rewarded with the lands east of the River Biferno; however, Civitate would have been granted to another potential ally of King Roger. My impression therefore is that Robert was the overlord of the eastern Molisian dominions after 1134 but was not allowed to keep his lordship in the Capitanata, as the king had other plans for it.

The other count mentioned among the king's allies, Count Roger of Ariano, provides another example of the intricate changes that may have occurred behind the scenes. Although he had resisted Roger II in the late 1120s, he is recorded here as a baron who fought on the king's side. Interestingly enough, Falco omitted this, despite his knowledge of, and previous references to, Roger of Ariano. He may have remained a royalist until Lothar's invasion in 1137, but the chronicler is again silent about his continuing changes of side and the attempted configuration of a kingdom's nobility.

We are told by Alexander of Telese that, by 1135, Robert son of Richard was a member of the king's army. At this time, the royal armed forces were near to Caserta, defending the Terra di Lavoro under the command of Emir John, having recently received reinforcements from Apulia of both knights and foot soldiers. Count Roger of Ariano is identified among the nobles in the royal army.[32] Robert was, however, not attested by Alexander of Telese as a count until after Roger II had granted the dignity of prince of Capua to his son Alfonso, when, while in Aversa, the king entrusted the command of the knights chosen to defend the northwestern territories to several counts he deemed trustworthy. These temporary commanders operated for set terms, and Robert son of Richard was appointed to the second of these periods in command.[33] As commander of the royal knights, Count Robert blockaded the borders of Naples 'with such military prowess and energy that its defenders never dared to sortie to inflict injury on their enemies'. He completed his two-month term of duty at Aversa, from November to December 1135, and then returned home – to the Capitanata, perhaps.[34] He was then succeeded by Count Simon of Monte Sant'Angelo in Gargano.

After the civil war, there is no further evidence besides Alexander of Telese that records the existence of either a count or county in Monte Sant'Angelo under Roger II. This Simon might have been Simon del Vasto, who is subsequently identified as Simon of Policastro, since he was the son of King Roger's maternal uncle Henry del Vasto, lord of Paternò and Butera.[35] Henry del Vasto belonged to the north Italian Aleramici family, as the brother of Roger II's mother Adelaide del Vasto.[36] The Sicilian lordships of Paternò and Butera had been associated with the Aleramici family since the time of Count Roger I.[37] Simon's parentage is confirmed by a September 1156 royal charter under which William I guaranteed the continued possession of the land held previously by Count Henry, father of Count Simon, to the church of the Holy Cross, which Simon had unjustly alienated.[38] It is striking that all the subsequent documents in which Count Simon is attested take place in Sicily, and the toponym 'of Policastro' is only recorded by Pseudo-Falcandus.[39] If the Count Simon in the Telesian testimony is the same Count Simon of Policastro, he was then soon removed from the mainland and returned to Sicily as lord of Butera, becoming thus the only known baron on the island with the comital dignity. This, however, might have just been the result of his temporary role as a royal commander during the civil war, which allowed him to keep the title he received on the peninsula, maintaining it as lord of Butera in Sicily. The references to his father as 'Count Henry' appear therefore to be given after Count Simon's activities on the mainland, and following his death the comital title seems to have lapsed. An alternative explanation is that Simon's father, Henry, could have been given the honorary title in recognition of his parentage, and also as a token of Roger's esteem. Henry was the son of Manfred del Vasto, brother of Marquis Boniface of Savona, and was married to Flandina, a daughter of Roger I by one of his first two wives – Judith d'Évreux or Eremburga of Mortain. Since Roger I died when Roger II was only five years old, his maternal uncle Henry must have played a leading part in the young duke's upbringing and in pressing forward the elevation of his nephew as a king. Alexander of Telese evidences this, as he narrates that 'those close to Duke Roger, and particularly his uncle Count Henry by whom he was loved more than anyone' were constantly suggesting that Duke Roger should be additionally honoured with the royal title.⁴⁰ Anyhow, Henry del Vasto does not appear to have been a count in the same way as the peninsular counts.

Another baron who is practically ignored in both Alexander and Falco and surviving charters, but who played a central role during this interwar stage, is Jonathan of Carinola. Jonathan was a relative – a son, according to Cuozzo⁴¹ – of Count Richard of Carinola, and duke of Gaeta – a title that this branch of the Capuan princely kin-group held between *c.* 1112 and 1135. This same Richard of Carinola issued a guarantee for the protection of the old Gaetan coinage to the people of Gaeta in November 1123, in which he regards himself as 'consul and duke of the city of Gaeta by divine mercy, son of the late Lord Bartholomew [brother of Prince Jordan I of Capua], of fond memory, descendant to the prince of Capua and to the counts of Carinola'.⁴² However, young Jonathan is attested in earlier dating clauses as the duke and consul of Gaeta.

As I have argued previously, Jonathan was the young duke of Gaeta from *c.* 1116 to 1120, who then was removed by his uncle Richard of Carinola, who also acted as count of Carinola. As a young survivor of the Drengot princely kin-group, Jonathan was still alive in the 1130s, and became the count of Carinola of the new kingdom – albeit the ducal dignity of Gaeta was not given to anyone.⁴³ Quid pro quo: Jonathan recovered the lordship and some of the titles to which he should have been entitled, and the Sicilian king tallied a noble Capuan collaborator to his side.

A ruthless king and the nascent nobility

In 1137, relative stability was replaced with the peril of a full-on German invasion. Lothar's marching army affected the Sicilian campaign, in that King Roger only came to the peninsula in September that year to avoid meeting the large invading and rebel forces. According to Romuald of Salerno, 'the emperor occupied the whole of Apulia without resistance'.⁴⁴ Lothar entered Apulia and captured Bari in 1137, having crossed the River Pescara after Easter, marching through the Adriatic coast and capturing Siponto, Rignano, Monte Sant'Angelo, Troia, Canne, Barletta and Trani.⁴⁵ It would be safe to assume that the entire coast from the Abruzzo to the Terra di Bari surrendered to the imperial invasion. Count Roger of Ariano, and possibly Count William of Loritello, joined the rebellion and welcomed the German emperor Lothar. This William might have been the same palatine lord that joined the imperial party, as the *Annalista Saxo* attests 'marquises Thomas and Matthew, together with their lord William, palatine [count]' (*Thomam et Matheum marchiones cum domno eorum Willehelmo palatino*) swore allegiance to Lothar II in 1137.⁴⁶ This is the episode Cuozzo refers to when assuming that Lothar took the lordship of Civitate from Robert son of Richard and gave it to Jonathan. Although I disagree with the latter, the former seems highly likely. As I argued in 2016, Roger II must have granted the lands and lordships that would later constitute the *comitatus* of Civitate to Jonathan of Carinola at some point between 1134 and 1137, after Count Robert son of Richard received some of the dominions of Hugh of Molise, but before the entire region was convulsed by Lothar's expedition.⁴⁷ The German Imperial invasion temporarily broke Roger II's rule on the mainland, forcing the barons of the occupied regions to surrender themselves.

The maintenance of the king's marginal resistance, and perhaps even the minimal governance of these provinces, was left in the hands of his local commanders, the territorial leaders left on the mainland. The royal garrisons were able to hold the invasion up until it withdrew in the autumn, allowing Roger II to recover what had been lost as the Germans retreated. The king returned to Sicily at the end of the year. Falco of Benevento states that this comeback was swift and ruthless: Roger summoned his army and immediately went to Salerno to march against Nocera, take all Count Rainulf's lands, furiously storm Capua, 'devastating it with fire and iron', recapture Avellino and Benevento, and devastate Montecorvino. The brother of Count Rainulf, Count Richard of Rupecanina, was forced out of his dominions. Duke Sergius of Naples (the *magister militum*) then rushed to the king's side, only to die soon after in Rignano fighting for the royal cause. Despite the initial drive of Roger's counteroffensive, there he lost again against Rainulf's army, on 2 October 1137.[48] After Nocera, Rignano was the second great defeat of the king's army against Rainulf of Caiazzo, but like the former, had no durable effect. Roger II restarted his campaign in the following year, crossing the frontiers of Apulia and moving into Capua and the Apulian lands still under Rainulf's control. Although this campaign proved again unsuccessful, Roger II was able to finally secure his hold over the entire mainland in 1139, after the spurious Duke Rainulf fell sick and died at his base, in Troia on 30 April 1139.[49]

The once rebellious nobility had been thus forcibly pacified. For almost a decade, the peninsular aristocracy defended the rights and privileges they had enjoyed for lack of an effective central rule. But things were different by the 1140s; a new authority had arrived and ultimately won. In September 1129, Roger II promulgated a comprehensive land peace at an assembly of mainland nobles in Melfi, by which these prominent lords swore to maintain peace and justice under the authority and assistance of the consolidated monarchy.[50] In 1140, Roger II was finally firmly in control of the entire southern third of the Italian peninsula and had achieved tranquillity in his mainland dominions. Once the dust settled, the king reorganized the lordships once occupied by his opponents. These regional leaders served as the basis of the reorganization of the mainland landholdings and the subsequent establishment of the peninsular counties.

Aristocratic survival in the aftermath of the war

In the wake of the creation of the kingdom, the composition and arrangement of the higher aristocracy had already changed considerably. His original conciliatory attitude towards the peninsular leadership, using both swords and words to secure and legitimize his kingship, had, by 1134, morphed into a more belligerent approach, which was then completely transformed after 1137 into the spoils system that allowed him to directly reward his supporters and punish any opposition without prevarication. First, the mainland was practically organized in three provinces after 1140 (Terra di Lavoro, Apulia, and Calabria; with Manopello and the Abruzzo as a separated region).[51] The counts of Ariano and Caiazzo were suppressed, as was that of Loritello, and the lands that were amassed under each comital title were confiscated by the crown and reassigned to other barons. The counts of Sarno disappear after 1139; it appears this lordship was also confiscated after Count Henry went into exile with the other rebels. The lords of Aquino, on the other hand, were allowed to keep their tenure, but not the comital title.

Count Roger of Ariano was defeated and imprisoned, and had his dominions confiscated.[52] Rainulf of Caiazzo died in Troia as the spurious duke of Apulia in 1139, leaving no acting successor to his lands or his position as head of the imperial party against the Sicilian crown. The lords of Aquino, after 1137, are solely referred to as *domini*, never again as *comites*. They are recorded only as lords in the *Quaternus* under a special section dedicated to Aquino.[53] Furthermore, the earliest reference to the lord of Aquino after the civil war is found in an 1148 charter that records a dispute between Montecassino and 'lord Pandulf of Aquino'.[54] After Henry of Sarno is recorded to have made a donation, as count and son of lord Richard of Sarno, in 1138 to Montevergine, there are no other counts of Sarno attested in the surviving evidence.[55] However, in a letter Conrad III sent to Manuel Komnenos *c.* 1144, transcribed by Otto of Freising, a certain Count Henry is mentioned among the Apulian barons known to the German king. Among other things, the Eastern emperor requested from Conrad information on south Italian exiles.[56] It is possible, hence, that Henry of Sarno remained an active count until 1139, due to his allegiance to Prince Robert of Capua. He was thus forced into exile with the other nobles who ended up in the German court as political refugees, namely Roger of Ariano, Richard of Rupecanina and Robert of Capua himself.

Andria was left vacant and perhaps temporarily merged into the royal demesne. The aforementioned William of Loritello welcomed and paid homage to the invading emperor; his lordship was later confiscated, presumably a result of this act of treason. Boiano, conversely, was restored to Hugh II of Molise. First, the chronicle of Santa Maria of Ferraria indicates that in 1141 King Roger married Hugh of Molise's sister, by whom he had his son Simon, the same son who was reportedly appointed prince of Capua.[57] Assuming that the date in the *Chronica Ferrariensis* is correct, it is not impossible that they got married, as this would have been after Roger's first wife Elvira of Castile died in 1135, and well before his marriage to Sibylla of Burgundy in 1149. Houben has suggested that she was in fact one of his mistresses.[58] In any case, Hugh of Molise may have negotiated the recovery of his extensive dominions with the king between 1139 and 1142, and certainly before 1144 – when he presided over a court at Trivento.[59]

Manopello, in Abruzzo, was given to a royalist Calabrian baron, Bohemund of Tarsia. The chartulary-chronicle of Casauria records that Roger II appointed 'Count Bohemund to the county of Manopello' (*comes Boamundus [...] comitatu Manupelli*), *c.* August 1140, and that the same count sought to interfere with the monastery, albeit restrained by the king.[60] Although his origins are uncertain, he was originally a Norman baron from Tarsia, Calabria, under the favour of Chancellor Robert of Selby.[61] Count Bohemund of Manopello was active in the first half of the 1140s as he interacted with the abbey of the Holy Saviour at M. Maiella in the Abruzzese Apennines. He first donated to this abbey in 1141; then, he intervened in favour of Prior Alexander during a dispute with the bishop-elect of Chieti in 1142; and finally, he restored the church of St Andrew to the abbey in 1144, under the king's direct instructions, and acting as his justiciar in Chieti.[62]

Conversano, in southern Apulia, was given to Robert of Bassunvilla during the civil war, and before the disastrous year 1137. He is attested in two documents from Cava, charters dated October and November 1136.[63] Alexander of Telese recorded, however, the existence of a certain Adam, King Roger's brother-in-law (*gener*), as count of Conversano, and temporary commander of the royal troops, *c*.1135–6.[64] His identity is unclear. Chalandon suggests Adam was in fact Adam Avenel, the son of Adelicia, daughter of Roger's sister Emma and Rudolph Machabeus.[65] Alternatively, Loud argues that Alexander of Telese may have made a mistake with the new count's name, and Robert would have therefore been appointed count slightly earlier than Alexander indicated.[66] Robert of Bassunvilla was not only already regarded as count of Conversano in April 1134, but he was Roger II's actual brother-in-law, married to the king's sister Judith.[67] Another less likely possibility may be that this Adam died soon after his appointment as commander of the royal forces in Aversa, because Robert of Bassunvilla was definitively the count of Conversano by the end of the civil war.

In the Capitanata, a Count William of Lesina was the new count of Lesina, before Geoffrey of Ollia was appointed as such. It is not certain who this William was; he could have been a descendant of the earlier counts from the 'son of amicus' kin-group, but this is unclear. Count William was the son-in-law of an erstwhile count of Lesina, Robert.[68] However, the connection between this Count Robert and the previous counts of Lesina is unclear; De Francesco suggests that he was a brother of Count Rao of Lesina, son of Count Peter, but this is just a hypothesis.[69] The only documented appearance of Count William of Lesina under Roger II's reign is found in the 1141 charter in which he is recorded as head of a court in Lesina.[70] This William of Lesina appears to be the same count who, according to Pseudo-Falcandus, was King William I's captive, held in chains at Palermo in 1156, and one of the royal palace captives released during the baronial conspiracy of 1161.[71]

The only comital positions that appear unchanged were Principato and Catanzaro. Count Nicholas of Principato made two documented appearances in 1141 and is also regarded as a ruling count in 1142. First, in March 1141, he and his brother William issued a confirmation (*preceptum*) of previously donated land to the archbishop of Salerno, for the salvation of the soul of their father, William II of Principato.[72] Later that month, as requested by a deputy of Archbishop William of Salerno, a certain Judge Peter certified in the presence of Count Nicholas a *preceptum* issued by the count in favour of the archbishop (i.e. the previous 1141 charter).[73] Unfortunately, these documents are highly suspicious in their present form. Both their latest editors, Giordano and Carlone, have identified them as fabrications in the form of authentic copies; the first as a copy inserted into a document issued in 1252 and the second as a forgery, possibly produced by the same scribe who participated in the reproduction of the *preceptum* given by Count Nicholas in 1141.[74] This possibility, however, should not justify dismissing the documents entirely, as a fabrication in the form of an authentic copy may still be based on an original and the information thus contained in subsequent reproductions cannot be assessed as reliable solely on the grounds of diplomatic criteria. The information that the 1141 charters contain on the archbishop of Salerno makes sense when contrasted with other surviving material. These charters appear to be based on original transactions, in that their prosopographical information is both accurate and significant. Cuozzo has identified most of the individuals attested in these legal transactions as local officials and barons allegedly established as members of the *entourage* of Count Nicholas.[75] Moreover, additional evidence confirms that Count Nicholas was still alive by 1141: a Greek charter from Auletta, dated May 1142, was certified 'in the time of our most pious Count Nicola' (ἐν τοῖς καιροῖς τοῦ ἐυλαβεστάτου ἡμῶν κώμιτος νικολάου).[76] Countess Adelaide of Principato, most likely Nicholas' wife, is subsequently attested as a donor to Cava in 1143 and 1146.[77]

In Catanzaro, the succession is harder to determine. It is, however, plausible to suggest that the Hauteville-Loritello branch kept the lordship throughout this period. Geoffrey of Catanzaro is last recorded in 1132, as a signatory in a royal charter.[78] A subsequent document suggests however that the title was vacated after his death, between 1143 and 1145. Geoffrey of Catanzaro was present in a royal court that heard a suit between Bishop John of Aversa and Abbot Walter of St Lawrence in November 1143, because the royal charter that records the ratification of the mediation presents him as a subscriber, as 'count of Catanzaro' (*comes Catacensis*).[79] Subsequently, his mother, Countess Bertha, made a donation in 1145 for the salvation of his son, the late Count Geoffrey.[80] Remarkably, Bertha is recorded both here and in 1112 as 'countess of Loritello', indicating not her actual lordship but her position as a member of the Loritello kin-group, which descended directly from one of the original conquerors, Geoffrey of Capitanata.[81] Besides Bertha, it is also possible that Geoffrey's brother Raymond succeeded him.[82] Raymond was the husband of Countess Segelgarda and the father of Clementia, the young countess.[83]

In 1140 there were only five confirmed counts on the mainland: three in Adriatic Apulia (Conversano, Lesina, Tricarico), one in the former principality of Salerno (Principato) and one in Calabria (Catanzaro). Furthermore, it was after 1140 when three more counts must have been reinstated and confirmed (Boiano, Carinola, and Civitate).[84] From 1140 to 1150, when the *quaterniones curiae* on the lords' land holdings that served as the basis for the *Quaternus magne expeditionis* were presumably drafted, the kingdom went through a phase of peaceful reorganization, which took over from the changes already introduced right after the end of the civil war.[85]

The gradual establishment of a hybrid comital class

Archbishop Romuald of Salerno states that the king 'created many new counts in his kingdom'.[86] Between 1140 and 1150, both continuity and readjustment can be documented in the activities and presence of the Italo-Norman counts. The *Quaternus magne expeditionis* implies the existence, by 1150, of eleven counts (Avellino, Boiano, Buonalbergo, Carinola, Civitate, Conversano, Fondi, Marsico, Montescaglioso, Principato and Tricarico). Although the counties of Alife and of Caserta are clearly recorded in the *Quaternus*, there is no evidence of a count of Caserta or a count of Alife before 1162, and I shall later argue in the two subsequent chapters that these counties in the Terra di Lavoro were created during the reign of William I.

Although the *Quaternus* seems to have been compiled by cataloguing lordships under either the duchy of Apulia or the principality of Capua – the two main provinces in which the mainland territories were divided – the lordships that were grouped under these comital titles were in some instances distributed in both provinces. The two most illustrative cases of this are the counts of Boiano and Carinola. The count of Carinola, whose seat was in the Terra di Lavoro, held the significant lordship of Conza in Apulia, and the lordships gathered under the Count Hugh of Boiano were included in the sections for Apulia and for Capua, because in these territories both provinces met on the northern borders. Additionally, Count Robert of Buonalbergo, whose comital seat was in the Apulian mountainous region of Irpina (northeast of Benevento), also held Acerra, Margliano and Sessola in southern Capua (between Naples and Avellino), because this recently created count must have held these lands previously as lord of Acerra in the same way his father Geoffrey of Medania did before him.[87]

At this time, additional counts are documented in the separated provinces of Calabria, in the south, and in the 'jurisdiction' (*justitia/comestabulia*) of the count of Manopello, the annexed province in central Italy known as the Abruzzo. Two comital seats were based in Calabria, the counts of Catanzaro and Squillace, whereas Count Bohemund of Manopello oversaw a handful of local overlords that also bore the title of count: Count Robert of Abruzzo (*Aprutium*), Count Theodinus of Sangro, Count Rambot of Loreto, Count Rainulf of Celano and Count Berard of Alba, among other overlords who were not recorded with the comital title.[88]

With regard to the count of Boiano, Hugh II of Molise presided over a court in 1144 at Trivento, according to a missing document from the archive of Montecassino. The document recorded a suit drawn against Maynerius of Palena and Matthew of Pettorano, two barons of the count of Boiano, and other tenants under the apparent jurisdiction of Hugh of Molise. The abbey finally obtained the restitution of the church of St Peter de Avellana at the hands of the barons, 'by *preceptum* and sentence of both the royal *curia* (*regalis curia*) and Count Hugh'.[89] Hugh of Molise is regarded here as both count and justiciar (*comes et justitiarius Ug. de Molisi*); this would be the only known instance in which the comital title is used alongside the title of justiciar during Roger II's reign, and though he is not explicitly attested as a 'royal justiciar', the court he presided over was both a king's and the count's court.[90] Count Hugh is additionally attested under King Roger's reign on three more occasions. Three Beneventan charters record him in 1147, 1149 and 1153. First, as 'Molisian count' (*comes Molisianus*), he presided over a tribunal in October 1147 that heard and witnessed an agreement at Limosano.[91] Count Hugh is then recorded in a privilege, dated March 1149, in which he confirms, at Boiano, as 'count of Boiano' (*comes Boianensis*), the *castella* of Castelvecchio, Toro and S. Giovanni in Galdo to the church of St Sophia in Benevento.[92] Hugh of Molise is also remembered in an agreement signed in Venafro,[93] in July 1153, in which the count, as 'Hugh by grace of God count of Molise' (*Hugo dei gratia de molisio Comes*), confirmed the *castella* of Castelvecchio, Toro, and S. Giovanni in Galdo to John, abbot of St Sophia di Benevento; the confirmation also stipulated the exclusion of a series of listed royal *placiti*.[94] All the places where these documents were produced – Limosano, Boiano, Venafro – and the locations they mention are found within what would later be known as the county of Molise, the historical basis of the current region of Molise. The lands of the region of Molise were situated in an important strategic area, located in the vertex of the northern border between the duchy of Apulia and the principality of Capua, connecting thus both the Terra di Lavoro and Adriatic Apulia, and the special justiciarate of the Abruzzo. Hugh of Molise is later attested as count of Molise by Pseudo-Falcandus, c.1160, who records that 'Matthew [Bonellus] was captivated by the beauty of an illegitimate daughter of King Roger who had been married to Count Hugh of Molise'.[95]

In none of the surviving documents concerning Count Hugh of Molise is the comital title clearly and solely referring to the 'county of Molise'. Instead, the term 'Molise' appears to have referred originally to the iconic toponym of the family of barons that came from Moulins-la-Marche (dép. Orne, cant. Tourouvre), in Normandy.[96] Hugh is attested in 1144 as both 'count and justiciar, Hugh of Molise' (*comes et justitiarius Ug. de Molisi*).[97] Then, in 1147, he is regarded as 'Molisian count' (*comes Molisianus*), and in 1153, he signs as 'Hugh, count of Molise' (*Hugo moilisii Comes*), which could still be referring to the toponymic name of Hugh's Norman family.[98] In the 1149 privilege, Boiano was still employed in the comital title – albeit it was issued in Boiano – and the designation '*comes Boianensis*' survived in a late thirteenth-century copy, when the county of Molise was a much clearer geographical and political unit.[99] It is unclear whether the dominions of the count of Molise were consolidated at this time as a 'county of Molise'. It does not help that the headlines for the county of Molise and the direct reference to Count Hugh of Molise are absent in the *Quaternus*, which to all appearances indicate a serious lacuna before the section for the principality of Capua in one of the subsequent copies of the document.[100] Though the composition of a rather large county for Hugh of Molise can be inferred from the content and structure of the *Quaternus*, the existence of a well-defined unit under the name of Molise cannot be confirmed at the time the first drafts of the *Quaternus* were made, c. 1150–67.

The restoration of the county of Hugh II of Molise must have diminished the lordships and lands that Count Robert son of Richard had amassed in the northern Capitanata, east of the River Biferno, under his comital title. It would have been necessary then to grant another lordship whose importance and extension matched that of his former holdings to one of the king's trusted allies, as Robert son of Richard was. The lordship of Civitate and its tenure in the Capitanata, which bordered the lands east of the Biferno, seem to have been an ideal alternative for Count Robert son of Richard, in that this was the original lordship Robert held before 1134. A charter dated January 1152 records Count Robert of Civitate, as 'the son of Robert, late count of Civitate by the grace of God and the king', restoring some land to Umfridus, abbot of *Terra Maggiore* (modern Torremaggiore), and agreeing upon some exemptions and privileges.[101] In addition to this, the document records the existence of a previous count of Civitate, who used to lawfully hold the title and the tenure corresponding to it: Count Jonathan. The latter is attested as count of Civitate in an imperial confirmation made by Frederick II in 1225 in favour of the monastery of St Mary of Pulsano. This charter records that 'late Jonathan, count of Civitate (*Civitatis comes*) by the grace of God and the king' donated land to the monastery.[102] Robert son of Richard is furthermore remembered in an early thirteenth-century testimony as an 'old count' (*vetus comes*) who had given land as a dowry for his daughter.[103] This land was in a place that used to host a monastery called *Sanctus Angelus in Vico*, in the vicinity of Lucera and Fiorentino. Fiorentino was the same town in the Capitanata which, according to Falco of Benevento, was taken by Robert son of Richard in 1127.

As I documented in 2016, Roger II used this opportunity to manoeuvre his nobles politically towards the consolidation of his rule over the mainland nobility by permuting Civitate and Carinola. The king would have returned Jonathan's previous dominions to Count Robert son of Richard, and Jonathan would finally be restored to his place of origin: Carinola.[104] However, Jonathan's ducal title of Gaeta was no longer employed, and the lordship over the coastal city was held directly by Roger II after 1140. The counts of Fondi would subsequently exercise their influence in Gaeta through the handful of *feuda* they held within the city limits, but no longer as dukes, 'consuls' or lords of the city. To compensate Jonathan of Carinola for the loss of Gaeta, Roger must have granted him a small but strategic lordship: Conza. Originally held by Geoffrey of Catanzaro, Conza was left vacant after his death. Count Jonathan then received Conza and held it *in demanio*.[105] The transfer of Conza was a problematic but rich episode in the transformation of the Italo-Norman nobility, which illustrates how liquid the delimitations of the counts' dominions were, and how closely the counties of Civitate and Carinola were weaved together.

Consequently, under Count Jonathan, the county of Carinola was enhanced with the lordship of Conza, a city that would play a crucial role in bringing together the count of Carinola's tenure in Apulia, and in the development of what would be known in subsequent centuries as the county of Conza. To summarize, I argue that Hugh II of Molise was either reinstated or confirmed as count of Boiano at some point between 1139 and 1144; Count Jonathan was restored to Carinola *c*. 1140, allowing thus Count Robert son of Richard to re-receive the county of Civitate; and to compensate Jonathan for the abolished ducal title of Gaeta he then received the lordship of Conza after 1144.

In Conversano, Robert of Bassunvilla had died by 1142, as a vineyard was granted in 1142 to the monastery of 'the hermits of Driene' (μονή τῶν ἐραιήτων δριένης) by Adelicia, who is attested as 'daughter of the most blessed [late] Count Robert of Bassunvilla' (ἀδιλασία ἡ τοῦ μακαριωτάτου κόμητος ροπέρτου βασαβύλλια θυγάτηρ).[106] His son Robert II of Bassunvilla succeeded his father soon enough, because in November 1143 he subscribed two royal charters in Capua and in Salerno, as 'count of Conversano' (*comes Cupersani*). The Capuan charter recorded an assembled royal *curia* which heard a suit between Bishop John of Aversa and the abbot of St Lawrence in Aversa.[107] However, the second royal charter from Salerno, by which the king assured St Mary a Capella in Naples of his protection – the only known royal charter of Roger II issued to a Neapolitan recipient – has been identified as a forgery by its editor, Brühl.[108] Its escathocol appears to have been copied from the Capuan charter; the dating clause was replicated almost verbatim, with the obvious exception of Capua having been substituted for Salerno, and the list of witnesses included in its *subscription* is almost the same, albeit with some omissions such as Count Geoffrey of Catanzaro and Count Richard of Avellino. It thus appears that the charter reportedly issued in Salerno was a fabrication. In any case, the existence of the first charter evidences the subscribers' presence in the royal *curia* held at Capua in autumn 1143.

Robert II of Bassunvilla was recorded in 1146, in what are now two lost donations, as having granted to the abbey of Venosa the churches of St Nicholas of

Terlizzi and St Mary, as count of Conversano and lord of Molfetta.[109] Additionally, a March 1148 charter records a confirmation of a grant made to the monastery of Cava by Robert of Bassunvilla, count of Conversano (*Cupersani comes*) and lord of Melfi (*civitatis mee Melficte*).[110] Robert II of Bassunvilla is subsequently attested in an 1153 reference as donating, as count of Conversano, the church of St Nicholas of Terlizzi to the abbey of Venosa.[111] In March of the following year, the same Robert made another donation to the abbey of Venosa, this time recorded also as lord of Molfetta.[112] Robert II of Bassunvilla seems thus to have been active as a prominent lord in Adriatic Apulia, around the *Terra Barese*. Similarly, just as the 'sons of Amicus' did from the conquest until the civil war, Robert of Bassunvilla exercised his lordship over Conversano and the city of Molfetta, but not over Andria and Lesina. The new count of Conversano's dominions were less extensive than the lands the original counts of Conversano and 'the sons of Amicus' held before the creation of the kingdom.

The old Lombard comital dignity for Avellino was used to create a new county from the former territories of the count of Sarno and given to the Norman family of Aquila at some point before 1143. Richard II of Aquila, the son of the old duke of Gaeta, Richard I of Aquila,[113] is recorded as count of Avellino (*comes Avellini*) in the list of subscribers of the aforesaid royal charter issued at Capua in November 1143.[114] The count of Avellino is attested in a series of transactions in the following years.

An August 1144 charter from Cava reveals that Count Richard of Aquila was involved in a suit against Alexios son of John *Coliander*, involving the house the latter had built on the outskirts of Avellino, next to the public road named 'Salernitana' (*fabricavit a foras civit. Avellini erga viam publicam que dicitur Salernitana*). One of the house's walls was built on the road, but the defendant denied it. Romanus, the count's *stratigotus* (and, hence, Avellino's *stratigotus*), was recorded instructing the defendant Alexios. The suit was heard by the same judges that sanctioned the charter: Bernard and John.[115] Was this *stratigotus* a civic or a comital functionary? The title suggests this was a position in the city's government, rather than an office in the count's entourage.[116] Romanus, however, is mentioned in this document as the count's own *stratigotus*, and he acted under the direction of the count of Avellino concerning a matter of both judicial and urban administration. The position of Avellino's *stratigotus* manifests then as a result of the overlap between the civic authority and that of the count in regard to Avellino's administration of justice.

In December 1149, Richard of Aquila, count of Avellino, donated the *feudum* and other holdings that used to belong to Jordan *Pinczast* in Pontecorvo to Montecassino.[117] This donation, although given under the title of count of Avellino, concerned land far from the town of Avellino; Pontecorvo was located on the western fringe of the principality of Capua, within the *Terrae Sancti Benedicti*, which was conceded to Montecassino in 1105.[118] Richard I of Aquila was originally established as baron in western Capua, even becoming duke of Gaeta between 1121 and 1129. A specific *feudum* held by Richard I of Aquila in the vicinity can be identified: the 1105 donation of Pontecorvo to Montecassino established that the *castellum* outside the town and *feudum* of Richard of Aquila were excluded.[119] Subsequently,

Richard of Aquila signed a written oath to Oddo, abbot of Montecassino, by which he committed to not harm the abbey, and to help him recover Pontecorvo.[120] An earlier donation charter recorded that in April 1091 Richard of Aquila, 'count' of the *castellum* of Pico, offered four monasteries to Montecassino.[121] The *castellum* of Pico must have been the same *castellum* recorded in the 1105 donation, because Pico is located just 10 kilometres to the west of Pontecorvo, and the 1091 donation was drafted by the notary of Pontecorvo, priest John. The county of Avellino had, therefore, a second, smaller *focus* in Capua because of the lordship Richard II of Aquila inherited from his father.

Back in his Apulian dominions, Count Richard of Aquila was recorded in 1152 exchanging some lands near Avellino and a house in the same town. First, Richard of Aquila, count of Avellino, exchanged in April three plots of land with a vineyard in *Allibergum* for another three plots of land with a forest (*arbustum*) and *iscla* in the vicinity of the *castellum* of Avellino, and a mill in the same *castellum*, on the River Cupo.[122] The official in charge of conducting this transaction was the same *stratigotus* Romanus mentioned in the 1144 charter from Cava. Then, in May 1152, the same *stratigotus* Romanus received 'on behalf of their lord, the count' (*pro parte domini nostri comitis*) a plot of land with an orchard located next to the River Cupo, the same river on which said *castellum* was located, in exchange for a house in the town of Avellino, near the church of St Lawrence.[123] Because the 1152 transactions were all conducted by the *stratigotus* Romanus, and Count Richard was neither present nor conducted the exchanges personally, it could be assumed that the count of Avellino was already ill by the first half of 1152, close to death – we know that Richard II of Aquila died in September 1152, and that he is the same baron attested in the *Quaternus* as the 'former' count of Avellino.[124] These exchanges also suggest that the count of Avellino had a plan to concentrate tenure in his own comital *caput*, in that he was clearly consolidating his hold on the *castellum* of Avellino and the lands around it, which in both 1152 charters is clearly distinguished from the *civitas* of Avellino.

The counts of Montescaglioso appear to have disappeared after Roger II took control of the town in 1124. As described earlier, the descendants of the last attested count of Montescaglioso did not bear the comital title and their lordships were not connected to Montescaglioso. However, Geoffrey of Lecce, son of Accardus, is recorded as count of Montescaglioso *c.* 1150.[125] This count of Montescaglioso descended from the lords of Lecce, and not from the original Norman lords that arrived during the conquest and used to hold Montescaglioso.[126] Additionally, Geoffrey of Lecce must have become count of Montescaglioso only after 1152, because, in May 1152, his daughter Alberada, *domina* of Lucera, refers to him solely as *Goffridus Licie*, without mention of his comital honour or his link to Montescaglioso.[127] In any case, a Sicilian marble inscription from 14 June 1153 records that 'Geoffrey of Lecce, the most serene count of Montescaglioso' (*Gosfridus Licii serenissimus comes Montis Caveosi*) consecrated the church of the Holy Spirit in Caltanissetta.[128] It can be argued then that the count of Montescaglioso had two peninsular foci by 1153: the lordship of Lecce that Geoffrey inherited from his family, and Montescaglioso, which was granted by the king when the lord of Lecce was created count in southern Apulia. Before 1150, Geoffrey had certainly taken the lordship of Lecce and Ostuni, as an 1148 inscription in the castle of Ostuni (now preserved in the atrium of the bishop's palace) reads as follows:

† REGIS HONOR VERI TIBI SIT REX MAGNE ROGERI
TEMPORIBUS CUIUS FABRICE LABOR EXTITIT HUIUS
QUAM SIC GOSFRIDUS LICII STATUIT SIBI FIDUS
ANNO MILLENO CENTUMQ(UE) QUATER DUODENO[129]

The dominions of Montescaglioso are located in the valleys of the Basento, the Sinni and the Agri, all of which flow into the northern part of the gulf of Taranto (the south of the instep of the Italian 'boot'), whereas Lecce and Ostuni are located in the Salento peninsula (the heel of the 'boot'). The count of Montescaglioso was hence an overlord in a pivotal territory that extended from the lands of the newly created count of Marsico, in the southern Cilento, to the easternmost boundary of the kingdom. Additionally, and most likely due to the fact that his sister, Emma of Lecce, was the mistress of Duke Roger III of Apulia, Roger II's firstborn and apparent heir to the throne until his death in 1148, Count Geoffrey's tenure was not limited to southern Apulia, as he was also later regarded by Pseudo-Falcandus as the lord of various towns in Sicily, including Caltanissetta, Noto and Sclàfani.[130] It is not certain when Geoffrey of Lecce became a lord of Sicilian lands, but a *terminus a quo* is provided by the marble inscription in Caltanissetta: 1153.

In the Principato, Countess Adelaide was presumably the widow of the late Count Nicholas of Principato and was presumably in control of the administration of the lordship until her last documented appearance in 1146. Nicholas's brother, William of Principato, may have been for whatever reason out of the picture at the time, to then suddenly reappear, first as a donor to the monastery of the Most Holy Trinity of Venosa in 1150, and then in a Palermitan prison in 1161. William of Principato is recorded in the March 1141 confirmation (*preceptum*) of land previously granted by his brother Nicholas to the archbishop of Salerno, in which William is referred to as 'heir and former son, in the same way, of the count [...] brother of mine [Nicholas]'.[131] This charter, identified by its editor and C. Carlone as a fabrication in the form of an original, was discussed previously. As was pointed out, the recorded transaction appears to be based on an original document.[132] William of Principato is subsequently recorded as a donor to the abbey of Venosa in 1150.[133] Afterwards, he is attested by Romuald Guarna in a prison in Palermo in 1161.[134] In the former, William of Principato donated, as count, a house in *Esculi* (nowadays Ascoli Satriano) to Abbot Peter II of the Most Holy Trinity of Venosa. This reference, nonetheless, survives only in an abstract prepared by Prignano. Although the source's nature is problematic, it does shed some light on the question of Principato in the 1150s. The hypothesis of this William of Principato being Nicholas's youngest brother is also supported and shared by Drell, who suggests that William may have served in his brother's comital court in some capacity.[135]

New counts were also created from other, lesser lords: Geoffrey, count of Tricarico, is recorded in 1139 and 1143; and Sylvester, count of Marsico, by 1150. Geoffrey of Tricarico subscribed the two aforementioned November 1143 royal charters as 'count of Tricarico' (*comes Tricarici*).[136] As was explained previously, the royal charter issued in Salerno has been identified as a forgery, but the existence of the first charter suggests the presence of a count of Tricarico named Geoffrey in a royal *curia* held at Capua in 1143. Furthermore, Count Geoffrey of Tricarico was recorded earlier in June 1139 as confirming under oath a concession granted by Duke Roger III of Apulia in favour of the archbishop and citizens of Trani, by which their urban customs were recognized, confirming thus the *preceptum et convenciones* his father Roger II bestowed before.[137] This is one of just three known surviving documents issued by Roger II's firstborn, and one of the earliest pieces of evidence not only for the count of Tricarico but also for young Duke Roger's role in the aftermath of the rebellion. This agreement with the city of Trani was made before Duke Roger defeated the papal forces at Mignano, a victory that led to the treaty by which Innocent II finally 'authorized' the creation of the kingdom of Sicily, inclusive of the duchy of Apulia and the principality of Capua.[138] Thus, the first count of Tricarico was not only a royalist, as would be expected of a position created by Roger II himself, but also a baron close to both the royal *curia* and the young Duke Roger.

The county of Tricarico was given to a Roger who granted, as count of Tricarico, a *feudum* to a Thomas Sarracenus within his own county, in 1154.[139] According to the *Quaternus magne expeditionis*, c. 1150, the lordships that Count Roger of Tricarico held *in demanio* were Tricarico (the *caput* of his dominions), Albano di Lucania, Pietragalla, Tolve, and *Sanctum Julianum*, and a *feudum* within the city of Andria.[140] It is unclear whether the *feudum* in Andria was already part of his family heritage, or if it was given to Roger of Tricarico at a later stage, perhaps after the death of the count of Andria in 1155. However, the rest of the places recorded in the *Quaternus* suggest that the count of Tricarico's dominions were located between the northern valleys of the Basento and Bradano rivers, in the modern province of Potenza. This area would have been the nucleus of the county of Tricarico.

The extension of Count Roger's dominions before 1150 is uncertain, as it is difficult to determine if all the entries in the *Quaternus* between paragraphs 108 and 134 were held *in servitio* from the count of Tricarico, or were independent lordships overseen militarily by Roger of Tricarico as royal *comestabulus*.[141] The current version of the *Quaternus* does not allow us to identify the original (*c.* 1150) delimitation of Tricarico. These changes are illustrated and discussed in following chapters. Moreover, there is a great deal of confusion surrounding the origins of this Count Roger of Tricarico, as the evidence is extremely scarce. The 1154 evidence is obscure, as it only survives in the eighteenth-century memory composed by Gatta, and the *Quaternus* does not provide any kinship relation for Count Roger. There is a considerable documentary silence until 1181, and only the chronicle of Romuald of Salerno and Pseudo-Falcandus refer to the count of Tricarico in the meantime. Romuald's chronicle placed Count Roger of Tricarico among the conspirators in 1159; again, no kinship is attested.[142] Notably, Pseudo-Falcandus omits the count of Tricarico entirely when providing his own list of rebel counts for the same conspiracy – Pseudo-Falcandus also omitted the Abruzzesi counts of Manopello and Sangro when naming the 1159 conspirators.[143] Pseudo-Falcandus, however, did record the activities Count Roger of Tricarico was involved nine years after, and on this occasion, he clearly was identified as the son of Robert of Lauro, count of Caserta and a member of the S. Severino kin-group.[144] However, is this Roger, son of Robert of Lauro, the same count of Tricarico recorded earlier? To answer this, one should first look at the S. Severino ancestry of Robert of Lauro.

The S. Severino kin-group also held extensive lands in the former principality of Salerno, both in the north (around Lauro, Montoro and S. Severino) and in the south (around Rocca Cilento, in western Cilento), as is revealed by numerous donations to the abbey of Cava.[145] An April 1105 donation by the late patriarch of the family, Roger of S. Severino, to the monastery of St Lawrence of Aversa, records in its witness list three of Roger's sons: Robert, Trugisius and Roger.[146] Roger of S. Severino must have died before 1125 as a major benefactor of Cava, as his son Henry is already recorded in 1125 as lord of S. Severino.[147] However, the family had several small branches, and Roger of S. Severino's estate was fragmented both before and after his succession. Lauro was given to Roger's son Robert before his father died; in 1119, Robert made a donation to St Angelo in Formis as 'Robert son of Roger of S. Severino, lord and resident of the *castellum* called Lauro'.[148] Portanova suggested that the Robert of Lauro who became count of Caserta was Roger of S. Severino's grandson, not Roger's son.[149] I agree; documents from St Angelo in Formis reveal that Robert II of Lauro was a minor, and his lordship was administered by Robert Capumaza before 1141.[150]

However, there is no concrete evidence to support the hypothesis that the Count Roger of Tricarico recorded in 1154 and 1159 was a member of the S. Severino family. On the contrary, it seems practically impossible for the son of a baron who was underage before 1141 and whose lordships were then limited to the *castrum* of Lauro to have been created count by Roger II in the 1150s. For a count that remained active until the 1190s, Roger son of Robert of Lauro must have been an infant when the first Count Roger of Tricarico was attested in 1154. One should not be surprised that two unrelated counts of the same county were both named 'Roger', as this was one of the most common names in twelfth-century southern Italy: a clear cultural consequence of the Norman presence in the Mediterranean. Additionally, both the *feuda* held *in demanio* by the count of Tricarico and the *feuda* held *in servitio* by lesser barons from the same count do not correspond or even neighbour the lands that S. Severino donated to Cava in southern Apulia. If anything, the lands which S. Severino held in Cilento must have been surrounded by the county of Marsico. The development of S. Severino's political and economic power is discussed further in following chapters; for now, it is enough to indicate the unlikelihood of Count Roger I of Tricarico being the same Roger of S. Severino who is attested from 1168 onwards.

On the other hand, Sylvester of Marsico is recorded in 1150 as having offered his vineyards in S. Juliani Calesia to St Stephen of Marsico, as 'count, by the grace of God, for the prosperity of the very vigorous King Roger and our own, and for the redemption of our deceased parents' souls'.[151] The same Sylvester of Marsico is recorded in the *Quaternus* as a count whose lordships held *in demanio* consisted of Marsico Nuovo, Roccettam, Teggiano and Sala Consilina.[152] The latter two are located in the eastern end of the Vallo di Diano,[153] and Marsico Nuovo is near the source of the River Agri. Three documents from the archives of Cava provide a useful and additional insight into the early development of the count of Marsico. In December 1153, Sylvester, regarded as count of Marsico, confirmed to the church of St Peter of Tramutola – subordinated to the abbey of Cava – all previous donations, sales and exchanges made by his predecessors and by the *boni homines* of Marsico [Nuovo], and he also granted additional lands to the monastery.[154] Count Sylvester of Marsico is later recorded in May 1154, as conceding to Abbot Marinus of Cava and to his successors pasturage rights (*glandes*) throughout the count's territory of Marsico for Cava's holdings of St Peter of Tramutola and the men of the *casale* of Tramutola; these rights consisted of an exemption from the swine pasturage fees (i.e. *glandaticum*), and the permission to collect gleanings.[155] This grant was made in his chamber at Ragusa (*in camera mea Ragusie*), which indicates that Count Sylvester was not only concurrently a lord in Sicily but also administering his peninsular county from his ancestral, insular lordship. A year later, in May 1155, the same Count Sylvester granted to the church of St Peter of Tramutola and to the men of the *casale* of that church the right for their flocks to pasture (*glandes*) and graze (*herbae*) and the right to take wood from the forests, in all the territory of Marsico, as the other men of Marsico enjoyed.[156] It is not clear where the 1153 and 1155 transactions were conducted, in either his chambers in Marsico or Ragusa, but the comital notary who drafted all these documents was the same: Lambert. Based on all this evidence, it can be safely argued that the nucleus of the county of Marsico was located on the southwestern fringe of the region of Cilento, between the River Agri and the Vallo di Diano. Additionally, the lands which, according to the *Quaternus*, other lords held *in servitio* from Count Sylvester were located in Caselle in Pittari, Gioi, Magliano Vetere, Monteforte Cilento, Novi Velia, Padula and Tortorella: all of these places are situated between the rivers Tanagro and Alento, southwest of the Vallo di Diano.[157] The domains of the count of Marsico extended from its nucleus to the west, covering thus southern Cilento.

It has been suggested by Cuozzo that some of the lands that were placed under Count Sylvester of Marsico belonged to the count of Principato until 1150.[158] Although it is possible that the lands of the original counts of Principato were more extensive than what is suggested in the *Quaternus*, this is not clear. The most compelling argument Cuozzo makes in favour of a partial expropriation of the Principato lands *c.* 1150 is the case of Auletta. Located at the core of the territory of the count of Principato's domains, the town of Auletta provides a rich collection of surviving Greek charters that illustrate the changes in the region. The May 1142 Greek charter is the last documented instance in which the authority of a count of Principato is regarded in Auletta before the reign of William II; the charters dated between 1148 and 1164 mention exclusively the royal authority and the *strategus* of Auletta, without making any reference to a count of Principato.[159] This would imply that after Countess Adelaide of Principato died, which must have occurred between 1146 and 1148, some lordships were taken from the heritage of the count of Principato. Even if it is the case that William, brother of Nicholas of Principato, inherited his brother's comital title and core lands, he would have then done so as overlord of fewer lords, losing for example Auletta and some towns in southern Cilento. Furthermore, since the first Auletta charter that ignores the count of Principato is dated 1148, the original *quaterniones* that served as a basis for the *Quaternus magne expeditionis* would have been drafted with a diminished entry for the count of Principato. To this point, the royal official who was in charge of assessing the *feuda* in Auletta was a chamberlain named Alfanus.

The *Quaternus* records Alfanus the chamberlain as being in charge of reporting the number of non-landed tenancy units held (i.e. *villaini* and *molendini*, as opposed to the *feuda*) and the military service owed by two barons: the unnamed son of John the notary and Aschettinus of Armo.[160] This royal chamberlain is the same Alfanus *Camerarius* who, according to the *Quaternus*, was temporarily placed in charge (*baiulatione*) of the *comestabulia* of Lampus of Fasanella, a position that was left vacant after 1156.[161] Additionally, Alfanus the chamberlain is remembered in an Auletta charter.[162] Alfanus was, however, responsible for the appraising of many other holdings across the region, including even some land north-east of Avellino, and was not limited solely to the *subcomestabulia* that would have corresponded to the dominions of the count of Principato. Hence, the documented appearance of Alfanus does not necessarily imply that he replaced the count of Principato at all, although it is possible that he was in charge of inspecting the military service alongside, or under, the royal constable (*comestabulus*) Robert of Quallecta.[163] What is clear is the noteworthy absence of a count of Principato after 1150.

If one ought to follow the tradition of Jamison and Cuozzo, the general territorial reform that may have taken place in the year 1142 in Silva Marca could have been the setting in which these changes were negotiated and took effect.[164] The possible existence of an assembly in Silva Marca is, however, very problematic. The only known piece of evidence that places Roger II in the so-called Silva Marca is a July 1142 charter given 'in the lands of Ariano, in the place called Silva Marca'.[165] The charter attests a royal confirmation bestowed on the nunnery of the church of St John in Lecce, of the possessions of the church of St Andrew in Mari, after Abbess Guimarca had presented her case. The document furthermore records that Roger II's court was convened at Silva Marca, with his son Alfonso, duke of the Neapolitans and prince of the Capuans, his counts, some other barons and most of the people of his kingdom, in order to correct disputes and injustices.[166] It appears, hence, that the king had assembled a large entourage during his stay on the mainland during the summer of 1142, and this extended court was hearing complaints and administering justice.

The correction of 'disputes and injustices' does not necessarily imply the introduction of a new military organization or the deliberate creation of new counties in the peninsula, and an open royal court held with many members of the different circles of power in the kingdom does not constitute a constitutional or reform assembly. It was customary for the king to not only hold open courts during his stay on the mainland – so the monarch could hear pleas, settle controversies and execute the royal judicial supremacy himself – but also invite the archbishops, bishops, counts, barons and royal functionaries to be part of his itinerant court. One might be tempted to assume from the language employed in this 1142 royal charter that some larger, sui generis gathering between the king and the peninsular aristocracy took place, but there is no testimony of such an assembly having occurred. However, Cuozzo takes this further, and argues that Silva Marca offers 'an explicit documentation of the Norman general assembly, which, following the model of the ancient Germanic assembly, resembles the gathering of all the freemen of the kingdom in a quadrille or troop unit (*quadrivio*)'.[167] Following this line of enquiry, Cuozzo proposes that there were three general assemblies summoned by Roger II: in 1140, 1142 and 1149.[168] The 1140 assembly is assumed from Falco of Benevento's testimony that in 1140, after Roger II rode to the Abruzzese region of Pescara, which had been recently captured by his sons, he went to Ariano and held a court with his nobles and bishops and dealt with a large number of different matters. According to Falco, among the other dispositions which he made there was a currency edict by which a 'terrible' new coinage was introduced: the ducat.[169] Again, this appears to have been more of a royal court that settled specific judicial controversies, including the standardization of the kingdom's currency, than a constitutional assembly in which the laws and government of the kingdom were generally established.

On the other hand, the 1149 assembly is assumed to have existed as a necessary legal preamble for the drafting of the military service *quaterniones* that were commissioned to oppose a potential invasion by Conrad III and Manuel Komnenos. Whereas Jamison has focused more on the role that these hypothetical assemblies played in the construction of a feudal language, to be implemented and enforced with the *Quaternus magne expeditionis*, Cuozzo has emphasized that it was in the assembly of Silva Marca where the centralizing design was enforced against the counts of the kingdom, and that this design entailed the systematic creation of a new feudal structure called a county in the two continental provinces of Apulia and Capua.[170] As a result, it became commonplace in south Italian historiography to assume that the county was a deliberate and designed creation of a centralizing monarchy in 1142, without careful regard for the available evidence on the counts' presence and activities.[171]

The territorial rights that the counts seem to have enjoyed during the Norman monarchy have also been understood by Martin, following Cuozzo's hypothesis, as a concession of non-military prerogatives and other *regalia* dues granted by the king, including the rights of *plateaticum* and *incultum*, and organized under the *feuda* recorded in the *Quaternus*. A market tax of Lombard origins, the *plateaticum* developed by the end of the eleventh century into a crucial prerogative of territorial lordship in southern Italy; even taxes considered 'public', such as the *incultum*, fell within the lord's authority, and eventually became rights that only the count could administer within his own lands.[172] The assumption here is that the newly created monarchy claimed that all agricultural and commercial fees, even those that had become seigniorial rights under the Norman lords, were part of the *regalia*, and as such the counts exercised these rights as a royal concession.[173] However, at least under the Norman dynasty, these territorial prerogatives were never executed or forgiven *ex parte regia* in the few comital donations that attest them, but simply as fees expected to be collected and controlled by the overlord of the land. Additionally, the *Quaternus* holding units make no reference to any territorial right. That the new royal authority allowed the counts to keep exercising these territorial rights does not necessarily imply that these fees were understood as royal taxes nor that these were unilaterally conceded during a constitutional assembly.

Be that as it may, the strongest argument against the hypothetical constitutional assembly of Silva Marca is the actual traceable chronology of the counts' activities, as was documented earlier; it is clear that there was no single year after which most of the counties had been established.[174] The appointment, confirmation and development of each comital position was an individual process, and although some groups of counts appear to have been either confirmed or made around the same periods of time, it is futile and even misleading to reduce the different stages of the social rearrangement into a single turn and constitutional assembly. This might have helped to push forward the impression that Roger II's monarchy was an administrative state with a clear centralizing agenda and a preconceived plan for government. However, the documentary evidence reveals a much less sophisticated reality that, although it may not explicitly deny the possibility that such a grand plan of Rogerian government ever existed, vindicates the role played by the upper aristocracy in the social control of Norman Italy and the contingent nature of the Hauteville royal authority.

The Abruzzo: A different animal, part II

An annexed province and the jurisdiction of Manopello

The delimitation of the scattered Norman lordships in the Abruzzo, and its boundaries with those that belonged to the counts of Loritello and Boiano, is a highly contested matter, and there is no available detailed evidence that could actually define the frontiers in this area.[175] The geographical treaty prepared by Muhammad Al-Idrisi for Roger II offers relevant information concerning the strategic value of the Adriatic corridor between the county of Loritello and the town of Chieti. Although the section concerning modern Abruzzo presents many problems of interpretation, Al-Idrisi revealed an interesting image of the kingdom's Adriatic border. The frontier area was set up from the River Sangro, passing though the *castellum* of Sangro (modern Castel di Sangro), up to Chieti and then stretched up to the west up to the town of Pacentro (*bâ'g.nn.rah*), in the hinterland and west of the Maiella range. The border sketched by Al-Idrisi did not extended to the valley of Pescara, but instead, rested on the Sangro. Also, the lordship of Manopello is not mentioned, although it is located between the Manopello and Maiella range.[176] This could have been the result of Al-Idrisi's sources having been drafted before Bohemund of Tarsia was appointed count of Manopello, and consequently, this pivotal area could not be sketched in detail, although it was identified and delimited. Pacentro was subsequently reordered in the *quaternion* for the Abruzzo as a *feudum* that was held by Manerio of Palena and later his sons, and although he was a local Abruzzese baron, Manerio's *feuda* were recorded as held *in servitio* from his overlord the count of Manopello.[177]

Count William of Loritello joined the rebellion during the civil war against Roger II and allied with Lothar II. Hence, it is almost certain that the count of Manopello followed the count of Loritello in opposition against the Sicilian monarchy. The recently created kingdom could not have been able to impose its authority over these territories before King Roger emerged triumphant; thus, the effective takeover of both Loritello and Manopello must have come after 1139. Falco of Benevento alleged that, in 1140, Roger II sent his son Alfonso, prince of the Capuans, and later his older son Duke Roger, beyond the city of Pescara (15 kilometres northeast of Chieti) with a large army of knights and infantry to subjugate that province to his power, a task that both of them ultimately accomplished. The notary from Benevento also described this province as 'close to the Roman frontiers' (*prope Romanos fines adiacens*). Falco further related that, in the summer of that same year, Roger II rode with 500 knights (*milites*) to Pescara, after having stayed in Capua and dismissed the troops of his army.[178] King Roger's temporary stay in the Abruzzo is also revealed by two surviving royal charters issued in August 1140. A transcription in the chartulary-chronicle of Casauria alleges that the king granted three *castella* (Colle Odoni, Casale Plano and Bolognano) and a privilege of liberty and protection to the abbey of St Clement in Casauria.[179] Another contemporary, although dubious, surviving charter attests the same royal privilege given to the abbey, and a confirmation of a long list of local properties and churches that allegedly belonged to the abbey of Casauria.[180] The pivotal role the count of Manopello and the town of Chieti played before in the Norman invasion was evidently still present during the time of the annexation of the Abruzzo to the kingdom.

The chartulary-chronicle of Casauria recorded that Roger II appointed 'Count Bohemund to the county of Manopello' (*comes Boamundus [...] comitatu Manupelli*), c. August 1140, as the monastic account alleged that the new count of Manopello sought to interfere with the abbey, but the king issued an order for him to stop the harassment against Casauria.[181] In addition, the new count of Manopello restored the church of St Andrew to the abbey of the Holy Saviour at Maiella in 1144, under Roger II's direct instructions, and acting as his justiciar in Chieti.[182] On 22 April 1148, Bohemund of Tarsia, alongside the Count Robert of *Aprutium* and two other local barons (Oderisius of Pagliara and Richard of Turgisio), recorded a suit between the abbot of Montecassino and the bishop of *Aprutium*, acting as royal justiciar (*iustitiarius domini regis*) in Chieti. The count of Manopello hence shared the responsibility for administering the king's justice with a lesser count and two Abruzzese lords, and the recorded suit was additionally subscribed by another local count: Count Berard of Chieti.[183] The titles and positions of the royal administration appear thus to have been given also to the Abruzzese barons, perhaps in a direct attempt to both use the indigenous structure and incorporate the local aristocracy into the kingdom's organization. However, this annexation effort must have been implemented through Count Bohemund, the Calabrese royal loyalist who had been given the gateway of the northern Adriatic frontier: Manopello.

The Abruzzese register of *feuda* and military service in the *Catalogus Baronum* constituted a different *quaternion*, with a particular and discrete structure, whose recorded barons appear to have been placed originally under the authority of Bohemund of Tarsia, count of Manopello. No inclusive geographical designation appears in the *Catalogus*, and the name *Aprutium* applied not to the entire province but to a single county and diocese. However, the record for all the Abruzzese lands brings out the unity of a region secured under the supervision of the new count of Manopello. According to Jamison, the modern editor of the *Catalogus*, a third scribe took up his pen with the section 'on the jurisdiction of Count Bohemund' (*De Justitia Comitis Boamundi [...]*), with different handwriting and different spelling, and a new and separate *quaternion* began there.[184] In this fresh *quaternion*, structural and textual elements that were not present in the preceding *Quaternus* are found. First, the register utilizes references to inner 'principalities' and uses the notion of 'county' (*comitatus*) as a geographical specification no longer corresponding to any specific political reality or major lordship. One example is the old Franco-Lombard counties of Penne, *Aprutium*,

Marsia and Rieti; the town of Rieti itself was destroyed by Roger II in 1148 and only rebuilt after the kingdom lost control of the territories in 1156.[185]

Furthermore, the social structure sketched by the Abruzzese records furnishes counts whose *feuda* were recorded as having been held *in servitio* of another count, Bohemund of Manopello, which implies the military subordination of counts to a peer who technically held the same comital dignity as them. In addition, the tenurial structure revealed here is generally stepped in three levels; the Abruzzese record presents a vast multitude of overlords who in turn held their *feuda* from other overlords, and a handful of them have other overlords subordinate to them. By contrast, the *Quaternus* for Apulia and the Terra di Lavoro reveals very few instances of third-level *in servitio* barons, and it does not record any count whose dominions and main *feuda* were held from other lords. However, such clear social distinction and superiority held by the south Italian counts appears to be disregarded in the register for the Abruzzo with the predominance of Count Bohemund.

The great majority of Abruzzese overlords did not bear the comital title, whereas in Apulia and the Terra di Lavoro the counts made up almost the entire social layer of overlords. If anything, the register of the annexed Abruzzo resembled the vague manner in which the comital title was traditionally employed by prominent lords in the lands of the Lombard principalities before the creation of the kingdom. Furthermore, the main *Quaternus* does not record any special 'jurisdiction' (*justitia*) like the one attested for the entire Abruzzo under Count Bohemund; the closest entity to this jurisdiction were the 'constabularies' (*comestabulia*) that are occasionally recorded in Apulia and the Terra di Lavoro, but the Abruzzese *quaternion* does not reveal the presence of any royal constable (*comestabulus*) in the province. In short, it is clear that the section in the *Catalogus* for the Abruzzo comprised a separate register, which, although employed for the same main goal as the original *Quaternus magne expeditionis* (i.e. identifying and mobilizing the continental armed forces), was drafted and administered differently, as the central Italian lands were annexed to the kingdom and controlled by the count of Manopello.

As a separated region, the Abruzzo was then annexed to the kingdom, rather than having been a constituent province, like Apulia, Capua and Calabria. The notion of 'annexation' has been employed before to refer to the question of the Abruzzo and the Sicilian kingdom; Rivera used that same term to describe the appropriation of the *Terre d'Abruzzo* to emphasize the regional individuality and sociopolitical singularity of the Abruzzo. The preceding and partial Norman occupation in the region does not appear to have been interested in attaching themselves to the social groups from which they emerged, either 'Norman' or Apulian, but instead in acquiring lands and enhancing their military power.[186] Hence, the partial presence in the Abruzzo of the followers of either the Hauteville-Loritello or 'sons of Amicus' did not significantly alter the local peculiarity of this region. Consequently, Roger II's takeover could not rely on the same social mechanisms that he had adopted and implemented in Apulia and the former principality of Capua. As long as the local customs and social setting inherited from the Carolingian duchy of Spoleto remained current, the province in central Italy could not have been controlled and incorporated into the kingdom in the same way as the rest of the continental territories.

Therefore, I understand the Abruzzo as a large border area, established as a special and separated jurisdiction. The whole region was thus no longer fragmented by boundaries of different states, between Spoleto and Benevento, as it was before its inclusion in the orbit of the Sicilian kingdom. As a result, the Abruzzo became a region that was less fully colonized by the Normans than the rest of the southern peninsula. It was consolidated by two of its main geographical features: its role as a coastal centre for the Adriatic routes, and its mountain passes that connected the kingdom and the northern territories of the peninsula, thanks to its position between the central highlands in the Apennines and the *Tavoliere delle Puglie* (i.e. the region of the Capitanata). This annexed province was set up as a march protecting the Adriatic borders of the kingdom from both the remnants of the duchy of Spoleto and the potential invasion from the Western Empire.[187] Under the Sicilian monarchy and on the basis of the military and political control exercised from Manopello, the reconstruction of the Abruzzese nobility was possible but gradual; in decades to come it would acquire a new role in the kingdom's politics. The local social order in the Abruzzo would be forcefully modified through a series of subsequent wars and rebellions on the peninsula after Roger II's death.

New counties and the comital status

A decade after Rainulf of Caiazzo died and King Roger consolidated his effective authority in 1139, some of the Capuan lands were distributed among the counts of Carinola and Fondi. The town of Airola must have been granted to Jonathan of Carinola, as he is recorded as its lord in *c.* 1150.[188] In this same border region, Fondi was given to the kin-group of Aquila in recompense for the duchy of Gaeta; Geoffrey, the son of Richard I of Aquila – erstwhile duke of Gaeta – is recorded dead, as count of Fondi, in 1149.[189] The *Quaternus* already attests Geoffrey's son Richard of Aquila as count of Fondi, and lord only of a *feudum* in Gaeta, *c.* 1150.[190] Precisely when these towns were granted is uncertain, but the documented pattern suggests that the additions to the lordships of Carinola and Fondi might have occurred under a rapid, new reorganization which may have been concluded around the year 1150. A similar situation can be observed in what used to belong to the counts of Ariano. The county of Buonalbergo was created from lordships that belonged to the former lordships of Ariano and given to Robert of Medania, *c.* 1150. The only known record that attests Robert of Medania as count of Buonalbergo is found in the *Quaternus*. Although this register presents his son Roger as the current count, this must have been changed in a subsequent revision of the *Quaternus* because a consecutive item in the same section for the county of Buonalbergo refers to his father Robert as the head of the county.[191] The dominions of this new count had two foci: Buonalbergo as the seat of their county and Acerra as the original lordship of the family.

Between 1140 and 1154, the kingdom's higher aristocracy on the mainland went from having five counts to being arranged in thirteen counties, and towards the end of Roger II's reign there were only some slight changes made to this structure. At some point before 1152, the count of Civitate, Robert son of Richard, must have been succeeded by his son, because Count Robert son of Robert was attested as the ruling count of Civitate by 1152. Richard of Aquila, count of Avellino and brother of Geoffrey of Aquila, died in 1152, and his son Roger inherited his lordship and succeeded him as count.[192] Roger of Aquila, his son, is remembered by Pseudo-Falcandus as the noble and very youthful (*nobilis adolescentulus*) count of Avellino, as he joined Matthew Bonellus against Maio in 1160.[193] Roger of Aquila is recorded in the *Quaternus* as well, *c*. 1167, replacing his father's original entries of *c*. 1150.[194] Robert of Medania, count of Buonalbergo, was succeeded by his son Roger at some point between 1150 and 1154, as the latter is recorded already as a count in June 1154.[195] In Calabria, the county of Squillace may also have been created before 1154, in that it is recorded by Pseudo-Falcandus that soon after Maio of Bari was created 'great admiral' by William I, he was particularly apprehensive of Count Everard of Squillace.[196]

The evidence on the counts of Andria after 1130 and before William II's reign is scarce. Kinnamos records a Count Richard of Andria as having been killed in combat during the Byzantine campaign in Apulia in 1155.[197] This Count Richard appears to be the same Richard of Lingèvres recorded by Robert of Torigni. The chronicler from Normandy had indicated that Richard of Lingèvres (*Ricardus de Lingheve*), described as an 'excellent knight' (*miles optimus*), joined King Roger's attack on Tripoli. Furthermore, Robert of Torigni attests that Richard of Lingèvres came from the county of Bayeux (*Baiocensi comitatus*), and that Roger II bestowed on him the 'county of Andria' (*comitatus Andri insulae*).[198] Robert of Torigni also attests Count Richard of Andria's participation in the war in Apulia in 1155.[199] Roger II, therefore, was not limited to employing only local peninsular barons from his military contingent for the creation of the new nobility, as Count Richard of Andria would have been a recent Norman immigrant who had joined the king's army. Andria thus would have been the fourteenth county created under Roger II before the king passed away.

The lordship that used to belong to Robert II of Loritello remained unassigned, perhaps incorporated into the royal demesne.[200] Although the available sources do not provide a picture of the actual extension and use of the royal demesne in the peninsula at this stage, the king appeared more interested in temporarily keeping it for subsequent redistribution to loyal supporters than in expanding it.

The basis for the territorial additions of the future counties of Gravina and Sant'Angelo dei Lombardi, which belonged to the Aleramici and Balvano kin-groups respectively, may have been set at this time, but the evidence for these comital titles before 1156 is scarce.[201] The case of the county of Sant'Angelo dei Lombardi is a misleading one. Count Philip of Balvano is recorded in the *Quaternus*, but this does not necessarily mean that he was already a count in 1150; Philip must have been made a count after 1167.[202] Philip of Balvano is recorded in the *Quaternus* as having declared to the *curia regis* the military service owed by his uncle Gilbert of Balvano, but he is not referred to as a count here.[203] On Gravina, Pseudo-Falcandus has recorded that the 'county of Gravina' (*comitatus Gravinae*) was given to Gilbert of Perche, a blood-relative of Queen Margaret, just before 1158.[204] Furthermore, there is no surviving evidence that records the existence of a count of Gravina before 1157. The kin-group that held the lordship of Gravina did so under the title of *marchio*; these lords of Gravina were descendants of

Marquis Boniface del Vasto, from the Aleramici family (the north Italian relatives of Roger II's mother Adelaide). Thus, before 1156, there was neither a count nor a county of Gravina. But, what exactly do we know about this 'marquis' of Gravina?

The title of 'marquis' was rare in the kingdom of Sicily, at least during the twelfth century. The marquis of Gravina was the only baron who bore such a title during Roger II's reign, because the lord of Gravina, Manfred, was the son of the renowned Boniface del Vasto, marquis of Savona and western Liguria. During the time of the conquest, Marquis Boniface was an ally of Drogo of Hauteville and Robert Guiscard; the marriage arranged between his niece Adelaide del Vasto and Roger I strengthened the position of both families and consolidated the alliance.[205] The branch of the Aleramici that settled in southern Italy could have thus enjoyed a special status among the south Italian aristocracy, due to the prestige their bloodline carried from the marquis of Savona and Liguria.

Manfred, son of Marquis Boniface, granted a mill to Archbishop William of Salerno in January 1146, with the consent of his wife Philippa and Bishop-elect Ursus of Gravina. The donation was made in the *castellum* of Gravina, and refers to the donor as 'Marquis Manfred, lord of the city of Forenza, by the grace of God and of the king' (*Manfredus marchio, gratia Dei et domini Rogerii magnifici regis civitatis Florencie dominus*).[206] The following year, in September 1147, the same Manfred, together with his wife Philippa, made a donation to the monastery of St Leo [the Great] at Bitonto. Manfred called himself 'lord of the city of Gravina, by the grace of God and of the king, and son and heir of Lord Boniface, marquis' (*Ego Manfredus marchio, gratia Dei et domini nostri magnifici Rogeri civitatis Gravine dominus, filius et heres domini Bonifacii marchionis*).[207] Marquis Manfred died before 1151, because five years later his wife Philippa is attested as 'marchioness, once wife of Marquis Manfred, lord of the city of Gravina' (*marchionissa, olim domni Monfridi marchionis uxor [...] civitatis Gravine*), in a privilege granted and confirmed to the bishopric of Gravina, in which she and her son Sylvester are recorded as signatories.[208] The same Sylvester is subsequently recorded in three charters of the monastery of Cava dated November 1155, in which he makes several donations, together with his mother *marchionissa* Philippa to the aforementioned monastery.[209] A donated estate (a vineyard) attested in one of these documents technically belonged to a certain Sinarcha son of Raynerius, but since the latter died without an heir, it was recorded that the vineyard 'reverted to their dominion [of the marquises of Gravina]' (*ad nostrum publicum*).[210] The lordship of Gravina thus enjoyed the legal possession of the land held by the barons in their territory. In all these documents, including their respective copies, the lord of Gravina is attested as marquis. None of these marquises played a prominent role during Roger's reign; they do however seem to have exercised authority over other, lesser barons. This can be inferred from the right of claiming inherited tenancy that is documented in one of the 1155 transactions, their relation with the bishop of Gravina and the archbishop of Salerno, and the tenure *in demanio* that they might have had *c.* 1150, as is suggested in a deconstruction of the *Quaternus magne expeditionis* (these holdings would have been the *feuda* of Gravina, Spinazzola and Forenza, each one valued as *feudum* of eight, four and four *milites* respectively).[211] The marquises of Gravina can, hence, be considered lesser counts who did not originally hold the prestige a count could enjoy under the traditionally ambiguous usage of the title. Nevertheless, they exercised a functional social role as major landholders and donors to the church, overlords of other barons and local authorities. Gravina consequently became a county that would play a major role during the subsequent rule of King William.

The counts established under the reign of Roger II also provided the highest stratum of the continental aristocracy with new kin-groups. With the new count of Buonalbergo, the Medania family and a branch of the Lombard princely family of Salerno attained a position among the kingdom's nobility. Count Robert of Buonalbergo was the son of the lord of Acerra, Geoffrey of Medania, and Sichelgaita (also documented as Sica). The maternal lineage of Robert of Medania is confirmed in a March 1125 charter, which recorded Henry of S. Severino swearing to respect the abbey of Cava's property, with Robert present as Henry's uterine brother.[212] Sichelgaita, granddaughter of Guaimar IV of Salerno, was married for a second time to Roger of S. Severino, most certainly after Geoffrey's death.[213] The count of Buonalbergo, Robert of Medania, was thus a descendant by the maternal line from the princely family of Salerno, but he was not directly tied to the Rogerian kin-group.[214] However, these two families, Medania and S. Severino, were strategic allies and loyal supporters of the king's activities on the peninsula. Their new status and power seem to have been a well-taken reward from Roger II with the county of Buonalbergo, which was made up with the remains of the former dominions of the count of Ariano.

Count Sylvester of Marsico was tied to both the Sicilian lords of Ragusa and the royal kin-group; his father, Geoffrey of Ragusa, was an illegitimate son of Roger I.[215] In December 1153, Count Sylvester of Marsico confirmed a series of donations made to the abbey of Cava, and he conducted this transaction 'for the soul of Count Roger I of Sicily, and that of his father Geoffrey' (*pro domni etiam Rogerii primi Sicilie comitis anime salute magnifici memorie et domni Goffridi nostri patris*).[216] This special consideration to Roger I is also attested in the other two donations made to Cava by Count Sylvester: in May 1154 the count made a donation for the salvation of the souls of Roger I, Roger II and Sylvester's unnamed relatives (*pro animarum magnifici Rogerii primi comitis Sicilie, necnon gloriosi regis Rogerii bone memorie salute, meique genitoris ceterorumque parentum salute*);[217] and in May 1155 he donated again 'for the relief and salivation of the first Sicilian count and the most glorious King Roger' (*pro remedio et salute animarum domni Rogerii primi Sicilie comes, domnique gloriosissimi regis Rogerii bone memorie*).[218] Additionally, Sylvester of Marsico must have inherited his father's lordships in Sicily, being at least lord of Ragusa, as he issued at least one donation as count of Marsico from his chamber in Ragusa. It is clear then that Sylvester of Marsico was a descendant of Count Roger I. Likewise, the new count of Montescaglioso, Geoffrey of Lecce, was tied to both a family of lesser barons and to the Rogerian kin-group; he was the son of Accardus, lord of Lecce and Ostuni, the brother of young Duke Roger's mistress – Tancred of Lecce's mother.[219] In this way, the newly established counties of Marsico and Montescaglioso allowed two of the illegitimate branches of the Hauteville royal family to climb up to the highest echelon of the kingdom's peninsular society, and, at the same time, brought along two families of lesser barons: the lords of Ragusa and Lecce.

The other new comital family incorporated by Roger II was the Bassunvilla.[220] Their already elevated position was further enhanced: Robert, count of Conversano, married Judith, the sister of King Roger.[221] The chronicle of Romuald Guarna, archbishop of Salerno, corroborates that Robert II of Bassunvilla was Roger II's nephew, in that it records that 'Robert of Bassunvilla, count of Conversano and cousin of the king' (*Robertus de Basavilla comes de Conversano consobrinus frater eiusdem regis*) was present at the coronation of William I, in 1154.[222] John Kinnamos likewise attests the familial connection: 'Roger [II] tyrant of Sicily had a nephew, by name [Robert of] Bassonville' (Ρογερίῳ γὰρ Σικελῶν τυράννῳ ἀδελφιδοῦς ἦ ὄνομα Βασαβίλας). Even the distant chronicler from Normandy Robert of Torigni acknowledged the fact that Robert of Bassunvilla was a relative (*cognatus*) of King William.[223] Robert II of Bassunvilla, the heir of the county of Conversano, was thus also related to the royal family.

Marriage ties appear, hence, to have also played an important role in the establishment of a new royal continental nobility. The new count of Conversano was not the only leading baron tied to the new monarchy by means of marriage. As indicated before, the count of Boiano was one of the first major overlords and territorial leaders who was soon tied to the Hauteville royal family through his marriage to an illegitimate daughter of Roger II and when his sister became a consort of Roger II, as suggested by the chronicle of St Mary of Ferraria.[224] The new count of Avellino, Richard II of Aquila, must have married Magalda, daughter of Adelicia of Adernò, at some point. The evidence for this is scarce, in that it is only Pseudo-Falcandus who elaborates on how the count of Avellino was related to the king, as the anonymous author explained that William I pardoned his 'blood-relative' (*consanguineum*) Count Roger of Avellino, because the king 'was moved by the pleas and tears of his cousin Adelicia, the same count's grandmother, who was terribly fond of her grandson because she had no other surviving heir' (*prece motus et lacrimis Adelicie consobrine sue, eiusdem comitis avie, que cum alium heredem superstitem non haberet, nepotem suum tenerrime diligebat*).[225] In turn, Adelicia was the daughter of Countess Emma, Roger I's daughter, and Rudolph Machabeus, the lord of Montescaglioso.[226] We also know that the name of Count Roger of Avellino's mother was Magalda, because the former made a donation in 1167 for the salvation of her soul (*pro remedio et salvatione anime comitissa Magalde matris mee [Rogerii]*).[227] Hence, Adelicia must have been Magalda's mother, and Magalda must have married Richard of Aquila at some point before the 1150s. For this reason, Count Roger of Avellino was subsequently remembered as a blood-relative, albeit a distant one, of the Sicilian kings. It is uncertain if King Roger played an active role in arranging the marriage of his young great-niece, but this union must have improved the proximity between the Avellino branch of the Aquila family and the monarchy.

Having explored the familial diversity of the old and new counts that constituted the kingdom's continental nobility, it is clear that there is no discernible majority of new comital appointees that were either royal relatives, or from Sicily or Calabria.[228] Only five new counts were technically royal relatives, but the only direct and legitimate blood-relative was the young Count Robert II of Conversano. The marital tie to Hugh of Molise certainly brought the count closer to the monarchy, but it did not yield any issue that would have secured the royal connection to his county.

Count Richard of Avellino's son Roger was also a royal relative, albeit a distant one. Count Sylvester of Marsico became a close figure of the royal *curia* in Sicily, but his position as a royal relative could have been questioned because his father was an illegitimate son. Geoffrey of Lecce, count of Montescaglioso, also became a close figure, mostly because of his residence in Sicily as lord of Ragusa, but his connection to the royal family was also tenuous given his sister's condition as a mistress of young Duke Roger.

The rest of the south Italian counts – Buonalbergo, Catanzaro, Carinola, Civitate, Fondi, Lesina, Manopello, Principato and Tricarico – were related to local Norman families. Also, it does not appear that there was a major placement of barons from Sicily and Calabria into comital positions. Only Sylvester of Marsico came from Sicily as a result of having held his father's original lordship of Ragusa, and the new count of Manopello, Bohemund of Tarsia, was a Calabrian royalist who was given authority over the annexed Abruzzo. It must also be highlighted that the counts of Catanzaro and Principato were the only two families of old counts tied to the larger Hauteville kin-group, but this connection did not have the same significance as it did in the preceding century; in the newly created kingdom, the only 'royal Hautevilles' were those that descended from Count Roger I of Sicily.

The dignity of *comes* was neither restricted to military commanders nor sufficient to secure an important baron's allegiance. Granting lands was not sufficient either. Although not all the counts were part of the 'royal nobility', since not everybody was related to the Sicilian branch of the Hauteville kin-group, they still occupied the highest place among the most prominent local lords. Securing certain territories and lords under the overlordship of a count was a strategy followed by the Sicilian monarchy on the mainland. However, how much of the comital organization can be attributed to King Roger's planning and implementation? Although there is no consistent and firm evidence to prove the existence of a royal project or policy for a specific social rearrangement, Roger II used the lordships and barons clustered together under these enhanced territorial leaders, that is the counties, to gather and organize his army, but not necessarily to command it.

The comital title transitioned from a local dignity to a distinction of power that emanated from a single authority to which all were accountable. The counts validated thus their higher social position over the rest of the barons under the new monarchy, and the crown secured certain territories and lords under the overlordship of a count. If a strategy can be reconstructed from the unfolding of the south Italian county this be one of symbiotic adaptation between the Sicilian monarchy and the peninsular aristocracy. Consequently, although the *comitatus*, the county, was not necessarily a fixed territorial demarcation at that point in history, it became a useful unit for organizing the powerful and loyal aristocracy and their tenure. The county under the early Hauteville monarchy was employed thus: as a unit of social power for manoeuvring with and against the upper strata of society. The counts, operating as heads of territorial clusters of lordships and landholders, commonly connected to a central authority, did not exist before the king. In this sense, there were no counties before 1140, only counts whose title referred to an authoritative lordship. Furthermore, after 1140, *comes* was neither a general and vague term used to denote a member of the upper aristocracy nor a simple honorary title. From this point onwards, the bearers of the comital title can be identified much more precisely.

The nobility's acquiescent strategy might have opened the door to the king's advance on the peninsula during the dawn of the Norman monarchy, but, at the same time, it allowed them to consolidate their authority as major landlords and territorial leaders, and the comital title was used as the ultimate confirmation of this condition. The counties, as clusters of local authority, operated as the 'connecting tissue' of a complex structure of social control on the Italian mainland. It was this attempted social structure upon which the successes and failures of the following generations unfolded.

3

Leadership and opposition under the count of Loritello

The restructuring of the baronial upper stratum had already started to be consolidated during the last years of Roger's kingship. The peninsular upper aristocracy cemented around the counts. Without having to depend on a royal office, such as that of *magister capitaneus* or *comestabulus regis*, these counts enjoyed the highest position among the peninsular landholders. The economic and political power brought about by the counts' numerous territorial holdings and subtenants was different from the authority held by the royal functionaries who were in charge of the mainland, such as the chancellor or the *magister capitaneus*. The confirmed and newly appointed counts appear to have been seen by the new monarchy as reliable leaders, worth keeping on top of the local society's structure. When Roger II died in 1154, there were eleven counts in the provinces of Apulia and the Terra di Lavoro (Avellino, Boiano, Buonalbergo, Carinola, Civitate, Conversano, Fondi, Lesina, Marsico, Montescaglioso and Tricarico), and two more in Calabria (Catanzaro and Squillace).[1]

An important additional comital title was granted during the transition period that followed Roger II's death. Although his son William I had been nominally co-ruling with his father as king since 1151, it was not until Roger's absence that the order of things started to change; according to the chronicle of Romuald of Salerno, William had reigned with his father for two years and ten months by the time of the latter's death.[2] The new changes that the south Italian aristocracy would go through during William I's time could not be solely the result of the new policies; the circumstances in which the kingdom was created, including the social rearrangements implemented on the mainland, were also consequential to these changes. This can be observed clearly in what became the first significant change to the peninsular nobility under William I: the creation of Robert of Bassunvilla as count of Loritello.

Robert of Bassunvilla: Twice a count

Robert II of Bassunvilla, originally the count of Conversano, was one of the direct results of King Roger's approach to bonding with the local peninsular leadership by way of marriage – he was the son of Judith of Sicily, Roger II's sister.[3] This Robert of Bassunvilla was the only member of the peninsular nobility who could have claimed direct membership to the royal kin-group. The other three counts who were related to the royal family – Hugh of Molise, Roger of Avellino and Sylvester of Marsico – were in a different, less secure position. Whereas both Hugh of Molise's and Sylvester of Marsico's ties to the king's kin-group were weak or distant (Hugh was related either as the brother of Roger's mistress or as the husband of Roger's illegitimate daughter, and Sylvester's father was an illegitimate son of Roger I), Count Roger of Avellino was too distant a relative of the royal family to be considered a potential candidate for the crown and a part of the king's kin-group. His mother Magalda was a great-niece of King Roger, making Roger of Avellino a grandnephew of William I only in the third degree. Count Robert I of Conversano was, on the other hand, married to a sister of King Roger himself. Robert II of Bassunvilla was in this way unquestionably a member of both the peninsular nobility and the Sicilian royalty.

As explained previously, Robert II of Bassunvilla must have inherited his father's lordship and title soon after his death and before 1142.[4] Robert II of Bassunvilla was also recorded in 1146, in two now lost donations as count of Conversano and lord of Molfetta.[5] As documented in the previous chapter, Robert II of Bassunvilla was active as a prominent lord in Adriatic Apulia, around the *Terra Barese*, and he exercised his authority over Conversano and the maritime city of Molfetta.

The creation of Robert II of Bassunvilla as count of Loritello was without doubt a turning point in the development of the south Italian county. First of all, the last dated documented appearance of a count of Loritello was in 1137, when William of Loritello confirmed what his grandfather Count Robert [I] and his father Count Robert [II] gave to the church of Chieti.[6] This William appears to have been the same lord recorded in two undated charters from the abbey of St Mary in Tremiti, and also the count who swore allegiance to Lothar II in 1137.[7] It has, therefore, been assumed that the king confiscated his county as a punishment for this disloyalty. Jamison was of the opinion that the lands of Loritello were merged with the demesne of the new crown for administrative purposes.[8] Very little is actually known about the royal demesne on the mainland at this stage, but Jamison assumes that the lands in which there is no surviving evidence of any count's activity or presence after the civil war were confiscated by the crown and held as royal demesne. Ariano and Loritello might have been attributed to the royal demesne, but many of the towns and lordships that fell under the authority of former counts were granted to other lords aligned with the monarchy, and so subsequently became parts of new counties.

In the case of Ariano, for example, we know that the newly created count of Buonalbergo, Robert of Medania, was the overlord of most of the territories north of the former comital seat. Notably, the *Quaternus* records that a handful of *feuda* south of Ariano (Contra, Flumeri, *S. Angelum*, Trevico and Vallata) did not fall under the lordship of any count, and their lord, Richard son of Richard – the brother of the former count of Civitate – held these lands *in demanio*, directly from the royal *curia*, and acted also as an overlord of two other lesser barons.[9] Albeit not a count, this Richard son of Richard is recorded as an overlord of two other lesser barons, and as such his military obligation is recorded to be of forty *milites* and eighty *servientes*, most of these due from the *feuda* near Ariano. Cuozzo has suggested that Richard's father was in fact Richard son of Guarin of Flumeri, who was also the father of Count Robert I of

Civitate.[10] Even though the *Quaternus* could in fact reflect a later snapshot in time, *c.* 1167, rather than when the original drafts might have been constructed, *c.* 1150, the county of Buonalbergo did not go through any apparent transformation, and no further county was created around the area. Conversely, the lands and *feuda* that are recorded in the *Quaternus* under the 'county of Loritello' appear to have been grouped as a small vacant county whose military obligation consisted of only sixteen *milites* and thirty *servientes*.[11] This vacancy could have been the case in either period of time or even both: so far as we know, Loritello remained vacant until 1154, and again after the events that would transpire in 1158 – those which are discussed in Chapter 4. In a nutshell, Loritello could have been the only vacant county whose original title preceded the kingdom's creation. Even though it is not certain just how these lands were preserved and administered, whether as a core lordship, unassigned and held by the crown, or as dismantled series of small lordships that were put together in 1154, a revived comital title for Loritello was used in 1154, and a county was created from it.

Three main narrative sources describe how Robert II of Bassunvilla was created count of Loritello: the chronicles of Romuald of Salerno, John Berard of St Clement in Casauria and Alexander of S. Bartholomew in Carpineto. Romuald Guarna's *Chronicon* recorded that 'after the death of his father, he [King William] summoned the magnates of his kingdom and was solemnly crowned at the next Easter [4 April 1154]. Robert of Bassunvilla, count of Conversano, the king's first cousin, was present at this court. King William gave him the county (*comitatus*) of Loritello and sent him honourably back to Apulia'.[12] Together with the appointment of Chancellor Maio of Bari as great admiral of the kingdom, investing Robert of Bassunvilla with the county of Loritello was William I's inaugural political manoeuvre. John Berard, in his chronicle appended to the *Liber instrumentorum* of the abbey in Casauria, reports that William I 'was a man of extraordinary wisdom and great courage, who wishing to benefit his relatives (*consanguineis suis*) made Robert of Bassunvilla count of Loritello, and placed both the whole of that county (*comitatus*) and the neighbouring lands under his rule, as he believed him to be loyal to himself and that he would be even more devoted if well-rewarded'.[13] This two versions seem to agree, and no further explanation on the possible reasoning behind this decision is presented. Alexander the monk expands this story in the chronicle of Carpineto, by explaining that Robert of Bassunvilla, the king's nephew, was made count by the explicit deathbed wish of Roger II.[14] Moreover, Robert of Loritello was recorded a couple of months earlier, before Easter, just as count of Conversano and lord of Molfetta, as he granted holdings to the abbey of Venosa in March 1154.[15] On the other hand, Robert's earliest documented transaction as count of Loritello is a concession he made to the bishop of Chieti in July 1154, exempting the cathedral of St Thomas Apostle of fiscal dues.[16]

This is a convenient point to note that, like many other monastic chronicles, the authors of the chronicles of Casauria and Carpineto, John Berard and Alexander, tend to interpret events as though their own monasteries were central to them. However, these accounts provide a useful corrective to the narrative of Pseudo-Falcandus, in that they present a positive view of William I as king. Together, these testimonies not only confirm the kinship bond between the Bassunvilla and the Sicilian crown and the creation of the former as count of Loritello but also provide a common picture in which the Apulian noble is the centre of attention of the monarchy, placing him at the same level of the 'emir of emirs', that is the great admiral, Maio of Bari, the most important office in the kingdom.

Why would the king pay so much attention to the count of Conversano and enhance his position and power by granting him a second county? It is not even clear if this decision was made by William I or by Roger II, if we ought to believe Alexander of Carpineto. Pseudo-Falcandus suggested, in the treacherous mouth of an ill-depicted Maio of Bari, that Roger II 'was said to have directed in one of his wills that if his son William should turn out to be useless or unsuitable, then they should put Count Robert, about whose abilities there was no doubt, in charge of the realm'.[17] John Kinnamos provides another take on the issue, albeit a muddled one. The Greek historian related that 'while Roger II lived, [Robert of] Bassunvilla had authority over [southern] Italy' and that after Roger died and the authority passed to his son William, Robert 'was constrained to continue as an assistant governor, while another controlled [southern] Italy. Refusing to endure the affront, he contemplated revolt'.[18] There is no indication whatsoever that the count of Conversano held any additional title, such as 'chancellor' or even 'master justiciar', so it is clear that Count Robert did not exercise any authority over the other counts of Apulia and the Terra di Lavoro, nor did he hold any sort of gubernatorial position. Kinnamos's confusion is most likely the result of a remote, retrospective view of Robert of Bassunvilla's pretensions and the role he exercised during the insurrection, as well as a convenient rationalization for Robert's opposition against William I. In any case, despite the inaccurate details of Robert's actual political position, the historian knew of Robert of Basunvilla's relationship to the royal family and of his rebellion on the mainland.

It seems feasible that behind Roger's presumed wish to make Robert of Bassunvilla count of Loritello was the king's scepticism about William's capacity to rule the entire kingdom, but this is not the only likely explanation. This passage, albeit hardly plausible due to the prejudiced nature of Pseudo-Falcandus's portrayal, may reflect Roger's desire to reward a potential heir, should his only surviving legitimate son die unexpectedly and without surviving issue. Nonetheless, the future William II was probably born in 1153, and he had an elder brother, Roger (d. 1161), making Robert of Loritello third in line to the throne at best.[19] However, the very young age of William's children could not have been a guarantee for succession. Perhaps the mainland dominions could have remained stable by strengthening the position of a loyal noble, and the control over the peninsular aristocracy would be guaranteed not only by royal functionaries but also by one of their own.

Also, there were enough reasons to believe that Robert of Bassunvilla's loyalty was reliable: after all, his father had been a loyal supporter of the king during the civil war, Conversano remained unproblematic throughout the rest of Roger's reign, and Robert himself was a royal relative. One can take this speculation even further and imagine that Roger II could have seen in his nephew a potential substitute for the crown in case William lacked both the ability and the support to be king. With this in mind, one should also assess the motives behind William's possible determination to make his cousin a double count. Was William I trying to dissuade a potential rival or rewarding someone who appeared to be a close noble ally?[20] Whether it was met with fear or confidence, the decision carried an inherent risk: tipping the scales of power in favour of a single aristocrat, and so disturbing the social equilibrium that had been created along with the rearrangement of the landholding aristocracy. In any case, the immediate consequences of creating a double count in Robert of Bassunvilla did not fulfil the possible expectations of either Roger II or William I, and instead unleashed a new period of instability.

This was the first time under the new monarchy that two comital titles were assigned to one noble. Furthermore, Loritello was not an insignificant lordship. Since the conquest, Loritello had been the gate to the northern Adriatic, connecting the Capitanata with the lands of the count of Boiano and the border region of the Abruzzo. It is reasonable to argue that many of the lords and lands that fell under the authority of the original Hauteville counts of Loritello were reassigned to other neighbouring counts (i.e. Boiano and Civitate), and hence the actual dominions granted along the Loritello title might have been less extensive than what was held by the original Loritello counts – just as the post–1136 county of Conversano was less extensive than the pre–1130 lands of the original counts of Conversano. In any case, the *feuda* placed under the county of Loritello provided a useful foothold to connect the lands in the southern Adriatic with the rest of the Italian peninsula. Robert II of Bassunvilla was therefore more than a simple baron honoured twice with the comital title; he became the most important lord of the Adriatic front of the kingdom. As such, he embodied the first manifest opposition in the kingdom since the civil war, as he rebelled against the Sicilian crown.

The barons' uprising, Loritello's leadership and the invasion of the kingdom

The rebellion of Robert of Bassunvilla spearheaded a fresh new period of instability, but the double count himself was not the only trigger. Frederick Barbarossa marched to Rome in the spring of 1155 for his imperial coronation. Both events seem to have sparked off a full-fledged revolt across all of the kingdom: Robert of Bassunvilla in the Adriatic coast, the exiled prince Robert of Capua who came back to recover the principality and invaded the Tyrrhenian front, and the supporters of Count Simon of Policastro on the island of Sicily. Although it is not the aim of this section to explain in detail and discuss what occurred during this period, it is necessary at least to relate the higher aristocracy's performance and transformation during these years of war.

The only sources that explicitly report a connection between Robert of Loritello and Frederick Barbarossa are John Kinnamos and the chronicle of Alexander of Carpineto. We are told by Kinnamos that, after contemplating revolt, Robert of Bassunvilla wrote to Emperor Frederick and 'promised to place the whole of [South] Italy and Sicily in the emperor's hands'.[21] Conversely, the monk of St Bartholomew in Carpineto records that soon after (*post modicum tempus*) Robert was given Loritello, he rebelled against his lord the king, and in order to oppose him, Robert placed himself under oath to the 'Roman emperor'.[22] The rebel count's hopes were thwarted however, because the emperor went back to Germany, and no effective support was provided. Although the chronicle of Carpineto does not elaborate on why Frederick did not come down to the Sicilian kingdom, we know that the German emperor left Rome after his imperial coronation on 18 June 1155 and retreated northwards at the end of July, apparently due to sickness in the German army and the explicit refusal of the German nobles to accept the pope's condition to consecrate Frederick after he had captured Apulia and Sicily.[23] Robert of Loritello hence appealed to another potential ally against the king: the emperor in Constantinople, Manuel Komnenos.

Alexander of Carpineto reports that the count's envoys to the eastern Roman emperor agreed to yield the naval cities of [Adriatic] Apulia and to place under the emperor's overlordship the rest of the towns; consequently, the emperor sent an army, with an immense amount of money, which encamped in the Apulian Adriatic coast, at Brindisi.[24] Kinnamos also recorded that after Robert of Loritello had achieved nothing in Barbarossa's court, he arranged a meeting with Michael Palaiologos – a member of the Greek emperor's council who held the rank of *sebastos* – in order to negotiate an alliance with the Greek Empire. They had already met and exchanged oaths in Apulia at Vieste (Βεστία), a coastal town on the tip of the Gargano peninsula which had previously been captured by Palaiologos' fleet.[25] Based on these two testimonies, Count Robert of Loritello made an initial offer to the Greek emperor, which allowed for a naval vanguard led by Palaiologos to set foot in Apulia before both parties had arranged the terms of their alliance.

By contrast, the chronicle of Casauria detailed Robert's unruly attitude as his unlawful action preceded his eventual rebellion. John Berard of Casauria related that the count of Loritello wanted to rule over the things which had not been granted to him, and thence 'he occupied the monastery of St Clement, and forced its men and some of the brothers to place themselves under oath before the count'. Accordingly, the chronicler states that the king became angry and indignant, and commanded Count Robert to refrain from this presumption and to leave the abbey of St Clement in peace, since it belonged to and was under the direct protection of the crown. The count of Loritello relented, and released its men and monks from the oath, but soon after he again 'acted treacherously against his lord [King William] and seized a great part of his kingdom'.[26] Robert of Bassunvilla was not the only aristocrat to participate in this uprising.

John Berard of Casauria provides a little more detail by recording that Robert of Loritello 'lured many counts into becoming associates in his wickedness and being more ambitious than one could imagine for a time he disturbed the whole country'. The war that resulted from the counts' sedition was destructive, as the chronicle of Casauria reports that fortresses were overthrown, villages left deserted and many abbeys harmed. Additionally, another count is specifically attested during this time by John Berard: Count Bohemund of Manopello. He is recorded as having lost his county (*comitatus Manupelli*) after having resisted the rebellion for a while. The invaders who 'took back' the county were described as those 'who had been driven out of the county of Manopello, and who thought that it rightfully belonged to them'.[27] These unnamed men would have been the descendants of Robert of Manopello, whom the same chronicle records as the ruling count in the late 1130s.[28] John Berard thus suggests that after the civil war, the heirs of the former counts of Manopello – who were related to either the 'sons of Amicus' or the Hauteville-Loritello branch – remained alive but were exiled from their own lands. Although John Berard tends to portray events as if Casauria was central to them, his testimony does supply us with a relevant local point of view; Casauria was at the centre of the Abruzzo: a region that, due to its geographical position as a border buffer zone and its proximity to the county of Loritello, became pivotal to Count Robert's rebellion.

An alternative reason for the insurrection of Robert of Loritello is provided by the archbishop of Salerno. According to Romuald's *Chronicon*, after the king had ordered his army to besiege Benevento some of the barons rebelled and some others returned home without permission. As the royal army was broken up, the count of Loritello abandoned the king, fearing that William I would have him arrested on the hateful suggestion of the admiral, Maio of Bari.[29] This episode is evoked in the chronicle of William of Tyre, in which it is told that the pope, in order to agitate the Sicilian king's own men after the latter had ordered them to lay siege to Benevento, 'persuaded the most powerful count of the realm, Robert of Bassunvilla, the son of the king's aunt, and many other nobles to rise against him [William I] by promising that they should never lack the aid and counsel of the Roman church'.[30] The chronicle of Romuald of Salerno furthermore suggests that the reason behind William I's order to attack Benevento, which happened after Easter in 1155, was the failed attempt of King William to make peace with the Roman curia after the election of a new pope, Adrian IV.[31] The Sicilian king refused to receive the papal mission sent to Salerno because the apostolic letters brought referred to William I solely as 'lord of Sicily', therefore denying him of his regal status.[32] As a papal city, Benevento was the central stage for any conflict between the papacy and the Sicilian kingdom. In this way, Robert of Loritello's desertion would have made him a crucial ally of the pope.

Pseudo-Falcandus furnishes a distinct and more nuanced, if rather partisan picture of the reasons behind Robert of Loritello's revolt. He starts by describing the ambitions and scheming of the great admiral of the kingdom, Maio of Bari. It is related that Maio was particularly afraid of three counts: Robert of Loritello, Simon of Policastro and Everard of Squillace. The reason behind Maio's alleged fear was rooted in what Pseudo-Falcandus describes as these nobles' 'good character', which made Maio believe he could not corrupt their loyalty through deceit or bribes.[33] Pseudo-Falcandus seems here to be identifying one aristocratic leader for each major geographical area of the kingdom: Simon for Sicily, Everard for Calabria and Robert for Apulia. As explained earlier, Count Simon was removed from the mainland soon after the end of the civil war, and returned to Sicily as lord of Butera, becoming thus the only known baron on the island who held the title of 'count' under the Hauteville monarchy.[34]

The image portrayed by Pseudo-Falcandus already conflicts with what was briefly said about the count of Loritello in the chronicles of Casauria and Carpineto. The count of Conversano and Loritello is no longer a treacherous and seditious lord, but the victim of a plot hatched between the great admiral and the archbishop of Palermo. It is then reported by Pseudo-Falcandus that the king crossed the straits, and many leaders went to visit the king in Salerno from many parts of the mainland. After Maio had turned the king's mind against Robert of Loritello, the latter was unable to have an audience with the king, which angered the count. William I then returned to Palermo leaving in the mainland provinces a displeased count and an army ready to oppose the German emperor. Although Pseudo-Falcandus does not make any explicit mention of Frederick Barbarossa's intentions, or even address the emperor by his name, he does attest that the potential threat of a sudden invasion was seriously considered. According to Pseudo-Falcandus, the royal army left in Apulia was commanded by the Chancellor Asclettin and Count Simon, neither of whom were members of the peninsular nobility.[35] Romuald of Salerno provides confirmatory testimony on Asclettin's role; we are told in his chronicle that just after his coronation William I committed the administration of Apulia (*Apulie amministrationem commisit*) to Archdeacon Asclettin of Catania, whom he had made chancellor, he was later ordered by the king to gather a great army and besiege Benevento.[36] Assembling and commanding the royal army appears here to be the substantial duty of 'administering' the peninsular dominions, hence Asclettin would have been as chancellor the commander of the king's armed forces on the mainland, just as Robert of Selby had been before.

Robert of Loritello's bloodline was definitely seen as a threat, and Pseudo-Falcandus uses this when explaining how Maio managed to manipulate the king against the count. On the grounds that Robert's uncle was Roger II himself, the count of Loritello was presented as someone who both wanted and could take control of the realm, at least according to Pseudo-Falcandus' Maio. The king purportedly summoned Count Robert to meet the royal commanders – Chancellor Asclettin and Count Simon of Policastro – in Capua. Here, Pseudo-Falcandus provides one of the most useful and interesting insights into the social system that equipped and mobilized the military power in the kingdom; the author reports that the chancellor went to Count Robert to tell him that

> it was the king's wish that he should transfer all the knights whom he levied from his *feudum* to the command of Count Bohemund [of Manopello]. The count was greatly annoyed by this, and replied that it was an offence and contrary to the custom for his own *milites* to be appointed to another commander (*dux*), as if he himself were considered a traitor or incompetent for war.[37]

It is unclear what the author means here with the term *feudum*, but if one bears in mind the vocabulary and structure of the *Quaternus magne expeditionis*, Pseudo-Falcandus must be referring to the *milites* that were required by the *feuda* of both his tenure *in demanio* as the lords that held their respective *feuda* from the count of Conversano or Loritello. The author also hereby implies that it was 'the custom' for a count to be the commander (*dux*) of the *milites* that belonged to his tenure. As a holder of two counties, the contingent of armed men that he could levy was surely considerable; if the details in the *Quaternus* accurately reflect the status of these counties *c.* 1155, then the barons grouped under these two titles would have provided for a contingent of at least around 80 *milites* and 100 *servientes* – and these figures do not include what the *feuda* held *in demanio* could have provided to the count of Loritello and Conversano.[38] We are told by Pseudo-Falcandus that Robert of Loritello refused to follow such orders, and then turned back and went into the Abruzzo. Perhaps it is after this episode that the events narrated in the chronicles of Casauria and Carpineto, both written by Abruzzesi monks, took place.

Just as the chronicle of Alexander of Carpineto did, Pseudo-Falcandus also records the Byzantine expedition in Apulia. He mentions too that the emperor of the Greeks was asked for support by Count Robert of Loritello, and that an army was dispatched to Brindisi, in which 'noble and very powerful men' were sent with enormous amounts of money.[39] We know from Greek sources that the imperial expedition of Constantinople for the occupation of Apulia was led by John Doukas and Michael Palaiologos, and reinforced by Alexios Komnenos, son of Nikephoros Bryennios and Anna Komnene. Alexander of Conversano, the former rebel who was defeated in 1132 and then in exile became a key mediator between the empires as a Constantinopolitan legate, is also recorded to have been present with the Greek army.[40] Alexander was described by Conrad III as 'accustomed to serve the empire with unbroken loyalty' (*imperio perpetua fidelitate servire manifeste consuevit*), and by Kinnamos as 'extremely devoted to the Romans [i.e. Byzantines] and the emperor's affairs' (Λογγιβάρδος μὲν τὸ γένος λίαν δὲ εὐνοϊκῶς ἔχων ἔς τε Ῥωμαίους καὶ τὰ βασιλέως πράγματα).[41] Alexander of Conversano was referred to in exile as 'count of Gravina' by John Kinnamos, Conrad III, Otto of Freising and William of Tyre.[42] It is not clear why Alexander's toponymic name changed; before 1132, he is attested as count of Conversano and lord of Matera, but without any overt reference to the inland town of Gravina. Perhaps Alexander wanted to avoid direct confrontation with the newly established continental nobility in his struggle to recover his former dignity against the Sicilian monarchy, because the title 'count of Conversano' was reused after 1140 by Roger II when he made Robert Bassunvilla a count. This was an exceptional situation considering that most of the titles of the other rebel and exiled nobles were abandoned, such as the counts of Ariano, Caiazzo and Sarno. Another possible reason is that the Byzantine emperor was expecting to exercise direct control over the maritime cities in the Adriatic in their plans to 'recapture' Apulia. Consequently, by supporting the exiles and rebels that would become subjects of the empire, at least nominally, the Greek Empire must have required the Italian nobles to confine themselves to the mainland. Remarkably, a Byzantine seal found in Dorostolon (modern Silistra, Bulgaria) bears the name of Count Alexander 'of Gravina' engraved on one side, and of St Catherine on the other.[43]

The count of Montescaglioso, Geoffrey of Lecce, was another nobleman who played a prominent role during this time. Count Geoffrey is personified by Pseudo-Falcandus as a benevolent, smart and outstanding warrior, who was nevertheless a fickle, disloyal and opportunist individual. Count Geoffrey's tenure was not be limited to southern Apulia; he is also recorded as lord of various towns in Sicily, including Caltanissetta, Noto and Sclàfani. This is backed up by the aforementioned 1153 marble inscription, in which the count of Montescaglioso was recorded as the patron of the church of the Holy Spirit in Caltanissetta.[44] According to Pseudo-Falcandus, Maio was able to persuade William I that it was too dangerous for the count to hold Noto, which had a well-fortified *castellum* that was ultimately confiscated.[45] In an attempt to circumvent Maio's machinations, the count of Montescaglioso obtained the loyal support of other aristocrats, such as Count Simon of Sangro, from the Abruzzo, and Roger son of Richard, from the family of the lords of Trevico.[46] The lordships gathered under the county of Montescaglioso were pivotal for the territorial control of the kingdom, in that it covered an extensive area around the gulf of Taranto. Additionally, this southern Apulian nobleman held a considerable influence in Sicily, in that his connection to the royal family via his sister – the late Duke Roger's mistress – was the main reason why he received the lordships on the island.

Count Geoffrey is subsequently attested as having attempted to assassinate Maio, and after having failed to do so, fled to Butera. According to Pseudo-Falcandus, Butera had been taken by Bartholomew of Garsiliato and other sympathizers of Simon of Policastro, in order to demand the liberation of Count Simon, who had been imprisoned by the king's command, on Maio's instigation. Geoffrey of Lecce's role during the siege and negotiations of the occupied *castellum* of Butera is unclear. However, the count of Montescaglioso went there to support the rebels, because after the surrender of Butera was negotiated, the royal party swore to him and his associates that the king would allow them to leave the kingdom unharmed. Count Simon was released following tremendous disturbances at Palermo, and his presence allowed the siege to be concluded and the negotiations to end successfully.

Another notable aristocrat is attested in the Butera episode: Everard of Squillace. Count Everard of Squillace, described as a man of 'unshakable loyalty', is recorded by Pseudo-Falcandus to also have been active in Sicily during the rebellion. According to the author, he was sent as a royal representative to Butera to negotiate with the rebels who had occupied the site's *castellum*.[47] Nonetheless, the Adriatic and Sicilian fronts were not the only theatre of war; Robert of Loritello's sedition also presented the opportunity the Capuan exiles had been waiting for since their defeat in 1139.

The confusion that came from the rebellion brought also instability to the principality of Capua and the former principality of Salerno. According to Romuald's *Chronicon*, the rebellion opened the gates for the pope and his army to enter the Terra di Lavoro and to recover papal control over Benevento.[48] The *Annales Casinenses* record that the former prince of Capua, Robert of Sorrento, 'captured the whole principality of Capua up to Naples and Salerno'.[49] Similarly, Pseudo-Falcandus relates that Robert of Sorrento was welcomed by the Capuans and took possession of the principality of Capua that belonged to him 'by right of inheritance'.[50] The word even reached Archbishop William of Tyre, as we are told in his chronicle that 'Robert of Sorrento, the Capuan prince' (*Robertus de Surrento princeps Capuanus*), was among the many illustrious and mighty-in-battle men who had been banished by William I and his father and who were then exhorted by the pope to return to the kingdom and regain the possessions which belonged to them by hereditary right.[51] The papal support came with a serious provision; according to the *Liber Pontificalis*, Pope Adrian IV received at S. Germano 'an oath of fealty, and homage from Prince Robert of Capua, Count Andrew [of Rupecanina], and other nobles from those lands [Terra di Lavoro]'.[52] Robert of Sorrento's return was confirmed by a princely donation issued by himself at Capua in April 1156, by which land was granted and confirmed to the nunnery of St John the Baptist in Capua; although we know of the transaction only from Monaco's transcription.[53] In this charter, Robert fashioned himself as 'Prince Robert II of Capua' (*Secundus Robertus Capuanorum Princeps*) and the recorded transaction was dated to the twenty-ninth year of his princedom; just as if his rule had never been interrupted since he was made prince in 1127. The return of Robert of Sorrento to his original principality brought the war to the other coast of the realm.

Together with Robert of Sorrento, other former members of the south Italian nobility came back to the Capuan province. The chronicle of Santa Maria of Ferraria recorded that 'Robert, the former Capuan prince, Robert, count of Loritello and a relative of the king, and Count Andrew, nephew of the late Rainulf [of Caiazzo]', invaded the kingdom alongside the Greek army, and subjugated all Apulia and the Terra di Lavoro.[54] In the same way, the German *Gesta Friderici* reports that 'the count of Capua, Andrew, a count of Apulia, and the other exiles from that province, entering Campania and Apulia with the emperor's [Frederick I's] embassy, received back the cities, castles, and the other possessions which they once had, without the opposition of the inhabitants who were supposing that the emperor would follow them'.[55] Andrew of Rupecanina is recorded thus as one of the invaders who marched into the *regnum* with the former prince of Capua during the first year of William I's reign. Even William of Tyre named 'Count Andrew of Rupecanina' (*comes Andreas de Rapa Canina*) as one of the exiled nobles who, together with Robert of Sorrento, returned to the kingdom.[56]

Andrew is attested with the comital title, and although there is no specific reference to where that title belongs, the rebel Count Andrew appears to have claimed the lordships that used to belong to his family as lords of Caiazzo, Alife and Airola. As a matter of fact, it was recorded that by this time 'count' Andrew had taken the town of Alife. The *Annales Casinenses* records that Andrew captured the 'county of Alife' (*comitatum Alifae*) once he heard that William I had allegedly died; the king was ill by this time, which not only secluded him for some months but also set off rumours of his death.[57] The other Capuan counts that could have either assisted the king's forces or joined the rebels seemed to be absent from the surviving records as well. Count Jonathan of Carinola, who is recorded as the lord of Airola in the *Quaternus*, was conspicuously inactive; no sources suggest he presented resistance to the rebel forces. On the contrary, Marius Borell, a lord who used to hold lands (*totam terram que fuit Gregorii Pagani*) of the count of Carinola does appear to have joined the rebels.[58] Marius, a relative of the Abruzzesi counts of Sangro, is recorded as having burned on 21 August 1155 the town of Arce, in the northern borders of the principality of Capua, north of Fondi and east of Ceccano.[59]

The other major aristocratic figure who could have played a central role during the rebellion was Count Hugh of Molise. The *feuda* that other lords held *in servitio* from Count Hugh not only comprised a major part of the northeastern territory of the Capuan province but also created a territorial bridge deep into the lands of the count of Loritello. He was a prominent overlord located in a strategic area, yet still his presence and activities during this time of instability and double-front war are conspicuously undocumented. Jamison suggests that Count Hugh of Molise could have been involved as a member of Maio of Bari's party because Hugh of Molise was a close friend of Archbishop Hugh of Palermo.[60] Such a claim is made on the basis of a thirteenth-century account of the *translatio* of the body of St Christina from Sepino to Palermo,[61] in which it is related that the archbishop of Palermo asked Count Hugh about the presence of this relic at the *castrum* of Sepino, and then requested that he allow the relic's transfer to the Palermitan church, where the remains of St Christina ultimately arrived on 7 May.[62] The date of the *translatio* is uncertain, but Hugh of Molise's reported communication with Archbishop Hugh must have taken place at some point before 1158, but certainly after Hugh of Capua became archbishop of Palermo in 1150, and not necessarily after Roger II's death. Be that as it may, Count Hugh of Molise is not attested in any surviving contemporary testimony as a participant in Robert of Loritello's rebellion; he could have been deceased by 1156, although the first clear record that he was dead comes only in October/December 1158. The *Necrologio* of Montecassino has two Count Hughs (*Ugo comes*) listed but it is not clear which one was Hugh II of Molise and which was Hugh I of Molise.[63] Pseudo-Falcandus's testimony confirms that Hugh of Molise's wife was a widow by 1160, in that it explains that Matthew Bonellus was captivated by 'an illegitimate daughter of king Roger who had been married to Count Hugh of Molise'.[64] Without the support of the *milites* of Count Hugh of Molise and Count Jonathan of Carinola, the king's barons could not stand a chance on his own against the rebel forces of the exiled Drengot family (i.e. the Quarrels) and the count of Fondi.

Sicilian rule on the peninsula appeared to be abolished during the climax of the war; in the words of Romuald of Salerno, 'one part by Prince Robert of Capua and the other by Count Robert, the whole land was occupied, except for Naples, Amalfi, Salerno, Troia, and Melfi, and a handful of cities and *castra*'.[65] However, just as rebellion sprung up everywhere, it was soon suppressed across the entire kingdom. After Butera was retaken, and the island pacified, the king's army crossed the straits, razed Bari and defeated the Greek army in Apulia. Before this, the former commander of the king's army, Chancellor Asclettin, fell from the king's grace and was thrown into prison. According to Pseudo-Falcandus, Asclettin was arrested and then sent to prison after being attacked and accused by Simon of Policastro, who in turn was manipulated by Maio.[66] Although one cannot be certain if Asclettin did in fact fall victim of a conspiracy from within the court, his activities in the peninsula ceased entirely, and that the king himself commanded the armed forces during the summer of 1156. William I's campaign stretched from May to June 1156.[67]

The alliance between the count of Conversano and Loritello and the Eastern Empire turned out to be a disaster, because the Constantinopolitan generals alienated the Apulian barons. According to Pseudo-Falcandus, the Greeks were cheated out of the help of Robert of Loritello, who did not join the battle between the king's forces and the invaders; Romuald of Salerno explained that Count Robert left Brindisi and went to Benevento after learning of William I's arrival, and John Kinnamos blamed the imperial defeat on the count's abandonment of the army.[68] The outnumbered opposing army was defeated at Brindisi, many of the Greeks and their generals were captured and sent to Palermo, and the Apulian rebel barons were scared away into the Abruzzo. William's capture of Brindisi on 28 May 1156 was a watershed in the rebellion's development.[69] The *Annales Casinenses* and *Ceccanenses* record that after the king had retaken Brindisi and Bari, he met with Pope Adrian IV in Benevento to negotiate the safe passage out of the realm of the count of Loritello and 'Count' Andrew [of Rupecanina].[70] The chronicle of Alexander of Carpineto confirms this incident, as it records that, after the Capuan prince was captured, King William 'headed ragingly towards Benevento as fast as a lion, laid siege to the aforesaid Count Robert and his companion Andrew, who, terrified of the royal power, fled to the pope. Thence, by intervention of Pope Adrian, the king granted them safe passage out of the realm'.[71] Furthermore, we are told by William of Tyre that Andrew of Rupecanina sought refuge with the German emperor.[72] Romuald of Salerno likewise explained in his chronicle that, on the pope's plea, the king allowed Robert of Loritello, Andrew of Rupecanina and the rest of the rebels who had taken refuge in Benevento to leave the realm.[73] Subsequently, the Capuan rebellion collapsed without even having directly to face the royal forces; the king's victories seemed to have shaken the hopes of the entire rebellion.

Pseudo-Falcandus provides an illustrative insight into the behaviour of the nobility during the rebellion, as the author relates Robert of Sorrento's capture. As the rebel prince of Capua was fleeing the realm, he travelled through the lands of the count of Fondi, Richard of Aquila; but as Robert of Sorrento was crossing the River Garigliano he was arrested on the count's orders and surrendered to the king.[74] Romuald of Salerno echoes this testimony, in that he recorded that Robert II of Capua was ambushed and captured by his own man (*homo*), Count Richard of Fondi, while the former was crossing the Garigliano.[75] The Garigliano was a natural border of the county of Fondi, since all the *feuda* recorded in the *Quaternus* that the count of Fondi held either *in demanio* or *in servitio* were exclusively located west of the river.[76] The county of Fondi was situated on the northwestern fringe of the kingdom, and it was the last major territory through which the Via Appia passed,[77] connecting the northern regions of Capua with the Gaetan shore and the Papal States to the north – today, the communes of Fondi and Gaeta are placed in the region of Lazio and not in the Campania, and the River Garigliano is the current border between these two modern regions. The county of Richard of Aquila was thus located in a crucial enclave, a mandatory passage for whoever wished to go to or from Rome. The count of Fondi did not stay loyal to the crown throughout the entire rebellion.

Pseudo-Falcandus relates that Richard of Aquila had 'greatly displeased the king before', and Romuald of Salerno referred to the count of Fondi as a 'man' (*homo*) of Prince Robert of Capua who, through an act of treachery (*proditionis genere*), recovered the king's grace, which he had previously lost.[78] This deed did not spare the count of Fondi a bad reputation, as Pseudo-Falcandus recorded that 'many people consider it to have been a criminal act for him to have vilely betrayed his lord [Robert of Loritello], a man of the greatest nobility and humanity, to whom he had in addition bound himself by an oath of loyalty (*sacramentum quoque fidelitatis prestiterat*)'.[79] Since this Count Richard of Aquila was the son of the late Count Geoffrey of Aquila, who died in 1148, the count of Fondi of this time could not have been tied to Robert of Sorrento before he had been deprived of his principality by Roger II in 1135. Hence, if what Pseudo-Falcandus reports is accurate, Count Richard of Fondi did betray the king and joined the party of the rebel prince of Capua. The count of Fondi is furthermore recorded as having, in 1155, in the midst of the rebellion's disorder, seized Suessa and Teano.[80] These two towns were located deeper into the Capuan territory, southeast of Fondi, and appear to have been royal towns; Teano is recorded in the *Quaternus* under the section of Capua, as a city that was under direct control of the crown. Two lesser barons are recorded in the *Quaternus* as having held in Teano two *feuda* directly from the royal *curia*: Raoul son of William of Capua, who held a *feudum* of two *milites* in

Teano, Octaiano and Fellino; and William son of John of Teano, who held a *feudum* of one *miles* in Teano.[81] Suessa, by contrast, has its own section in the *Quaternus*, and was clearly under direct control of the king; all the barons who held *feuda* in the city are not placed under any other major lord, and what appears to be a royal official, Ebolus the chamberlain, had recorded the value and service of many of the town's *feuda*.[82] His betrayal of Robert of Capua seems to have been the reason why Count Richard of Fondi survived and kept his title and position after the rebellion.

The consequences of the 1155–6 aristocratic rebellion

By the autumn of 1156, William I had 'expelled many of his enemies from the realm, sent others to prison, and received the rest back into his grace and love' (*Rex autem plures de inimicis suis de regno expulit, quosdam in carcere posuit, quosdam in sua gratia et amore recepit*).[83] The count of Conversano and Loritello left the kingdom, lingering around the northern Adriatic border. Count Geoffrey of Montescaglioso, the insular Count Simon and Count Everard of Squillace were out of the picture once stability returned to the kingdom. We are told by Pseudo-Falcandus that Geoffrey of Montescaglioso was, first, prevented from leaving Messina while the king was on campaign, against what was guaranteed to him during the Butera negotiations, and then imprisoned and blinded at Maio's behest.[84]

Although there is no certainty beyond Pseudo-Falcandus's testimony that Geoffrey of Lecce was in fact blinded, he did lose all his lordships. He does not appear in any surviving document as conducting any activity on either the mainland or the island. The only piece of evidence that attests him after 1156 is a funerary inscription from the cathedral of Palermo, dated 8 April 1174, in which he is recorded as 'Count Geoffrey of Lecce' (*Comes Licii Gosfridus*). Garufi arrived at the conclusion that the usage of the comital title here was given as a mark of respect to the defunct, in that he was the uncle of Tancred of Lecce, who had acquired a considerable degree of influence in the king's *curia* by that time.[85] It is safe to assume then that Geoffrey stayed in Sicily, deprived of his lordships and the county of Montescaglioso, and died in Palermo, perhaps after having been released from prison by 1169. Count Simon, on the other hand, is recorded by Pseudo-Falcandus as having died after he was summoned to court, just before he arrived in Palermo.[86] Simon's death is attested in the same 1156 royal document in which his parentage is confirmed.[87] Everard of Squillace survived sometime after the realm was pacified, but soon after he too fell from the king's grace and was imprisoned. According to Pseudo-Falcandus, Maio inflamed the king's suspicions after Count Everard had left the court 'without permission' with a contingent of *milites*, as reportedly he went out to hunt. Everard was then summoned to court, arrested, had his eyes gouged out and his tongue cut off.[88] Such a sudden and gruesome fate could be more a figment of Pseudo-Falcandus' rhetoric than an actual testimony of what occurred; it does however indicate the deposition of the count of Squillace. There is no further evidence that records any count for Squillace before 1176.

In the principality of Capua, there was no discernible change in the configuration of the local upper aristocracy. After hearing the news of William's victories in the

Adriatic front, Andrew of Rupecanina left Alife and the kingdom. The silence around most of the Capuan counts forces us to rely solely on the conjecture that they were neither involved with the rebels nor mobilized themselves to face the rebellion without the direct command of the royal army. Thus, after 1156 the upper aristocracy of the province of Capua had the same members and arrangement as it did before the rebellion.

The Adriatic front must have been an arena of intense conflict during this period; from the *Terra Barese*, where the invading Greek army had obtained a foothold, to the River Trigno (the border between northern Apulia and the Abruzzo), where Robert of Loritello was active. The lords who were grouped under the count of Conversano might have joined the rebellion as part of the reinforcement the rebel count meant to send to the Greek army, but there is no evidence of any major confrontation or battle taking place in the valleys of the gulf of Taranto (located in the instep of the Italian 'boot'), where many of these lords held their respective *feuda*. The count of Andria, on the other hand, was active in fighting on the king's side.

The count of Andria, Richard of Lingèvres, is recorded by Robert of Torigni as having participated in the destruction of Apulia, alongside Robert II of Bassunvilla.[89] The Norman chronicler nevertheless mistakenly asserts that Count Richard presumed the king was dead and ravaged Apulia together with the count of Loritello. Conversely, John Kinnamos provides a more detailed and closer look at the activities of Count Richard of Andria. The Greek historian recorded that a certain Richard, who was in command of the 'fortress' of Andria ('Άντρου φρουρίου), opposed the Greek advance in Apulia and joined with other counts (κόμητες) and the 'logothete' Asclettin in the recovery of the city of Trani – the maritime city of Trani is adjacent to the northeast to the town of Andria. This commander of Andria was assuredly the same Count Richard that Robert of Torigni attested as count of Andria. Kinnamos furthermore indicates that Richard was originally followed by an army of 2,000 knights (ἱππεῖς) and a myriad of soldiers, and that his intervention shifted the balance of the war; Richard later retreated to Andria followed by 2,800 knights and a large group of foot soldiers. The count of Andria was nonetheless pursued and ultimately defeated by the Byzantine army and the contingent of the count of Loritello. We are also told by Kinnamos that after Richard of Andria was killed, Andria and its troops went over to the invading Greek army.[90] After this, no other baron is remembered to have been created count of Andria during William I's reign.

The count of Civitate, Robert son of Robert, is conspicuously absent from the surviving evidence. As the county of Civitate appears to have been intertwined, or at least juxtaposed, with the county of Loritello, Count Robert II of Civitate would have been placed at the centre of the rebellion's arena. He is nevertheless omitted by the narrative accounts and does not appear in any subsequent document. Robert son of Robert may either have joined Robert of Loritello and then been killed in combat or fled the realm, or alternatively he might have supported the royal resistance and then been killed in combat like the count of Andria. Had the former been the case, his heirs, if he had any, would not have been allowed to inherit the county, or even to stay in the kingdom; had it been the latter, the rebel forces of the count of Loritello would have taken his lands and removed any potential local rivals and heirs. Whichever the case, it is clear that Count Robert II of Civitate was out of the picture after the rebellion, and his county remained vacant through William I's reign.

Finally, the count of Lesina, a neighbouring overlord of both Civitate and Loritello, does make an appearance in Pseudo-Falcandus's testimony. Count William of Lesina is reported to have already been taken prisoner in Palermo, together with Bohemund of Tarsia, the defeated count of Manopello, as King William was concluding his campaign on the mainland. John Berard furthermore recorded that Count Bohemund was captured by William I, and then put in chains.[91] Hence, Count William of Lesina either took part in the rebellion as an ally of the count of Loritello, or failed to defend his lands from the rebels, and been consequently deprived of the county and his freedom. By 1156 a new count of Lesina had been created: Geoffrey of Ollia, the son of the former royal justiciar Henry of Ollia.[92] Count Geoffrey of Lesina is mentioned in an October 1156 charter when Robert, his chamberlain (*Robertus, Malfridi filius, totius terre comitis Guffredi Alesine camerarius*), was recorded to have heard a legal case made by the abbot of the monastery of St John *in Piano* against the abbey of Tremiti.[93] Additionally, a March 1173 charter was issued by the same Count Geoffrey in the eighteenth year of his countship.[94] This Geoffrey of Lesina was the same count of Lesina and royal justiciar (*Comes Alesin[us] et Domni Regis Iustitiarius*) who maintained correspondence regarding land distribution with Abbot Leonas of St Clemente of Casauria at some point after 1157.[95] Hence, the Adriatic front must have comprised a corridor of six counties, starting from Manopello in the Abruzzo, going through Loritello, Lesina and Civitate, all the way down to Andria and Conversano, which were adjacent to the maritime cities of Barletta and Trani, and the whole Terra di Bari. From this geographical perspective, it makes sense that the prominent barons recorded as major players during the rebellion of the count of Loritello and Conversano were in fact the counts in this corridor. With the exception of Count Robert II of Civitate, the counts of Manopello, Lesina and Andria are attested as having been actively involved in the armed conflict, and all of these noblemen either ended up in prison or died in combat; again, the count of Civitate might have been involved in the war, and his subsequent absence could have been the result of his participation in the conflict.

There are no major recorded activities related to the rebellion on the Tyrrhenian coast and Central Apulia. The count of Buonalbergo, Roger of Medania, is recorded in an 1154 local transaction as the overlord of a certain Constantine Aczarulus. He remained in place after the rebellion, as a June 1158 donation attests him as a benefactor of the monastery of Cava, in which he is recorded as 'count of Buonalbergo, by the grace of God and the king' (*Rogerius gratia Dei et regia Boni Herbergi*).[96] Roger of Medania was mentioned months earlier, in a May 1158 transaction, according to which the bishop of Caserta granted the churches of St Mary and St Marcianus, at Cervino, in the territory of Maddaloni and within the bishop's diocese, to the abbey of Cava, by request of Countess Judith – the widow of Count Robert of Buonalbergo – and her son Count Roger.[97] Likewise, the activities of the count of Avellino during this period are scarcely documented; after Count Richard of Aquila died in 1152, the earliest attested presence of his successor, Roger of Aquila, is found in Pseudo-Falcandus, relating to the events of 1160. In a similar way, the recently created count of Marsico is recorded just after the rebellion; in December 1157, in the Palermitan *curia*,

Count Sylvester of Marsico was recorded as witness of a royal charter.[98] In a similar way, Count Roger of Tricarico is only recorded in 1154, and nothing is heard of him until Romuald of Salerno refers to him in his chronicle while relating a subsequent rebellion in 1159.[99]

The only county in this area in which there was some changes during this period is Principato. Unfortunately, there is no surviving evidence that records any activity conducted after 1150 by a count of Principato. Cuozzo and Houben have hypothesized that Count William, brother of Count Nicholas of Principato, joined the rebellion against William I in 1155-6 and was subsequently imprisoned in Palermo, on the basis that he is recorded to have escaped from prison in Palermo in 1160 in order to join another rebellion.[100] Although it seems likely that the Count William of Principato who was attested years later in a Palermitan prison was the same Count William recorded in 1150, this is no evidence that he was actively involved in the 1155-6 rebellion. Additionally, Cuozzo has suggested that the royal justiciar and *comestabulus* Lampus of Fasanella was involved in the rebellion as a 'loyal man' of the family of the counts of Principato.[101] However, there is no actual evidence that Lampus conducted any activity during this period, apart from the fact that he does not appear in any surviving document after 1153.[102] The point to make here is that, as royal justiciar, Lampus of Fasanella would have been in charge of overseeing the lands that corresponded to the former Lombard principality of Salerno. Hence, he must have acted not as a man of the count but as a delegate of the king's authority when he subscribed, alongside the *stratigotus* of Eboli, a judicial authentication of a *preceptum* issued by the count of Principato.[103] As the head of an extensive county, covering a territory that went from Salerno to the lands of the count of Tricarico, if Count William of Principato had been involved in the uprising, a new front would have been open in the Salernitan region and southern Apulia. On the contrary, we do not hear about any important action taking place here, nor was the role of the count of Principato mentioned in any surviving narrative source. It is more reasonable on the other hand to assume that Count William was imprisoned later, between 1156 and 1160, perhaps falling victim to the plots and conspiracy Pseudo-Falcandus so vividly attests as having taken place in Palermo. Hence, the counties of Avellino, Buonalbergo, Marsico, Tricarico and, perhaps, Principato appear to have remained unchanged in 1156.

The barons' rebellion thus ended with some very significant but not numerous changes to the composition of the peninsular nobility. Pseudo-Falcandus recapped the state of affairs among the aristocracy: by the end of 1156 'opposition died down throughout the kingdom; all those brave men whom the admiral thought he had cause to fear had either been imprisoned or forced into exile'.[104] Only a handful of the Rogerian nobility appear to be explicitly recorded as participants in the rebellion on either side. Count Robert of Loritello and Conversano was the leader of the rebellion in Adriatic Apulia and was then forced into exile in the Abruzzo. Count William of Lesina and Bohemund of Tarsia were both taken prisoner after the king's successful campaign in the Adriatic. Although the former was apparently an ally of Robert of Loritello, Bohemund of Tarsia was not; he was blamed for failing to conduct the defence effectively in the country of the Abruzzo. Count Richard of Andria died in combat against the rebel Count and the Greek army. Count Richard of Fondi joined Robert of Sorrento when the latter captured Capua, and then betrayed Robert to regain the king's favour. Andrew of Rupecanina had joined the invasion of Robert of Sorrento, the rebel prince of Capua, only then to surrender and return to exile. Geoffrey of Ollia was, soon after the rebellion, created count of Lesina. Thus, only the counties of Civitate, Conversano and Loritello appear to have been left vacant by the end of 1156.

The overall picture of the peninsular nobility during this period of instability is thus one of limited changes but generalized disaffection. The absence of recorded incidents in Central Apulia and the former principality of Salerno, and of activities performed by most of the upper aristocracy, might suggest a nobility that had remained loyal, but still one that was rather passive and alienated. Were these major landholders and territorial leaders capable of maintaining both their social status and control over the land even in times of rebellion and shifting central authorities? Trouble is attested only when the forces of Palermo clashed directly with those of the foreign powers and the rebels. It was not until King William and his army crossed the Strait of Messina that effective and lasting resistance was exercised against the opposition. Consequently, the main core of the royal military forces during this campaign would have come from Sicily and Calabria, and also perhaps from the southern counties of Marsico, Montescaglioso, Principato and Tricarico.

Kinnamos's account is the only surviving narrative testimony that provides a deeper insight into the local military mobilizations before the king's army reached the Adriatic coast by land from Messina to Bari. The Greek chronicler alleged that the count of Andria not only commanded a considerable armed force – of 2,000 to 2,800 knights and a large group of foot soldiers – but that he also marched from his principal fortress to the defence of the city of Trani, which would have been the closest Adriatic bastion to his county. Contrary to the Greek narrator, the *Quaternus magne expeditionis* provides different figures. According to the military service records, the count of Andria under Count Bertram (*c.* 1167–8) had to provide 72 *milites* and 200 *servientes* for the *feuda* he held directly (i.e. *in demanio*), plus 50 knights for the *feuda* held by his 16 subtenants (*in servitio*).[105] The 122 knights that the count of Andria was formally obliged to mobilize *c.* 1167–8 falls deeply behind the 2,000 ἱππεῖς Count Richard supposedly commanded in 1155. Even if one assumes that the subsequent count of Andria was granted fewer *feuda* and had acted as overlord of fewer barons than those held by Richard of Lingèvres, no county in the *Quaternus* is recorded to have been responsible for a number of *milites* even close to one thousand. Thus, Kinnamos must have exaggerated the size of the ultimately defeated army of the count of Andria. Even if Kinnamos was correct and Count Richard did in fact lead the large army the chronicler attests, it can be inferred that Richard of Lingèvres must have been a commander not only of his own knights and barons but also of a larger division of the royal peninsular armed forces. In any case, and despite the count of Andria's apparent impressive military strength, he was still defeated by the rebels and the invaders.

This episode of the 1155–6 war suggests that the peninsular counts might have been effective foci of military mobilization only under direct command of the king's forces. As overlords, the counts appear to have played a vital role in guaranteeing social stability during times of peace, acting as hubs within the regional economic and political structures. At this moment of crisis, however, the counts do not appear to have been effective commanders of autonomous royal military forces. The count of Andria, in Adriatic Apulia, and the count of Manopello, in the Abruzzo, appear to have led their own military contingents against the rebellion, albeit unsuccessfully. The transition from times of peace to times of war resided in the counts' integration with the forces of the royal *curia*. Only a handful of noblemen openly rebelled against the crown in 1155–6, but that was hardly an indicator of domestic stability. The following years proved just how manifold and capricious were the aristocratic forces that the centre at Palermo was believed to have under control. The rebellion of 1155–6 hence opened the gates for a new period of political tension and social rearrangement.

4

Coalition and survival of the nobility

As the most important baron on the mainland and the leading count of the realm, Robert of Loritello provided a rich insight into the development of the nobility in the years following Roger II's death. His case, however, does not illustrate the condition of the kingdom after 1156; the great count of Conversano and Loritello went from being a linchpin of the aristocracy's structure to a rebel and finally an exile and a marauder. During the apparent peace after the rebellion, Robert of Loritello was constantly occupying and leaving the kingdom as he harried the northeastern border. Pseudo-Falcandus reports that Count Robert attacked the Abruzzo and the adjacent districts of Apulia (the county of Loritello must have been one of these adjacent Apulian 'districts'), the reason for which an army had to be retained in Apulia.[1] As the former count of Loritello was raiding the northern border, his *comestabulus* Richard of Mandra and the bishop of Chieti were arrested and taken to Palermo. Considering that Count Robert of Loritello made a donation in July 1154 to Bishop Alan of Chieti, the captured Bishop and supporter of the rebel count was probably this same Alan of Chieti.[2] Robert of Loritello continued his career outside the borders of the kingdom, and the remaining members of the upper aristocracy, including Richard of Mandra, went into another stage of change and ascent without him. The stability left by the royal army became an evanescent accomplishment undermined by an unsteady nobility. The same counts that appeared passive to the count of Loritello's rebellion and the invasion in Capua started to become restless actors in the political arena. The absent leadership left by Robert of Loritello's defeat was soon occupied not by another single powerful baron but by a coalition of counts, with the newly created count of Gravina in the midst. This chapter explores and discusses the activities that lead to a different stage of coalitions and rebellion and the new position acquired by a conflictive comital nobility.

The activities conducted on the island have been vividly narrated by Pseudo-Falcandus, although his dramatic testimony may contain figments of the courtier's political imagination. In any case, most of the reported events in this source are centred on the court in Palermo. The Great Admiral Maio and his circle of royal functionaries have been studied in depth; however, the unfolding of the peninsular affairs has been eclipsed by the emphasized leadership of Maio of Bari. Our exploration, by contrast, directs its attention to the continental dominions of the realm, and follows the actual documented actions of those magnates and barons that stood at the top of the social structure outside of the island itself.

The county of Gravina

Soon after 1156 an important change took place on the peninsula: the creation of the count of Gravina. We are told by Pseudo-Falcandus that the 'county of Gravina' (*comitatus Gravinae*) was given to Gilbert of Perche, a blood-relative of Queen Margaret, just before 1158.[3] Furthermore, there is no surviving evidence that records the existence of a count of Gravina before 1157. The kin-group that held the lordship of Gravina appears to have done so under the title of *marchio*; this lordship was held successively by the descendants of Marquis Boniface, from the Aleramici family.

In the kingdom of Sicily, after the civil war period and the consolidation of Roger II's reign, *comes* was no longer a vague term indicating a leader of the upper aristocracy or simply a baron with an additional dignity, but a title denoting a member of the highest level of the nobility and the head of a *comitatus*. Although the lords of Gravina did not appear to have been key actors in the process of creating and imposing a new order under Roger's kingship, they must have been pivotal aristocrats who would have gradually allowed for the control and mobilization of local barons and their respective knights. In other words, the marquises of Gravina were counts in the making; after the first rebellion William I faced, Gravina became a new county ready to play a major role in the kingdom's development.

An additional piece of evidence suggests that the count of Gravina was created before the appointment of the queen's relative Gilbert. A charter issued in March 1157 to the monastery of Cava records an Albert son of Marquis Boniface as 'count, by the grace of God and the king', in which said Albert confirmed a donation previously made to Cava by his nephew Marquis Sylvester.[4] The document refers to all previous lords of Gravina as 'marquises', but Albert himself employs the comital title and signs as a count, even though he was a son of the original Marquis Boniface. Hence, during the turmoil of the Greek invasion (between 1155 and 1157), Sylvester either died without leaving any heir or was removed from his position, and his uncle was placed in his stead as count. There is not enough evidence safely to hypothesize on Marquis Sylvester's role in the rebellion and the invasion, but it is certain that the king allowed and even utilized the promoted lordship of Gravina as a county when he created Gilbert a count. We can hence presume Sylvester's uncle Albert was given the comital title as Sylvester's successor. By the mid-twelfth century, the previous notion of bearing a prestigious but politically ambiguous dignity fell behind the new social significance and prominence of being a count of the realm. The subsequent vacancy of Gravina was in all probability the result of Albert having died *c.*1157, and Sylvester's heirs being either inexistent or banned. Sylvester's mother Philippa continued to hold an estate in Forenza, a nearby town of which Boniface was originally a lord, until her death before 1168, as she was remarkably recorded in the *Quaternus* as the 'former' (*quondam*) Marquioness of Gravina, whose *feudum* in Forenza would revert (*revertetur*) to Count Gilbert of Gravina on her death.[5] It is probable then that the family of the sons of Boniface of Gravina died out just before Gilbert became count of Gravina.

We are told by Pseudo-Falcandus that King William summoned Gilbert of Perche from Spain in order to take the comital position of Gravina.[6] His familial relationship to

Queen Consort Margaret was rather distant, although certain. Gilbert's father Bertram was an illegitimate son of Count Rotrou II, who in turn was the son of Count Geoffrey II of Mortagne, counts who later adopted the style counts of the Perche.[7] Count Rotrou II was the brother of Juliana of Perche, who stood for his brother while the former participated in the crusade led by King Alfonso of Aragón and Navarre and acted as a lord of Tudela through the 1120s. This legacy was presumably the reason why his illegitimate son and his grandson were residents and lords in Navarre.[8] Count Rotrou II also arranged the marriage of Margaret, daughter of his sister Juliana and Gilbert of L'Aigle, with García Ramírez, a member of the former royal dynasty of Navarre.[9] Hence, when García Ramírez secured his claim to the throne of Navarre in 1135, Margaret of L'Aigle became the queen consort of Navarre, whose daughter Margaret was to become the wife of William I and queen consort of Sicily.

The count's coalition against the Sicilian rule

The appointment of this Hispano-Norman relative of the queen initially backfired against William I; Count Gilbert of Gravina was soon enough involved in a coalition against the Sicilian regime. Both Romuald of Salerno and Pseudo-Falcandus recorded the formation of a coalition of counts in the midst of a conspiracy against the Great Admiral Maio of Bari. Romuald recorded that, in 1159, the group of conspirators consisted of 'Count Jonathan of Conza, Count Gilbert of Gravina, Count Bohemund of Manopello, Count Roger of Acerra, Count Philip of Sangro, Count Roger of Tricarico, and other barons'.[10] Similarly, we are told by Pseudo-Falcandus that the conspiracy consisted of 'Count Jonathan, Count Richard of Aquila, Count Roger *Acerranus*, and other counts and powerful men. Together with them there was also Count Gilbert.'[11]

Count Jonathan here is the count of Carinola who was granted some of the Apulian lands that used to belong to Geoffrey of Catanzaro, as well as Conza. Count Roger of Acerra was in fact count of Buonalbergo, but he also held Acerra, a lordship that had belonged to his family before the comital title was granted to his father, Robert of Medania. Count Philip of Sangro must have been the son and heir of Simon of Sangro, the same Abruzzese Count Simon recorded in the *Quaternus*, who had sided with the former count of Montescaglioso, Geoffrey of Lecce, during his feud against Maio of Bari. Being both a baron from the Abruzzo – a region where authority was in fluctuating disarray between the exiled Robert of Loritello and the remaining royal loyalists since the rebellion broke out in 1156 – and a son of a sympathizer of an imprisoned rebel nobleman, Philip of Sangro would have been an ideal candidate to lead an uprising against the Sicilian rule. One could even suspect that Count Simon of Sangro either died as a combatant or was captured during the rebellion led by Robert of Loritello in the region; however, there is no surviving evidence or explicit testimony that would prove any of this. Count Roger of Tricarico, on the other hand, does not appear to have been engaged in any of the partisan disputes during the previous years; his last recorded presence is found in an 1154 donation made to a certain Thomas Sarracenus.[12] Pseudo-Falcandus does not explicitly list Roger of Tricarico as a member of the coalition, leaving Romuald's chronicle as the sole piece of available evidence that overtly records the involvement of the count of Tricarico in the uprising. The Richard of Aquila recorded by Pseudo-Falcandus was Count Richard of Fondi, the same baron who had recovered the king's grace by betraying Robert of Sorrento and handing him over to the royal government.

The Count Bohemund of Manopello mentioned by Romuald of Salerno is not the same count that was taken prisoner after the previous rebellion, Bohemund of Tarsia. The disgraced Bohemund of Tarsia was replaced in Manopello by another Bohemund. According to the chronicle of Casauria, the first Count Bohemund was soon spared by the king and then released from prison, but went back to his native Tarsia, in Calabria, where he unexpectedly died. Additionally, it is mentioned that Bohemund of Tarsia's heirs were not allowed to succeed him; John Berard alleged that this was the result of the offences the former count of Manopello committed against the abbey of St Clement and the church of Pescara.[13] Certainly, this rationalization can be expected from a monastic chronicler who would constantly overemphasize the role of his own abbey; the explanation however pinpoints the fact that the county of Manopello was confiscated, perhaps for the same reason that William I imprisoned Bohemund of Tarsia in the first place. Cuozzo has hypothesized that this Count Bohemund was related to Tancred of S. Fele (*Sanctus Felex*), a lesser baron from central Apulia who held S. Fele, Agromonte and Ricigliano, and *feuda* in Bella and Muro Lucano.[14] Cuozzo identified this Count Bohemund with a certain *Boamundus Sancti Felis*, and on that premise he assumes the connection with the barons of S. Fele.[15] I have, nonetheless, been unable to confirm this, as Count Bohemund II of Manopello is not attested with such a patronymic label in either the *Chronicon* of Casauria nor in Pseudo-Falcandus, and no other surviving diplomatic evidence indicates the actual descent or origin of this Bohemund.

Although the conspiracy claimed justification because of the great admiral's alleged tyranny, it was nevertheless ultimately aimed against a royal *curia* that attempted to rule from Palermo. Romuald of Salerno reported that even though the king ordered the conspirators to desist in their attempt against his trusted and loyal admiral, the counts refused to sustain the admiral's 'rule and government' (*amirati dominium et amministrationem*).[16] Regardless of the chroniclers' rationalization, whether this was against only Maio of Bari or actually against King William, the counts and their league were rebelling against the regime of the Palermitan *curia*. And the counts of the kingdom were not alone in their efforts against the Sicilian rule: Andrew of Rupecanina returned.

The new insurgency was assisted by a previous invasion led by Andrew of Rupecanina, who had taken the comital title and invaded the kingdom during the 1154–6 rebellion and kept raiding and occupying the northern territories of the principality of Capua even after his defeat in 1156. We are told by the chronicle of the Fossanova Abbey in Ceccano (*Annales Ceccanenses*) that in November 1157, Count Andrew crossed the Capuan border alongside 'Romans, Greeks, and many other allies', captured all the land of Fondi (i.e. the county of Fondi), burned down Traetto (modern Minturno),[17] vengefully seized the lands of St Benedict (Montecassino's land), reached Comino, burned down *Posta* and *Campuri*, and marched to Atina, finally retreating to

Aquino (a border lordship on the northeastern fringe of the kingdom, right to the west of Montecassino).[18] Kinnamos confirmed the Greek involvement in this campaign, as the Greek contemporary historian recorded that in 1157 Alexios [Axouchos], the imperial protostrator, sent Constantine Otto and 'Count' Andrew from Ancona to Apulia, where they raised a large mercenary force to subdue numerous cities, including S. Germano.[19] The same *Annales Ceccanenses* also recorded that on the fourth Sunday after Epiphany of the following year (January 1158), Count Andrew marched against the town of S. Germano, on the foot of the hill of Montecassino, and fought and defeated the king's knights, from whom Andrew seized more than 200 men and all their spoils, at the same time as some others fled to the abbey of Montecassino. Count Andrew then gained control of S. Germano and climbed up the hill and occupied the abbey of Montecassino. Andrew stayed there until the feast day of the Forty Martyrs (10 March), when he abandoned the occupied lands and went to Ancona. After this he went to meet the emperor Frederick Barbarossa, who at that time was besieging Milan.[20] The Greek support for this campaign must have been short-lived, because the Greek war prisoners that William I captured in 1156 brokered a peace treaty between the kingdom and Constantinople by which the prisoners were released.[21]

The *Annales Casinenses* confirm Count Andrew's invasion: they recorded that in November 1157 Andrew seized the land of Fondi, Aquino, the land of Montecassino and Comino. Later, according to the same *Annales*, on 6 January 1158 the same count captured S. Germano, forcing Abbot Rainulf of Montecassino, Archbishop Alfanus of Capua and many others to retreat to Montecassino. The land of St Benedict then surrendered itself to the invading count who the following day ascended to the abbey and fought fiercely, but did not accomplish anything; afterwards, Count Andrew left the kingdom.[22] The *Annales Casinenses* do not specify if Andrew of Rupecanina went to Frederick Barbarossa, yet they do mention that the German emperor was besieging Milan.[23] Pseudo-Falcandus has echoed these recorded events, and he alleged that, after being in exile in Campanian territory, Andrew of Rupecanina gathered some knights and captured Aquino, captured S. Germano and from there marched as far as Alife.[24] Alife, together with the region in general, was closely tied to the former dominions of his family, the Drengot kin-group, in that Andrew's uncle was Count Rainulf of Caiazzo.

Therefore, it is clear that the territory of the Principality of Capua was temporarily taken away from the king's authority in 1157–8, and after Andrew of Rupecanina started a war in the northwestern territories. As a result, the counts of Carinola and Fondi must have been pressured into joining the unruly coalition of nobles. Andrew, the invader count, returned to the Capuan province in 1160, as the *Annales Casinenses* recorded that in the same year that Matthew Bonellus assassinated Admiral Maio in Palermo, Count Robert of Loritello and Count Andrew entered the kingdom.[25] It appears thus that Pseudo-Falcandus was summarizing Andrew of Rupecanina's activities from late 1157 to 1160. In any case, Count Andrew would have crossed the Garigliano and taken the rest of the Capuan province, including Alife, after he returned to the kingdom in 1160. Count Richard of Fondi must have remained on the invader's side, because Fondi was not reported to have been captured again in 1160, and although Count Andrew had left the kingdom after 1158, the pressure of his constant presence and imperial support would have been incentive enough to oppose the king's armed forces. However, by 1160, the heads of the Capuan counties of Carinola and Fondi had openly joined the rebellious coalition.

We do not hear about Count Jonathan of Carinola before 1160. He may have either opposed Andrew by commanding the king's knights that the *Annales Ceccanenses* recorded in 1157, or simply stayed in his dominions on the southern side of the River Garigliano (in either Carinola or Conza), away from the lands Andrew took in 1157–8. Soon thereafter, Count Jonathan made a donation during the last stage of the widespread rebellion. According to a now lost charter, which survives only as a transcription made by Ughelli, in February 1161 Jonathan granted the church of St Andrew and the *castrum Petre Pagane* to the cathedral of St Mary of Conza. In this donation, Jonathan called himself 'count of Conza, by the grace of God' (*Dei gratia Compsie Comes*) and mentioned neither the regnal year nor the grace of the Sicilian king. Additionally, the donation was made together with, and was subscribed by Jonathan's wife Stephanie, 'countess of Conza' (*Compsie Comitissa*), and his sons Richard and Geoffrey.[26] Although the document only survives as a modern transcription, it correctly reflects contemporary practices of other comital charters from a diplomatic point of view, including the fact that Count Jonathan's son and future heir Richard was already of age to subscribe in cruciform his father's transaction. Moreover, no elements of the charter's content are contradicted by any other surviving piece of evidence. For these reasons, Cuozzo has defended the position that this document is indeed a copy of an original.[27]

However, the document does not refer to Jonathan's other title as count of Carinola nor to his Capuan dominions, which suggests that during the rebellion Jonathan must have resided in central Apulia, further from the active northwestern arena. This is the first-known charter in which the title of 'count of Conza' was employed; before this, Pseudo-Falcandus and Romuald of Salerno were the only contemporary sources that spoke of Count Jonathan of Conza. Perhaps, it was the turbulent years of Andrew of Rupecanina's constant incursions and provocation that pushed the count of Carinola closer to his other cluster of lordships in central Apulia. What was initially a handful of scattered lordships in the inland valleys of Ofanto and Cervaro, granted to the restored count of Carinola, developed over the years into a second county within the dominions and under the authority of Count Jonathan: the county of Conza. The lands and lordships under Count Jonathan became thus a 'polynuclear' county with two emblematic centres: Conza and Carinola.

Comital presence and commotion in Palermo

In addition to the Capuan dissident counts, we are told by Pseudo-Falcandus that Count Sylvester of Marsico supported the plan of the 'Apulians' – a term employed by Pseudo-Falcandus when referring to the rebel barons – and promised to help them. The count of Marsico, however, did not dare to act on these alleged intentions and is described by Pseudo-Falcandus as 'the timidest of men' (*hominum timidissimus*).[28] In this passage, Pseudo-Falcandus attests another supposed count who had likewise hidden his true intentions against Maio of Bari: Roger of Craon. The latter's comital title must have been an oversight of Pseudo-Falcandus, because Roger of Craon is not attested anywhere else as such. This lesser Sicilian baron was the son of William of Craon, and he is recorded in May 1142 in a legal case before Roger II as he and his mother Rocca held a dispute against the canons of Agrigento.[29] Furthermore, he appears in a forged document, dated July 1143, in which the rights of the church of Messina were confirmed by King Roger.[30] Although this is a forgery, Roger of Craon is not recorded here as a count. Nor did the people who were identified as his possible relatives by Ménager in his *inventaire* bear the comital title in any documented instance.[31] It is clear, therefore, that Roger of Craon was neither a count nor a member of the peninsular upper aristocracy.

The activities of the count of Marsico must be highlighted here. At some point between 1154 and 1157, Count Sylvester had been in Sicily and was part of the royal entourage; the count of Marsico had already issued a donation from Sicily in May 1154, in his chamber of Ragusa.[32] Pseudo-Falcandus's testimony is not the only piece of evidence that suggests the count of Marsico's involvement in the king's close circle. In December 1157, Count Sylvester witnessed in Palermo a royal charter, by which William I granted a *feudum* of six *milites* to Archbishop Hugh and the church of Palermo Brocato; he subscribed the document as 'count of Marsico' (*Silvester comes Marsic[i]*).[33] The donation was drafted by Matthew of Aiello, the notary, and issued by the Great Admiral Maio, and was also witnessed by Matthew Bonellus, Admiral Stephen son of the Great Admiral Maio, another Admiral Stephen (seemingly Maio's brother) and a series of archbishops and bishops.[34] Alongside all the notable heads of the south Italian church, there are two other counts whose origins are uncertain: Count Simon of Mileto and Count Roger of Yscla.

There is no other evidence to attest the existence of another 'count of Mileto' or even to suggest that Mileto was a seat of a county by this time. This Simon could, however, have been the same 'Count Simon' Pseudo-Falcandus recorded to have been a son of Roger II by a concubine and kept in the royal palace at Palermo.[35] Jamison has suggested that the concubine mentioned here was a sister of Count Hugh of Molise.[36] As I have explained earlier, Hugh of Molise offered the hand of his sister to King Roger to recover the monarch's grace after the civil war.[37] Moreover, Pseudo-Falcandus ambivalently referred to 'Count' Simon as 'prince', and also alleged that it was with that title that 'he was addressed' (*Symonem quem principem appellabant*).[38] The usage of the comital title here is thus rather confusing and unclear, since Count Sylvester was the only actual count in the *subscriptio*. What does seem to be clear is that there was neither a county of Mileto nor a county of Yscla in the kingdom of Sicily during the twelfth century – although Mileto could be a reference to the old Rogerian lineage, as it was one of Roger I's comital *capita*. I have not been able to accurately identify this 'Yscla', although it could be a reference to the island of Ischia (*Isclia Maior*), near Napoli, or to any other island or town near Sicily or Calabria. In any case, the royal donation indicates that Count Sylvester of Marsico – present together with the king, the royal officials and the high-ranking members of the south Italian church – had become a close component of the Palermitan *curia*. Sylvester's lineage might explain his presence in the royal circles, since the count of Marsico was a member of the royal family – his father, Geoffrey of Ragusa, was an illegitimate son of Count Roger I of Sicily.[39]

In order to oppose the raids and subsequent occupation of almost all of Apulia that Count Robert of Loritello appeared to have been leading since 1158, Maio's brother Stephen was placed in command of the knights of Apulia; at least according to Pseudo-Falcandus.[40] We are told by the same anonymous author that the great admiral's power was consolidated during the apparent peace that followed Count Robert's rebellion. Maio of Bari's brother Stephen had risen to the rank of admiral, and his brother-in-law, Simon the seneschal, was appointed 'master captain' (*magister capitaneus*) for Apulia and the Terra di Lavoro.[41] Based on the testimonies provided by both Pseudo-Falcandus and Romuald of Salerno, Jamison has suggested that Simon's appointment occurred just after the summer of 1156.[42] As the *magister capitaneus*, Simon would have replaced Chancellor Asclettin and the king himself as commander of the royal armed forces in the peninsula, albeit without holding the title of chancellor as the previous peninsular commanders did. Instead, as Pseudo-Falcandus records, Simon the seneschal became the *magister capitaneus totius Apulie et principatus Capue*. Simon is nevertheless last attested in October 1158 as 'royal seneschal and master captain of Apulia' (*dominus Simon regius senescalcus et magister capitaneus totius Apulie*) in a court case involving the monastery of St Sophia in Benevento, held at Capua.[43] The chronicle of Casauria similarly described Simon the seneschal as 'master captain of the whole realm' (*totius regni magister Capitaneus*), when he presided over a court at Salerno, at some point between 1156 and 1160, to hear the monastery's complaints in its dispute with Count Bohemund II of Manopello.[44] Jamison has also suggested that Simon's appointment as *magister capitaneus* may be reflecting a second stage of the office's development.[45] If this is the case, the development of this 'office' would have thus been hindered by the counts' rebellion.

Having Stephen, and not Simon, in command of the peninsular knights after 1159 might be an indication of a sudden change of the *magister capitaneus* during the crisis of the counts' coalition, as whoever was supposed to be in command of the royal forces had been already cornered and surrounded. Furthermore, Pseudo-Falcandus reported that a fear of the counts had forced Simon the seneschal (the actual 'master captain') to retire into a very well-defended town. Even the main places that had stayed loyal to the king in the past swayed against the royal *curia*: the city of Salerno and the region of Calabria. Marius Borell, one of the leading members of the counts' coalition, persuaded the majority of the Salernitan citizens into taking the same oath the conspirators had taken against the great admiral. Calabria, whose 'loyalty had previously hardly even been shaken' (*cuius antea fides difficillime consueverat vacillare*), also sided with the opposition.[46]

The well-known (or rather intensely narrated) episode of Matthew Bonellus's involvement in the assassination of Maio of Bari provides a number of insights into the Calabrian nobility. According to the chronicle of the archbishop of Salerno, the Apulian counts promised Matthew Bonellus the hand of Countess Clementia of Catanzaro, in exchange for his active participation in Maio's assassination.[47] The narrative sources do not go into too much detail on the development of the insurrection on the mainland, as they mostly focus on the plot executed by Matthew Bonellus on the island and the assassination of the great admiral. Yet, we are told by Pseudo-Falcandus that Matthew Bonellus, who was allegedly related to several noblemen from Calabria by lineage, was offered the hand in matrimony of the countess of Catanzaro (*comitissa Catacensis*) by Roger of Martorano, a prominent man who acted as the spokesman of the conspiring Calabrians.[48] Although there is no agreement on who actually offered him the empty comital seat of Catanzaro, it does seem that the Calabrian county was effectively used as a bargaining chip in the plot against the great admiral of Sicily.

After Maio of Bari was assassinated in November 1160, Pseudo-Falcandus relates that Count Sylvester of Marsico disclosed the malign intentions of Admiral Maio to the king, following which he pardoned Matthew Bonellus and arrested Maio's brother and son, both admirals and both named Stephen. Again, we do not hear any more about the great admiral's brother-in-law, Simon the seneschal, which strengthens the hypothesis that the nominal *magister capitaneus* was either routed or removed from its charge during the last years of Robert of Loritello's rule. Pseudo-Falcandus had put in the mouth of Matthew the notary the pragmatic reason behind the king's pardoning of Bonellus; the latter had both popular acclaim and the support of all the counts and of Calabria who had rebelled against the great admiral.[49] Even if the words of the anonymous author might have been skewed against Matthew the notary, whom he disliked, the reasoning provided by both contemporary writers serves to support the assertion that Matthew Bonellus became the charismatic leader of the rebellion. Having the peninsular nobility as de facto military rulers of all the mainland territories ('Count' Andrew of Rupecanina in the Principality of Capua, and Count Robert of Loritello and the leagues of counts in Apulia and Calabria) was anything but a simple task, even during the lowest point of the civil war of the 1130s King Roger did not lose Calabria.

Once the apparent reason for the counts' rebellion was removed, it became much clearer that the nobility's opposition went further than simply going against Maio of Bari, regardless of how wicked the great admiral was depicted by Pseudo-Falcandus. Even in the year after Maio's assassination, turmoil continued to convulse Sicily. A subsequent plot was brewed in Palermo, and this time William I himself was the person under attack. We are told by Pseudo-Falcandus that Roger of Avellino, count of Avellino, a 'young noble' (*nobilis adolescentulus*), joined Matthew Bonellus and the bastards 'Count' Simon and Tancred. The latter two were alleged by Pseudo-Falcandus to have practically been prisoners of the king, in that they were not allowed to leave the palace at Palermo. Simon was the son that Roger II presumably had had with his concubine, Hugh of Molise's daughter, whereas Tancred was the son of Duke Roger, the firstborn of Roger II who had died in 1148, and his mistress Emma of Lecce. As has been detailed before, the young Roger of Avellino was a distant relative of William I, on account that his grandmother Adelicia of Adernò was a cousin of the king.[50]

This is a convenient point to emphasize the vague nature of the titles borne by Simon and Tancred. As children of King Roger II and young Duke Roger respectively, they could have been considered direct members of the kingdom's royalty, despite their condition as illegitimate offspring. Pseudo-Falcandus expands on this issue, asserting that Roger II had left in his will (*testamentum*) the princely dignity of Taranto (*principatus Tarenti*) to his bastard Simon, and that later on William I took it away from him. Houben has suggested that the princely title of Taranto was left vacant after William was made 'prince of Capua' following the death of his older brother Alfonso *c.*

1144.⁵¹ Furthermore, Pseudo-Falcandus explains that 'the princely dignities of Taranto and Capua should have only been conferred upon legitimate children, although it was not unworthy for even natural sons to be granted counties or other royal dignities'.⁵² This reasoning could reflect the mentality by which Simon and Tancred used, or rather were allowed to use, the comital title under William I. Throughout the chronicle of Romuald of Salerno, Tancred and Simon are only referred to as 'counts', and Pseudo-Falcandus relates that Simon was called prince during the attempted coup d'état in Palermo. Neither Simon nor Tancred were proper counts, in the sense that they were not overlords of other barons and did not seem to exercise any authority over other lordships. Even if the comital title granted was attached to a specific toponym, if we believe that this is the same 'Count Simon of Mileto', being forced to stay within the walls of the royal palace would not have allowed them to exercise any sort of role on the mainland.

The scheme of Count Roger of Avellino and Matthew Bonellus planned the release of the noble prisoners that were held in the palace dungeons, and the deposition of William I. We are told in the chronicle of Romuald Guarna, archbishop of Salerno, that on the fifth day of Lent (9 March), the dungeons of the Palermitan palace were opened, and then the king was captured and imprisoned. Among the noblemen who were reported to have been released and later involved in the plot against the king were Count William of Principato, Richard of Mandra, Alexander 'the monk' and 'Count' Tancred of Lecce.⁵³ Pseudo-Falcandus recorded additionally that among the noble prisoners were (former) Count William of Lesina, 'a most atrocious man' (*vir atrocissimus*), together with Robert of Bova and Richard of Mandra, the former *comestabulus* of the rebel count of Loritello and Conversano. It was during this episode, narrated in detail by Pseudo-Falcandus, that Richard of Mandra beat off an attack of William of Lesina and Robert Bova against the king himself.⁵⁴ This gesture undoubtedly explains his subsequent successful career, and the favour of the Sicilian king towards a man who had previously been a commander for one of the worst enemies of the royal government. The prominent position of Richard of Mandra is part of a later stage in the nobility's development, and it is discussed in Chapter 5. Although the king was held prisoner in his own palace by the conspirators and the escaped prisoners, he was soon released. The prisoners fled and took refuge in Caccamo – a town east of Palermo and just south of the port of Termini.

Without having to go into too much detail relating the events once again of the momentary coup d'état in Palermo, it is fundamental to highlight the consequences the plot had for the composition of the upper aristocracy. Romuald of Salerno's chronicle alleged that King William I had counts William, Simon and Tancred of Lecce, as well as 'the many others that were unwilling to remain in the country' taken out of the realm by galley under safe-conduct, most probably embarking from Termini, to either Terracina (a coastal town near Rome) or the kingdom of Jerusalem.⁵⁵ Conversely, we are told by Pseudo-Falcandus that Matthew Bonellus and some of the conspirators who were involved in the king's capture stayed in Caccamo, and that, after the barons there expressed their displeasure, they negotiated their expulsion from the kingdom, whereas Matthew Bonellus returned to Palermo. The names Pseudo-Falcandus recorded as having been in Caccamo were 'Prince' Simon (referred to here as a prince and not a count),⁵⁶ Tancred, William of Lesina, Alexander of Conversano and Roger Sclavus, the son of the disgraced Count Simon del Vasto.

Alexander of Conversano may have been the same Alexander 'the monk' recorded by Archbishop Romuald as having been released from the dungeon in the palace. In addition, this Alexander could have also been the same former count who rebelled against the nascent kingdom and who later came back together with the Greek army in 1156. Although there is no direct reference to the capture of the previous count of Conversano, Alexander's presence in Apulia with the invading Greek army – as commander of the 'French' contingent (Γερμανοί) – was recorded by John Kinnamos.⁵⁷ As William I decisively defeated all the opposing forces when his army recaptured Brindisi, Alexander of Conversano must have escaped to Ancona, avoiding thus the king's wrath when the other Greek generals were captured and taken in chains to Palermo. When Manuel Komnenos dispatched Protostrator Alexius (Axouchos) to Ancona to lay claim again to Italy in 1157, his last attempt to make war in the peninsula, Alexander was used by Alexius to negotiate with the people of Ancona.⁵⁸ In all likelihood, Alexander was part of the Greek contingent that assisted Andrew of Rupecanina in the latter's raiding campaign in 1157. However, soon after the peace treaty between Sicily and Constantinople was made later that year, Alexander of Conversano must have stayed in Italy, insisting in making war against the kingdom. Alexander hence ended up in a Palermitan prison after this point, perhaps being captured after participating in some of the incursions that Andrew of Rupecanina led on the kingdom's border between 1157 and 1158. After his release, Alexander of Conversano must have returned to the Greek court. Alexander of Conversano did not return to the kingdom after 1161, and he finally admitted defeat and stayed under the employment of Constantinople. Alexander is only attested again in 1168, 1169 and 1177 when, according to William of Tyre, he was sent to the kingdom of Jerusalem as an imperial envoy by Manuel Komnenos.⁵⁹

Simon is likewise attested as having gone to the Constantinopolitan court in 1166: Kinnamos recorded that after William I had died, his brother (ἀδελφὸς) approached Emperor Manuel Komnenos in order to receive his assistance to rule Sicily; Manuel however did not support the king's brother, as the Greek emperor was ensuring the good will that had been achieved with the peace treaty agreed by both rulers after the failed Apulian expedition in 1158.⁶⁰

Finally, Roger of Aquila, count of Avellino, was pardoned and allowed to stay in the kingdom. Pseudo-Falcandus explains that William I considered his betrayal a mistake rather than a misdeed on the grounds of his young age. Also, as mentioned earlier, Roger of Aquila's grandmother Adelicia of Adernò was William I's cousin, and she intervened in order for her only surviving heir to recover the king's grace.⁶¹ Roger of Avellino was henceforth the only nobleman who, after having been actively involved in the king's capture, was allowed to stay in the realm without losing his lordships or comital dignity. Yet, the count of Avellino angered King William once again; Pseudo-Falcandus reveals that Count Roger of Avellino married the daughter of Fenicia of S. Severino without royal permission, and both Count Roger and his brother-in-law William of S. Severino fled the kingdom to avoid the king's anger when the latter marched across the peninsula later in 1162. However, the countess of Avellino was taken to Palermo as a prisoner alongside her mother Fenicia, after defending her besieged *castellum*; it is unclear if Pseudo-Falcandus referred here to the *castellum* of Avellino or the *castrum* of S. Severino.[62] Count Roger's wife, it should be noted, was called Marocta.[63] This episode, however, did not mean the end of the turmoil in the peninsular dominions. The counts were not even close to allowing the king to have his rule back on the mainland, at least not without another war.

After William I had recovered from the attempted coup d'état, he was ready to launch a counterattack against what still was a rebellion against the Palermitan government. According to Pseudo-Falcandus, the king's *familiares* at this time were Bishop-elect Richard of Syracuse, Henry Aristippus and Count Sylvester of Marsico.[64]

As pointed out earlier, Count Sylvester of Marsico formed part of the court's entourage since at least 1157; his role and prominence in the Palermitan court was however not clear.[65] The count of Marsico must have become a *familiaris* of the king and a regular resident in Palermo after the assassination of Maio of Bari. A July 1176 charter from Palermo records a sale made to the *duana baronum* by Count William of Marsico, son of Count Sylvester, in which it was remembered that Sylvester, 'by the grace of God and the king, count of Marsico' (*Silvester Domini et Regis gratia Marsici comes*), had purchased Maio of Bari's house in Palermo, near to the churches of St Mary of the Admiral and St Cataldo.[66] Furthermore, Count Sylvester had an infant daughter of just nine months, who died in Palermo in 1161 and then buried in the same church of St Cataldo. A funerary inscription made in her honour and marking the place where she was buried survives to this day in St Cataldo.[67] The inscription reads:

† EGREGII COMITIS SILVESTRI NATA MATILDIS
NATA DIE MARTIS MARTIS ADEMPTA DIE
VIVENS TER TERNOS HABUIT MENSES OBIITQ(UE)
DANS ANIMAM C[O]ELIS CORPUS INANE SOLO,
HEC ANNIS D(OMI)NI CENT(U)M UNDECIES SEMEL UNO
ET DECIES SENIS HAC REQUIEVIT HUMO.[68]

Since St Cataldo in Palermo was founded by Maio of Bari, this church must have been also acquired by Sylvester of Marsico, having been subsequently used as the resting place of her late daughter.

Sylvester's presence in Palermo and his position at the head of the royal *curia* should, however, not automatically be interpreted as an act of representation for the kingdom's nobility. His comital title does not serve to support the presumption that 'class consciousness' of the upper aristocracy existed by this time and that he acted as its representative. As argued by Pio, the members of the royal inner council of the king did not represent the social echelon from where they came; they were instead prominent members of the social circles that were already close to the king.[69] Sylvester of Marsico had been present in the Palermitan court for some time before, most probably because of his status as a member of the royal family, and his involvement during the counts' rebellion was at most marginal. Sylvester of Marsico does not appear to have intervened directly as a mediator between the king and the other counts. Pseudo-Falcandus even suggested he was in fact in favour of the rebels' intentions. The count of Marsico was neither a spokesman of the peninsular nobility nor the most powerful count of the kingdom; he was, nonetheless, an ally of the king both as a royal relative and a major landholder and overlord who could offer the economic and military support his position could guarantee. Pseudo-Falcandus related that Count Sylvester opposed Matthew Bonellus's presence in the court and persuaded the monarch to arrest Matthew Bonellus under the presumption that the latter was somehow involved with the rebellion that Roger Sclavus was leading in the southeastern lands of the island. Roger Sclavus thus did not leave Caccamo with the rest of rebels, but instead went back to Butera once again to lead the insurgency in the region.[70]

A defeated nobility and the rise of the count of Gravina

As Sicily was mired in unrest, Apulia and the Terra di Lavoro were submerged in war once again. According to Romuald of Salerno's chronicle, Count Robert of Loritello occupied Apulia without meeting any resistance, whereas Andrew of Rupecanina invaded the Terra di Lavoro. Robert of Loritello came back with a vengeance; he marched as far as Salerno in the west, although the Salernitans refused to receive him, and by 1161 he had invaded the territory all the way to Taranto in southern Apulia.[71] Pseudo-Falcandus agrees with this, because he recorded that the count of Loritello invaded most of the kingdom, reaching Orgeolo, a place on the borders of Apulia and Calabria.[72] The *Chronica* of Archbishop Romuald records that the king sent the archbishop himself to Apulia to appease the counts, whom the king feared would rebel yet again. Romuald of Salerno was, according to his chronicle, so zealous in convincing the peninsular barons to 'bow to the royal love and fealty' (*ad amorem et fidelitatem regiam uehementer adtraxit*), that 'all of them wanted to travel to Sicily and vindicate the injury done to him [the king]' (*quod unanimite volebant in Siciliam pergere et regis iniuriam vindicare*). The emollient words of the archbishop of Salerno appear to have been less effective in practice; we are also told by Romuald that at Easter the king ordered the counts to abjure the oaths (*sacramenta*) they had made when they formed the rebellious coalition. However, most of the counts, except Count Gilbert of Gravina and Count Bohemund of Manopello, rejected the royal command, despairing of recovering the king's grace. They went to Count Robert of Loritello, and after the counts paid homage to Robert (*facto ei [Roberti] hominio*), they invaded and occupied the king's land with him.[73]

The *Annales Ceccanenses* add little to this, but they at least tell us that by the time that Robert of Loritello had reached Taranto, 'many counts attached themselves (*coniunxerunt se*) to Count Robert'.[74] Pseudo-Falcandus explains that all of the counts who had rebelled because of Admiral Maio's wickedness joined the count of Loritello because they despaired of being restored to William I's favour, except for Count Gilbert of Gravina who obtained the king's favour as a result of the pleas of his relative, Queen Margaret.[75] Again, this is a convenient explanation for a long-standing opposition against the royal government from the mainland counts. However, there is no clear indication in the surviving evidence that the Sicilian government ever recovered its control over the mainland after the assassination of Admiral Maio. The unstable state of Palermo and the *curia* would not have allowed the king to settle the quarrel with the peninsular nobility in the meantime. The great exception in this persistent insurgency was the count of Gravina, and it was through him that the Sicilian king responded to the counts.

In December 1162, Count Gilbert made a donation of some lands near Polignano to Abbess Scolastica of the nunnery of St Benedict in Polignano.[76] Gilbert called himself here both 'count of Gravina, by the grace of God and of the king, and great constable for all Apulia and the principality of Capua'. His charter was subscribed not only by the count of Gravina but also by his son Bertram and Milianus the seneschal – most likely Gilbert's seneschal, although he did not refer overtly to the count as his lord and he was not attested among the comital seneschals in a subsequent transaction.[77] Three years later, in January 1166, Count Gilbert of Gravina granted a mill to the same nunnery of St Benedict in Polignano, still in the hands of Abbess Scolastica. On this occasion, Gilbert employed a very similar title as great constable, referring to the 'principality of Capua' instead of to the Terra di Lavoro, and he also called himself lord of the town of Polignano. The transaction was subscribed by both his family and comital officials: his wife Countess Stephanie, his sons Bertram and Bartholomew and his seneschals Pagan and Bernard.[78]

We are told by Pseudo-Falcandus that Count Gilbert of Gravina was admitted back into the king's grace by intervention of his relative Queen Margaret. He subsequently deserted the rebellion and commanded the (king's) army in Apulia.[79] By contrast, Romuald of Salerno records that William I commissioned Aquinus of Moac to retain knights on the mainland and resist the enemy, which would have made the latter the effective commander of the royal forces, responsibility that nominally fell under the authority of the 'master captain' (*magister capitaneus*).[80] These two events are not necessarily mutually exclusive, in that Aquinus could have been a co-commander, operating in a different region, most likely the former principality of Salerno and the Terra di Lavoro. The count of Gravina therefore would have operated in the Adriatic front during this contingency. After the king was able to stabilize the island and suppress the rebellion led by Roger Sclavus in Butera, he gathered his forces and crossed over to Apulia. William I was able to capture Taverna, in Calabria, and Taranto. Taverna was a bastion of the counts of Catanzaro, and it had become the first fortified resistance to the king's advance into the peninsula. Countess Clementia of Catanzaro was recorded by Pseudo-Falcandus to have joined Robert of Loritello, just as the other counts did, and reinforced Taverna to oppose the royal army. The siege of Taverna, which took place in March 1162, resulted in a royal victory, allowing William to advance through Calabria into Apulia, not without capturing the rebels first.[81] These included Roger of Martorano, the countess, her mother and her maternal uncles, Alferius and Thomas. The latter two were identified as the heads of the affair (*principes*); Alferius was handed over for punishment, whereas Thomas was immediately hanged at Messina. Conversely, the countess of Catanzaro was sent with her mother Segelgarda to Messina and then to Palermo to be kept in prison.[82] This would mean that the king's army crossed the Messina straits, went through Calabria and marched over the southern regions of the peninsula.

The royal incursion was impressive enough to scare Robert of Loritello back into the Abruzzo, after having been based previously around the lake of Salpi, on the Adriatic coast, below the Gargano peninsula. Romuald of Salerno explains that Count Robert of Loritello retreated because he feared that the barons of Apulia would desert him, 'as was their custom' (*barones Apulia ipsum solito more relinquerent*).[83] In the same way Pseudo-Falcandus relates that the count of Loritello mistrusted the divided loyalties of the south Italians, and he preferred to retreat rather than relying on untrustworthy soldiers. Robert of Loritello then went back to Taranto, later to return to the Abruzzo.[84] At this stage it was not Aquinus of Moac but Richard of Say (*Riccardus Ysaiae*) who is recorded to have been commanding the king's army as it pushed the rebels away into the Abruzzo.[85] The presence of 'the Say' family in Sicily dates back to 1094, when Geoffrey of Say (*Gofridus de Sageio*) – who was perhaps Richard's grandfather – granted, with his wife's consent, three villeins in Caccamo, and also witnessed a charter of Roger I of Sicily to the abbey of Lipari.[86] Richard of Say had been employed before as a royal commander and administrator for the province of Calabria, in that he is recorded in January 1157 as 'constable and justiciar' (*comestabulus et justiciarius*), exercising 'judicial supremacy by royal prerogative' (*regali potestate primatus iudicorum*) alongside Carbonellus of Tarsia and Roger of Sangineto, the royal justiciars (*iustificatores/regalis iusticiarii*) for the Val di Crati, in Calabria.[87] The rebel count of Loritello was able to flee the realm before the arrival of Richard of Say.

Likewise, we are told by Pseudo-Falcandus that Count Jonathan of Conza (and of Carinola), Count Richard of Fondi, Count Roger of Acerra (of Buonalbergo), Marius Borell and the other barons who had associated with Robert of Loritello fled into either the Abruzzo or the (Papal) Campania, terrified by the king's approach.[88] King William himself marched over the Terra di Lavoro, as Romuald of Salerno recorded that the king and his army went to S. Germano, which lies beneath Montecassino, and expelled the count of Fondi, Richard of Aquila.[89] The *Annales Ceccanenses*, furthermore, describe William I's activities in the northern territories in 1162: the king went to a hill identified as *colle Aponis*, appointed some knights to the custody of Montecassino, sent the 'count of Lauro' (i.e. Robert II of Lauro) together with an army, took Monte Arcano in Fondi and captured Count Richard of Fondi's wife and many others who were found in that location.[90] This is the first reference made to Robert II of Lauro as a count, and this is the same Robert who would later become a count in the former principality of Capua as well.[91] Although his role during the first uprising of Robert of Loritello is not clear, Robert of Lauro is conversely recorded as an active member of William's army during the counts' insurrection in the Tyrrhenian front. Robert II of Lauro would, henceforth, have become a prominent baron as one of the king's men during the opposition against the invading forces of Andrew of Rupecanina and the rebellion in Capua.

By 1162, William I was able to subjugate the county of Fondi, the northernmost region of the principality of Capua, and the gates into the kingdom from the Tyrrhenian coast. The invader Count Andrew must have already left the realm by this stage, in that there is no subsequent report of him engaging in any confrontation or battle against the king's armed forces, but instead he was recorded in 1161 as having left his lands behind and gone to Constantinople.[92] Kinnamos also related that the Greek military campaign, which reinforced Andrew of Rupecanina's invasion, ended because the notables Doukas and Komnenos, prisoners of war held captive in Sicily, brokered a peace treaty between William I and Constantinople. Although Emperor Manuel disgruntledly accepted, the agreement finally halted the wars between the kingdom and the Eastern Empire.[93] In this way, the Sicilian monarch re-established his control over the mainland and forced the rebel counts back into exile.

Additional changes were made to the peninsular nobility in and after 1162. Robert of Lauro was already regarded in the *Annales Ceccanenses* as a count by 1162, as the king gave him an army to capture the last bastion of the count of Fondi (Monte Arcano). The 'county of Lauro' did not exist as such, but what the *Annales* from Fossanova must be referring to is the fact that Robert of Lauro was rewarded with the rank of count for his role as an ally against the rebels during 1162. He was the son of Sarracena and Lord Robert I of Lauro, who in turn was son of Roger of S. Severino and Sichelgaita (also known as Sica), the daughter of Landulf, son of Prince Guaimar IV of Salerno.[94] Robert II of Lauro is recorded in 1141 as an underage holder of land administered by Robert Capumaza (Sarracena's husband by that time); in the following year he made a donation as 'Robert son of Robert, lord of Lauro'.[95] Robert II of Lauro was not just a local baron who acted as a military leader on the king's side, but the member of a family, the S. Severino, that had been gradually climbing up the ladder of the peninsular aristocracy since the time of Roger II. The S. Severino kin-group held extensive lands in the former principality of Salerno, both in the north (around Lauro, Montoro and S. Severino) and in the south (around Rocca Cilento).

Robert of Lauro does not appear to have held the county of Caserta before his active participation in William's army in 1162. His earliest record as count of Caserta was found in a now lost document from the nunnery of St John Baptist of the Nuns in Capua, in which he is regarded as 'count of the Casertans and many others'.[96] The same title is employed in a July 1165 transaction, when Count Robert, by intervention of Bishop John of Caserta, made a donation to St Angelo in Formis.[97] It could have been possible that Robert of Lauro employed the comital title before receiving Caserta, because the *Annales Ceccanenses* already referred to him in 1162 as count, and also a February 1159 *memoratorium* made by Benedict, the prior of St Peter of Scafati, recorded that 'Count Robert' had questioned the father of chaplain William.[98] However, in all pre-1163 instances, Robert is recorded only in the vicinity of Lauro, which is located east of Avellino and north of Salerno. Robert of Lauro's record as count of Caserta in the *Quaternus magne expeditionis* must have then been included when the register was put together *c.* 1167–8.[99]

The county of Caserta might also have been created later from lordships that belonged to the former count of Caiazzo and which Andrew of Rupecanina had reclaimed and occupied between 1160 and 1161. Additionally, some of the lands held *in demanio* by the count of Caserta had previously belonged to Nicholas Frascenellus, as the record in the *Quaternus* indicated. This Nicholas Frascenellus was the original lord of Caserta and of the many *feuda* in the vicinity, including in Telese and Solopaca, but after the turbulent years of rebellion and invasion, he lost all of these, either because he had died or as a result of his participation in the rebellion. In this way, the head of the Lauro branch of the S. Severino family was finally able to enjoy comital rank, and additionally received a county of his own in the Capuan province that he helped to reclaim. The title and the county were perhaps granted by William I as a reward and incentive for his support during the peninsular rebellions. The 'many others' to which

Robert's comital title referred after 1163 must have indicated that this new county of Caserta comprised also the ancestral dominions that Count Robert originally held in Lauro. This is a convenient point to remember that, contrary to Robert of Lauro's case, another member of the S. Severino family left the kingdom to avoid the king's anger: William of S. Severino, son of Marocta of S. Severino, fled with his stepfather Roger of Aquila, count of Avellino.[100]

By this time, after the province of Capua was finally recovered and the rebels and invaders had been expelled, William I took this opportunity to rearrange and modify the local nobility. The county of Caserta was not the only creation, but the county of Alife must have been also granted after 1162. The town of Alife, a town once held by the former counts of Caiazzo and Andrew of Rupecanina, and its surrounding smaller lordships were given to Malgerius son of Richard, as the latter was recorded in the *Quaternus* as a count in Alife. The recorded county of Alife was small (four *feuda in demanio* and one baron, Polido de Thora, holding four small *feuda* from him [*in servitio*], being obliged to thus levy a total of 86 *milites* and 250 *servientes*), and hence the new county would not have been as powerful as the former dominions of Rainulf of Caiazzo and Andrew of Rupecanina, but it was big enough to mobilize an additional contingent of the king's knights against any other possible invasion.[101]

Malgerius is additionally remembered in a January 1170 recorded legal sentence (*iudicatum*) of a complaint (*querimonia*) that John Bova presented against Odoaldus *Carbonarii* to a court convened by Lord Peter of Revello, the chamberlain (*camerarius*) of the count. In this sentence, it was remembered that the aforementioned John and his father held in the time of Lord Malgerius these same lands that Odoaldus had seized, a situation that they presented to their count. As this unnamed count heard their plea, he ordered Peter of Revello to make justice for them; hence, the comital chamberlain, with the count's order, conducted the interrogation in the presence of judges and other *bones homines* so he could decide whether John Bova and his father were correct on this issue.[102] It is unclear whether the count who originally heard the complaint and ordered the chamberlain to take action was the same Lord Malgerius during whose rule the lands were lawfully held. However, the fact that the entire legal complaint was presented in one court only and that throughout the document the count presiding over the court remains unnamed, suggests that Count Malgerius was either dead or removed by 1169, before John Bova and his father initiated the legal complaint but after the *iudicatum* was finalized, and that the comital chamberlain, Peter of Revello, was left in charge temporarily. Malgerius would therefore have been created count not in 1167, but before, precisely after Andrew of Rupecanina and the rebel counts of Fondi and Carinola were pushed out of the realm. The Capuan territories must have been redistributed after the province had been shaken up during the invasion of Count Andrew. This redistribution meant that new smaller counties were created in Capua, adding two new clusters of lordships between Carinola and Fondi, and northwestern Apulia.

The defeated nobility left a profound mark on the territorial structure of the kingdom. We are told by Pseudo-Falcandus that, by the end of 1162, 'some of the king's enemies had crossed over to Greece, others had fled to the German emperor with the count of Loritello, and many remained impoverished in the papal Campania'.[103] Moreover,

William I appears to have imposed over the defeated 'redemption fees', in that Pseudo-Falcandus recorded that, after the king's death, the queen abolished the 'unbearable burden of redemption fees' (*redemptionis onus importabile*) that had shaken Apulia and the Terra di Lavoro with utter despair.[104] This implies not only that the rebel towns and rural aristocracy on the mainland were subjected to an economic penalty for the rebellion but also that there were lesser barons who must have participated in the insurgency, who nevertheless stayed in the kingdom. The remaining upper aristocracy was hence consolidated in a handful of lordships, organized around significantly fewer counts than when William I become the sole Sicilian king. Starting with the province of Capua, two new counties were created from the remnants of older lordships, between the counties of Fondi and Carinola: Alife, given to Count Malgerius, and Caserta, given to Count Robert of Lauro.

The other two Capuan counts, Roger of Fondi and Carinola, had to forsake their counties in their exile. There is no surviving evidence for either before the end of William I's rule. The Apulian lands of the count of Carinola (i.e. the lordship of Conza) were not given to either the *comestabulus* Gilbert of Balvano or to Roger of Medania, count of Buonalbergo and Acerra, as has been suggested by F. Scandone when he speaks of the '*comestabulia* of the count of Conza', and the lands of the lord of Montella.[105] Roger of Medania held some lands east of Conza, as lord of Nusco, but evidence that is discussed in the following chapter indicates that the county of Carinola would be restored to Jonathan's heir, and Conza was included in the dominions returned to him.[106] Another major baron with tenure in the province of Capua was Roger of Aquila, count of Avellino. Count Roger of Avellino must have returned to his county after 1162 and before William I died, as a 'Count Roger' is mentioned in an 1165 land delimitation concerning some lordships near Avellino (*ab uno latere fine Rogeri comite*).[107] This is not unlikely considering also that Roger of Aquila had been pardoned before by William I, just after his participation in the coup d'état in Palermo, and that, according to Pseudo-Falcandus, he fled the kingdom during William I's march over the peninsula because he had married Marocta of S. Severino without the king's permission. Although he appears to have disobeyed the monarch just after being pardoned, he was not regarded as a rebel by this stage, which places him at a different level than that of those insurgents who were driven into exile. Perhaps Adelicia of Adernò (Roger of Aquila's grandmother and William I's cousin) intervened again in favour of this mischievous young count, or simply Count Roger returned to his lands without the explicit permission of the king. Whatever the case here, the count of Avellino must be distinguished from the rest of the nobles exiled in 1162.

The other two major barons forced into exile were Roger of Acerra, count of Buonalbergo, and, of course, the count of Conversano and Loritello, Robert II of Bassunvilla. These counties remained vacant through the rest of William I's rule. Other comital dominions in Apulia appear to have been left vacant as well, but the evidence is even scarcer; these include the counties of Civitate, Molise, Montescaglioso and Tricarico. Civitate and Montescaglioso were already vacant before the second rebellion faced by King William, as Geoffrey of Lecce must have been deprived of the county of Montescaglioso when he was sent to Sicily as a prisoner, and Count Robert II of Civitate disappeared after 1156. It has been suggested by Cuozzo that during this vacancy the county of Civitate was administered by Guarmundus son of Walter, a chamberlain recorded in Cava charters between 1146 and 1180; this suggestion is founded on the fact that the *feuda* the count of Civitate held in Campomarino (near the mouth of the River Biferno) and in the area northwest of Biccari were accounted in the *Quaternus* by testimony of Guarmundus.[108]

The county of Hugh of Molise had remained vacant since the death of the count *c.* 1158, leaving this pivotal lordship at the margins of rebellion and turmoil. Nevertheless, a son of Robert of Molise, who consequently was also a cousin of Count Hugh II of Molise, was active in this county, and their descendants remained in his lordship. Hugh of Molise, lord of Sepino and son of Robert of Molise, made a donation in November 1143 to the church of the Holy Cross.[109] Although this Hugh was a relative of Count Hugh II, and a lord of a central town within the dominions of Boiano, he does not appear to have been part of the count's entourage. The available documents for Count Hugh II of Molise do not attest the presence of this Hugh of Molise, and the charters from St Cristina of Sepino that record the latter's transactions do not confirm that the count personally exercised his authority in Sepino. Interestingly enough, after Count Hugh II of Molise died, the lords of Sepino continued to remember their relative Hugh of Molise as a count. Two charters from St Cristina, one issued by Hugh of Molise in 1150 and the other by his son Robert of Molise in 1175, recorded transactions made for the salvation of the soul of Count Hugh of Molise.[110] Although the county of Hugh of Molise was no longer in the hands of the Molise family, the familial connection the lords of Sepino had to the old count remained in their memory. Additionally, the charters of Robert of Molise, ranging from 1175 to 1189, do not make any reference to the actual contemporary ruling counts of Molise.

The role played by Count Roger of Tricarico during the uprising is unclear; the only overt reference to his involvement is found in Romuald's chronicle, where he is named among the conspirators in 1159.[111] However, Count Roger was not identified as a leader of the rebellion by Pseudo-Falcandus, and there is no record of the count of Tricarico after 1159 and before 1168. Moreover, it is not clear if in 1159 this Count Roger of Tricarico was either the same Roger created count before 1154 or the son of Robert of Lauro, who was awarded the comital title and Caserta by 1162. Of course, it is possible that father and son could have stood on different sides during the upper-baronial war, but Robert of Lauro's son might not have been old enough by 1159, and not least because it would have been extremely unlikely for Roger to become a count before his father did in 1162. Considering it is almost impossible for Roger, son of Robert of Lauro, to have been the same count of Tricarico in 1154, and that the latter may have been involved in the rebellion, Roger II of Tricarico must have been made count at some point after 1162, but before William I died, in 1166. Robert of Lauro's recently acquired position as count of Caserta, and the favour he enjoyed after having been the king's commander in Capua and a royal ally during the rebellion, must have allowed him to convince the king to grant his son the vacant county of Tricarico, securing thus the comital title for both of his sons. This would explain why Pseudo-Falcandus does not mention Roger's appointment as count of Tricarico during the regency when several counts were created, *c.* 1167–8, but the same Roger was then attested in Messina in 1168 as count of Tricarico and son of the count of Caserta.

The corridor of counties that had been created along the northern Adriatic coast of the kingdom (Manopello, Loritello, Lesina, Civitate, Andria and Conversano) were temporarily dismantled after 1162, leaving the count of Lesina as the only major baron in the whole region between the border with the Abruzzo and the Terra di Bari. The area of influence of Geoffrey, count of Lesina, was restricted to the northern Capitanata, closer to the Abruzzo and far from the coastal cities of Adriatic Apulia. Count Geoffrey was recorded in documents regarding the abbeys of Casauria, in the Abruzzo, and Tremiti, on an island north of the Gargano peninsula; soon thereafter Count William of Lesina was captured and removed from his county in 1156, Geoffrey was already regarded as the ruling count of Lesina in an October 1156 charter concerning the abbey of Tremiti.[112] Count Geoffrey of Lesina was also recorded in the *Chronicon Casauriense* as having sent a letter to the abbot of St Clement in Casauria at some point after 1157.[113] The chartulary-chronicle of the same abbey of Casauria subsequently attests a donation of some lands around the swamp of Lesina, free of taxes and *plateaticum*, made by the count of Lesina in 12 February 1165, in which he was recorded both as 'Geoffrey, by the grace of God and the king count of Lesina, and royal justiciar' (*Goffridus Dei et Regis gratia Alesinae Comes et Regius Iustitiarius*).[114] As the son of a royal justiciar, Henry of Ollia, and as a justiciar himself, Geoffrey was not originally a member of the upper peninsular aristocracy, and instead he was a member of the circle of royal functionaries that, in the middle of the social turmoil caused by the count of Loritello's rebellion, was elevated to the comital rank.[115] His new title and lordship over Lesina could have been more prestigious than his office as a justiciar, but in all surviving evidence he does not omit his original position. Count Geoffrey of Lesina thus held these two positions in parallel, serving as both a representative of the king's justice and a major local landholder and overlord. Perhaps his lack of military protagonism and his role as justiciar in the region allowed him to stay away from the counts' coalition and survive first the insurgency and then the king's march over the mainland.

A new type of count had thus emerged from the counts' rebellion, a social overlapping that did not exist during Roger II's reign: the royal functionary and the count. The blurred lines between the military responsibilities of a count and those of an appointed royal commander allowed for their roles to be constantly changing and superimposing throughout the multiple wars and rebellions. Military offices had been granted before to peninsular counts (e.g. the temporary commanders Roger II left on the mainland during the civil war period, and Count Gilbert of Gravina being made *magister comestabulus* by William I), and loyal royal commanders had been awarded before with a county (e.g. Richard of Lingèvres, count of Andria and Robert of Lauro, count of Caserta). However, never before had an administrator of justice been elevated to the upper social echelon and allowed to be at the same time a local overlord with direct military and economic control over other barons. What could have started as a contingent solution to displace rebel counts and as an attempt to keep local structures close to the crown during times of lost social control became a situation thereafter normalized in the Sicilian kingdom.

Another count who consolidated his position after the rebellion was Sylvester of Marsico. As explained earlier, Count Sylvester stayed close to the king as a member of his *curia* in Palermo. The few surviving documents that record his activity as count of Marsico during the first years of William I's reign were issued in Sicily, in his chamber of Ragusa, and Pseudo-Falcandus's testimony and the December 1157 royal charter indicate that the count was a regular member of the Palermitan royal *curia*. Furthermore, Count Sylvester appears to have moved his residence to Palermo, as it is suggested by the purchase he made of Admiral Maio's houses in the city and the gravestone of his late infant daughter in St Cataldo.[116] The count of Marsico was made a royal *familiaris* after Maio's assassination, and kept this position in the wake of the rebellion.

According to Pseudo-Falcandus, the king's *familiares* accompanied William I in his march across Apulia, and then reached Salerno after the rebellion was suppressed. Mathew the notary, who is recorded as one of these *familiares* of the royal *curia* (as Henry Aristippus lost the king's favour after the attempted coup d'état and been subsequently arrested and sent back to Palermo during the king's campaign on the mainland), addressed the other *familiares* Richard, bishop-elect of Syracuse and Count Sylvester, so they could help him to convince the king to be lenient with the city of Salerno, which had shown support for the counts and to Marius Borell during the insurgency.[117] Salerno was ultimately spared, and William I and his *familiares* returned to Sicily. Nonetheless, Count Sylvester's consolidated position as royal minister was truncated by his own death. According, again, to Pseudo-Falcandus, not long after the kingdom was pacified, Sylvester of Marsico died. He must have died then at some point after 1162, but considerably before 1166, when William I died. The vacancy left after Count Sylvester's death was not taken by another count – another argument against the suggestion that the count of Marsico joined the king's court as a representative of the peninsular nobility. Instead, we are told by Pseudo-Falcandus that the other two remaining *familiares* (Bishop-elect Richard and Matthew the notary) monopolized the king's council and the 'administration of the realm' (*disponebant regni negotia*), and that Qaid Peter, the master chamberlain of the palace (*magister camerarius palatii*), was then associated with them.[118] Sylvester's son, William of Marsico, must have then inherited his father's title and lordships, but it is not exactly clear when he did so, or even if the new count of Marsico also resided in Palermo.

In the province of Calabria, changes were naturally expected to take place; after all, the members of the Calabrian nobility had played an actual role against Maio of Bari and during the insurgency. After Clementia, countess of Catanzaro, and her mother Countess Segelgarda had been imprisoned, there is no further account of her condition or of that of the county of Catanzaro. It has been suggested by Cuozzo that both countesses were pardoned and released at some point before 1165, as a Greek charter from that same year indicates that they were back in their county.[119] The cited document, however, does not refer to either of the countesses as a contemporary ruler. The charter issued 10 August 1165 records a judicial inquiry and mandate made by Michael, the 'chamberlain' of Badolato (καπριλλίγγος εἰς τὸν Βαδουλάτον), against the 'labourers' (δουλευτὲς) and 'tax collectors' (απέτιται) of Badolato; it was recorded that the 'colonists' (πάρ[ο]ικος) of the monastery 'of the mountain' (ερημίτες του όρους) held in Badolato were being unjustly taxed by the men of said town.[120] These men were summoned by the chamberlain, and they were remembered as the collectors 'from the time of Count Geoffrey and the countess' (ἀπό τόν καιρόν τοῦ κόμητος ἰοσφρὲ καὶ τη[ς] κομητίσσης). Furthermore, Geneisos the notary was especially remembered as a tax collector during the time of Countess Segelgarda (νοτάριος γένεισος, ὁ ὤν απετιτὴς εἰς τον καιρόν σικληγαίδας κομητίσσης). On the monastery's part, it was declared under oath that such exactions did not take place at the time of either count or countess. Therefore, in 1165, the countesses of Catanzaro were remembered as the former rulers of this Calabrian region. Moreover, a ruling count would have been expected to be the authority figure to mediate these sorts of disputes, or at least one of his or her officials; yet, the inquiry does not make any contemporary reference to a comital authority, but instead presents this 'chamberlain' as a mediating authority among, or even over, the local officials – the charter attests among its witnesses Sideros, the judge of the town of Badolato and the *strategoi* of the towns of Stilo and S. Caterina dello Ionio, all localities south of Catanzaro. The presence and role of Michael the chamberlain were justified by the absence of a count or countess of Catanzaro. He was thus acting not as a municipal administrator but as a provisional regional authority appointed by the royal *curia* after the rebellion.

The county of Catanzaro was hence left vacant throughout the rest of William I's reign. The status of the other Calabrian comital position, Squillace, is even more obscure, in that Pseudo-Falcandus is the only surviving source that attests Count Everard, the only known count of Squillace, before 1176. It appears then that, after Everard was deposed in 1156, there were no counts for Squillace until the time of King William II.

The kingdom's two centres of power

During the first eight years of William I's reign, royal control over the peninsular territories was fragmented and even interrupted. Although it is not clear to what extent the peninsular nobility shook off Sicilian authority during the first rebellion of Robert of Loritello, it would be impossible to claim that the royal *curia* was in control of the aristocracy of Apulia and the Terra di Lavoro between 1160 and 1162. As has been narrated by both Pseudo-Falcandus and Romuald of Salerno, for three years the Sicilian king and his men fought against the coalition of nobles and cities whose insurrection lasted beyond the assassination of Maio, which happened in November 1160. Whether out of frustration, or because they despaired of recovering William I's grace, the counts stayed in open rebellion. Both narrative testimonies, Pseudo-Falcandus's and Romuald's, agree on the resistance the king still had to face on the mainland, and how it was not until William I marched himself with his Sicilian army that royal control was reestablished in both Apulia and the Terra di Lavoro. Therefore, the implication of this continuing insurgency was more severe than in Sicily. The focus in Pseudo-Falcandus's narrative is, however, primarily on the events unfolding on the island; after all Palermo was the main stage for the coup d'état and the plots of the royal *curia*. Romuald Guarna, archbishop of Salerno, does pay proportionally more attention to the situation on the mainland, but the focus of his 'universal' chronicle is still divided between affairs in Rome and the development of the rebellion in Sicily.

Nevertheless, from the point of view of the nobility's activities, the kingdom of Sicily was split between opposing effective authorities: the Sicilian royal government and the league of counts led by Robert of Loritello in Apulia.

The activities in the Terra di Lavoro are less clear, and there is no explicit indication that Count Andrew of Rupecanina was the leader of the counts in this province. Nevertheless, Andrew must have exercised a conspicuous role as head of the revolt in the Terra di Lavoro because of his familial connections to the former princes of Capua and the counts of Caiazzo, and his political connections with both the Greek and German emperors.[121] Additionally, Count Andrew expanded his alliance strategy through marriage; Count Andrew 'of Comino' is recorded to have accepted in marriage the daughter of Count Berard of Alba in October 1160.[122]

This marriage has several, significant implications. First, this confirms Andrew's presence at the northern border of the realm in 1160. Second, Count Andrew, regarded here as 'count of Comino', established a base in a pivotal region (the Comino valley), distant from the centre of the Capuan province but strategically located in the inland northern vertex between the Abruzzo, central Italy and the kingdom, where he would have been able to coordinate the incursion into the Capuan principality from a safe position behind the Abruzzese mountains. Third, Andrew's activities were not merely military but also political; he was rallying to his cause a local baron from a region that had been practically severed from the kingdom, but that had played a vital role as a buffer zone between central Italy and Apulia and as a base for Robert of Loritello's incursions against the kingdom. The marriage seems to have sealed both a settlement and a partnership between Andrew and Berard of Alba, as it was also recorded that Berard gave money to Andrew for which the former had his lands restored and dominion over his lands conceded, after which Berard went to Comino and then plundered the town of Schiavi di Abruzzo (*Sclavi*). Subsequently, both Andrew and Berard raided the region as they marched over the lands of the abbey of St Vincent in Volturno and burned many towns down.[123] Although it is impossible to confirm the extent of Andrew of Rupecanina's control over the Capuan province, he definitely acted as a major leader of the insurgency and a key broker between the rebels and the external political forces. For three years the peninsular territories of the kingdom appear to have escaped from the Sicilian rule, and instead to have been under the independent control of the counts.

The Abruzzo must have been a lost province during this eight-year period (1154–62). As a border area, established as a northern march, the Abruzzo was predisposed to instability and a lack of centralized control in times of turmoil and invasion. The special jurisdiction (*justitia/comestabulia*) led by the count of Manopello could have been the only royal post in the region; the rest appears to have been land submerged in chaos and plunder. After Count Bohemund I of Manopello was defeated, the great lords of the region, the Abruzzese counts, benefited from Robert of Loritello's rebellion and the lack of royal control as they plundered the neighbouring churches and the lands of the major monasteries (e.g. Casauria and Carpineto). Unsurprisingly, the Abruzzo became a safe zone for the rebel count of Loritello. The frontier province hosted Count Robert of Loritello after the royal army defeated his insurrection and served as a centre of operations for the expelled rebels.

What was the actual state of the kingdom's government on the mainland during these three years (1159–62)? There is no evidence that would indicate that either Count Robert of Loritello or Count Andrew of Rupecanina claimed the royal title for themselves. They appear instead to have been more interested in shaking off royal authority, and much less in appointing a new figure of central authority, not even from among themselves. Their military leaderships were not translated into a claim to the throne. The league of counts did not constitute a substitute for government but instead were a military alliance which prevented the enforcement of the king's authority. Neither Robert of Loritello nor Andrew of Rupecanina would have been interested in taking over responsibility for the administration of the entire kingdom; what concerned them was not being placed under the effective control of any overlord or military commander. Like Count Robert II of Loritello, son of Rao, and Rainulf of Caiazzo during the early decades of the same century, the dissident counts might have been willing to acknowledge a nominal figure of authority, as long as in practice they were allowed to rule autonomously, commanding their own armed forces and controlling the lesser barons in their vicinity. After all, it was the former count of Loritello who, before the arrival of Roger II and the creation of the kingdom, regarded himself as 'count of counts'. The rebellion of the peninsular nobility against Maio of Bari and William I was thus an aristocratic movement against the expanding institutional control of the Sicilian government, and not a political organization or federation that intended to provide a substitute for the functions of the Palermitan *curia*.

This opposition to the king's control did not necessarily imply a class-conscious effort from the nobility against the court's officials, but instead a real effort for their survival and consolidation. Count Richard of Fondi, for example, was constantly switching sides throughout this period, but his apparent political fickleness could have been more sensible than cynical. Given the county of Fondi's exposed but strategic position on the Tyrrhenian border of the kingdom, and the seemingly considerable external support for the exiled prince, and then the exiled count of Rupecanina/Caiazzo (from Rome and both the German and Greek empires), Count Richard may have had little choice but to join the rebels. As keeper of the gateway between the kingdom and the papal lands, the count of Fondi was liable to become a major actor in the insurrection, whether he wished to be or not. Also, the role played by Robert II of Lauro, who did not join the coalition and fought alongside the king's forces, and Sylvester of Marsico, who was directly involved in the Palermitan *curia* despite his condition and status as a count. Pseudo-Falcandus seems to have struggled with Count Sylvester's closeness to the royal *curia*, in that this undermines his categorical assertion that all barons and nobles were against the tyranny of the royal government. This might have been the reason why Pseudo-Falcandus rationalized Count Sylvester's absence from the counts' rebellion on the grounds of his timidity. In any case, it is certain that the count of Marsico neither joined the league of counts nor openly opposed the king's control over the mainland.

The rebel counts would not have needed to reject or repudiate their king overtly; they fought against the effective rule of his court officials, namely his great admiral or any other of the royal commanders and high officials. The rebels' desperation to be restored to the king's favour could have justified their continuing insurrection, but this would have meant that the enemy to defeat was the king's ability to exercise his will, not the existence or legitimacy of his kinship. The existence of a nominal king who would stay in Sicily and the dissipation of economic and military restraints seem to have been the purpose of the league of counts. Pio called them the 'centrifugal force';[124] however, the peninsular nobility was not necessarily a unified hierarchy that acted as a self-aware class against the central bureaucracy, but instead a coalition in favour of a strong but local military command. It is fundamental to pinpoint that the leadership of Robert of Loritello was not simply a matter of *primus inter pares*, but a recognized subordination. The attachment and the homage that the other counts made to the count of Loritello and Conversano suggest that a degree of at least military subordination was acknowledged by other barons, who appear to bear the same nominal authority and distinction. Thus, Robert would have become a true 'count of counts'. Effective military leadership requires a centre of authority. It was this political realization that allowed the unity of the kingdom to survive and the Sicilian king partially to recover his control of the territories across the Straits of Messina. If William I wanted to control the counts, he needed to do so through an indirect deputy, one from the counts' own echelon.

According to Pseudo-Falcandus, King William only pardoned two counts: Roger of Aquila, count of Avellino, and Count Gilbert of Gravina. In both instances, the former rebels were admitted back into the king's grace because of the direct plea their relatives made to William. In both cases, however, they seem to have taken little part in the rebellion. Count Roger was recorded back in the kingdom, near Avellino, in 1165.[125] It was the king's pardon that allowed Count Gilbert to switch sides. The defection of the count of Gravina was the next, necessary step in the redefinition of the relationship between the Sicilian royal government and the peninsular aristocracy. Count Gilbert was a recent addition to the kingdom's nobility, and his familial ties to the queen made him a natural ally of the king.

Since the kingdom's creation, neither the high offices for the military command nor those of the administration had been occupied by a member of the peninsular nobility. According to Alexander of Telese, the counts who were entrusted with the command of the king's knights to defend the northwestern territories were to succeed each other for set terms. These commanders however were temporary, and they do not appear to have kept their positions after the imperial invasion of 1137. The role played by these counts was limited to the civil war period, and this rotating command would only have been a reality during the stage before the rearrangement and consolidation which was implemented after 1139. However, in 1162, the count of Gravina was made the *magister comestabulus* for Apulia and the Terra di Lavoro. Count Gilbert and Richard of Say, the same royal commander who led the offensive against the rebels after Aquinus of Moac, were subsequently recorded in 1165 as royal commanders. We are told by the *Annales Ceccanenses* that the two came into the papal Campania with the army of the Sicilian king to recapture the lands that the imperial commander, Chancellor Christian of Buch, and a Count Gonzolinus had taken and harried before, so that these territories would swear allegiance to the anti-pope Paschal III and the German emperor.[126] The two appear to have captured Veroli (north of Ceccano), and marched all the way to the S. Lorenzo valley; after they burned the *castrum* of S. Lorenzo, each one returned to their own place. Outstandingly, William I seems thus to have assisted Pope Alexander III against Frederick Barbarossa and Paschal III, with an army partially commanded by the count of Gravina. This confirms both the military role taken by Count Gilbert as *magister comestabulus* and the survival of Richard of Say as a royal commander during the final years of William I's reign. However, it is uncertain whether Richard of Say was still a constable and royal justiciar in Calabria by that time, or if he had acquired the same title as Gilbert. It is also not clear what specific role the count of Gravina played during the royal incursion.

Although it was reported that Gilbert of Gravina joined the king's cause and was made a commander, Aquinus of Moac and Richard of Say were the ones recorded as active captains of the royal army. What is more certain is that after the counts and Robert of Loritello had been defeated and expelled, Count Gilbert was left as both a leading count and the king's man on the mainland. Neither Aquinus of Moac nor Richard of Say appear to have been part of the kingdom's upper aristocracy, and their lack of both an honorary title and a county meant that they did not have the economic means to consolidate their own authority. Their authority derived only from the king, and even though they were commanders of the army on the mainland, in times of peace they were only lesser barons with a royal appointment. Conversely, Gilbert of Gravina was not only a *magister comestabulus* but also a local authority and an overlord. He could thus recall and mobilize the lords and their respective knights who held lands *in servitio* of the count of Gravina, not to mention the wealth that all the lands he held *in demanio* could produce. This was the first occasion since the creation of the kingdom that a count was appointed not only as commander of the armed forces but also as a continuing overseer for the royal government. Although this may appear at first reading to be counterintuitive, mostly since it has been presumed that Roger II was keen to detach the peninsular nobility from the central government in order to avoid creating uncontrollable magnates, it was not until both social layers overlapped in the figure of Count Gilbert that a lasting peace with the upper aristocracy was achieved. By the end of 1162, the peninsular territories had a new master and commander; Count Gilbert of Gravina was the royal governor on the mainland for the remaining years of William I's reign.

Although his remit did not extend to Calabria and the separated region of the Abruzzo, Gilbert of Gravina had hence become the most powerful commander on the peninsula. While the role the count of Gravina played as a royal ally during the pacification of 1162 is not clear, Gilbert was the man left in command after William I had won the war and returned to Sicily. We do not hear much more about these captains later on, but the *magister comestabulus* Gilbert became a central actor in the kingdom's politics and administration. The power that the count of Loritello and Conversano would have wanted to wield on the mainland was now in the hands of the count of Gravina. William I was ultimately forced to concede and relinquish the direct control the royal *curia* exercised over the two major provinces in the Italian peninsula, as the new royal commander was neither a functionary of the court nor a lesser baron with a temporary appointment, but a nobleman who resided on the other side of the Straits of Messina. Thus, Count Gilbert of Gravina became the additional centre of power through which William's reign could continue, without any further insurrection or internal challenge.

5

New spheres of comital action under Margaret's regency

Before King William passed away, he appointed his queen consort, Margaret of Navarre, as the regent and guardian of his sons, all minors at the time of his death. By this stage, the existence of only three counties can be confirmed (Caserta, Gravina and Lesina), although the counts of Alife and Marsico must have been also active until *c.* 1163–6 (before their respective deaths), and a new count of Tricarico was most likely appointed before 1166. The rest of the counties appear to have been left vacant during the remaining years of William I's reign.[1] In the spring of 1166, the eldest son William, who was then twelve years old, succeeded his father on the throne.[2] The policy of the new regime radically changed the Palermitan *curia*'s attitude towards the peninsular nobility.

We are told by Romuald of Salerno in his chronicle that Queen Margaret 'opened the prisons, freed the numerous captives, restored the lands to those liberated, forgave debts, recalled to the kingdom the counts and barons that had been banished, and gave them their confiscated lands back'.[3] The royal *curia* also granted royal lands to the churches, counts and barons. In the same way, Pseudo-Falcandus explained that the queen granted copious favours, such as opening the prisons and abolishing the 'redemption fees' imposed by William I on Apulia and the Terra di Lavoro, in order to make both the people and the nobles grateful and loyal towards her and her son.[4] Many of the benefits that were thus conferred by the queen and her court seem to have been made to turn the page from William I's reign, and make the young William II a beloved king and his kingdom a peaceful polity. However, in the midst of the subsequent changes and arrangements made in the Sicilian court and Qaid Peter's apparent predominance over the other royal *familiares*, the count of Gravina did not stay idle either, and crossed the Straits of Messina into Sicily.

The count of Gravina versus the count of Molise

We are told by Pseudo-Falcandus that the reason Count Gilbert had come to the royal *curia* was to be appointed 'master captain of the whole kingdom' (*magister capitaneus totius regni*) and to administer the affairs of the court in the top position after the queen (*negotia curie post reginam principe loco disponeret*).[5] Furthermore, it is explained that since the count of Gravina did not bring enough knights (*milites*) with him, and that the queen was not willing to put Qaid Peter, the master chamberlain of the royal palace, in second position to anyone, Count Gilbert was not able to exclude the other *familiares* from the court against Queen Margaret's wishes. Hence, even as a commander on the mainland, far from the royal palaces, the count of Gravina would still be considered a *familiaris* of the queen. Also, this passage suggests that Count Gilbert's title as 'great constable' (*magnus comestabulus*) was a military position and did not carry an administrative responsibility that a 'master captain' would have done, as was explicitly put by Pseudo-Falcandus when he described Gilbert's intention to be put in charge of the administration of the affairs of the *curia*. Although the surviving evidence for the last years of William I's reign is scarce, the count of Gravina is not recorded as presiding over any court on the mainland or as conducting any mediation or issuing any mandate outside his county. He was nevertheless remembered in the *Annales Ceccanenses* as a commander of the king's armed forces in the peninsula.[6] The count of Gravina would, however, acquire the position to which he was aspiring at a later stage; the chronicle of Casauria recorded that Count Gilbert, 'the current master captain and governor of the whole realm' (*Comes Gilisbertus [...] tunc temporis Magistrus Capitaneus et gubernatore totius regni*), presided over a court at Foggia to follow up the long-running controversy between the monastery of Casauria and Count Bohemund II of Manopello, just as the previous master captain, Simon the seneschal, had done before him.[7] At least it is clear from Pseudo-Falcandus's testimony that the count of Gravina, after William I's death, wanted to improve his position and expand his authority through his relative, the queen.

The real extent to which the titles of 'great constable' and 'master captain' differ is unclear. Both Jamison and Takayama agree that there was no practical difference between these two titles. Jamison suggests that 'captain and constable were titles equally applicable to the new governor [of the mainland]', and Takayama simply assumes that the master captains, constables and justiciars were part of the same institution of two general governors, originally established under Maio's administration and subsequently consolidated as the 'viceroys' overseeing Apulia and Capua.[8] These assumptions present a neat image of the royal administration and an understanding of a designed central office; nonetheless, the terminology and context of the surviving evidence presents a less elegant and more contingent institutional development. The case of the count of Gravina illustrates this. It serves not only as an example of the possible difference between the titles of 'great constable' and 'master captain' and their particular military and administrative functions but also as an example of the political environment in which the royal *curia* revived the office of 'master captain of the whole of Apulia and the Terra di Lavoro'. This title was last documented before Maio of Bari was assassinated and his brother-in-law, Simon the seneschal, the original *magister capitaneus*, disappeared from the political arena. Gilbert of Gravina seems thus to have taken advantage of the confusion following William I's death, by aspiring to the gubernatorial office created under Admiral Maio's administration, and thence merging it with both his military rank as peninsular commander-in-chief and his socio-economic position as a member of the kingdom's nobility. Such an ambitious agenda must have been the reason behind Gilbert's presence in Sicily and Qaid Peter's concern and precautions.

The kingdom's two centres of power were thus in confrontation one with another soon thereafter William I died, with Qaid Peter standing on the side of the Sicilian court. According to Pseudo-Falcandus, 'the barons and the rest of the nobles who held any estates or *feuda* preferred the count of Gravina to be at the head of the court and be appointed captain, whereas the salaried knights, alongside their constable [Richard of Mandra], and except for a few from the north of the Alps, preferred the rewards of Qaid Peter'.[9] Such a testimony not only provides an insight into the composition of the royal contingent of hired soldiers, which was made up partially of transalpine knights, but also reveals to some extent the administrative and political division of the kingdom's armed forces, between conscripted and contracted. Additionally, Gilbert himself came from across the Alps, as he was a member of the kin-group of the counts of Perche and had come from Spain; one might have expected, therefore, that some of these transalpine knights empathized with Gilbert of Perche.

Count Gilbert of Gravina stood in a position that no other nobleman had enjoyed since the creation of the kingdom. Robert of Bassunvilla, the former count of Loritello and Conversano, had previously attempted to shake off the control of the royal functionaries. The consequence of this, however, was the insurgency and ultimately Gilbert's rise to power. Making Count Gilbert, a relative of the queen, a 'great constable' in the midst of a punished and reduced nobility, allowed Gilbert to consolidate himself among the other remaining counts. Now that William I had died, and rapid changes were taking place in the *curia*, the count of Gravina sought to take a further step and seize the authority of the royal government itself. Just as the upper peninsular aristocracy appeared hence to attempt to take over the political source of the kingdom's social control, the chief *familiaris* of the royal *curia* responded symmetrically by 'infiltrating' the nobility and placing one of his own men in charge of one of the economic and military sources of control on the mainland: Richard of Mandra was appointed count and given the county that used to belong to Hugh of Molise. This interpretation does not solely rely on the ties Richard of Mandra had with Qaid Peter and the royal *curia*, but also on Pseudo-Falcandus's own impression of the affair; we are told by the anonymous historian that Qaid Peter planned to have Richard of Mandra 'made a count and use him thus as a defence against the count of Gravina, so that count could resist the other count with full authority, as if from horseback'.[10] Even if one is sceptical of Qaid Peter's role in the nomination of Richard of Mandra, being cautious of Pseudo-Falcandus's detailed and politically charged account, it is clear that as an appointed official of the royal government, Richard of Mandra was not powerful enough to face the influence of the count of Gravina. The rationale presented here reveals the contemporary core understanding of what a count was: a knightly military force (*ex equo*) and a baron with full authority (*plena auctoritas*). The authority that a royal functionary could have wielded as a representative of the court, either as a military commander (*comestabulus*) or as an administrator (*justitiarius* or *camerarius*) was not enough, or even complete; only as a count could Richard have 'full authority'. Making Count Gilbert a 'great constable' (*magnus comestabulus*), and thus a general of the king's army, unshackled the system that throughout Roger II's reign and the first seven years of William I's rule had allowed the crown to consolidate its pre-eminent jurisdiction over the whole mainland and restrain the nobility while, at the same time, acknowledging the local authority, prestige and overlordship of the nobility, which was recognized as such through the comital title. The Sicilian royal *familiares* decided then to fight fire with fire and granted Richard the constable the extensive dominion of the late Hugh II of Molise, including Boiano and Venafro, creating as a result a powerful noble to rival Count Gilbert on the mainland.

This episode additionally provides a fascinating insight into the procedure of making a count. As recorded by Pseudo-Falcandus, Richard was made a count 'with trumpets, drums and cymbals going in solemn procession before him, according to custom' (*tubis tympanis cymbalisque de more solepmniter preeuntibus*).[11] Such a scene must have been similar to the image of the triumphant entry of King Tancred I into Palermo in 1190, which was preceded with cymbals, drums and trumpets, as was depicted by Peter of Eboli in his *Liber ad honorem Augusti*.[12] The comital dignity was accompanied with a ceremony that matched the gravity of the appointment. The evidence is tenuous, and Pseudo-Falcandus's words are the only indication of such a ceremony having taken place in the creation of a count. However, this was the case in the other comital appointment, as in the kingdom of Sicily it was undoubtedly the king who created and confirmed the counts. It is uncertain if this ceremony had to have taken place on every occasion, perhaps in Palermo as the permanent seat of the royal *curia*, but it would not come as a surprise to assume that some of these processions took place in other cities, while the monarch held courts on the mainland.

We are also told by Pseudo-Falcandus that Count Gilbert of Gravina stayed in Palermo, allegedly hatching some major plot against Qaid Peter, together with the bishop-elect of Syracuse. As a result, the chief royal *familiaris* fled during the night alongside a few eunuchs, with a considerable amount of money, and sailed across to Africa to the king of the Muwahids and of Morocco (Caliph ʿAbd al Mu'min).[13] Qaid Peter's escape intensified the drama in Palermo, as Count Gilbert took the opportunity to publicly denounce the great danger that it was to have a 'Muslim slave' (*servus Saracenum*) in a position of power. Countering the imputations made by the count of Gravina, Count Richard of Molise defended the Qaid and thence both counts began arguing, to the point that the new count of Molise 'called the count of Gravina a coward and unworthy to be one to whom the king's army could be entrusted'.[14] Here, the specific nature of Count Gilbert's position is again made clear, in that it is implied that the royal armed forces were entrusted to him, a position that Count Richard reportedly was opposing very forcefully. The escalated argument between the counts of Gravina and Molise ended with Queen Margaret's orders and the appeals of the magnates of the *curia* to both sides to simply forgive each other's injurious statements.[15] However, the appeased confrontation with Count Gilbert of Gravina was far from being over.

In the meantime, the expelled Capuan counts resumed the attacks against the kingdom. Andrew of Rupecanina and Richard of Aquila, the former count of Fondi, were recorded as having invaded the dominions of the Sicilian king immediately after William I's death. According to the *Annales Ceccanenses*, both counts besieged Pastena, and after not being able to capture the town, they marched to Pico and burned it, and then captured Itri and Traetto (modern Minturno), to finally return to Ceccano.[16] All of these places are located on the Capuan border, around what would have been the county of Richard of Aquila. Pastena and Pico are north of Fondi, whereas Itri and Traetto are found on the southeastern route towards the River Garigliano, on the Via Appia – Traetto had been taken before by Andrew of Rupecanina in 1157.[17] The records do not provide any detailed account of the kingdom's reaction to this invasion, except that 'the knights of the king burned Traetto'.[18] Although the royal army's general on the mainland, the *magister comestabulus* Gilbert of Gravina, must have been engaged at this time with the politics of the royal *curia*, the invading counts not only stopped their advance before they crossed the River Garigliano but also appear to have retreated back into the papal Campania.

It is uncertain whether the incursion led by Andrew of Rupecanina and Richard of Aquila, former count of Fondi, was originally meant to be a harrying expedition to exercise pressure on the recently appointed regency, or part of a larger campaign against the Sicilian kingdom. We know that after William I's triumph over the rebel and invading forces, and the retreat of Frederick Barbarossa in 1155, Pope Adrian IV was forced to come to terms with the Sicilian king at the Treaty of Benevento.[19] Since both the Sicilian monarchy and the papacy were seemingly wary of Emperor Frederick's agenda on the Italian peninsula, an exercise of realpolitik and a recognition of common interests must have been necessary for such an agreement to be finally reached. The practical, shared motivations behind this treaty seem clear: to avoid future mutual confrontations and to prepare for a common front against the German emperor and his allies. Even though Andrew of Rupecanina was a papal ally and was able to escape the king's wrath in 1156 thanks to the pope's intervention, he was also a baron close to the German emperor. Furthermore, we are told by Kinnamos that Andrew had antagonized the pope before, when Alexios the protostrator sent him to Apulia to subdue numerous cities in 1157.[20] Andrew's subsequent attacks and harassment must have taken place without support from Rome, but with the implicit backing of Frederick Barbarossa. In any case, Andrew of Rupecanina does not appear to have had another chance to reclaim his ancestral domains after 1162.

The last documented appearances of Count Andrew are found in 1167. First, when the German army marched through Italy in 1167, as the imperial chancellor Rainald, and then Frederick himself, besieged Rome. Andrew participated in the battle of Monte Porzio on the side of the emperor, as a soldier in Christian of Buch's army to fight against Pope Alexander III and the Romans.[21] Additionally, Andrew of Rupecanina witnessed two charters issued by Frederick I in the same year, one in Rimini in April, and another in Pisa in August.[22] Consequently, a potential invasion led by the German emperor could have seemed a real danger, but due to both the accord between Rome and the Sicilian monarchy, and the hostilities between Rome and Frederick Barbarossa, the exiled barons had to neglect their campaign against the *regnum* and assist the emperor, their main – if not only – political patron. In any case, Barbarossa's campaign was halted by the sudden outbreak of an epidemic, which effectively destroyed the German army and drove the emperor back north of the Alps.[23]

It was the threat of a German invasion that, according to Pseudo-Falcandus, was announced in a false letter composed and presented to the court by Matthew the notary, in order to provide the queen with a reasonable justification for ordering

Count Gilbert to go to Apulia as soon as possible. The count of Gravina was finally appointed 'captain of Apulia and the Terra di Lavoro' (*capitaneus Apuliae Terraeque Laboris*), together with his son Bertram, who had recently been granted the county of Andria (*Andriae comitatus*).[24] Although these two concessions appear to have been downplayed by Pseudo-Falcandus's narrative, these must have been as important as the creation of Richard of Mandra as count of Molise. Not only did Count Gilbert acquire the title and power he had been demanding since his arrival in Palermo, but his son also received one of the counties in the sensitive Adriatic line, a position that had been left vacant since the late Count Richard of Andria died in 1155 fighting against the Greek army.[25] This must have created a considerable block of lordships and dominions around the Terra di Bari, extending from the central Apulian Adriatic coast to the hinterland, bordering with the Cilento region, which had also been placed under the comital authority of Gilbert of Perche and his son.

Gilbert of Gravina's power was thus consolidated as the de facto governor of Apulia and the Terra di Lavoro, in exchange for his 'departure' from Palermo and the royal *curia*. We are told by Pseudo-Falcandus that in Count Gilbert's place the queen made Count Richard of Molise a *familiaris* of the court, 'since he had cherished great loyalty for Qaid Peter, and granted him greater power than the other *familiares*'.[26] Richard of Mandra took not only Gilbert's place but also Qaid Peter's membership of the council of royal 'ministers'. By temporarily appeasing the confrontation between the count of Molise and the count of Gravina, the queen's government further consolidated the two centres of power that had been developing since the last insurgency. On the one hand, Gilbert and his family enjoyed the overlordship of two adjacent counties, and Gilbert himself became the first documented 'great captain' of the kingdom since 1158, when the royal affairs were under Maio of Bari's administrative control. On the other hand, Richard had not only acquired the extensive county of the late Hugh II of Molise but also been anointed as a royal *familiaris*, thus, becoming one of the most influential men in the court of the regent queen. There is no evidence, however, that Richard of Mandra conducted any specific activity, or held a court, in any of his recently given peninsular dominions, at least before 1170. During this stage of the regency, the count of Molise was engaged with affairs of the court at Palermo, rather than spending his time on the mainland.

It must have been at this time, in 1167, after the count of Gravina was made great captain, his son Bertram count of Andria and Richard of Mandra count of Molise, and while Emperor Frederick was campaigning in central Italy, that the *Quaternus magne expeditionis* was put together, transformed from the original drafts or *quaterniones* made c. 1150 to the core structure in which it survives to this day. The *Quaternus* already attests Bertram as count of Andria, and the counts of Alife and Caserta recently created by William I during the last rebellion, but it still does not name any count of Loritello, Conversano or Principato. However, the entire document was not updated, as many entries still made mention of counts who had either died or were in exile by that time (e.g. Count Sylvester of Marsico, dead before 1166, and Richard of Aquila, the exiled count of Fondi). Also, the entries for the county of Molise appear to begin abruptly, without any subheading or introduction, and the rest of the register does not make any overt mention of the name of the count of Molise. All of this may suggest that the surviving recession of the *Quaternus* was left incomplete, perhaps after the ensuing turmoil at the royal *curia* during Easter 1168.

Collective comital nominations

The unfolding of the year 1167 was turbulent and confusing. The chronicle of Romuald Guarna, archbishop of Salerno, does not expand on the arrangement made by the royal *curia* at this time in much detail. Conversely, Pseudo-Falcandus provides a thorough, albeit confusing summation of the changes that took place before the appointment of a new chancellor by the regent queen. The most relevant passage to this inquiry is the list of new counts provided by Pseudo-Falcandus. He wrote that the queen

> created eight counts in that one year [1167]: Richard of Mandra, the count of Gravina's son Bertram, Richard of Say, Roger son of Richard, Jocelyn, Simon of Sangro, Count Sylvester's son William, and her relative Hugh of Rochefort, a man devoid of every virtue who had recently arrived from France; in addition she restored to their previous dignity Count Roger of Acerra and Count Roger of Avellino.[27]

First of all, Pseudo-Falcandus employs the comital title in a rather relaxed manner, and this is not the first time he assigns this dignity to a man that clearly did not belong to the same rank as the kingdom's counts (i.e. Roger of Craon). Hugh of Rochefort is another of these instances, as nothing certain is known about him. Loud and Wiedemann have provided an exploration of Hugh's possible origins in France, and have proposed, on the basis of a suggestion made by Cuozzo, that he may have received the county of Alife; although this is not impossible, there is no evidence or even indication that this Capuan county was given to this transalpine foreigner.[28] Furthermore, an April 1170 charter records a donation made to the church of St Mary of Monte Drogo (della Grotta) by Roger son of Richard, count of Alife.[29] It is even more unlikely that Hugh of Rochefort would have received Alife to then lose it to a Roger son of Richard without any overt reference of this in any surviving contemporary testimony. However, this Count Roger son of Richard must not be confused with the Roger son of Richard who, according to Pseudo-Falcandus, was made count in 1167, because the 1170 charter of the count of Alife was dated in the first year of his countship. This other Roger son of Richard was instead related to the original Norman counts of Caiazzo.[30] It has been generally assumed that the Roger son of Richard that Pseudo-Falcandus remembered here was in fact given the county of Alba, in the Abruzzo. But, before I explain this possibility, it is necessary to discuss the group of Abruzzese counts listed by Pseudo-Falcandus.

Cuozzo, Loud and Wiedemann have identified Roger son of Richard, Jocelyn and Simon of Sangro as the counts of Alba, Loreto and Sangro, respectively.[31] The separate *quaternion* for the Abruzzo, appended to the *Quaternus magne expeditionis* and likewise edited in the *Catalogus Baronum*, provides the direct reference for these identifications. The case of Count Simon of Sangro is straightforward; his toponym already provides the answer for the core lordships of this recently created count, and the Abruzzese *quaternion* records 'the county of Simon, count of Sangro', and the same Count Simon, 'son of Count Theodinus', is found as the lord, among many other lordships and barons, of the *castellum* of Sangro.³² Jocelyn is an uncommon name among the Lombard, Greek and Norman aristocracies of southern Italy – there are only eight different *Joczelinus* recorded in the entire *Quaternus*, all lesser barons. Besides, there is no record of any count named Jocelyn in Apulia or the Terra di Lavoro, and only one Count *Joczelinus* can be found in the Abruzzese *quaternion*: the son of Rambot, lord of Loreto – this Rambot appears to have been a descendant of Drogo 'the Badger', son of Geoffrey of Capitanata (death *c.* 1063).³³ Notably, Count Jocelyn's entry in the *Quaternus* explicitly mentions that he held his *feuda* 'from the king' (*tenet a domino Rege*). Hence, there is no reason to doubt the identification by Pseudo-Falcandus of this new count Jocelyn as the Abruzzese count of Loreto. However, the case of Roger son of Richard is less clear.

The *quaternion* for the Abruzzo records a Count Roger of Alba, 'who says that he held *in demanio*' Alba, and many other *feuda* in Marsia; however, by the end of the entry the name of another count is recorded: Count Berard of Alba. This is a common situation in the records for the *magna expeditio*, whereby the previous entries from original drafts were not updated in subsequent references to the military service owed by the same lordships and counties. Also, earlier, in 1160, Andrew of Rupecanina (count 'of Comino' by that time) is recorded to have accepted in marriage the daughter of Count Berard of Alba; afterwards, both counts raided southern Abruzzo and the northern part of the county of Molise.³⁴ It is clear that Count Berard of Alba was involved in the insurgency, and it is probable that he was expelled, or even killed, in the wake of William I's campaign on the mainland, thus leaving the lordships of Alba and Marsia vacant *c.* 1162–6. Nonetheless, there is no certainty as to the relation between this Count Roger and Count Berard, or for when Count Roger received Alba.

The identification of this Count Roger of Alba and Roger son of Richard found in Pseudo-Falcandus is essentially based on two pieces of evidence. First, an Abruzzese charter issued on 1 April 1198 by Count Peter of Celano, son of Count Berard, confirmed the holdings that the church of St Cesidius of Trasaco lawfully took when 'late Count Roger of Andria granted those fisheries to the said church in the time when he held the county of Alba' (*Comes quon. Rogerius Andreae ipsas Piscationes, iam dictae Ecclesię dedit eo tempore, quo tenebat comitatis Albae*).³⁵ Second, the fact that the latter's given name is also Roger and that he was created count in 1167. Roger son of Richard was mentioned earlier by Pseudo-Falcandus as one of the barons who were staying in Palermo and who were on the side of Geoffrey of Lecce, by then the count of Montescaglioso, when the latter was plotting against Maio of Bari.³⁶ On that occasion, Pseudo-Falcandus named him together with Simon of Sangro, an Abruzzese baron. Since Geoffrey of Lecce was later arrested, and many barons involved in that rebellion were either imprisoned or forced into exile, it is quite probable that Roger son of Richard was in exile after 1156. Roger son of Richard must have returned to the realm at the same time as the first batch of pardoned counts were accepted back by the queen regent. Moreover, Cuozzo has argued that Roger's father was the same Richard son of Richard attested in the *Quaternus* as lord of Trevico, Contra, Flumeri, Vallata and *Santum Angelum* (a region in Apulia, south of the county of Buonalbergo), overlord of two barons, and placed under the *comestabulia* of Guimund of Montellari.³⁷

Richard son of Richard was the brother of Robert son of Richard, the loyal supporter of Roger II who was made count of Civitate. Hence, this Roger son of Richard was also the cousin of Count Robert II of Civitate, who most likely also joined the rebellion in 1155–6. Even though the count of Civitate does not appear to have recovered his lordships after the debacle of 1156, his cousin Roger found a way to return to the kingdom and be pardoned by the new regime.

It is not surprising that Roger son of Richard would have received a vacant county in the Abruzzo on his return. On the one hand, the status of his father as an overlord and his cousin as count of Civitate must have helped Roger son of Richard to justify his membership within the comital rank; his kin-group was already part of the upper aristocracy. On the other hand, Roger son of Richard had previously become acquainted with some nobles from the Abruzzo (such as Simon of Sangro) while he stayed in Palermo supporting Geoffrey of Lecce, which must have made him a candidate already familiar with the Abruzzese aristocracy. A Count Roger of Alba is subsequently attested in Pseudo-Falcandus as the military commander who, together with Richard of Say, would chase Count Gilbert out of the realm. This episode is discussed in the section 'A comital takeover: Richard of Molise and Henry of Montescaglioso'; however, the point to make here is that Roger son of Richard's political career appears to have escalated speedily enough, because in less than two years he went from being an Apulian rebel in exile to an Abruzzese count, who was then temporarily made a royal general.

The testimony of Pseudo-Falcandus also attests that two former counts were restored to their position at this stage: Roger of Acerra, count of Buonalbergo, and Roger of Aquila, count of Avellino. Count Roger of Avellino had returned to his dominions before William I's death, but this might have happened without the full approval of the royal *curia*, which he received after under Queen Margaret's regency. Roger of Medania, count of Buonalbergo, would then be the first exiled nobleman recalled back to the kingdom by the new royal administration. A donation of some land and a mill, made on 25 May 1166 by Roger of Medania to the abbey of the Holy Saviour at Goleto (modern S. Guglielmo al Goleto), remembered the latter as 'count of Acerra and lord of the city of Nusco' (*Rogerius de Medania, comes Acerrarum et dominus civatis Nusci*).[38] Subsequently, on 2 May 1167, Roger of Medania was recorded as having granted some land and timber rights to the same abbey as 'count of Acerra and lord of Nusco, by the grace of God and the king' (*Rogerius de Medonia Dei et Regis gratia Acerrarum Comes et Nusci Dominus*).[39] Although the original comital seat of the county created by Roger II was located in Buonalbergo, northwest of Ariano, and the *Quaternus* recorded it as the 'county of Buonalbergo', the ancestral lordship of the Medania family in the principality of Capua (i.e. Acerra) gradually became the toponym of his comital title. Pseudo-Falcandus always regarded Roger of Medania as count of Acerra, and this 1167 donation does not employ Buonalbergo as part of Roger's dignity. Perhaps the comital seat was transferred after Roger of Medania was restored to his original lordships. Hence, after Roger of Medania returned from exile, the former county of Buonalbergo was transformed into a cluster of three geographically separated lordships: Acerra in the principality of Capua, and Buonalbergo and Nusco in the duchy of Apulia.

Of the other recently made counts recorded by Pseudo-Falcandus, we already know how Richard of Mandra was made count of Molise and Bertram, Gilbert's son, was made count of Andria. The remaining two, Count Sylvester's son William and Richard of Say, can be clearly identified. Count Sylvester of Marsico died at some point between 1162 and 1166; perhaps his son stayed in Marsico while his father was residing in Palermo as a member of the royal *curia* and had not been able to go to Sicily in order to receive properly his father's comital title beforehand. William of Marsico inherited his father's lordships on the island, as he is much later recorded as lord of Ragusa.[40] William of Marsico was mentioned in 1168 as the overlord of Laverius, priest of Marsico, in his condition as count and son of Count Silvester.[41] It is clear that the county of Marsico was inherited by Sylvester's son William, and that the confirmation, and possibly the appointment ceremony, of his comital dignity took place in 1167.

Richard of Say, on the other hand, had been attested in Palermo by Pseudo-Falcandus, pursuing the annulment of his marriage with the sister of Bartholomew of Parisio so he could marry the niece of the archbishop of Capua. According to Pseudo-Falcandus, Richard of Say had remained unshakeably loyal and never deserted the king as 'captain and master constable for Apulia' (*Apuliae capitaneus et magister comestabulus*). The title of 'master constable' (*magister comestabulus*) must have referred to his position as general of the royal army on the mainland, both during the last insurgency and when William I sent his army to assist Pope Alexander III in 1165, and was equivalent to the title of 'great constable' (*magnus comestabulus*) that Gilbert of Gravina once held. It is unclear, however, why Pseudo-Falcandus would have given Richard of Say the title of 'captain' (*capitaneus*). Although, it is certain that Richard was by no means a 'master captain' or governor for Apulia and the Terra di Lavoro, in that not only Pseudo-Falcandus overtly used the adjective *magister* uniquely and specifically for his condition as 'constable', but there is also no evidence that he exercised such responsibility or employed that title. Perhaps the distinction of 'captain' used by Pseudo-Falcandus reminisced Richard of Say's previous gubernatorial role for Calabria as both master justiciar and constable for that province. We know for sure that Richard of Say received the county of Fondi, as Pseudo-Falcandus explicitly explained that, due to his loyalty, the regent queen received him favourably in Palermo and invested him with the county of Richard of Aquila, the exiled count of Fondi.[42] The lands of the county of Fondi were invaded as soon as William I died, and the incursion was led by Andrew of Rupecanina and Richard of Aquila himself. Consequently, the responsibility of the new county must have included the mobilization of the local knights to resist the Capuan exiled counts and protect the realm's gates between the province of Capua and the papal Campania. Richard of Say's previous experience as both a general of the royal armed forces and an envoy to the papal Campania must have been one of the central reasons why, of all vacant comital seats, he received the county of Fondi. Also, given the strategic importance of the county of Fondi discussed before,[43] the appointment of an experienced and reliable commander to his county would seem a sensible move.

This was the rapidly changing scenario taking place in the Sicilian royal *curia* and the nobility of the kingdom. But as if things were not escalating quickly enough already, things went from turbulent to uncontrollable yet again: Stephen of Perche, another relative of the queen, was appointed chancellor of the realm.

The chancellor from Perche and the count from Navarre

The chancellorship of Stephen of Perche opened the door for the asymmetric power on the mainland, unleashed first with the appointments of Gilbert of Gravina and Richard of Mandra, to be resolved in the midst of incipient conspiracies and rebellions taking place on the island of Sicily. Pseudo-Falcandus, and to a much lesser extent Romuald of Salerno, have provided a detailed image of the activities and conspiracies that took place in Sicily during Stephen's chancellorship.

Chancellor Stephen, a relative of the regent queen, Margaret of Navarre, did not come from Navarre, but from the county of Perche, between Normandy and Maine. Stephen of Perche was, according to Pseudo-Falcandus, the son of the count of Perche, Rotrou [II] (d. 1144), making him a paternal uncle of Count Gilbert of Gravina.[44] As was pointed out before, Gilbert was a grandson of Count Rotrou II of Perche, who had participated in the crusade led by King Alfonso of Aragón and Navarre and acted as a lord of Tudela between 1123 and 1133. Although one cannot be completely certain of who Count Gilbert's father was, he must have been fathered by Count Rotrou while he stayed south of the Pyrenees – it has been hypothesized that his name was Bertram.[45] Furthermore, Pseudo-Falcandus confirms these familial ties when he subsequently relates that Stephen of Perche, on his way to Sicily, had stopped with the count of Gravina, 'his brother's son', who gave Stephen many gifts and briefed him about the state of affairs at the *curia*.[46] The chronicle of the archbishop of Salerno, by contrast, just mentions that Stephen was the son of the count of Perche and a blood-relative of the queen, without any overt relation to Gilbert of Gravina. However, Romuald's chronicle summarized Stephen's presence in Sicily by saying that, in a very short space of time, the chancellor from Perche, whose subsequent election as archbishop of Palermo was arranged soon thereafter, 'had become so favoured and close to the [minor] king and queen that he administered the whole kingdom as he wished'.[47] Since the regent queen was herself the daughter of Margaret of L'Aigle, niece of Count Rotrou II, Stephen of Perche and Queen Margaret were hence cousins once removed.[48]

Stephen of Perche's first records as chancellor are dubious. A November 1166 charter for the monastery of St Mary of Nardò that records Stephen as chancellor, edited in Coleti's *addenda* to *Italia Sacra*, is an eighteenth-century forgery.[49] Moreover, it is clear from the surviving testimonies of Pseudo-Falcandus, and Romuald's chronicle, that Stephen arrived in the kingdom in 1167. A second royal charter given in Palermo by Chancellor Stephen in August 1167, by which King William II granted the destroyed *castrum* of Montecorvino to Archbishop Romuald of Salerno, appears to be a falsification in the form of an original.[50] The most recent editor of the document, Giordano, provides a comprehensive list of the palaeographic characteristics that sustain the forgery hypothesis. In addition, Giordano has indicated other elements in favour of this suggestion, such as the absence of the title *notarius domini regis* to indicate the scribe of the royal document;[51] and the presence of an 'f' on the *verso* of the parchment that seems to be the abbreviation for *falsum*.[52] What we do not know is whether this document was an outright fabrication or an 'improved', retrospective version of a genuine original. By November 1167, Stephen was archbishop-elect of

Palermo, and his appointment to his position had already been made *c.* July.⁵³ Although it is impossible to pinpoint exactly and accurately the month in which Stephen started to exercise his chancellorship, it is very probable that he became chancellor in the summer of 1167.

The superior role taken by Chancellor Stephen is clearly confirmed by Pseudo-Falcandus. Reportedly, the regent queen ordered that all the business of the *curia* should first of all be brought to the new chancellor in the first place (*iussit ut universa curiae negotia deinceps ad eum principaliter referrentur*). Additionally, it was noted that Stephen undertook 'the burden and the honour of presiding the royal *curia*, only after the queen, after having attained two of the great dignities of the kingdom [chancellorship and the archbishopric of Palermo]' (*duas regni maximas dignitates adeptus, totius curie post reginam onus et honorem suscepit*), and 'the foremost position of power and government of the entire realm' (*potestatis prerogativa et totius regni cura*). This caused a negative reaction, as the magnates of the *curia* complained about Stephen's appointment, 'saying that it was a disgrace that this foreign-born boy had occupied the highest position of the court' (*dicentes indignum esse puerum hunc alienigenam, maximis curiae dignitatibus occupatis*).⁵⁴ Hence, a foreigner but a relative of the queen had precipitously become the head of the royal government.

Another blood-relative of the queen had arrived in the kingdom and was staying in Palermo by this time; Henry, Margaret's natural brother, received the county of Montescaglioso, which used to belong to Geoffrey of Lecce, and the hand of one of the daughters of Roger II.⁵⁵ We are told by Pseudo-Falcandus that this other 'Spaniard' relative brought with him many 'Spanish' knights and that he was never recognized by the king of Navarre, García Ramírez, as his son. Moreover, this apparent illegitimate son of the king of Navarre was originally named Rodrigo, but this was a name that 'the Sicilians did not like because it was unknown to them and laughed at as barbarous; so the queen told him to call himself Henry'.⁵⁶ The mainland was left again on the margins of the narrative focus of the surviving testimonies. The peninsular aristocracy did appear to have played a leading and active role in the kingdom's affairs, but this time the noblemen from the peninsula were the ones who meddled in the Sicilian *curia*, and not the other way around.

As expected, important changes took place under Stephen's administration. After Richard of Mandra, the former chief constable of the king's military entourage (a position which Pseudo-Falcandus refers to under the title of *magister comestabulus*), was made count of Molise, Berengarius was appointed as the new chief constable of the royal *curia*. This appointment, however, must have been transitory, because we are told by Pseudo-Falcandus that Stephen put Roger of Tiron in Berengarius's place when the latter went away across the Straits of Messina to visit the lands that the *curia* had granted to him.⁵⁷ According to the *Quaternus*, Berengarius of Gisay (also attested as Peregrinus of Giso) regarded as a 'constable' (*comestabulus*) had acquired Viggiano, and held *Sarconem* and *Pertecara*, all *feuda* located in the Agri valley (south of modern Basilicata).⁵⁸ For Berengarius to have been recorded in the *Quaternus* both as a 'constable' and a baron with holdings in southern Apulia, he must have been appointed chief constable of the royal household soon enough after Richard of Mandra and Bertram, son of Gilbert, were made counts. On the other hand, Roger of Tiron was a descendant of a family that originally came from modern Thiron-Gardais (dép. Eure-et-Loir, cant. Nogent-le-Rotrou), in the region of Perche, and that held lands in Sicily, near Vizzini, and in Calabria, in the Stilo region.[59] Although Pseudo-Falcandus does not elaborate on the reaction that this replacement caused directly, it must have been seen negatively by the Apulian aristocracy and, of course, by the replaced Apulian baron.

Pseudo-Falcandus expands on the reported dissent that arose on the mainland, as he explains that while intrigue was developing in the Sicilian territories, another conspiracy was being formed in Apulia, supported by a large party aggrieved by Richard of Mandra's sudden elevation to a pinnacle of so much honour – 'the most noble county of Molise' (*nobilissimus Molisii comitatus*).[60] In other words, the other counts did not like the idea of having a lesser baron, who had been a military commander (constable) on the sides of both the rebel Count Robert of Loritello and the Sicilian *curia*, among their rank. This is the first-known testimony of the upper aristocracy's opposition to the creation of a count, and the first occasion that a lesser baron from a questionably loyal past had been elevated to the peninsular nobility; previously, the kingdom's counts were either members of noble families (old counts or royalty) or loyal royalist allies. Regardless of how impressed and grateful William I could have been after Richard of Mandra saved his life during the attempted coup d'état, the former combatants who witnessed the insurrection on the mainland must have remembered his role as constable of Robert of Loritello. Pseudo-Falcandus does not name all the leaders of this new conspiracy, but he identified several of them: Count Bohemund of Manopello, William of Gesualdo and Richard of Balvano.[61] Remarkably, Bohemund is the only count clearly identified as a conspirator by Pseudo-Falcandus, but it is hard to believe that he would have been the only count who opposed Richard of Mandra. This Richard of Balvano must have been the son of Gilbert of Balvano recorded in the Quaternus, whose military service was originally declared (when his father Gilbert was still alive) to the *curia regis* by his cousin, Philip of Balvano.[62] Gilbert of Balvano was a peninsular baron who had acted as an official of the Sicilian royal government, as he is attested as one of the 'royal justiciars' who were present in 1149 in a court held at Melfi, presided by Chancellor Robert (of Selby).[63] Richard's father Gilbert of Balvano was also recorded as a *comestabulus* in the *Quaternus* c. 1150, whose *comestabulia* comprised a region with two core areas: the lands east of Avellino and the lordships around Conza.[64] Although it is not clear whether Richard's cousin Philip of Balvano had been created count by this stage, the fact that Pseudo-Falcandus named Richard and not Philip may indicate either that the counts of Apulia were keeping a low profile during this conspiracy or that Philip had not yet acquired the comital dignity. Be that as it may, the figure which these conspirators were inciting as the spearhead of their movement was the queen's brother Henry, the recently appointed count of Montescaglioso.

We are told by Pseudo-Falcandus that the conspirators drove Count Henry of Montescaglioso by telling him that he had more right to be in charge of the kingdom's administration, in that he was both the queen's brother and the king's uncle. Count Henry armed his Spanish knights, and then crossed over to Sicily, accompanied by the barons explicitly mentioned earlier as some of the leaders of the conspiracy. However, Chancellor Stephen managed to defuse the entire situation, making Count Henry's associates return to Apulia, winning the favour of Count Bohemund of Manopello and keeping an appeased Henry with him in Palermo.[65] Turmoil was, nevertheless, far from coming to an end. The peninsular nobility had another chance to clash against the Sicilian establishment in Messina.

The counts' ambitions in Messina

According to Pseudo-Falcandus, on 15 November 1167, the king and his entourage set off for Messina. Conversely, Romuald Guarna's chronicle recorded that the king and the queen, together with the magnates of the *curia*, went to Messina around Christmas (1167).[66] The first royal charters issued by William II in Messina were in January 1168. The first one was given on 7 January to the Greek monastery of SS. Elias and Anastasius, in Val Sinni (northern Calabria, now southern Basilicata).[67] The second Messina charter was issued on 18 January to another Greek monastery, St Philip in Val Demone (northwestern Sicily).[68] In his narrative surrounding the court at Messina, Pseudo-Falcandus relates many tensions and conspiracies, not only providing many details but also constructing a reality that fits classical rhetorical models (notably Sallust and Plutarch). It is neither useful nor pertinent to the current exploration to discuss Pseudo-Falcandus's intertextuality or to focus too much on the alleged speeches delivered by courtiers and nobles during these sessions. What is relevant to this study is the prosopographical information provided for the peninsular nobility and the concrete confrontations in which they were involved.

The noblemen who were attested in Messina by Pseudo-Falcandus are Count Gilbert of Gravina, Count Robert of Caserta with his son, Count Roger of Tricarico, Count Bohemund of Manopello, Count Roger of Avellino, Count Henry of Montescaglioso, Count Simon of Sangro, an obscure and unattested Count Roger 'of Gerace' and, of course, Count Richard of Molise. There is no further evidence of this so-called count of Gerace; he was one of the several otherwise unattested characters upon which the anonymous author incautiously assigned the title of count. Gerace is a town in southern Calabria, and since the Calabrian documentation is very fragmented and scarce, it could be possible for such an important lord as the bearer of the comital title to have escaped record in that area.[69] However, unlike the case of Squillace, there is no subsequent evidence that would reveal the existence of a count of Gerace at any time in the kingdom of Sicily.

One of the matters that was attended to during this Messina court was a land dispute among the S. Severino kin-group. William of S. Severino, this time remembered as the cousin of Robert of Lauro, count of Caserta, had recently been recalled from exile, and was occupying *feuda* that Robert of Lauro was claiming to be legally his.[70] This is the same William of S. Severino, son of Fenicia of S. Severino, who earlier Pseudo-Falcandus remembered as the brother-in-law of Roger of Aquila, count of Avellino, and who in 1162 fled the kingdom to avoid the king's anger when the latter marched across the peninsula.[71] William of S. Severino was recorded in the *Quaternus* as son of Henry of S. Severino and lord of S. Severino, a *feudum* of eight *milites*, Rocca

Cilento, a *feudum* of six *milites*, and Montoro, a *feudum* of thirteen *milites*.[72] According to Pseudo-Falcandus, Count Robert of Caserta approached the court to argue that Montoro and the *castrum* of S. Severino and 'other towns' (perhaps referring to Rocca Cilento) were being held by William, and that 'William's father had taken control of these illegally and by force' (*Willelmi pater iniuste ac violenter eadem [Montorium et castrum Sancti Severini ceteraque opida] possedisse*).[73] William's father Henry of S. Severino was a baron active in the northern region of the former principality of Salerno, and a benefactor of Cava and Montevergine, between 1125 and 1157.[74] Henry is attested as lord of S. Severino and Montoro in March 1125.[75] Nothing is known about his death, but in March 1157 his widow Fenicia was recorded as the head of the S. Severino *feuda*.[76] It is clear then that Henry of S. Severino was the lord originally recorded in the 1150 *quaterniones* of the military levy and that his son William was added into the *Quaternus c.* 1167–8, after the regent queen and the royal *curia* had pardoned the first group of exiled counts. This means that the royal administration had acknowledged William of S. Severino as the lord of these three *feuda* during Queen Margaret's regency. Consequently, the allegation that Robert of Lauro, count of Caserta, was making about the unlawful holding of these lands by Henry of S. Severino was indeed a challenge to the inheritance of the S. Severino domains that occurred before the kingdom was founded, in 1125.[77] It took more than forty years for Robert of Lauro, grandson of Roger of S. Severino, to confront the descendants of Henry in an old but seemingly dormant family inheritance feud.

The case presented by Count Robert of Caserta against his cousin William of S. Severino did not prosper, as Pseudo-Falcandus reported that Chancellor Stephen did not want William, whom he knew was a 'loyal supporter' (*fideles sibi [Stephano]*), to sustain any loss. Hence, the royal *curia* 'restored' to William of S. Severino his inheritance, which can be attested in the *Quaternus* as William's lordships. However, Stephen of Perche did not want to give Count Robert of Caserta an excuse for causing trouble, so he arranged for Robert to be granted other land in Apulia, on the condition that the matter of William's inheritance would never be contested again.[78] The *Quaternus* records a *feudum* of only three *milites*, composed of two towns, Mandra and Pulcarino, as belonging to Count Robert of Caserta; Mandra does not exist today and has not been identified yet, but Pulcarino (modern Villanova del Battista) is located southeast of the county of Buonalbergo.[79] This entry is a separate record from both the section for the county of Caserta and the entry for Lauro, Robert's original lordship.[80] Moreover, it is clear that this dual *feudum* was neither within the county of Caserta nor in the proximity of the *feudum* of Lauro. Consequently, it is safe to assume that Mandra and Pulcarino were the Apulian lands which, according to Pseudo-Falcandus, were granted to Count Robert of Caserta at Messina in 1168.[81] Lauro was officially (i.e. according to the *Quaternus*) located within the province of the principality of Capua, though adjacent to its southern border with the former principality of Salerno, north of Sarno and west of Avellino. Hence, even if the *feudum* granted was much smaller than the S. Severino lordships, it definitely gave Robert, a Capuan lord and count, the tactical advantage of having a foothold in the Irpina region. Thanks to the conciliatory nature of Chancellor Stephen's position, the count of Caserta was able to at least expand his dominions into central Apulia.

Count Gilbert of Gravina did not go to Messina unaccompanied, as we are told by Pseudo-Falcandus that he brought 100 of the best knights of Apulia and the Terra di Lavoro (*de nominatissimis Apulie ac Terre Laboris militibus multis cognitos bellis elegerit*) – as the master captain on the mainland, this must have been an easy task for Gilbert to coordinate.[82] The chronicle of Archbishop Romuald also recorded that Count Gilbert of Gravina, remembered as the blood-relative of both the chancellor and the queen, and the master captain of all Apulia (*regine et cancellarii consanguineus, qui tunc capitaneus erat totius Apulie*), arrived in Messina with a large force of knights (*cum magna manu Militum*). We are also told by Romuald's chronicle that Count Gilbert 'advised' Chancellor Stephen to arrest his nephew Count Henry of Montescaglioso and imprison him on the other side of the Messina straits, in Reggio Calabria. He was later accused of having plotted the deaths of the count of Gravina and the chancellor.[83] Contrastingly, Pseudo-Falcandus relates that Count Gilbert was instead summoned by Stephen of Perche, alongside Count Bohemund of Manopello and Count Roger of Avellino, to be briefed on the whole affair related to an alleged plot led by Count Henry of Montescaglioso, the regent queen's brother, against Chancellor Stephen. However, Count Henry resumed not only his opposition against Stephen of Perche but also his demand for a better political position. According to Pseudo-Falcandus, Henry claimed that 'the county of Montescaglioso could not meet his expenses and financial distress, and he asked to be granted either the principality of Taranto or the "county" that Count Simon [son of Henry del Vasto] had once held in Sicily' (*comitatum Montis Caveosi sumptibus vel angustiis non posse sufficere, petiitque principatum Tarenti vel comitatum quem in Sicilia Symon comes olim tenuerat sibi concede*).[84] Again, one ought to be very careful when reading Pseudo-Falcandus's words here.

It is possible that Henry of Montescaglioso, the king's uncle, may have requested the princely title, which before had only been used as an appanage for a junior member of the royal family; as far as we know, this title had only been used by William I while his two older brothers were still alive, and each had the titles of duke of Apulia and prince of Capua, and by Simon, the illegitimate son of Roger II. Up to this point, the title of 'prince of Taranto' was created *ex novo c.* 1140 as a royal distinction but a legal nullity. The principality of Taranto never formed a specific administrative division, and its title did not carry any specific land tenure or authority over an actual province or delimited district. Apart from the prestige that this princely title had, this appanage must have consisted of a gift of money for the maintenance of the prince, which might have come from the south Apulian lordships that some barons held directly from the king.[85] Likewise, when Pseudo-Falcandus talks of the 'county that Count Simon used to held in Sicily', this does not mean there was a county within the island, but, as explained earlier, instead referred to Butera and Paternò lordships that Henry del Vasto, Roger II's maternal uncle, and then his son Simon, had held in Sicily. The comital dignity these two enjoyed was associated with their Sicilian estates, but this did not imply that these lands were organized in the same manner as counties. Additionally, the former count of Montescaglioso, Geoffrey of Lecce, was also a landholder in Sicily; Geoffrey has been attested as patron of the church of the Holy Spirit in Caltanissetta, and by Pseudo-Falcandus as lord of Caltanissetta, Noto and Sclàfani.[86] There is no available evidence on Henry's Sicilian possessions, and it is unclear if the new count of Montescaglioso was also granted Geoffrey's lordships in Sicily, but perhaps the petition alleged by Pseudo-Falcandus echoed an actual case presented by Count Henry, in order to hold the entire estate once held by the former count of Montescaglioso.

The situation escalated rapidly, and Henry of Montescaglioso was accused by Gilbert himself of being both a disturber of the realms and a rebel against the royal majesty and was subsequently kept under guard within the palace. The chancellor ordered both Gilbert's knights and his own to assemble in front of the palace, which scared off the Spaniard's knights, supporters of Henry of Montescaglioso – a large number of them seem later to have perished in the snow in the forest of Sila, a mountain range in southern Calabria. In this way, Stephen of Perche used his nephew, Count Gilbert, to neutralize the regent queen's brother, Count Henry. Gilbert of Gravina, however, did not stay idle, and in return he attempted to use the court to push his own agenda. We are told by Pseudo-Falcandus that the time had come for Gilbert to settle a pending score with Count Richard of Molise.[87] Count Gilbert did not stand alone in his fight against Richard of Mandra; Bohemund II of Tarsia and Count Robert of Caserta publicly spoke against the count of Molise. Bohemund II of Tarsia was the son of the former Count Bohemund of Manopello, who had been removed of his authority and county in disgrace after having been defeated by Robert of Loritello; William I had imprisoned the defeated count of Manopello in 1157.[88] After this, there is no further record for Bohemund I of Tarsia.

Since Richard of Mandra was the constable of the rebel count of Loritello, and the former was almost certainly involved in the military conflict that caused Bohemund of Tarsia's disgrace, his son must have seen this as an opportunity to take revenge. Hence, Bohemund II of Tarsia testified against Richard of Mandra, accusing him of having acted disloyally towards the *familiares* of the *curia*. Similarly, Robert of Lauro, count of Caserta, claimed that Richard of Mandra had illegally occupied (*invadere*) and secretly held Mandra, as well as some of the other towns belonging to the king in the territory of Troia. Count Richard of Molise replied that Qaid Peter, the previous highest-ranking royal *familiaris*, had conceded Mandra to him in exchange for an annual fee, and that the Troian towns were given to him by Turgisius, the [royal] 'chamberlain' (*camerarius*) of that territory.[89] We already know from the *Quaternus* that Mandra, together with Pulcarino, was later held as a *feudum* by Count Robert of Caserta and that these towns were presumably granted during this time at Messina.[90] Robert of Lauro's grievance reinforces the assumption that Mandra and Pulcarino were the lands given to him in return for dropping his claim over the S. Severino inheritances, not only because these towns would have been available to be given as part of the royal possessions in Apulia but also because this reveals the special interest the count of Caserta had in Mandra. Conversely, Richard of Mandra must have been especially interested in holding Mandra as well, the town of his namesake, as Richard's origins must have been connected to this town.

Even more interesting is the mechanism that Pseudo-Falcandus attests for Richard of Mandra's sentencing. The accusations had been made before the royal *familiares*, the royal officials and the noblemen gathered at the open court. These noblemen also heard Richard's response and even questioned Chamberlain Turgisius, who happened to also be at the Messina gathering. Subsequently, we are told that

> all the nobles, with the exception of the *familiares* of the *curia*, were ordered to withdraw in order to bring a judicial sentence on these charges that had been made against the count [Richard]. The following were those who rose to pass judgment: Bohemund, count of Manopello; Robert of Lauro, count of Caserta; his son Roger, count of Tricarico; Roger, count of Avellino; Simon, count of Sangro; Roger, count of Gerace; Roger of Tiron, master constable [of the royal guard]; and Florius of Camerota; as well as the master justiciars Tarentinus the judge and Abdenago, son of Hannibal.[91]

It is not clear who actually ordered the nobles (*proceres*) to withdraw, but it would be safe to assume that it was Queen Margaret who instructed for the verdict to be delivered. The king's *familiares* were also instructed to recuse themselves from the sentencing, which reveals a very interesting insight into both the kingdom's judicial procedures and the prerogatives of the upper aristocracy. It appears hence that a nobleman could only be judged by his peers and that the ecclesiastical figures and palace employees were excluded from this process; the other *familiares* of the king's *curia* were Bishop-elect Richard, Matthew the notary, Qaid Richard and Qaid Martin.[92] However, even though the *familiares* excluded themselves, royal authority was still present among the jury with Roger of Tiron, Florius of Camerota and the master justiciars; none of them were upper aristocracy, and only Florius came from the mainland. Florius of Camerota became a key player on the peninsula as a justiciar and constable, but he was not a major baron or an overlord – one of Florius's *feuda* was held *in servitio* from William of S. Severino.[93] Consequently, Florius's presence in court and on this jury must have been the result of his role as a royal official on the mainland.[94] Also, since Florius was an experienced royal justiciar, he could have been considered an expert by both the *curia* and the nobles.

We are also told by Pseudo-Falcandus that Count Bohemund proclaimed the jury's judgement, 'in the presence of the king and on behalf of all and with their approval', and that Bohemund forbade Count Richard to reply that the verdict was unjust or false, as 'this insult reflected not on them, who had delivered the verdict, but on the crown'.[95] It is clear, hence, that Richard of Mandra was judged by the other counts, although this judgement was reinforced by four legal officials, representing the royal administration. This reveals the importance and relevance that comital authority had even in the presence of the monarch and the royal *curia*, in that neither Chancellor Stephen nor Queen Margaret herself was able to use the royal prerogative to dismiss the charges brought against the recently appointed count of Molise. Richard's new status as a count implied a requirement that he needed to be judged by his own peers, which allowed Count Robert of Caserta to be both accuser and juror in this instance. Count Gilbert's absence is conspicuous, although he was not a member of the court's *familiares*. Perhaps also his superior position as 'master captain' for Apulia and the Terra di Lavoro, and the fact that he had verbally attacked Richard of Mandra before, forced him to keep a low profile during the entire process.

The verdict delivered against Richard of Mandra basically ratified the accusation made against him, placing him at the king's mercy with regard to the lands that he held in secret, after Qaid Peter had fled the kingdom, and for those others that he occupied on his own authority, contrary to the loyalty he owed to the monarchy. However, the counts did not appear to have set the penalty, but instead the archbishops and bishops present were ordered to decide a just penalty, not only for the verdict that confirmed his unlawful occupation of land but also for contempt – he insulted the crown by saying that the court's judgement was false. The ecclesiastical figures decreed, 'in accordance to the constitutions of the Kingdom of Sicily' (*iuxta Constitutiones regum Siciliae decreverunt*), that Count Richard was liable with respect for both the lands he held and his limbs and body. Consequently, Count Richard was arrested and ordered to be taken to Taormina (in Sicily).[96] Romuald of Salerno's chronicle summarized the whole affair by only recording that, about the time when Count Henry was arrested, Count Richard of Molise, among some other lesser barons, was also arrested and imprisoned.[97] There is no known contemporary provision that would overtly stipulate that in the kingdom of Sicily the verdict of a noble charged of a crime should be delivered by his peers, or that the sentence must be decided by churchmen. However, the role exercised here by the archbishops and bishops can be explained on the grounds that contempt against the court's judgement was considered sacrilege. The collections of laws that contain the legislation of Roger II stipulates what ought to be considered to be sacrilege; the relevant articles on committing sacrilege read:

Cod. Vat. Lat. 8782
Art. 17. Concerning Sacrileges. There should be no dispute about the judgement, purposes, decrees or deeds of the king; for it is comparable to sacrilege to dispute his judgements, decrees, deeds and purposes, or to dispute whether the king chosen or appointed [official] is worthy. Many laws have punished sacrilege most severely, but the penalty must be moderated by the decision of the one who is judging, unless perhaps the temples of God have been openly and violently despoiled, or gifts and sacred vessels have been stolen at night, for in that case the crime is capital.

Cod. Cassinese 868
Art. 11. Concerning Sacrilegious Purposes. There should be no dispute about the judgements, purposes, decrees or deeds of the king; such dispute is deemed the same as sacrilege. Many laws have punished sacrilege most severely, but the penalty must be moderated by the decision of the one who is judging, unless perhaps the temple of God has been openly and violently despoiled, or gifts and sacred vessels have been stolen at night, for in that case the crime is capital.[98]

From the first sentence, the law appears to have been taken from Justinian's *Codex*, book 9, title 29, article 3.[99] However, the Sicilian legislation significantly altered the original statute, not only in shape but also in content, as the original referred only to the emperor's administrative appointments – the preceding statute speaks generally of observing the divine law and the following one specifically refers to the provincial offices appointed by the emperor. In the Sicilian instance, sacrilege is being paired with any sort of judicial action taken in the name of the crown; the version of the Montecassino text does not even elaborate on the crime being extended to the king's appointees. Furthermore, the Rogerian statute explicitly contextualized the dispute against royal judgement with the actual desecration of churches, although with the provision that the former should not be punished as severely as the latter. Regardless of the actual extent to which Roman law influenced the Sicilian legislation, it is clear that arguing against the resolution or deliberation of a royally sanctioned body was legally considered sacrilege. Hence, this could explain why the ecclesiastical leaders present were ordered ultimately to sentence Count Richard of Molise.

After Count Richard had been temporarily neutralized in this way, Pseudo-Falcandus reports that another count was appointed during the Messina court: Hannibal of Celano.[100] This Abruzzese count was approved to inherit the comital dignity and lands of his father, Count Rainulf of Celano, who had probably died shortly before 1168.[101] Count Hannibal was thus the third Abruzzese count present in the royal court at Messina; the others were Bohemund of Manopello and Simon of Sangro.

The count of Gravina was not done yet, however; before the king left Messina, Gilbert of Gravina had one more ambition to satisfy. We are told by Pseudo-Falcandus that Count Gilbert was emboldened by the fact that the chancellor had survived his enemies thanks to him, and that no danger remained, and as a result he put in a request to the *curia* that he be given the county of Loritello.[102] It is not made clear in Pseudo-Falcandus's narrative whether or not Gilbert was in fact granted all the lands that the then exiled Robert Bassunvilla used to hold as both count of Conversano and Loritello. Romuald of Salerno's chronicle, in contrast, recorded that the royal *curia* did indeed grant Gilbert the notorious county of Loritello. We are told by Romuald of Salerno that Gilbert obtained the county of Loritello 'with everything belonging to it' (*comitatum Loritelli cum omnibus suis pertinentiis*), and he did so 'on the advice and with the help' of Chancellor Stephen (*consilio et auxilio cancellarii*).[103] Again, it is unclear whether this 'county of Loritello' also comprised the lands of the county of Conversano, which had previously been held by Robert II of Bassunvilla. Whichever may be the case, the *magister capitaneus* had left Messina and returned to the mainland as the new double count: Gilbert, count of Loritello and Gravina.

Pseudo-Falcandus added that, by taking the county of Loritello, Count Gilbert provoked the jealousy and the relentless animosity of the nobles and cities of Apulia, because Gilbert had thus obstructed the reinstatement of Robert II of Bassunvilla, whose return they all very keenly wanted.[104] There is no further evidence on this alleged romanticizing of the former and exiled count of Loritello and Conversano, or if there had been some negotiations between the royal *curia* and Robert of Loritello before. Nevertheless, the other nobles must have been at least sceptical and weary of all the political and economic power Queen Margaret's second cousin had amassed in two years of the queen's regency. Reminiscing the former count of Loritello and Conversano, the new count of Loritello and Gravina became the strongman of the south Italian peninsula. This time, the tenure of two counties came alongside one of the most important appointments of the royal government on the peninsula, as he had become the master captain of Apulia and the Terra di Lavoro. This was the first time since the creation of the kingdom that a high-profile nobleman occupied the position equivalent to a royal governor on the mainland. From being count of Gravina, to becoming the *magister comestabulus* and *magister capitaneus totius Apulie*, and then being granted the county of Loritello, Gilbert used both his relationship to the queen and the position he was given as a general to intervene in the affairs of the royal *curia*. He then used his influence in the Sicilian government to enhance and consolidate his authority as a prominent member of the kingdom's nobility. The endgame here emerges, and just as the count of Loritello and Conversano attempted to do before him, Count Gilbert aimed to exercise his authority over the mainland, above the other counts, and separately from Sicilian control. The zenith of Count Gilbert's career was nevertheless ephemeral; he is recorded to have been expelled from the realm in the year after he became the governor in Apulia.

A comital takeover: Richard of Molise and Henry of Montescaglioso

In the spring of 1168, William II and Margaret, together with their entourage, returned to Palermo. With regard to the regent queen's brother, Count Henry of Montescaglioso, Pseudo-Falcandus relates that the queen decided to give him 1,000 ounces of gold, and to arrange his transportation from the fortress of Reggio, where he was being held captive, back to Spain. After this, Pseudo-Falcandus recorded that the king left Messina on 12 March, and reached Palermo on 20 March.[105] Likewise, Romuald's chronicle reports that the chancellor, together with the king and queen, was back in Palermo around Easter (which in 1168 fell on 31 March).[106] The last surviving royal charters issued at Messina in 1168 were given by Chancellor Stephen in March, but the specific dates are not attested. First, William I and his mother Queen Margaret granted exportation privileges (i.e. an exemption from paying *plateaticum* or *portaticum*) that allowed the monks of St Mary de Latina at Jerusalem to export specific and limited goods from Messina to Jerusalem. Also, they confirmed the said house's possessions and privileges.[107] According to a third royal charter, the monarchs granted Casale del Conte (modern Torregrotta) to the nunnery of St Mary of Scala at Messina.[108] The end of their stay in Messina, however, came with yet another period of turmoil.

Another rebellion broke out in Sicily just after the counts of Montescaglioso and Molise were arrested and imprisoned. Without having to go into the details provided by Pseudo-Falcandus about the palace conspiracy against Stephen of Perche, it is important to highlight how the unfolding of this rebellion affected the composition of the aristocracy. The *Chronicon* of the archbishop of Salerno reported that, during the Octave of Easter of 1168, the people of Messina rose in rebellion and went to Reggio to free Count Henry of Montescaglioso, and to Taormina, on the Sicilian east coast, to release Count Richard of Molise from the prison.[109] We are also told by Pseudo-Falcandus that, during the uprising in Messina, the Greeks were busy slaughtering anyone from north of the Alps they could find, until Count Henry forbade this by threatening to punish them. After this, the people of Messina occupied Rometta (west of Messina) and approached Taormina (south of Messina) to set free Count Richard of Molise; afterwards, the people of Messina took control of the castle (*castellum*) of Taormina and of the count himself.[110] This Sicilian rebellion managed thus to quickly release the counts disgraced in Messina, but the unrest had still to take one more victim.

After having heard of this uprising, the people of Palermo also rioted, and attacked and cornered Chancellor Stephen and all his men. The regent queen and young William

II had to intervene, ordering the chancellor and his transalpine allies to leave the kingdom by sea; he then boarded a ship and sailed to (the kingdom of) Jerusalem.[111] According to Pseudo-Falcandus, the otherwise unattested Count Roger of Gerace and the very well-known Count Roger of Avellino participated in the conspiracy against Chancellor Stephen.[112] This suggests that the count of Avellino, Roger of Aquila, did not return to his dominions, but instead had accompanied the king back to Palermo, and stayed there during the uprising of Messina. The last documented appearance of Roger of Aquila in Apulia before he went to Messina is found in an August 1167 donation he made in his *castellum* of Avellino. As count of Avellino, he granted two plots of land (*pecie de terries*), an orchard (*ortum*) in the church of St Basil, and a vineyard (*vinea*) in *Orrita*, near the *castellum* of Mercogliano, to the abbey of Montevergine, for the salvation of the souls of his parents Count Richard and Countess Magalda, and his wife Countess Marocta. Count Roger of Avellino's donation also stipulated that the same abbey had the right to take water from the 'public' aqueduct (*publicus aqueductus*) that came from Mercogliano; the use of public infrastructure in this sense, at least in the county of Avellino, was a comital prerogative.[113] Furthermore, we are told by Pseudo-Falcandus that Count Roger of Avellino kept riding up and down outside the royal palace in the midst of a city confused by rumours, and when the supporters of Qaid Richard saw him, they attacked him. The rioters were already pointing their spears at the count of Avellino when William II, who had gone to the palace windows to see what the ruckus was about, ordered the mob to bring the count to him unharmed. The king then ordered Count Roger of Avellino to be kept under close guard in the Castello a Mare.[114]

Chancellor Stephen's allies did not only include transalpine sympathizers, but, according to Pseudo-Falcandus, Bohemund II of Tarsia, his brother Carbonellus and William of S. Severino 'were always closely attached to Stephen' (*semper ei [Stephano] familiarius adherebant*).[115] Bohemund, who had testified against Richard of Mandra, and William of S. Severino, whose lordships were protected by the *curia*'s decision to dismiss the count of Caserta's accusation, must have known that the chancellor's enemies were their enemies as well. Perhaps this is the reason why William of S. Severino had not gone back to his Apulian dominions after the court of Messina was adjourned, and rather followed the royal *curia* and Chancellor Stephen to Palermo. The tension left after the arrest of counts Henry and Richard of Mandra, and the role that Count Robert of Caserta played during the Messina courts, might have pushed William of S. Severino to retreat temporarily in Sicily, regardless of whether the royal chancellor had confirmed his lordship over S. Severino, Montoro and Rocca Cilento.

After the upheaval and violence in Palermo escalated to the point that Stephen and his party were trapped inside a bell tower, we are told by Pseudo-Falcandus that the conspirators offered the chancellor terms for his surrender. It was agreed that the chancellor should sail to Syria in an armed galley with a few men of his choice, the other Frenchmen were to be given ships to cross the sea, and the noblemen of the kingdom of Sicily who were with the chancellor were to keep their lands safely and freely. That these terms would be fulfilled was sworn by Bishop-elect Richard of Syracuse, Matthew the notary, Qaid Richard, Archbishop Romuald of Salerno and Bishop John of Malta. Ultimately, Stephen of Perche left Sicily and made the journey safely to Syria.[116] Not only is Stephen's arrival in Jerusalem attested in the chronicle of Romuald of Salerno, but William of Tyre also recorded that, in the summer of 1168, Stephen of Perche arrived in the kingdom of Jerusalem attended by a small retinue. Stephen was thereby remembered as 'chancellor of the king of Sicily and bishop-elect of the church at Palermo, [...] a brother of Count Rotrou of Perche, and a young man of fine appearance and excellent natural ability' (*domini regis Sicilie cancellarius et Panormitane electus ecclesie, [...] domini Rotoldi comitis de Percio frater*). Stephen, however, was overcome by a serious illness after his arrival and died, according to William of Tyre; he was buried at Jerusalem with fitting honour, in a chapel of the *Templum Domini* (i.e. the Dome of the Rock, on the Temple Mount).[117] The life and career of the regent queen's relative, royal chancellor and archbishop-elect of Palermo was thus abruptly terminated.

Counts Richard of Molise and Henry of Montescaglioso went to Palermo upon their release, where, according to Romuald of Salerno, the king pardoned them and granted them their lands back.[118] Pseudo-Falcandus detailed their arrival: both counts arrived at Palermo with twenty-four armed galleys from Messina, relying on their power (*vires*) they altered the composition of the *curia*, and appointed ten *familiares*, three of whom were counts – Richard of Molise, Henry of Montescaglioso and the otherwise unattested Roger of Gerace.[119] The counts of Molise and Montescaglioso not only greatly expanded the number of royal *familiares* but also forced their own inclusion into this high-ranking royal council.

Under the new administration imposed by the queen regent's brother Henry and Richard of Mandra, Gilbert, the mainland's *magister capitaneus* and count of Gravina and Loritello, saw the end of his dominance. We are told simply by Archbishop Romuald Guarna's chronicle that after Chancellor Stephen left, Count Gilbert of Loritello, with his son Count Bertram of Andria and all his men, abjured their land, to then go to Jerusalem.[120] The *Annales Casinenses* likewise recorded that, in 1168, Count Gilbert (without making an overt mention of any of his counties) and his son Bertram were expelled from the kingdom, and went to Jerusalem.[121] This sudden and drastic withdrawal was a predictable result of the similarly sudden change in power at Palermo. Pseudo-Falcandus related that the first decision of the newly constituted *curia*, which was under the power of Richard of Molise and Henry of Montescaglioso, was to expel Count Gilbert of Gravina and his son Count Bertram from the realm. The royal *curia* also threatened Gilbert to use the kingdom's full force 'if he should resist by making use of force and gathering his knights' (*si viribus uti et militibus adunatis reniti presumpsisset*). Pseudo-Falcandus manifestly omitted many details of such a large and drastic operation, mostly compared with the previous testimonies of the events in Palermo just before Stephen left the kingdom. He only narrates that the matter was assigned to Roger, count of Alba, and Richard of Say, count of Fondi, who assembled accordingly 'an enormous army from all the cities of Apulia, and besieged Count Gilbert in a certain fortress to which he had retreated together with his wife'.[122]

It would have been very illustrative to the understanding of both Count Gilbert's activities and the development of the counties of Gravina and Loritello to have known the location of the fortress to which the count retreated during this reported siege. Likewise, it is notable that Richard of Say and Roger son of Richard, the recently appointed counts of Fondi and Alba, respectively, suddenly became Gilbert's royal replacements, in that they acquired what was the central entitlement of either the *magister comestabulus* or the *magister capitaneus*: assembling an army from the Apulian draft. Richard of Say had been in that position before, as he was a long-standing royal official, a general during William I's last uprising, and had commanded the royal army alongside the *magister comestabulus* Count Gilbert of Gravina in 1165. Roger son of Richard had also recently acquired the comital rank and had been involved with the Palermitan royal *curia* before. However, he joined the rebellion against William I's regime and been in exile just before 1167. Perhaps Richard of Mandra did not consider this to be a deterrent but instead a shared circumstance that could potentially serve as an incentive for Roger son of Richard to support his takeover.

Pseudo-Falcandus further explains that all the knights (*milites*) deserted Count Gilbert as soon as they heard the '*curia*'s order' (*curiae mandatum*) and that he had attracted a great deal of jealousy from the nobles and severe hatred from the cities. Consequently, Gilbert realized that there was no hope left, and then chose to submit himself, together with all his goods (*thesaurus*), to Count Richard of Fondi, on the agreement that Gilbert would be allowed to cross over to Syrian lands with his wife and children.[123] Hence, if we ought to believe Pseudo-Falcandus, all the knights in the peninsula were informed, bypassing the head of the structure that was put in place to control the knights. The knights' desertion could have operated that smoothly only if their lords and commanders had reached them without any regard for their master captain. In other words, the *comestabuli* and the counts must have almost unanimously tolerated Richard of Mandra and Henry of Montescaglioso's takeover, in order to have ignored Gilbert's royal title as master captain and, at the same time, have cornered a family that technically held the Adriatic corridor of lordships that extended from the border with the Abruzzo, in Loritello, all the way down to the Terra di Bari, with Gravina, Andria and, perhaps, Conversano. This must have made up the largest county in the kingdom thus far. Nonetheless, the great count of Gravina and Loritello, also the father of the count of Andria, was all of a sudden left powerless, cornered in a fortress.

The '*curia*'s order' could not have been the main reason behind the knights' desertion, in that even if these orders carried all the weight of the royal authority and its supremacy, a structure and mechanism were required for these orders to be transmitted and headed. The counts' rebellion during William I's reign clearly revealed how royal orders did not prevent the rebels from gathering their own knights and assembling their own armies in their war against the command of the Sicilian *curia*. If anything, the peninsular insurgencies demonstrated the vulnerability of the king's military appointments and the fleeting control the royal *curia* exercised over the nobility. Count Robert of Loritello was both supported by many counts and even acknowledged as their leader. The new count of Loritello, however, was not even slightly close to have been regarded in the same way. Like many of the royal favourites, the privileges that Count Gilbert had acquired so much and so swiftly had won him few allies and a lot of enemies; besides, he was an outsider. No other single episode could better illustrate the importance of the south Italian nobility and the role the counts collectively played in the effective control of the aristocracy than the swift removal of Gilbert, count of Gravina and Loritello and master captain for all Apulia and the Terra di Lavoro. Just as Count Gilbert had used the royal *curia* to push his own agenda and undermine Richard of Mandra, the latter used it to avenge his previous downfall and remove the man who appeared to be the most powerful count of the kingdom.

We cannot know for sure what the position and wishes of the monarch or the queen regent were. Pseudo-Falcandus is not explicit here, but it can be assumed that Queen Margaret would not have agreed on her own to attack and expel Stephen and Gilbert, both of whom were their blood-relatives. The royal *curia* was thus taken hostage by the opponents of the chancellor and the counts released by the mob of Messina. William of Tyre provides an external but useful perspective on this issue, as he explained that Stephen 'had been made the victim of a conspiracy on the part of the combined nobles of Sicily, who by their intrigues had succeeded in driving him from that land. This was done contrary to the wishes of the young king, a minor, and his mother, but they were powerless to prevent it.'[124] If William II and his mother Queen Margaret were indeed powerless, the counts of Molise and Montescaglioso, the new members of the kingdom's nobility, must have arranged an alliance with the already established nobility – including both the counts made by William I and the former rebel counts who were pardoned by the new regency – to counteract Count Gilbert.

The same counts who had sat in judgement against Richard of Mandra were now on his side; without Robert of Caserta and Roger of Avellino, the operation against the *magister capitaneus* could not have been possible. This, in hindsight, made political sense. Robert of Lauro, count of Caserta, must have been aware both of the power Gilbert had concentrated from his multiple appointments, and that the tables had turned in Palermo. Even though Robert of Caserta had testified against Richard of Mandra, changing sides should not have been a problem; guaranteeing the stability of the position he and his family enjoyed as counts, and perhaps also his tenure of Mandra, would have been incentive enough to support the takeover. Roger of Aquila, count of Avellino, had been involved before in Robert of Loritello's rebellion and then temporarily exiled during the last years of William I's reign, so he would have been inclined to support Richard of Mandra and oppose Gilbert, the master captain who rose into prominence after the rebel counts were exiled in 1162. The otherwise unattested Count Roger of Gerace was a member of the jury that condemned Richard of Mandra, but he was also involved in the conspiracy against Stephen of Perche, and as a result he had to associate with the leaders of the mob that facilitated the chancellor's expulsion. The other counts who were involved in Richard of Mandra's judgement were from the Abruzzo: Bohemund of Manopello and Simon of Sangro. They, together with Roger son of Richard for the time he held the county of Alba, appear to have been part of a new and increasingly significant role that the Abruzzo played in the kingdom's new equilibrium of power.

The other change made to the kingdom's upper aristocracy by the new *curia* dominated by Richard of Mandra and Henry of Montescaglioso was the attempted expulsion of Hugh Lupinus, count of Catanzaro. We are told by Pseudo-Falcandus that, after Gilbert's expulsion, the 'magnates of the *curia*' (i.e. Richard of Mandra and Henry of Montescaglioso, and their followers) decided to exile Count Hugh of Catanzaro, because he was a 'relative of the chancellor' (*cancellarii consanguineus*), but since Hugh reportedly was 'a stupid and violent man whom they feared as someone who would plot in secret or else undertake some reckless act on impulse', he was spared, hoping that by this Margaret's anger would be in some way restrained.[125] There is no certainty around this Calabrian county at this stage, but a July 1167 charter attests the presence of Countess Segelgarda and her daughter Clementia, administering what would have been her husband's ancestral land. Segelgarda was the wife of the late Count Rao of Catanzaro, and the mother of Countess Clementia, and it had been reported that both she and her daughter were imprisoned by William I when the latter marched over the mainland to recover control of the territory.[126]

Countess Segelgarda made a donation at her deathbed on 28 July 1167 to the church of St Christopher at Deliceto (*ecclesia sancti χpofori, quo est sita ante portam eliceti*), and she called herself 'once wife of R[ao] comitis' (*quondam uxor .R. comitis*).[127] Rao of Loritello, count of Catanzaro and Segelgarda's husband, held lands around Deliceto, lordships that used to be held by the Catanzaro branch of the Loritello family; Segelgarda also made a donation in September 1158, as the 'countess of Deliceto' (*domina Sikelgarda deliceti comitissa*), to the church of St Ephrem – Deliceto itself is found in the *Quaternus magne expeditionis* as a *feudum* that both the count of Civitate and the count of Carinola held, most likely at different stages.[128] In any case, Segelgarda was released from prison at some point after 1162, most probably after William I's death. The deathbed donation made by Segelgarda was entrusted to Bishop Robert of Catanzaro, who attested how he received the charter from Segelgarda and her daughter Clementia.[129] It appears then that Segelgarda was staying in Calabria, although she apparently did not recover any authority over the county of Catanzaro, in that neither she nor her daughter subscribed the donation as countesses of Catanzaro. Even though it is unclear if Segelgarda or Clementia recovered Catanzaro, this reveals that Segelgarda was allowed to hold some of the lands that corresponded to her husband's ancestral inheritance.

There is no surviving testimony about the creation of a new count of Catanzaro, or even on Clementia's marriage. However, Count Hugh of Catanzaro was present in the same judicial case arbitrated by the master justiciars Abdenago and Tarentinus at Messina in February 1168 that heard the dispute between the Calabrian monasteries of Bagnara and St Euphemia. Count Hugh of Catanzaro was recorded in this resolution as the judicial instance who had previously heard this case, as 'master justiciar and constable of the entire Calabria' (*[…] iussum fuerat ab illustri comite Hugone catanzarii, magistro iusticiarii et comestabulo totius Calabrie*).[130] It does not appear as if Count Hugh attended the court in Messina, in that he was not recorded as having personally testified before the royal *curia* there and did not subscribe the judgement. This would also explain why he was not attested by other testimonies as being present in Messina, or among Stephen's supporters during the Palermo riots. Count Hugh must have stayed in Calabria, acting as the top royal official for that province.

Pseudo-Falcandus did not mention either a Count Hugh or a count of Catanzaro having been appointed during the regency's first batch of new counts. Count Hugh's sudden appearance however can be explained if he was indeed appointed during Chancellor Stephen's administration. Moreover, as a blood-relative only of Stephen of Perche, Hugh must have arrived in the realm with the transalpine contingent who accompanied Stephen to Sicily, and been consequently appointed royal governor for

Calabria, with the title of master justiciar and constable – the same office that Richard of Say had once occupied. The implication here is that the master justiciar and constable for Calabria married Countess Clementia, the surviving heir of an apparently vacant though crucial county in Calabria, instead of being unilaterally assigned the county of Catanzaro. Hugh then must have taken the comital dignity as a result of being the spouse of Countess Clementia.[131] If Count Hugh was in fact a relative of Stephen of Perche, it is probable that he was also a relative of the queen, and his expulsion must have antagonized Queen Margaret further. However, Hugh's role as both royal governor for Calabria and count of Catanzaro and the fact that he must have been in Calabria during the development of these events were practical and strong considerations that Richard of Mandra, Henry of Montescaglioso and their followers must have made when they decided to 'spare him'.

This picture, however, would not be complete without addressing the role played by Count Roger of Alba. It is almost certain that the Count Roger of Alba recorded in the *Quaternus magne expeditionis* is the same Count Roger of Alba who was reportedly assigned, together with Count Richard of Fondi, the task of assembling the Apulian army. It also should be considered that, in Pseudo-Falcandus's own account of Count Gilbert's surrender, Count Roger of Alba is omitted. Although the same author related before that both Richard of Say, count of Fondi, and Count Roger of Alba were appointed as some sort of de facto peninsular great constables, we are told that Gilbert of Gravina chose to submit himself only to Count Richard. The logistics of such a potential military mobilization forces us to consider that had Roger of Alba taken a more significant role during this operation, he would have been in the lead of the Adriatic front, while Richard of Say would have operated on his side of the peninsula, in the Terra di Lavoro and the former principality of Salerno. However, it was the commander on the other coast, Richard, who marched to the Adriatic lands, where Gilbert's fortress must have been located between Loritello and Gravina. It appears, hence, that Roger of Alba was simply placed in command of the knights from the Abruzzo during the takeover by Richard of Mandra and Henry of Montescaglioso, instead of appointing the other leading Abruzzese counts who had been previously closer to the royal *curia* – Philip of Sangro and Bohemund of Manopello – but were directly involved in Richard of Mandra's trial.

The count of Manopello would have been expected to lead the Abruzzo contingent, because he had been the institutional figure on whom the royal administration relied for control of this border province, as is attested by both the role the count of Manopello played during Robert of Loritello's rebellion, and the *quaternion* of the 'jurisdiction' (*justitia/comestabulia*) of Count Bohemund of Manopello, the register in which the *feuda* and military service of the Abruzzo were recorded. Nonetheless, during this time of turmoil and rapid change, Count Richard of Molise and Count Henry of Montescaglioso appear to have relied on the apparently less important count of Alba to mobilize the Abruzzo in case Gilbert's opposition turned into a full-on rebellion that could have destabilized the northern border province, just as Count Robert of Loritello had done before. The reassignments of the counties of Gravina, Andria and Loritello-Conversano were a matter for a different stage of the nobility's establishment, and although Richard of Say might have used his role in bringing the count of Gravina down as political leverage, this entire episode does not directly justify the subsequent concession of another county to Richard of Say – at that time count of Fondi. Likewise, the fact that Roger son of Richard was made afterwards count of Andria must not be regarded as an unequivocal result of his momentary position as a count in the Abruzzo.

The earliest evidence that attests the existence of at Roger as count of Andria is an 1175 charter that records a donation made by Roger, son of the late Richard, and count of Andria, to the nunnery of St Mary of Porta Somma in Benevento.[132] Similarly, the earliest-known piece of evidence that still attests Richard of Say as a count after 1169 is found in a Montecassino document from September 1173 in which a 1172 royal mandate was copied, by which William II gave orders to his great constables and master justiciars, Count Richard of Say and Count Robert of Caserta.[133] The latter document does not make any reference to Richard of Say's specific county, but it has been assumed that he received Gravina at some point because his wife Theodora was recorded as countess of Gravina in 1178, and his descendants held it subsequently.[134]

The profiles of both Richard of Say and Roger son of Richard were similar; barons who did not belong to comital families but had served in royal *curia* as appointed regional officials, and who had subsequently been commissioned in high-ranking administrative positions thanks to the role they played in political conjunctures. Richard of Say had been a loyal royal official, both as master justiciar and constable for Calabria and as commander of the royal army in Campania, and Roger son of Richard was an overlord close to the Sicilian court who would have returned alongside the barons who had played an important role on Apulia before having been exiled by William I. As a result, the economic position and social prestige of both of them was enhanced by granting Fondi to Richard and restoring Roger son of Richard to the lordships that belonged to his father, perhaps even giving him the comital title. Overall, the creation of the new counts of Andria and Gravina is a matter that belongs to a different stage in the kingdom's development and was not a direct result of the takeover by Richard of Mandra and Henry of Montescaglioso in 1168.

6

Consolidated counties during the reign of William II

Archbishop Romuald of Salerno mentioned in his chronicle that after the expulsion of Chancellor Stephen and Count Gilbert, the realm remained in peace and tranquillity.[1] By 1169, the peninsular aristocracy started to enjoy a new period of stability, during which time the nobility's composition was cemented upon a new type of relationship between other local authorities on the mainland and the Sicilian monarchy. From this point of view, we face a different type of count. This was a nobility qualitatively different from the previous one, although most of its members came from it. Also, an additional smaller phase of change occurred around this time, when a new inclusion to the comital rank was agreed by Queen Margaret and William II: Robert II of Bassunvilla was allowed back into the kingdom.

This chapter presents a detailed exploration of the new and consolidated ruling elite in the mainland, covering each county separately from 1169 to 1189. The numbers of counts occupying their respective counties remained relatively stable. By 1175, there were seventeen confirmed counts in the provinces of Apulia and the Terra di Lavoro (Alife, Andria, Avellino, Buonalbergo/Acerra, Carinola/Conza, Caserta, Civitate, Conversano and Loritello, Fondi, Gravina, Lecce, Lesina, Marsico, Molise, Principato, S. Angelo dei Lombardi and Tricarico), and two more in Calabria (Catanzaro and Squillace); by 1189, only four of these counties appear to have been left vacant (Avellino, Conversano, Lesina and Loritello).[2] The following discussion provides both a sequential account of all the documented activities of the southern Italian counts and an analysis of each county's development and the consolidation of the comital authority by the end of the William II's reign.

The palatine county of Loritello and Conversano

Romuald's chronicle records that after the rebel Count Robert of Loritello had repeatedly begged for King William's grace without success, the queen and young king took pity on him, restored their grace to him and finally 'gave him back the county of Loritello, just as his father [William I] had granted it to him [Count Robert], and out of the abundance of his grace added to this the county of Conversano'.[3] The chronicle of the archbishop of Salerno suggests here that the 'county of Conversano' was a gift bestowed upon the forgiven count, when in fact it was his original lordship: the title he had inherited from his father Robert I of Bassunvilla, count of Conversano. This must have happened after the convulsions of Stephen of Perche's chancellorship were finally resolved, but before 1170. According to the *Annales Ceccanenses*, Robert of Loritello made peace (*concordia*) with the Sicilian king in March 1169; the *Annales Casinenses* agree with this, although without mentioning any month in particular.[4] The count of Loritello and Conversano had thus returned. At this stage, it is not clear on what terms this peace was reached nor on what was the extent of the counties of Loritello and Conversano on Robert's return. However, one can be certain that both territories and dignities were restored, and that from this point onwards Robert's comital title would always bear the additional dignity of 'palatine' (*palatinus*).

The earliest-known transaction of Count Robert after his restoration is a now lost February 1173 charter. Reportedly, Robert, 'palatine' count of Loritello and Conversano, lord of Casone (*Casalinovo*), granted an exemption from all dues normally owed to the church of SS. Philip and James in Casone.[5] The town of Casone (now an abandoned *masseria*) is located east of San Severo, around 40 kilometres east of Loritello.[6] Casone is recorded in the *Quaternus* only as a town where a *feudum* of just one *miles* was held by a lesser baron, Gualdimus Malacorona. He held this unit directly, not from an overlord.[7] However, this entry is both contextually very close to the section for the county of Loritello in the *Quaternus* (¶¶ 357–62), and geographically near to Loritello. As argued previously, the 'county of Loritello' of the *Quaternus* appears to have been grouped as a small vacant county, which could reflect either snapshot in time: *c.* 1150 or *c.* 1167.[8] Consequently, either the dominions of the former counts of Loritello were divided and reduced by Roger II before these were granted to Robert II of Bassunvilla in 1154, or William I fragmented the county of Loritello as a corrective and punitive measure against the insurrections led by the head of the county between 1155 and 1162. Evidently, there is not sufficient evidence to reconstruct the composition of the county of Loritello as held originally by Robert of Bassunvilla. Nonetheless, the 1173 transaction sheds some light on this question. It is very unlikely that the royal *curia* would have granted additional lordships to Robert of Bassunvilla on his return, but, instead, both parties must have agreed to restore Robert's county as it was constituted before the rebellion – perhaps even a reduced version of it. Hence, if Robert of Loritello was also lord of Casone by 1173, and was exercising local fiscal authority in the area, in all likelihood his county included this town, and perhaps many more than the few locations recorded in the *Quaternus* as part of the county of Loritello's demesne.

In the same year, in April 1173, Count Robert, attested also as lord of Molfetta, granted the harbour of Molfetta to the church of St James.[9] Then, in July 1174 the 'palatine' count of Loritello and Conversano, again as lord of Molfetta, made a donation from his demesne lands in Molfetta to the church of St Mary of Bagnara.[10] The transaction was conducted in the count's *castellum* of Rignano (Garganico), and was subscribed, among others, by Nicholas the priest, the count's castellan. It appears, hence, that one of the residences of the count of Loritello was Rignano, which was kept by a comital castellan. According to an April 1175 charter from Cava, Robert, as 'palatine' count of Loritello and Conversano and lord of Molfetta, granted land next to the city wall of Molfetta and numerous olive trees in diverse places to his 'loyal man' (*fidelis*) Petrarch of Taranto.¹¹ This last document was issued in Casone and drafted by the count's notary Griffus of Molfetta. Additionally, it was subscribed by William of Rapolla, seneschal of the count.

In April 1179, Robert, 'palatine' count of Loritello and Conversano and lord of Campomarino, declared that he had received a lease from the Abbot Absalom of Tremiti. This *preceptum* was subscribed by men who can be described as members of the comital administrative staff: Leonasius the 'justiciar of the palatine count' (*palatini comitis iustitiarius*); Lucasius the constable (*comestabulus*); Cedemarius the chamberlain (*camerarius*); Thomas son of Gilbert, chamberlain of the palatine count (*palatini comitis camerarii*); and William, judge of Loritello.¹² The 'palatine' count brought to Campomarino not only his own attendants but also his judicial administrator and even a judge from his northern comital *caput*. Perhaps Thomas son of Gilbert came from Loritello as his main administrator, while Cedemarius was Robert's local official in the lordship of Campomarino. Furthermore, Count Robert made some administrative appointments in the city: a scribe appointed by 'palatine' Count Robert, named Palmerius, drafted a private sale charter (*cartulam scripsi ego Palmerius a domino palatii comite Roberto ordinatus*), issued in Campomarino on 5 December 1191.¹³ Campomarino, as a *feudum* of six *milites*, belonged to the county of Civitate, as indicated by the *Quaternus*.¹⁴ The counties of Loritello and Civitate were adjacent to each other; their *capita* were just 25 kilometres apart, and it can be expected that some of their respective dominions would intertwine. It is unclear why the lordship of Campomarino changed hands at some point between 1167 and 1179, but it is possible that this Adriatic town used to belong to the original county of Loritello, and after the latter was confiscated following Count Robert's defeat, the town was given to the neighbouring county of Civitate. In any case, this 1179 transaction confirms that the county of Loritello, at least by the 1170s, was larger than the *Quaternus* suggests.

Another April 1179 charter recorded that the 'palatine' count of Loritello and Conversano, along with, on this occasion, the lord of Bovino, made a donation to the cathedral of St Mary of Bovino while in Fiorentino (*Florentinum*).¹⁵ The transaction was subscribed, among others, by Bishop Giso of Fiorentino, Bishop Robert of Civitate and Abbot Matthew of *Terra Maggiore* (modern Torremaggiore) – ecclesiastical figures who must have witnessed this donation to the bishopric of Bovino as heads of the local churches; Civitate and Torremaggiore are neighbouring towns of Fiorentino. Concerning the same area, in the following month, May 1179, Count Robert issued a fiscal concession by which he exempted the men of the abbey of St Leonard in Siponto from paying the local agricultural and commercial fees (i.e. *adiutorium, forisfactura* and *platea*), and granted that the herds of the church of St Mary of Olecino should graze and have free use of water in the territory of Dragonara¹⁶ and Fiorentino.¹⁷ This transaction was subscribed, among others, by two interesting administrative figures: Philip, the count's marshal (*palatini comitis manescalcus*), and a certain 'constable' (*comestabulus*) Roger Tisonus. They must have been part of the military entourage of Count Robert of Loritello: Philip as the commander of the count's own armed forces, and Roger as a military functionary in charge of the regional contingent of knights. Moreover, an October 1180 charter for the monastery of St Mary of Gualdo, issued in the same Dragonara, was dated in the time of their lord Robert, 'palatine' count of Loritello.¹⁸

Back in Molfetta, fashioning himself again as the lord of this coastal city, the 'palatine' count of Loritello and Conversano issued a confirmation of a fiscal exemption in March 1180 to the abbey of Cava.[19] According to Prignano, the count of Loritello and Conversano subsequently made another donation to Cava, in 1182, but to my knowledge there are no further surviving charters of Count Robert in the archives of Cava.[20] This is the last documented appearance of Robert II of Bassunvilla, 'palatine' count. A papal confirmation, issued on 27 September 1181 and by which Lucius III confirmed all the donations and privileges the church of Larino had received thus far, referred to the holdings of the 'palatine' count of Loritello, which appear to have been part of the said church's lands.[21]

The usage of the specific title of 'palatine' was unprecedented in Norman Italy, at least under the Sicilian monarchy. The only known exception is found in the *Annalista Saxo* when it related that the rebel William, 'palatine [of Loritello]', swore allegiance to Lothar II in 1137.[22] One might be tempted to make a connection between this dignity and the lordship of Loritello, but no other source attests the 'palatine' title for the Norman counts of Loritello before the kingdom's creation. The palatine title used by Robert of Bassunvilla must have been then an additional dignity conferred to him in the peace treaty he made with William II, to distinguish the king's cousin from the rest of the counts and confirm the royal nature of Loritello's concession without granting him any additional power over other noblemen or within the royal administration. The count of Loritello and Conversano was not a 'count palatine' in the imperial and German sense of the term, but simply a count related to the royal palace by means of bloodline and royal favour.

Nonetheless, a dubious document from Montecassino, dated 10 September 1175, attests Count Robert acting as a royal official. Robert, as a 'master justiciar' (*magister justitiarius*), but still palatine count of Loritello (*Palatinus Comes Rotelli*), presided over a judicial court in *Aternum*, in the Abruzzo, which judged a dispute between Montecassino and Raynald and Alexander of Troia concerning the church of St Angelo of Barano.[23] Jamison argued that this was a forgery, on the basis that she thought it is impossible for Count Robert to be a master justiciar for the king, as well as because of the strangeness of the *intitulatio*'s wording and the abnormality in the notary's naming (i.e. *scriptum per manus Roberti notarii nostra curia juratus iussimus scribi*).[24] Petrucci added that its mistaken *datatio* provided a day and followed the Roman calendar, something unusual in Count Robert's charters and uncommon in twelfth-century south Italian documents generally.[25] This charter might be a forgery, but this does not exclude the possibility that an original act which served as a basis for this document could have existed, mostly considering that Count Robert's judicial duties to the crown are confirmed in a letter appended to the chartulary-chronicle of Carpineto, which King William II sent to Count Robert on 5 June 1173, issued in Messina – a document which both Jamison and Petrucci seem to have ignored.[26] The king referred here to Robert as both the 'palatine' count of Loritello and his own blood-relative and loyal man (*palatinus comes Lorotelli, dilectus consanguineus et fidelis suus*). The letter relates that Abbot Oliver of Carpineto had complained to the king's *curia* about the barons of Civitaquana, located also in the Abruzzo, saying that they had invaded the abbey's holdings.[27] The king exhorted Count Robert to investigate and resolve this issue. Perhaps Count Robert never received an official royal administrative appointment, or even the title of 'master justiciar', but he was at least, according to this royal letter, serving the royal *curia* as a procurator of justice in the Abruzzo. After Robert returned to his county, and Count Bohemund II of Manopello died *c*. 1170, the Sicilian government must have relied incidentally on the count of Loritello as their main gateway and communication channel with the aristocracy of the Abruzzo.

Count Robert of Loritello must have died at some point between 1182 and 1184. First, a charter from the chartulary-chronicle of Carpineto, dated 1184 and regarding the market dues (*platea*) of the Abruzzese town of *Aternum*, does not refer to the ruling count of Loritello, but instead attests the existence of an acting 'chamberlain' for the whole county of Loritello: Robert of Varo (corr. Baro).[28] Second, an 1187 concession of pasturage rights made by Adelicia, lady (*seniora*) of Fiorentino, to St Sophia in Benevento and the men of the *casale* of S. Salvatore recorded the former as the daughter of the late Count Robert of Loritello, confirming that Robert II of Bassunvilla was dead by that time.[29] It appears that Count Robert did not have a male heir, and his daughter was not given nor allowed to inherit either county. Perhaps this was another condition agreed by the peace agreement made in 1169, and part of the peculiar nature of the palatine title: the granting of these two counties was a royal prerogative and not a hereditary holding.

The new 'palatine' count did almost everything as both count of Loritello and Conversano, regardless of whether he was in the Capitanata or in southern Adriatic Apulia, and even if he was conducting a transaction as lord of Bovino, Campomarino, Casone or Molfetta. During Count Robert's second period, the counties of Loritello and Conversano practically merged into a single political unit and territorial cluster. However, after Robert II of Bassunvilla passed away, these two comital dignities were separated again; Tancred of Lecce, as the newly elected Sicilian king, would grant the county of Conversano, without Loritello, to Hugh II Lupinus, son of Count Hugh of Catanzaro.[30] There is also a charter, from the monastery of St Benedict in Conversano, that attests the existence of a royal administrator for the county of Conversano by the final year of William II's reign. In September 1188, Thomas of Frassineto, lord of Turi, made a donation to St Benedict, before the presence of Robert of Baro, 'royal chamberlain of the count of Conversano' (*dominus Robbertus de Baro comitis cupersani regius camerarius*), among others.[31] There is no further known evidence for this Robert of Baro; although both Jamison and Takayama cited this document, neither of them identified a royal chamberlain with this name.[32] It is possible that Robert of Baro, as a royal chamberlain, was placed in charge of the 'vacant' county of Conversano at some point after Robert of Basunvilla's death, and although he administered this Adriatic county, he did not receive the comital rank or become the official count of Conversano. Perhaps a more correct version of his title should have been *comitatus Cupersani regii camerarii*. Whichever may be the case, this royal functionary was soon displaced after 1189 by an actual count, Hugh II Lupinus.

The county of Acerra (formerly known as Buonalbergo)

Roger of Medania must have died soon after his return to the kingdom in 1167, because in the same year a new count of Acerra is recorded. Richard of Aquino, son of Roger of

Medania's sister Cecilia, reportedly made a donation in 1167 to the former Neapolitan abbey of the Holy Saviour in 'Castro Lucullano', as 'count of Acerra' (*Riccardus dei gratia comes Acerrarum*), according to a seventeenth-century summary of the now lost charter.[33] It is known that this count of Acerra was Richard of Aquino because in two subsequent transactions Count Richard described himself as the heir of his uncle Roger of Medania. First, in September 1171, Count Richard of Acerra made a donation to the abbey of Montevergine. Richard is recorded here as 'count of Acerra' (*Acerrarum comes*). He reportedly made this donation for the salvation of his soul and that of his parents, and that of his maternal uncle Roger, the late count of Acerra.[34] A Vicencius the castellan is recorded in the eschatocol as a subscribing witness; as both a castellan and one of the count's witnesses, Vicencius must have been a comital official in charge perhaps of Count Richard's residence. Then, in July 1174, Richard of Aquino made another donation while in the land of Goleto, as son of Raynald of Aquino, count of Acerra and lord of Nusco (*filius R[ainaldi] A[quini] domini Dei et regia gratia Acerrarum comes et Nusci dominus*). This donation was to the abbey of the Holy Saviour at Goleto, and the charter was written by his notary, Robert.[35]

Richard of Aquino, the new count of Acerra, must have held not only lands near Montella and Nusco but also the nucleus of Robert of Medania's original county: Buonalbergo. The *Quaternus magne expeditionis* is the latest known source in which the comital title of this family is linked to Buonalbergo. There is no evidence to suggest that either Roger of Medania or his nephew Richard of Aquino lost the cluster of lordships that used to belong to the Norman counts of Buonalbergo. Even though Richard of Aquino is only attested in the surviving evidence with the title of count of Acerra, this must have not excluded his hold of Buonalbergo. Thus, throughout the reign of William I and the first decade of that of William II, the ancestral lands of the Medania family became the emblematic focus of the counts of Buonalbergo, and the lordship of Acerra eventually became the main identifier of this comital position.

Richard of Aquino became a central actor in William II's reign by its final decade. The prominent role Count Richard of Acerra played during the war against the Byzantine Empire in 1185 was soon confirmed and enhanced after William II died and Tancred of Lecce took over as the new Sicilian king. An August 1190 charter recorded the count of Acerra (*comes Acerrarum*) as the captain and master justiciar of Apulia and the Terra di Lavoro (*capitaneus et magister iusticiarius Apulie et Terre Laboris*), an office which he shared with Count William of Caserta.[36] With this title, Count Richard of Acerra became one of two royal governors on the mainland. Such a promotion must have been the result not only of the role he played during William II's reign and the responsibilities he acquired in this period but also of his familial tie with King Tancred: the consort queen was Richard of Aquino's sister.[37] During the succession war that followed William II's death, Count Richard of Acerra became the general of an army supporting Tancred of Lecce, made war with and captured Count Roger of Andria in 1190, and then handed the rebel over to Tancred. During this episode, several chronicles overtly remembered Richard as the brother of Tancred's wife.[38] His status as both a count of the kingdom and a royal relative made Richard of Aquino a crucial ally of King Tancred during the upcoming wars.[39] Furthermore, Richard's position offered a strategic location in two different key areas: in the Terra di Lavoro, north of Naples, and in Buonalbergo and Montella, in Irpina.

The county of Alife

A certain Roger son of Richard made in April 1170 a donation to the church of St Mary of Monte Drogo (della Grotta), located in the territory of the count's *castrum*. The donor, calling himself count of Alife and many others, granted and confirmed a *cesina* (non-arable land) into the hands of Prior Robert. This charter was dated 'in the first year of the countship' of Count Roger son of Richard, and was written on the count's order, by Regitius the judge, who must have been a judge of Alife.[40] This Roger son of Richard hence received the county of Alife c. 1169–70. Cuozzo has suggested that this Roger was in fact the son of Richard of Rupecanina, the father of Andrew of Rupecanina and brother of Rainulf of Caiazzo, which is possible but unproven.[41] If this was the case, he must have been allowed to take control of his ancestral lordship and bear the comital title after the expulsion of Stephen of Perche and Gilbert of Gravina. It is not clear whether his presumed uncle, the infamous Andrew of Rupecanina, was still alive by that time, but he most certainly would have been excluded from any royal pardon on account of his many offences against the Sicilian kingdom. However, his house had not entirely been proscribed, and one of his relatives was accepted back into the former principality of Capua and given one of the counties that had been made from the remnants of his uncles' once extensive lordship. Of course, this Roger of Rupecanina did not employ the family name that his uncle had practically turned into a synonym for rebellion and plundering.

A subsequent document from October 1181 offers further evidence for the count of Alife: Count Roger is remembered as ruling count in a document (*instrumentum*) presented as evidence in a suit for the payment of *terraticum* in *Monte Drogi*. Peter of Velletro (corr. Revello) is recorded here as the *camerarius* of the count.[42] This is the same Peter of Revello who was recorded in a January 1170 legal sentence as the *camerarius* of an unnamed count, in which it was also remembered the time of Lord Malgerius, the former count of Alife.[43] This *camerarius*, Peter of Revello, appears thus to have been a comital official who served first Count Malgerius and then stayed under the new count, administering seigniorial justice in the county of Alife even during the transition period between Malgerius and Roger son of Richard, c. 1169. Not only did the lesser strata of the aristocracy remain unchanging, but the functionaries that served the count's authority also continued in office. These comital officials must have been pivotal for the preservation of the local social control in the midst of rebellion and political change, in that they bridge the ruling periods of previous and newly made counts.

The county of Andria

The earliest reference to the count of Andria after Gilbert's son Bertram was expelled from the realm is an 1175 donation made by 'Roger, son of the late and fondly remembered Richard, and count of Andria by the grace of God and of the king' to the nunnery of St Mary of Porta Somma in Benevento.[44] As discussed earlier, this Roger son of Richard was most likely the son of Richard, son of Richard, an overlord of two other lesser barons whose *feuda* was located in central Apulia, south of Buonalbergo. It is unclear exactly when Roger was made count of Andria. However, this appointment must surely have happened after Robert of Loritello's return, *c.* 1169–70.

Unfortunately, there is no surviving diplomatic evidence for the county of Andria nor regional private charters that would attest the presence of Count Roger. This documentary void is, however, partially supplemented by Roger's activities in his ancestral domains. The 1175 transaction was conducted in his ancestral lordship of Flumeri, in his quality as lord of Trevico and Flumeri. Nicholas, judge of Benevento, and *Finees*, judge of 'all the count's holdings' (*Finees iudex totius patromonii nostri*), validated the charter, which was also subscribed by his brother Philip and other *boni homines* from Benevento and *castrum* Flumeri: Richard of Vallata, William of Vallata and Michael of Benevento. Even if any of these lesser barons were part of Count Roger's entourage, none of them were actually tied to Andria or its county in the Adriatic coast of Apulia. The count's ancestral domains had their own judge, rather than a comital one who came from Andria, or a city judge from Benevento. *Finees* must have acted as the judge of the lordship of Trevico, since he is attested as judge of all the holdings of Trevico in an 1183 legal controversy that involved the bishopric of Trevico, which he still subscribed as 'judge of all the count [of Caserta]'s holdings' (*Ego Finees judex totius patrimonii Domini Comitis*).[45]

Fortunately, a lead seal of Count Roger of Andria survived in the collection of the Royal Palace of Turin. The seal has the same imprint on both sides: a profile of a clean-shaven man facing right, surrounded with the inscription: 'Roger, son of Richard, count of Andria by the grace of God and the king' (✠*ROG FILIV RICC DI ET REGIA GRA COMES ANDRI*).[46] As pointed out by Cuozzo, the count's depiction in his seal follows a classical model, as if it were a precursor of Frederick II's *augustalis*.[47] This uncommon piece of evidence illustrates how developed the count's chancery was, despite the lack of surviving documents. It also sheds some light on the way comital authority was self-depicted in Norman Italy, as in the case of Andria title and certification appears to have been aggrandized with a personal image.

Count Roger of Andria's dignity and political power was not limited to his comital authority by 1183, but was additionally enhanced as he became a central functionary for the royal *curia*.[48] Following a trend that began under William I's concessions after the last rebellion and was normalized under the regency of Queen Margaret, the new count of Andria became also the king's master justiciar and royal constable in the peninsula.

The county of Avellino

Roger of Aquila, as count of Avellino, made a donation in March 1174 in Calvi to Montevergine. This comital donation stipulated that Montevergine would receive a series of privileges from the count's authority. First, the monks were exempt from any service attached to the donated land, and they received *licencia et potestas* to dispose of the land and the mill as they wished, without the count's previous consent. Second, the abbey's court (*curia*) was authorized to judge cases in which Montevergine's men injured the count's men or knights (*milites*), whereas the count retained jurisdiction over the cases in which his own men injured Montevergine's men.[49] In the traditional terminology of feudalism, this concession would be referred to as an allodial title, as opposed to the conditioned ownership identified as 'feudal', even though the document does not employ the term *feudum* at all. However, besides the flexibility and specificity with which land donations could be made by an overlord, the concession given by Count Roger is also particularly revealing in terms of delimiting local jurisdictions. The count of Avellino displayed here his faculty not only to pass judgement over civil and territorial injuries but also to guarantee the judicial rights of a third party, which in this case was the abbey of Montevergine.

The other important aspect revealed by this donation is the geographical extent of the count of Avellino's dominions. As a member of the Aquila family, Count Roger of Avellino must have inherited some of the ancestral holdings that the original Aquila lords held in the principality of Capua. The *Quaternus* records a Count Richard of Aquila as the lord of Calvi and Riardo and an overlord of fourteen lesser barons in these same Capuan towns.[50] Although it is unclear from the register itself whether this Richard is the count of Fondi or the count of Avellino, this 1174 donation confirms that Calvi and Riardo belonged to the counts of Avellino, and that the Count Richard in the *Quaternus* was in fact the father of Count Roger of Avellino. The county of Avellino must have had then a second, lesser *focus* in the Capuan province, around Calvi, because of its counts' ancestral lordships.

The familial holdings of Count Roger of Avellino were not limited to the mainland. He also inherited some Sicilian lordships from his mother's side – Count Roger's mother was Magalda, daughter of Adelicia of Adernò. According to a December 1177 confirmation, Roger of Aquila re-granted the church of St John, located in the plains of Adernò, and the church of St Mary of Catania, located in the old town of Adernò, to the Order of the Hospital of Saint John of Jerusalem,[51] confirming thus what his grandmother Adelicia had reportedly donated before.[52] The plains around Adernò were an external territorial *focus* of the domains of the count of Avellino. By this time one cannot speak of a 'county of Adernò', in that there were no counties on the island during the Norman period; instead, these lands were simply the Sicilian lordship that a count happened to hold because of his maternal heritage. So, the connection between Adelicia and Count Roger of Avellino must have been the reason behind the subsequent attachment of the comital title to Adernò.

Although it is unclear in its current form where this document for Adernò was issued, additional evidence from Montevergine suggests that Count Roger of Avellino was not present in the county during that same year. A May 1177 charter, issued by five judges of the city of Avellino, records a donation the count of Avellino made to Montevergine.[53] The charter also indicates that the count of Avellino sent two letters by which he ordered the transaction to be made. In the first letter, the count instructed his 'master bailiff' (*magister baiulus*), Raymarius, to grant a plot of land with a hazel orchard (*nucelletum*), located in a place known as Cerreta, which the count claimed to have bought from Bernard the *stratigotus*, to Abbot John. In the second, the count requested that the judges of Avellino convene to draft and authenticate the donation. It is hence clear not only that the Count Roger of Avellino was not present in Avellino at the time and conducted his business by means of correspondence but also that he used the city judges as representative of his authority and his bailiff as the overseer of his estate. Therefore, Count Roger's residence was not limited to his comital *caput*, and he visited the other foci of his dominions (i.e. Calvi and Adernò) to administer them personally, at least throughout William II's reign.

The master bailiff of the count of Avellino is further attested in an April 1181 charter, issued in Mercogliano. In what was a court composed by the judges of Mercogliano and the count's master bailiff Simon Filiolo, the 'justiciar' of the Terra di Lavoro, Grimoald, accused a monk and notary of having unlawfully held a plot of land.[54] The document records that both parties reached an agreement before the judges and the bailiff passed any judgement on the case.[55] Furthermore, two subsequent charters, issued in Avellino in August 1181, record a donation made to Montevergine by a certain Bernard, who called himself a former *stratigotus* (*stratigus*) and son of the late Bernard, who was called a 'viscount' (*vice comes*).[56] The document does not provide any further information about the activities of either Bernard, but the title of 'viscount' is puzzling.

A *stratigotus* named Bernard was attested earlier in the 1177 donation as the seller who originally conceded the land that the count of Avellino was donating to Montevergine at that time. It is uncertain when in the past this previous transaction had occurred, and consequently one cannot be sure if this *stratigotus* was the son or the father. It is possible that the younger Bernard occupied the same post as his father. Given that Richard of Aquila had been away from the core focus of his county, either in exile or personally administering his ancestral dominion, it is possible that the *stratigoti* of Avellino partook the responsibility of representing the count's authority just as the city judges did. Likewise, although it is not clear to what extent the functions of the count's appointed bailiff and those of the city *stratigotus* overlapped, it is possible that during the count's absence both figures were accountable for the lands that fell within the orbit of Avellino as the *caput* of the county.

The county of Avellino thus developed a body of comital functionaries, which exercised the count's authority during his constant absences. While Count Roger of Aquila conducted business in his other ancestral dominions, either in the Terra di Lavoro or in Sicily, the judges of the cities of the county filled the gap with their authority and the bailiffs administered the count's lands and business. After having become count of Avellino at quite a young age, *c.* 1152, Count Roger of Aquila had died by 1184 when a legal case from Avellino recorded him as deceased. The role played by both the bailiff and the city judge is furthermore revealed in this subsequent document.

A judicial settlement in January 1184 recorded that William, judge of Mercogliano, had received a letter from Count Roger of Andria, attested here as master constable and justiciar for Apulia and the Terra di Lavoro (*magister comestabulus et iustiarius tocius Apulie et Terre Laboris*), written in response to a petition from the sons of Pagan the judge. The count ordered both William and the bailiff of Mercogliano to investigate and resolve an alleged usurpation of land committed by the late Count Roger of Avellino against Pagan the judge.[57] The letter reported that Pagan had produced another letter that the king and his vice-chancellor Archbishop Walter of Palermo had previously sent to the late Count Roger, which ordered the latter to return the lands. The judge of Mercogliano issued a sentence in favour of the sons of Pagan. Outstandingly, he did so together with the bailiff of his same city, and his sentence ordering the restoration of their property was corrected on the advice of Jacob, the judge of Avellino. The judge of Avellino appears thus to have had some jurisdiction over Mercogliano: the latter being a smaller town that was deemed to be part of the territory of Avellino. After what must have been the recent death of Count Roger of Aquila, no comital successor took control over the county. Perhaps this was the reason why Avellino's judge had the authority to correct the sentence from another town and oversee local estates.

A countess of Avellino is subsequently attested in the town of Taurasi during the first years of the Hohenstaufen dynasty. Perrona, 'once countess of Avellino', and Matthew of Castelvetere, her son and the lord of Taurasi, made a donation in January 1196.[58] There is no actual evidence that would reveal the relationship between Perrona and Count Roger of Avellino; Scandone has assumed that she must have been the daughter of Roger of Aquila, but the documents he cited attest neither her ancestry nor her alleged rule as countess of Avellino or before Henry VI's reign. Since she was the mother of Matthew of Castelvetere, it is safe, at least, to assume that Perrona was married to Roger of Castelvetere, lord of Taurasi and Rocca S. Felice. Hence, Scandone suggested that Roger of Castelvetere became the new count of Avellino during the turmoil that followed William II's death, on the basis of his wife's alleged connection with Roger of Aquila. After Roger of Castelvetere disappeared in 1194, his wife Perrona opposed Henry VI, and consequently both she and her son were deprived of their dominions.[59]

However, Scandone's assumption is misleading. In a charter of May 1200, in which he remitted the labour service owed by a certain Alferius the priest, Matthew was described as 'son of Count Roger of Avellino and by the grace of God lord of Taurasi and other places'. This suggests, therefore, that Perrona had been married first to Count Roger of Aquila and then, after his death, to Roger of Castelvetere. Consequently, Perrona would have been Count Roger's second wife, as Marocta of S. Severino was his original spouse. Another point of interest concerning the May 1200 charter is that it was not dated according to the regnal year of any ruler, and Matthew described his lordship as being conferred upon him only 'by God's grace', with no reference to the king.[60] This was probably a reflection of the weakness of royal authority in the early years of King Frederick's minority. Although this charter may confirm Roger of Castelvetere's temporary position as count of Avellino, it also indicates that his family was allowed to keep their original lordships, and hence did not lose Taurasi, as Scandone supposed. In any case, one can be certain, at least, that the house of Aquila no longer possessed the county of Avellino.

The dual county of Carinola and Conza

The timeline for the succession of Count Jonathan of Carinola is quite hazy. The last documented appearance of Count Jonathan is when, according to Pseudo-Falcandus, he joined the rebellion and then left the realm *c.* 1162, terrified by the king's approach.[61] Count Jonathan's last documented donation (1161) was made and subscribed also by his son Richard, who then became his father's successor.[62] The earliest dated document in which Richard is attested as count of Conza is a June 1168 charter by which he granted an *iscla* located near *Castellum Caletri* (modern Calitri),[63] to the abbey of St Mary in Elce, by then in the hands of Abbot Roger.[64] This implies that at some point before June 1168, Jonathan's heir was allowed to both return to his lordship and bear the same comital dignity that his father had held since the time of Roger II. Although the available narrative witnesses are silent on the restitution of the county of Carinola and Conza during Margaret's regency, Jonathan's son must have been allowed to inherit his father's dominions and title at the time that the other counts were pardoned and created, either in early 1167 or during the chancellorship of Stephen of Perche. It is unclear if Jonathan died at some point after he left the realm as a rebel in 1162, or if he was simply not allowed back, but instead a compromise was reached between his family and the Sicilian royal *curia* that allowed Richard to recover his father's 'polynuclear' county. Whichever the case may be, by 1168 the count of Conza and Carinola was back and active.

Count Richard's donation was also subscribed by a Thomas of Carbonara, who must have been the same Thomas, son of the (former) count of Catanzaro (*filius Comitis Catacensis*), recorded in the *Quaternus* as the baron who held from Count Jonathan of Conza two *feuda* of three *milites* each: *Monticulum* (possibly modern Monticchio Sgarroni)[65] and Carbonara (modern Aquilonia).[66] This Thomas must then have been the illegitimate son of Count Geoffrey, son of Rao and Bertha of Loritello.[67] As an illegitimate son, Thomas must have not been allowed to inherit his father's comital title or his core dominions in Calabria, but instead he was given some of these minor *feuda* that belonged to his father's ancestral lands, in the vicinity of Conza.[68] Thomas of Carbonara was thus part of the comital entourage of his overlord, and consequently, he must have been close to both Count Jonathan of Carinola and his son Count Richard.

Although the earliest documented activity of Richard son of Jonathan as a count only attests him as count of Conza, he is subsequently mentioned also as count of Carinola in a charter of the cathedral of Cefalù; this is the same document in which the donation made by Countess Segelgarda to the church of St Christopher at Deliceto is found.[69] This peculiar document was made up of three different transactions: the first section comprised Segelgarda's deathbed donation, dated 28 July 1167; the second is a donation made by a certain Pagan, priest and chaplain of Count Richard, to Bernard, canon of Cefalù; and the third is an incomplete letter sent by Count Richard to Bishop Guido of Cefalù. Segelgarda's donation to the church of St Christopher at Deliceto was included here for it was the church that Pagan donated to the bishopric of Cefalù. In his donation, Pagan called himself priest and chaplain of Count Richard of Carinola. Pagan made this generous donation before going on pilgrimage to Jerusalem, to visit the Holy Sepulchre for the redemption of his soul. Count Richard of Carinola then sent a letter to the bishop of the endowed see to confirm Pagan's gift. Such a donation appears to have required the approval of either the donor's overlord or the count of the region acting as the relevant local authority. This letter must have been issued in or after 1178, and before 1191, when Count Richard was captured by the invading army of Henry VI, and remained thereafter a prisoner.[70]

A lost Neapolitan charter, a summary of which survives in Prignano's work, recorded a donation that Count Richard reportedly made in 1175 to the abbey of the Holy Saviour at Goleto.[71] Likewise, an 1180 charter of the lost archive of the abbey of

Venosa recorded that Count Richard, as lord of Deliceto, granted some of his lands and possessions in Deliceto to Venosa.[72] Count Richard is recorded again in 1185 as a donor to Montevergine, recorded as count of Conza and son of the late Count Jonathan. The transaction was conducted before the judges of S. Martino (Philip and Durantus, according to the escathocol), and John son of Tancred, the count's judge (*noster iudex*) of Airola; it was subscribed, among others, by Borell and John, the count's *nutriti et camerarii*.[73] The land of S. Martino and the town of Airola were actually located within Count Richard's Capuan dominions, that is the sub-county of Carinola; however, Richard styled himself on this occasion using the toponym of Conza. More importantly, this document illustrates how, as a count, Richard was able to summon the judges of two different towns. Furthermore, Richard of Carinola had a small entourage of comital functionaries, such as the protégés and chamberlains who subscribed this donation.

Five years later, during the turbulent year that followed William II's death, Count Richard made another donation to the abbey of Venosa. The original document is also now lost, but according to the later register of *privilegia* of the abbey of Venosa, Richard, count of Conza (*Consia Comes*) was a patron of the abbey in 1190.[74] In the letter appended to the Cefalù document, Count Richard employed only the Carinola toponym, omitting Conza, even though this affair concerned holdings in Apulia, which were much closer to Conza than to Carinola in the principality of Capua. Nevertheless, the political context of the letter is considerably different from that of the donations made in 1161 and 1168.

First, Count Jonathan must have been involved in the last rebellion but kept his distance from Andrew of Rupecanina and the disorderly Terra di Lavoro. Hence, he must have stayed in the Apulian parts of his county, as count of Conza. Likewise, Count Richard might have stayed in Conza during the first years of his restitution and of Margaret's regency, staying away from trouble. With the passing of years during William II's reign, Richard must have acquired a more stable position, perhaps even managing to claim Carinola back after 1169. Additionally, in his letter Count Richard was not issuing a transaction himself, but simply confirming what his former chaplain had granted within his dominions around Deliceto, in the valley of Cervaro. Located in central Apulia, the valley of Cervaro is not close to Conza, and was thus an outlying territory of the Carinola-Conza cluster. Therefore, either toponymic title could have been used without any particular expectation of one in particular. In the now lost transactions of 1175 and 1180, Prignano recorded Count Richard 'of Conza' as the donor. In any case, Richard's county was represented by two different geographical centres: Carinola in the Terra di Lavoro and Conza in the principality of Salerno (which was administratively deemed to be part of the province of Apulia).

The counties of Caserta and Tricarico

A handful of charters have survived that attest the economic and social activity of the count of Caserta after 1169. In 1172, Count Robert of Caserta granted the inheritance of the late Richard *Menzonis* to William, abbot of the monastery of St Peter of

Piedimonte, who was required to pay, in return for this 'donation', 100 Amalfitan tarì.[75] Two years after, in October 1174, Count Robert conceded and confirmed some land, located in Campus de Puczano and Piczone, to the church and nunnery of St John Baptist in Capua. Robert described himself in these documents as 'count of the Casertans and many others' (*Casertanorum aliorumque plurium comes*).[76] The only person who was expressly named among those who were present at this transaction was the judge of Caserta, John, described as one of the count's loyal men (*noster fidelis*). The same judge John of Caserta, Robert's *fidelis*, was present in an earlier donation that Count Robert made to St Angelo in Formis, in July 1165.[77] The same count subsequently 'granted', in September 1176, some land in the *casale* of Ventosa to Peter of Capua, in return for a lump sum of thirty Amalfitan tarì and an annual fixed fee of two tarì. The concession was issued in Caserta and drafted by a different notary, Jacob the cleric, but subscribed again by Basil, judge of the city of Caserta.[78] Regardless of who occupied this position, it is clear that the judges of Caserta must have been important figures to the comital entourage, because they were the primary civic authorities of the county's *caput*.

Two documents from Cava in September 1178 further attest Count Robert's activities outside his Capuan dominions, closer to his ancestral lordship of Lauro, in the former principality of Salerno. First, Count Robert of Caserta issued a confirmation of two tenant-farmers (*homines censiles*) living at Solofra.[79] The charter further relates that they had been previously ceded along with their wives, children and property, by the count's late mother Sarracena to Cava, and that these two men should no longer work for the count or his heirs, but in future for the abbey, just like its other ceded men. Sarracena had, in March 1159, given these and other tenant-farmers, inhabitants of the village (*vicus*) of Solofra, to Cava. She had also granted some land in the appurtenances of Solofra; we know of this donation only from a confirmation of April 1164.[80] Consequently, after Count Robert had inherited his mother's dower, at some point before September 1178, the abbey must have wanted to be reassured that these two specific tenant-farmers would stay working on the abbey's land and not on the count's.[81] The second September 1178 charter, seemingly sanctioned by the same Judge John, records an exchange of some lands and houses in Capua that Count Robert made with Cava.[82] The count's sons, William and Richard, were present here; additionally, Count Robert and these two were recorded as the guarantors of the transaction.

A papal bull, issued on 14 August 1178 by Alexander III, placed the church of St James of Caserta under apostolic protection, and confirmed the holdings and rights that had been granted by both Count Robert and Bishop Porfirio of Caserta. Reportedly, it was Robert of Caserta who originally requested this, because the count himself had built the church for the salvation of his soul and in memory of his late wife, Countess Agnes.[83] This church in Caserta was in fact consecrated in the same year, and it must have been the result of the count's very generous patronage, as it was a substantial edifice.[84] The following year, in November 1179, Count Robert made a donation to this church.[85] This donation also recorded that the recipient, the church of St James, had been built on the suggestion of the count's late wife. In none of these charters did Count Robert employ the title of his royal office as either great constable or master justiciar, even though he had held these positions since at least 1171.

Robert II of Lauro, count of Caserta, must have died by 1183.[86] According to a September 1183 charter, William of Lauro, son of the late Count Robert of Caserta, confirmed a disposition that his father had made in favour of the abbey of Cava. This charter was read out before all those that were present in the palace of the *castellum* of Lauro, including the judges Richard and Gilbert, who sanctioned the entire transaction by which William of Lauro finally gave the charter of sale to Abbot Benincasa of Cava. Richard and Gilbert must have been the city judges of Lauro.[87] As the ancestral lordship of the family, Lauro was a second *caput* of the county of Caserta, located north of the former principality of Salerno, and its palace must have been a second residence for this count. This is evident if one reads the list of those present in the *castellum* of Lauro at this time: Bishop Porfirio of Caserta, the bishop of Telese (?),[88] and knights (*milites*) and *boni homines* from the contingents of the county's two foci – Caserta and Lauro – accompanied William in Lauro. However, throughout this entire document, William was not referred to as count of Caserta nor even given the comital title.

The creation of a new count of Caserta after Robert II of Lauro's death might simply have been delayed while the news reached Palermo and the king's approval received on the continent; there is no direct evidence that Count Robert's succession was problematic. Nonetheless, there is no actual documented certainty of who was the firstborn among his three sons: Richard, William and Roger II of Tricarico. We know that Richard accompanied his father and subscribed both of his charters of 1178 and 1179, whereas William only subscribed the latter. Conversely, Robert's son Roger is not attested in any transaction in the county of Caserta before 1182, but let us not forget that Roger was already a prominent noble. When he had accompanied his father to the king's court in Messina in 1168, he was described as count of Tricarico.

The September 1183 charter does not refer to Richard as 'late' or 'deceased', but the *Necrologio* of Salerno shows that he had died in October 1182.[89] Perhaps, William, as the younger son, would not have been considered until that point as the next in line to rule the county, and one cannot be sure that Count Roger of Tricarico did not have any objection to the change of power in in his father's dominions. This would not be the first time that the S. Severino family had to deal with a succession dispute among legitimate heirs. In any case, William of Lauro, even though he was yet formally to become count, promptly surrounded himself with some of the key actors within the county, namely the bishop of Caserta and the barons and knights of both Caserta and Lauro; he made sure this prestigious entourage would accompany him while he executed his father's last dispositions inside his palace of Lauro.

William of Lauro was finally attested as count of Caserta two years later. On 7 July 1185, Count William of Caserta (*Gulielmus comes Caserte*) made a donation in the presence of his wife Joetta, and on the advice and in the presence of his son Robert, to Cava, which consisted of a plot of land with a house in the city of Salerno, near the cathedral.[90] The transaction was conducted before and subscribed by John the judge. This same judge sanctioned another charter from Cava, dated 8 January 1187, by which the monastery sold some lands and houses in Capua to a certain Geoffrey Pliarinus. This property had reportedly originally belonged both to Count William and to his father Count Robert and was then granted by the former to the abbey.[91] It is uncertain when this previous donation occurred, but it might have been connected to the exchange of some lands and houses in Capua that Count Robert made with Cava in 1178.[92]

While the abbey of Cava possesses an outstanding collection of twelfth-century charters, there is a real danger that the social image of medieval southern Italy that one can construct from the surviving documentary sources will therefore be overly dependent on the evidence from this one particular Salernitan abbey. It is, however, clear that the abbey of Cava was by no means the only monastic foundation that was patronized by Count William of Caserta. We know, for example, that he made a donation to the abbey of SS. Severino and Sossius in Naples in September 1188. William, recorded as 'count of the Casertans and many others', was in his comital *caput* of Caserta, together with his son Robert, when made a donation to the Neapolitan abbey.[93] The count's son also subscribed the charter, calling himself 'Robert of Lauro'. Even though Count William conducted this transaction using his title as count derived from a location in the principality of Capua, and it concerned lands in the Terra di Lavoro, his son and successor still referred to the Salernitan town of Lauro as his toponymic denomination – a tradition that began when his ancestor, the first Robert of S. Severino, became lord of Lauro.

Count William's brother Count Roger of Tricarico did not stay away from his father's ancestral dominions, as one might have expected. Once Count Robert of Caserta died, Roger of Tricarico was involved alongside the count of Caserta in some transactions in the Salernitan region. According to a September 1187 charter, while Count Roger of Tricarico was in his *castrum* of Montoro, Abbot Benincasa of Cava requested that he and his brother Count William of Caserta grant permission for the abbey's tenant-farmers at Montoro or Solofra to appear at the monastery's court at Montoro.[94] However, the monastery's court was bound to do justice in front of either the judges of Montoro – regarding the men from Montoro – or Serino – regarding the men from Solofra.[95] This transaction was subscribed not only by the two counts but also by the aforementioned Robert of Lauro, Count William's son.

Likewise, Count Roger of Tricarico and Count William of Caserta ceded, in June 1188, all the land in Montoro which Palmerius of Auriconta held at the time of his death to Alexander of Alife, son of the late John.[96] The charter does not state where the transaction was conducted, but this must have been done also in Montoro, not only because his brother Count William subscribed this concession but also because both charters were sanctioned by the same three judges: Gervase, Guerrasius and William. These must have been the judges of Montoro. Besides these two 1187 and 1188 charters, the September 1183 charter cited earlier, in which William of Lauro was recorded after his father had died, attested that the castellan of Montoro, Eustace, acted as a deputy of Richard de Lauro, the other son of Count Robert. Along with these charters from Cava, another document from the same abbey, dated March 1194, recorded that the aforesaid Judge Guerrasius sanctioned the sale of four plots of land to Alexander of Alife, and that this land had been previously donated by Count William of Caserta and Count James of Tricarico – Count Roger's successor.[97] Furthermore, a May 1179 papal document referred to a church of St Thomas, in the territory of Montoro, which the count of Caserta built.[98] This must have antagonized William of S. Severino as lord of Montoro, but the evidence suggests that Montoro had changed hands in the late 1170s.⁹⁹ Throughout William II's reign, Count Robert of Caserta, as one of the top functionaries of the royal *curia* on the mainland, was one of the most influential nobles in the kingdom, and as such he must have been able to leverage his old claim over the ancestral S. Severino dominions.

Count Roger II of Tricarico, by contrast, is attested in only a handful of transactions during the last decade of William II's reign. Tricarico was the least documented county of the Norman period; the only known transaction that Count Roger of Lauro made in his comital *caput* was a donation made to the bishopric of Tricarico in 1181.¹⁰⁰ However, some of the actions of the count of Tricarico can be discerned through the ties his family had with Cava after Robert of Lauro's death.

Roger, as count of Tricarico, and together with his wife Countess Sibylla, made a donation to Cava in November 1186.¹⁰¹ In February 1188, a year after he and his brother Count William had issued a judicial concession to Cava,¹⁰² Count Roger of Tricarico, for his salvation and that of the souls of his parents and late wife Countess Roagia, made a donation to the church of St Dominic at Cociano: a Cava obedience. The charter was drafted by Leo, curial and public notary of Tricarico, and subscribed, among others by John of Aversa, the count's seneschal, Eustace the chamberlain and castellan, and the count's son James – whose subscription was placed at the charter's heading.¹⁰³ John of Aversa and Eustace, in their quality as comital officials, must have been members of the comital entourage, administering the count of Tricarico's property and residence.

It is unclear whether Countess Roagia was Count Roger's first wife and Sibylla his second, or if he had remarried after 1186 and Roagia had died soon afterwards. Most probably the former was the case, since it would have been fitting for his son James to witness a transaction given for the salvation of his mother's soul. This charter offers another example of the reach of the comital authority, both in terms of seigniorial jurisdiction and the capacity from the overlord to surrender jurisdiction over villeins and labourers to ecclesiastical courts. Even if the men were subordinated to a church's holding as their tenant workers and were not directly the count's lordship, the count still held the prerogative to administer justice over all the men inhabiting his dominions.

The still-existent county of Civitate

After Count Robert II of Civitate had, most probably, joined the rebellion in 1155–6, the county of Civitate was left vacant until the regency of Queen Margaret. However, the *Quaternus* records a certain Count Philip in the county of Civitate.¹⁰⁴ There is no additional information about Count Philip's origins; he could have been appointed either during Stephen's chancellorship or just after *c.* 1169, but Philip is not attested by any contemporary narrative nor in any transaction in the Civitate region. To my knowledge, there are no surviving charters in which Count Philip is recorded. The earliest piece of evidence for the county of Civitate after 1169 is a charter from Montevergine in 1178. Bishop Rao of Volturara Appula, together with Count Henry of Civitate and his mother Countess Sica, recognized the church of the Holy Spirit in

Celenza (Valfortore) and made a donation to it, on 25 February 1178.[105] Bishop Rao of Volturara concurred in this concession by request of Count Henry and his mother.

Count Henry of Civitate was surely a second-generation count, given that, throughout this document, Henry's mother Sica was associated with her son's transactions and was herself called 'countess'. A subsequent document confirms that Count Philip of Civitate died at some point before 1179, and that his son, Count Henry, was left as the head of the county of Civitate; consequently, Count Philip must have married Sica no later than 1161. Henry, as count of Civitate and lord of Montecorvino (modern Pietramontecorvino), and son of the late Count Philip (*Civitatis Comes et Dominus Civitatis montis corvine olim domini comitis Philippi bone memorie filius*), sold a vineyard to his 'loyal man' (*fidelis*), John Priniataro, in April 1179. The sale was conducted in the presence of Robert, their judge (*noster iudex*), and the charter drafted in Montecorvino by Umfridus, their public notary (*noster publicus notarius*).[106] Although Count Henry referred in this sale charter to both the judge and the notary as 'his' (*nostri*), most certainly they were not agents of comital power, but civic officials of Montecorvino. However, the town's functionaries must have been subordinated to the count in his condition as lord of Montecorvino.

It appears that Henry was the count of Civitate for the remainder of William II's reign. However, the last surviving notice we have of Count Henry is a donation that he made in December 1180 to the monastery of St Mary of Gualdo Mazzocca, for the salvation of the soul of his father, Count Philip.[107] This monastery was located near S. Bartolomeo in Galdo, 25 kilometres southwest of Montecorvino, and hence Count Henry must have issued this charter in the latter town, as its lord.[108] It is noteworthy that these last two transactions dealt with lands around Montecorvino, suggesting that this lordship had become an important location within the county of Civitate.

The counties of Fondi and Gravina

It is uncertain whether the county of Fondi remained in the hands of the trustworthy Richard of Say, great constable and master justiciar, in the immediate aftermath of the convulsions of 1168. However, the county was returned to the Aquila family at some point before 1171. First, the count of Fondi was remembered in the, admittedly later, chronicle of Richard of S. Germano specifically as Richard of Aquila.[109] Second, an April 1178 charter recorded that Lady Theodora, countess of Gravina, ordered to concede some land to Cava, for the soul of her late husband Count Richard.[110]

That is the first-known transaction relating to the county of Gravina since the time of Count Gilbert; however, this Count Richard must have been Richard of Say, former count of Fondi. We know this because his son Tancred of Say, as count of Gravina, and son and heir of Richard of Say, count of Gravina, made a donation in September 1189 to the church of Gravina.[111] Then, in September 1189, the same Count Tancred granted some lands, between the rivers Maiore and Valione, to the same church.[112] Consequently, Countess Theodora must have been the niece of the archbishop of Capua, who according to Pseudo-Falcandus Richard took as a wife after his first marriage was annulled.[113] Moreover, the descendants of Richard of Say are attested as counts of Gravina in the thirteenth century.[114] There is thus no doubt that Richard of Say was 'transferred' from the county of Fondi to Gravina before he died; however, he surrendered Fondi before 1171.

A royal mandate addressed in 1172 to Richard as one of the two *magni comestabuli et magistri justitiarii* referred to him only as Count Richard of Say (*de Sayguine*), without specifying which county he headed at that time.[115] In the twelfth century, the Sicilian royal government never had two master justiciars from the province of the Terra di Lavoro; it was not in vain that the full title came with the specification 'of all Apulia and the Terra di Lavoro'. After the last *magister capitaneus* was expelled, the great constables and master justiciars who replaced him and can be documented under William II were Count Robert of Caserta between 1171 and 1182, Count Richard of Say in 1172, Count Tancred of Lecce between 1176 and before 1185 and Count Roger of Andria in 1184 and before 1185.[116] Richard of Say thus served as a master justiciar when he was already an Apulian count.

Richard of Aquila, who had been exiled by William I, must have been pardoned and allowed back into his former county between 1169 and 1171, probably around the time Robert of Bassunvilla was pardoned. In July 1173, Count Richard of Fondi granted a site for building a church and a hospice to the papacy.[117] The count of Fondi was also present at William II's wedding in 1176 and subscribed the charter specifying the dower of Joan of England.[118] These documents, however, do not provide any additional toponym that would allow us to discern directly whether this Richard was 'of Say' or 'of Aquila', but, as argued earlier, this must have been the latter. In any case, the count of Fondi was expressly identified in 1178 and 1179 as Richard of Aquila.

On 14 December 1178, Richard of Aquila, as count of Fondi, issued a concession to Bishop John of Fondi. The count granted pasturage and timber rights (*pascua utenda [...] lignamina ad incidendum*) to the bishop and the men in the bishopric's lands.[119] There appear to have been important reasons behind this exemption of agricultural dues. A papal letter of June 1211 sent by Innocent III to the bishop of Fondi related that Richard of Aquila's son Count Richard confirmed a transaction from the time of William II between his father and Bishop John 'through the royal *familiares*' (*per ipsius Regis [Willielmi] familiaries*), granting various liberties to the bishopric.[120] Although there is no absolute certainty that Richard II of Aquila was referring to the same 1178 concession, the intervention of the king's *familiares* must have been part of a continuing attempt from the royal *curia* to prevent the count of Fondi from overstepping his authority and acting in disregard of the sovereign's prerogatives and the customs established by the kingdom's new order.

A royal privilege issued on 7 November 1179, by which the customary practices in the county of Fondi were guaranteed in favour of the subjects, attested the presence of Richard of Aquila, count of Fondi, in Palermo. Reportedly, Count Richard was summoned by the king's *curia* to answer, before the king, for all the damages the count had allegedly inflicted severely upon the people of Traetto (*populus Traiectensus*) and many *boni homines* of Fondi; these damages included the incarceration of individuals and alienation of their holdings. The royal court that heard this case condemned the count's oppression. The count of Fondi was therefore exhorted to limit himself to request a guarantee of a pledge from the perpetrator of a crime, without resorting to incarceration, and likewise reminded that judgement over those charged with murder, theft, arson and forest destruction was a matter for a royally sanctioned court. Accordingly, Count Richard was told by the Sicilian authority not to alienate any goods, impose fines – unless livestock had been damaged – or obstruct the exercise of usage rights of land, forest and marshes. He was to hold his dominion following the good customs, and not demand contributions from his own men, unless these were for the marriage of a daughter or for a royal expedition.[121] This rare piece of evidence illustrates the collision between the comital and royal authorities: a situation that may have been more common than the surviving evidence suggests, although this case may have been complicated by the fact that the abbey of Montecassino also had a claim to Traetto (modern Minturno).[122]

This judicial record demonstrates the supremacy of the royal prerogative over the counts' jurisdiction: it not only claimed to be the only authority that could try and give judgement upon serious 'criminal' offences such as murder, theft, arson and forest destruction, but also that a count, or any other local authority, could not incarcerate anyone 'because the people's bodies belong to the king' (*quoniam corpora domini regis sunt*). Nonetheless, the count of Fondi was neither punished nor penalized. The royal *curia* clearly confirmed his judicial supremacy and the boundaries of social control the count was allowed to exercise within his own county and did not proceed further against the count. William II and his officials would not necessarily have considered Richard of Fondi a trustworthy noble – after all, he had rebelled against the monarchy before – but in what was a hallmark of this royal government, they allowed the count to make amends for his mistakes and submit again to the sovereign, without interfering economically or militarily in his county.

The county of Lecce, on the foundations of Montescaglioso

In the *Quaternus*, Montescaglioso and Lecce were regarded as two different and separate counties, although at the beginning of the entry for Lecce it was recorded that Geoffrey, the former count of Montescaglioso, held the *feuda* that Count Tancred of Lecce held *in demanio*: Lecce, a *feudum* of ten *milites*; Carovigno, one of three *milites*; and Ostuni, one of seven *milites*.[123] This does not imply that Count Geoffrey had held an additional county, but that he kept these three lordships in Salento while also being the count of Montescaglioso. There are, furthermore, some entries in the *Quaternus* that indicate the existence of the so-called principality, and of a *quaternion* that recorded the *feuda* of this territory, which were scattered around the town on Taranto, both in the Basilicata and the Salento peninsula.[124] The so-called principality of Taranto must have been a territorial indicator rather than a judicial entity, and much less a separate administrative province. It was originally a princely title, tied to the royal family, which was subsequently used to refer to the southern Apulian dominions of Count Tancred of Lecce. There is evidence of neither the lands held *in demanio* of the principality nor of any actual royal official whose office was dedicated exclusively to administer the principality. Therefore, this principality must have started as a regional grouping of tenants that would later be tied to the actual comital dominions Tancred of Lecce held after 1169.[125] However, the core territorial unit of Tancred's cluster of lordships was the county of Montescaglioso, whose count Geoffrey of Lecce had held Lecce and Ostuni as his original lordships. The county of Lecce was hence a subsequent creation, an expanded county of Montescaglioso as it were, given to Tancred of Lecce, who was both a relative and heir of Geoffrey of Lecce, and a royal relative who at some point held the princely title of Taranto.

Tancred must have been granted his uncle's former county of Montescaglioso before the end of 1168, because the previous count, Henry of Navarre, was already attested in December 1168 as count of Principato.[126] The new count of Lecce was related not only to the Sicilian royal family, as the illegitimate son of William I's elder brother Roger, but also to the count of Acerra, in that Tancred had married Sibylla of Aquino, Count Richard of Acerra's sister.[127] Richard of Acerra was subsequently remembered as the brother of Tancred's wife (ὁ τῆς γυναικὸς τοῦ Ταγκρὲ κασίγνητος), Tancred's brother-in-law (*frater uxoris regis Tancredi*) and his relative (*cognatus*).[128] Palumbo has already offered an extensive and comprehensive study on Tancred and the county of Lecce. For this reason, I focus here on the county's development and Tancred's activities.[129] In the 1170s, Tancred was engaged in various judicial and military activities, serving the Sicilian monarchy; however, his transactions as count of Lecce are not documented until 1178.

First, the intercession of Count Tancred was recorded when Alexander III on 15 June 1178 confirmed the holdings of the nunnery of St John the Evangelist in Lecce and its direct dependence on Rome. This last had previously been granted by Anacletus II, but such an action by an 'anti-pope' would not, of course, have been considered completely valid.[130] Emma, abbess of this nunnery between 1152 and 1193, was Tancred's maternal aunt; Tancred made this relationship clear in May 1190, when he granted a *casale* near Lecce to the same nunnery.[131] Tancred of Lecce also built and endowed the monastery of SS. Nicholas and Cataldo in Lecce, something which was recorded in two inscriptions: one on the lintel of church's main gate and the other over the cloister's door, which date the foundation to 1180.[132] This is confirmed by the foundation charter of the monastery, granted by Tancred in September 1180, noting his role as its founder and benefactor.[133] In October of the same year, Tancred made another ecclesiastical donation, this time to the bishopric of Lecce.[134]

Count Tancred made a series of subsequent donations (January 1182, February 1185 and May 1185) to the monastery he founded, constantly expanding its holdings and securing its position.[135] One of the points to make here is that the May donation was dated to the sixteenth year of Tancred's countship (*comitatus nostri anno sextodecimo*), which confirms the fact that Tancred received the county of Montescaglioso in 1169. An undated *privilegium*, but which was issued during the reign of William II, records Count Tancred of Lecce, acting also as lord of Ostuni (*Comes licii et Ostunii dominus*), granting building and residence licences to the 'free' men (*franci homines*).[136] In none of these transactions did Count Tancred employ his title as a royal official; he did this only when he exercised a judicial role outside his own county.

Although the former county of Montescaglioso was in practice absorbed into Tancred's new county of Lecce, a specialized royal functionary appointed to serve in the territory of Montescaglioso. Richard of Balvano attended a court held by Count Tancred of Lecce in Barletta, in November 1183, as 'royal constable and justiciar of the justiciarate of Melfi and the honour of Montescaglioso' (*Justiciariatus melfie et honoris mantis caveosi Regio Comestabili et Justiciario*).[137] It is unclear what the actual geographical extent of Richard's jurisdiction was; he was subsequently attested as a royal justiciar and constable in March 1187, when he made a donation to the church of St Mary of Perno. At this time, he called himself *Regius Comestabulus et Iusticiarius*, without specifying any regional jurisdiction.[138] Towards the end of William II's reign, another royal official for Montescaglioso is attested: a donation made in September 1189 to the monastery of St Benedict in Conversano was made in the presence, among others, of Lord Robert, royal chamberlain of the honour of Montescaglioso (*domnius Robertus tituli honoris montis scaveosi regius camerarius*).[139] Since the county of Montescaglioso had technically disappeared into the extensive countship of Tancred of Lecce, the royal *curia* must have called the territory in the valleys of the gulf of Taranto (modern Basilicata) that used to belong to the count of Montescaglioso an 'honour' as part of a reorganization of its administration in Apulia. In this way, the royal administration was able to distinguish the Basilicata area from the rest of the county of Tancred, which also had holdings and lordships in the Salento and on the Adriatic coast, without splitting up Tancred's comital authority or designating Montescaglioso as the seat for another count.

The county of Lesina and the honour of Monte Sant'Angelo

Count Geoffrey of Lesina was one of those who survived the turmoil of Queen Margaret's regency. In March 1173, he issued a confirmation charter to Cava, into the hands of Guido, prior of St Egidius. In this document, he was described as count of Lesina and royal justiciar (*Lisine comes regalisque iustitiarius*), son and heir of lord Henry of Ollia. The charter was dated in the eighteenth year of his countship.[140] It is unclear where this transaction was issued, but it must have taken place in the vicinity of Varano, in the Gargano peninsula. The count of Lesina was attested again in October 1175, in the coastal town of Peschici, in the northern fringe of the Gargano. Here Geoffrey of Ollia, count of Lesina and royal justiciar, made a donation to the abbey of Tremiti in the presence of his *milites* and *boni homines* of Peschici.[141]

In this same year, 1175, Count Geoffrey made another donation, but on this occasion to the abbey of Casauria. Once again, he was described both as count of Lesina and as a royal justiciar. The charter was given on 8 June 1177 and subscribed by the judge of Lesina, William of Isclitella, and by three men that must have been part of Geoffrey of Lesina's comital entourage: the count's chamberlain (*camerarius*), William Flanditius, and two of the count's 'companions' (*socii comitis*), Roger of Baro and Albericus.[142] According to a now lost charter of the monastery of St John in Piano Count Geoffrey of Lesina confirmed in 1179 a donation that a Count Peter had previously made to this monastery.¹⁴³ This original donation dated back to before the creation of the kingdom of Sicily, because the donor must be identified as Count Peter of Lesina (d. 1092) son of Walter son of Amicus, count of Lesina.¹⁴⁴

Geoffrey of Ollia died at some point between 1179 and 1182. In November 1182, Countess Sibylla, widow of the late Count Geoffrey of Lesina (*Sibila comitissa uxor quondam domini Comitis Goffridi Alisine*), issued a confirmation charter to Cava, into the hands of Guido, prior of the church of St Egidius. The countess of Lesina ceded half the share of a fishery with all its produce – both regular and nocturnal – and fishing rights, on the River Varano, the other half of which had previously been granted to St Egidius. She had been informed that this had previously been granted to this church, but because of the carelessness (*incuria*) of the church's rectors, it had remained in her power. Sibylla of Lesina thus confirmed that the entire fishery was to be held by this dependency of Cava.¹⁴⁵ One of its *testores*, *fidelis* and *miles*, Romanus, had already witnessed a comital transaction, Count Geoffrey's 1173 confirmation; he must therefore have been one of the *milites* in the count of Lesina's military entourage.

We have no other surviving document that attests further transactions for a count or countess of Lesina during the remainder of William II's reign. It is not clear whether Geoffrey of Ollia had any issue, or whether his widow Sibylla died soon afterwards, or was simply removed from the countship. The county of Lesina eventually disappeared. This may simply have been a consequence of Geoffrey and Sibylla not leaving an heir. But it may also have been connected with William II's grant of the Gargano peninsula, together with all the holdings of the count of Lesina and the towns of Siponto and Vieste, as an honour included in the dower for his new queen consort, Joan of England, in 1177. This newly created lordship was named using a revived title: the honour of Monte Sant'Angelo.¹⁴⁶

Since the first decade of the kingdom, when Alexander of Telese talked about Count Simon of Monte Sant'Angelo, neither this comital title nor the name of the county had been employed.¹⁴⁷ The dowry charter provides a detailed description of the county's composition. First, the lands held *in demanio* by the county's titular were the cities of Monte Sant'Angelo, Siponto, Vieste, together with all their respective holdings and belongings. The honour also included the *servitium* of the holdings of Count Geoffrey of Lesina: Peschici, Vico, Serracapriola, Varano, Cephalicchia and 'all other [places] recognised as held by the count of the honour of the county of Monte Sant'Angelo'. The king also enhanced the 'honour' with the following dependent lordships (*in servitio*): Candelaro, S. Quirico, Castel Pagano, *Bersentium*, Cagnano and the monasteries of St John of Lama and St Mary of Pulsano.¹⁴⁸ The county of Monte Sant'Angelo was thus renewed as an honour and expanded, absorbing the county of Lesina, and its nominal holder was the queen consort Joan. This is the first occasion since the kingdom's creation that a count was placed within the domains of another county. Notably, the charter does not refer to the 'county' of Lesina but only to the holdings of the count of Lesina; a careful distinction that most likely was meant to avoid the incongruity of having a county situated inside another county or lordship, while making the holder of this honour, the queen consort, the overlord of a count.

This nominal overlordship was not mentioned by Count Geoffrey or Countess Sibylla in either of the transactions discussed earlier, those of June 1177 and of November

1182, nor does the confirmation of 1179 provide any relevant information. It does not seem, therefore, that the queen's dowry had any immediate impact on the composition of the county of Lesina or the activities of its count. Count Geoffrey was already under the king's dominion, as any other count would be, and as a royal justiciar he must have been a baron who was particularly trusted by the royal government. There is no indication that Queen Joan or her officials administered this honour separately from the royal *curia*, as the actual countess of Monte Sant'Angelo. On the contrary, the king's administration must have kept the honour, including the county of Lesina, under its own jurisdiction. This is suggested by the fact that during a court held by the master justiciars in Barletta, in November 1183, Guimund of Casteluzzo and Bonismirus of Siponto were called 'royal justiciars of the honour of Monte Sant'Angelo'.[149] The fact that the newly created county in the Gargano was in theory an 'honour' must have allowed the king to create this extensive cluster of lordships and manage it without opening the opportunity for a noble to claim this comital position in the future – just as with the honour of Montescaglioso. Only after William II died, did Joan's dowry have any effect on the kingdom's politics. King Tancred refused to concede the honour of Monte Sant'Angelo to be held autonomously by Joan of England, on the grounds that these lands were unalienable from the Sicilian crown. (After all, this was a county with a strategic position that lay on the route connecting Apulia with the rest of the Adriatic Italian coast.)[150]

The county of Marsico

The son of the late Count Sylvester of Marsico, William, must have remained as head of the county after 1168, and he is documented as active both in Sicily and in his county. According to a July 1176 charter, William as count of Marsico (*comes Marsici*) sold property near the church of St George in Palermo that his father had bought from the king, and that previously belonged to Maio of Bari, to the *duana baronum*, into the hands of Qaid Mataracius, chamberlain of the king's palace. For this, the count of Marsico received 8,000 Palermitan (Sicilian) tarì. His charter was witnessed by the master justiciars of the king's *curia* and Nicholas son of Qaid Peter, who was the Greek *magister* of the *duana de secretis*.[151] This property was part of one of the many donations King William subsequently made to the church of Monreale. He transferred it to the church only a month later, in a diploma witnessed by Count William himself.[152] After this, the count of Marsico made a series of donations to Venosa, c. 1177–8.

First, at some point between September 1176 and February 1177, Count William of Marsico granted the church of St Mary of the Fountain, built for the salvation of the count's father, to the abbey of Venosa. Then, in February 1177, Count William, at the request of the abbot of Venosa, issued another concession to the same church of St Mary. In the same year, Count William issued a concession allowing the churches of the abbey of Venosa to collect timber from the count's forests. Soon thereafter, in 1178, the count of Marsico exempted in perpetuity the dues owed by a series of men. Finally, in 1178 Count William issued a charter of unknown content.[153]

Eight years after, in January 1186, Alfana 'countess of Marsico by the grace of God' (*Alfana dei gratia comitissa marsici*) declared that Peter *vesterarius* of Cava, following Abbot Benincasa's orders, had leased the church of St Nicholas of Scaviano, in the Vallo di Diano, together with all its men and holdings, to her for nineteen years. Robert the notary, the countess's 'loyal man' (*fidelis*), drafted the declaration, and it was certified with the seal of 'her dearest husband' Count William (*sigillo domini egregii comitis Willielmi karissimi viri nostri*).[154] It is unclear how Countess Alfana and Count William of Marsico were related, but considering that she applied William's comital seal and that he might have been in Sicily, either in his ancestral lordship of Ragusa or in Palermo, it is probable that she was either Count William's wife or sister. Portanova has indicated that Count William of Marsico had a sister, Elizabeth, who married William of S. Severino; it was from this union that the baronial family of S. Severino inherited the county of Marsico in the subsequent century.[155]

William of Marsico was finally attested in his mainland county in 1190. While Count William of Marsico was in his *castellum* of Rocchetta, the Prior of St Peter of Tramutola – the monastery that had been donated with all its holdings and men to Cava by his father Sylvester – requested that he prevent the many nuisances and insults with which his bailiffs and foresters had hitherto troubled the monastery and his men. After considering the matter with his *fideles*, William forbade his bailiffs or foresters from further disturbing the church.[156] The charter was drafted by the count's notary John, and it was subscribed by several comital officials: Robert Valencis, the (count's) seneschal (*senescalcus*); John of Marsico, castellan (of Rocchetta) (*castellanus*); and Herman, the constable of Marsico (*comestabulus*). It was also subscribed by two other local men who appear to have been part of the comital entourage of Marsico: Geoffrey the knight (*miles*) and Robert son of William of Sala – Sala Consilina was not only part of the county but also one of the *feuda* that the count of Marsico held *in demanio*.[157] In practice, what the count of Marsico did was to surrender both his comital prerogatives to exact agricultural dues, which his bailiffs and foresters must have been in charge of collecting.

The county of Molise

Following the death of Count Hugh II of Molise, his county was left in a marginal position. After Richard of Mandra was made count and received this county, the situation does not appear to have changed and Count Richard remained attached to the king's *curia* as a minister. Richard's activities within his county are documented in only one known document from Montecassino. In February 1170, Richard, as count of Molise and royal *familiaris*, held a court in Isernia by royal mandate, together with the bishops of Boiano, Isernia and Trivento (Robert, Raynald and Rao, respectively), and the count's justiciars and barons (*Justiciarii et Barones nostri*). This confirmed a series of royal concessions concerning the tenancy and liberties of the churches of St Lawrence in Anglona and St Nicholas in Vallesurda. The judicial record was subscribed by the same bishops, and by Robert of Molina.[158] Robert of Molina was a comital official, who was attested in 1185 as the count's constable.[159]

A 'master bailiff of all the land of Count Richard of Molise' (*magister baiulus totius terre domini Riccardi Mulisani comitis*) is attested on the Adriatic coast of Apulia. In, May 1167, a certain Anuncius, carrying this administrative title, stated that the count sent a letter to Angelo, catepan of the town of Terlizzi, ordering him to distribute and assign the (count's) demesne land in Terlizzi among the town's citizens. A subsequent baronial transaction conducted in January 1170, also in Terlizzi, referred to the land of 'their lord, Count Richard'.[160] Hence, Richard of Mandra was also a lord in Adriatic Apulia, as not only did he hold lands in the territory of Terlizzi but its citizens also referred to him as their lord. He had the capacity to address its catepan directly, and he maintained a 'master bailiff' who administered the lands. Perhaps Richard of Mandra's status as *royal familiaris* allowed him to send an order directly to a catepan, but his baronial prerogatives must have overlapped with the town's local government; after all, his land donations directly concerned the interests of Terlizzi and its citizens. It is unclear if Anuncius was also the administrator of the county of Molise while Count Richard was in Palermo. His title states that he was the bailiff 'of all the land of Count Richard of Molise', but this could simply have referred to all the lands that Richard of Mandra held in this Adriatic area, not to the actual county.[161] Anuncius the bailiff is not attested in the county of Molise, and Terlizzi does not appear to have been attached to the county of Molise afterwards.

Due to the extension and location of this county, and the fact that it remained vacant for a long period (throughout William I's reign), it is understandable why there would be comital justiciars in charge of the administration of local authority. Moreover, Count Richard called himself here a royal *familiaris*, which indicated he was still part of the royal *curia* and the king's closest circle; and indeed, he subscribed three royal charters alongside other *familiares* in 1169.[162] As a *familiaris* he must have spent most of his time with the king's entourage in Palermo, making the existence of comital justiciars necessary. However, the last mention of Count Richard of Molise comes in a charter for St Sophia in Benevento, in November 1170, issued from the medicinal baths at Pozzuoli.[163] It may be that his presence there suggests that his health was failing. Certainly, he was no longer listed among the royal *familiares* in a diploma of October 1170, and he may well have already been dead, or have died soon afterwards.[164] However, his successor in the county is only attested in 1185; thus, for fifteen years nothing is known of a count of Molise.

Although there is no evidence for an active 'vice-count' in this county, it is clear that the administration of justice could not rely on the city judges of the count's towns alone, like it was the case in the county of Avellino. The county of Molise not only was larger than that of Avellino but also appears to have been less centralized around a single comital *caput*, and instead was divided among relatively minor urban centres such as Boiano, Isernia, Sepino, Trivento and Venafro.[165] However, the boundaries between the royal and comital jurisdictions in the domains in the county of Molise appear to have been blurred after more than a decade of vacancy and royal management. The extensive domains of the late Count Hugh II of Molise were thus consolidated as an administrative territory that remained in royal hands until 1167, only to be granted to the constable of the royal guard, who stayed in Palermo as a royal *familiaris*. This territory, the county of Molise, was in this way essentially different from the other kingdom's counties. Hugh II of Molise was a remnant of the *ancient regime*, when the counts were the superior source of social control, while Richard of Mandra was a product of the Sicilian regime and an external agent, active primarily as a member of the royal *curia*. The county was thus unable to develop like the rest under William II. One should not confuse Count Hugh's inherited capacities and negotiated position with the role the new counts of Molise played in subsequent centuries. If Richard of Mandra exercised the king's justice in his county, it was not the result of any alleged inherent right as the count of Molise, but his condition as an almost absent royal minister of a county that had been managed previously as a royal jurisdiction.[166] Hence, the counts of Molise in the second half of the twelfth century appear less as influential noblemen than as figureheads who appear to have been absent from their county. It is therefore hardly surprising that we lack evidence for the economic activities of the counts of Molise during this period. This could explain why the counts of Molise became hereditary officials of the king, and the county of Molise was conferred and administered under the subsequent royal dynasties as a special justiciarate.

A Count Roger of Molise is attested in a May 1185 charter that recorded the judgement of a suit brought by Abbot William of St Sophia in Benevento against Roger Bozzardi, lord of Campolieto, in regard to the *adiutorium [...] domini nostri Regis* demanded from the villages and churches of St Lucy and St Mark. In the presence of Count Roger, the matter was heard in a court held in Boiano, composed of local barons and judges; the judges who passed judgement and subscribed the charter were John of Venafro, 'master judge of the county' (*comitatus magister [iudex]*), and William and Bartholomew, judges of Boiano. Roger Bozzardi claimed the right to exact *adiutorium* because he had previously won this case when it was heard before the master justiciars of Apulia and the Terra di Lavoro, Counts Tancred of Lecce and Roger of Andria. The abbot, however, denied this, and claimed that the lord had failed to establish his right at a subsequent hearing before two royal justiciars. Judgement was finally given in favour of the abbot.[167] Count Roger of Molise subscribed the charter and commissioned Garardus, a public notary and *advocatus* of Boiano, to record the judgement. Likewise, the count of Molise's entourage must have assisted the court's activities, since the document was also witnessed by the county's constable (*comestabulus comitatus*) Robert of Molina.[168] Also, the barons of Boiano who attended the court and witnessed the act must have been part of the comital entourage.

This charter exemplifies both the dues that fell under comital jurisdiction and the nature of the *adiutorium*. The abbey of St Sophia must have appealed to the count's justice after having been disappointed by the judgement of the king's provincial court presided over by the provincial master justiciars. Consequently, the count of Molise summoned a court in Boiano for the local judges to resolve this issue. It was the count of Molise who ordered his notary to be the court's scribe and provided subscribing witnesses from his entourage. This legal dispute must also have needed the count's approval because it was in regard of the *adiutorium*, an extraordinary seigniorial due that fell within the count's authority, just as the *plateaticum* or *terraticum* did.[169] The legislation of Roger II made an explicit reference to this *adiutorium*, when, as a general caution on how to treat subjects (*III. Monitio generalis / 2. Ut domini subiectos humane tractent*), the king exhorted that all those who have citizens, burgesses, peasants and men of any sort subject to them should treat them decently and mercifully, 'particularly when collecting the *adiutorium* owed, as they should demand this in moderation'.[170] This legislation confirms both the extraordinary character of the *adiutorium* and that it was levied by the overlords themselves, not necessarily by royal officials. However, this law does not specify either the precise form of the tax or the substance of the contribution demanded.

Jamison assumed that this *adiutorium* must have been the same as the military levy for the royal *magna expeditio*. She hypothesized that Count Roger of Molise came from Palermo on this occasion to supervise the levy of an extraordinary *collecta* for William II's military campaign against the Eastern Empire of 1185.[171] There is no indication, however, that Count Roger of Molise was a member of the royal *curia*, as his predecessor Richard of Mandra had been fifteen years earlier. Nevertheless, since in the charter the *adiutorium* was described as pertaining to the king (*adiutorium domini regis*), it could have referred to the *augmentum* of the royal military levy. This would explain why the controversy involving St Sophia was judged both by a provincial court of royal jurisdiction presided by master justiciars and by a comital court presided by the count of Molise.[172] Roger Bozzardi, as lord of Campolieto, must have been the successor of Raynald of Pietrabbondante, who in the *Quaternus magne expeditionis* was recorded as lord of Campolieto, a *feudum* of only one *miles*, which was held directly from the king (*tenet de domino Rege*).[173] For this reason, the lord of Campolieto had appealed directly to the king's justice, but since this was still an issue of seigniorial dues, the abbey of St Sophia was then able to appeal to the local authority embodied in the comital court. The gathering of the *magne expeditio* was a highly sensitive issue that required the coordination of both spheres of control, because this was a royal entitlement that depended on the coordination and authority that a count offered as a local source of power.

The origins of this Count Roger of Molise are a mystery. He was quite probably Richard of Mandra's son, but there is no evidence that would suggest this relationship except for the fact that he succeeded him as count of Molise. Also, the fifteen-year gap complicates the matter even further, because, as we have seen, Richard of Mandra probably died *c*. 1170, when he ceased to be attested as a royal *familiaris*, while Count Roger might only have received the county just before 1185. A December 1183 charter, recording a court hearing at the *castellum* of Serracapriola, mentions a certain Gaitelgrima as countess of Molise, but provides no further information as to her connection either with Count Richard or with Count Roger. At this court, a certain Simon of Molise, sitting with the judges of Venafro, heard a suit against Ylaria, daughter of Geoffrey Cervus, who was accused of taking the holdings of the daughters of William Englisus. Ylaria, in response, declared that she had already proven her claim when she was accused of the same issue in the presence of Gaitelgrima, countess of Molise.[174] Simon of Molise acted here as an agent of comital authority, in that he was able to summon the judges of the town of Venafro and hold a court in Serracapriola to pass judgement on a dispute about landholding and inheritance, involving a case that had been heard before by the countess of Molise herself. However, the charter states neither Simon of Molise's title or office nor his relationship with the countess. Gaitelgrima could have been Richard of Mandra's widow, who acted as the head of the county while Roger was still a minor, and Simon of Molise could have assisted her as the county's bailiff, but all this is speculation. The only certain thing is that a certain Roger was count of Molise for the remaining years of William II's reign.

The resurgence of the county of Principato

After having been left vacant for a long period of time, the county of Principato was 'revived', enabling Tancred of Lecce to acquire his uncle's county of Montescaglioso and to provide the current holder of that latter county, Henry (Rodrigo) of Navarre, with a more than satisfactory replacement. In contrast to what happened in the county of Molise with Richard of Mandra, Henry of Navarre was not subsequently attested in Palermo as a member of the royal *curia*, but instead appears from the first to have been active in his new county of Principato. In December 1168, Henry, calling himself count of Principato and brother of Queen Margaret (*comes Principatus et domine Regine Margherite frater*), confirmed a donation made by one of his predecessors to the church of St Erasmus, in the *castellum* of Campagna. The charter further remembers that the county's lands used to be in the king's hands.[175] Although the 'transfer' of Count Henry from Montescaglioso to Principato occurred soon after Count Gilbert of Gravina was expelled during the takeover orchestrated by him and Richard of Mandra, it was not quite immediate. A July 1168 charter, most likely issued in the vicinity of Auletta, declared to have been enacted in the time of Octavian son of Nicholas Vitziusos, the *stratigotus* of Auletta, and 'Viscount' Peter Gitzos.[176] The latter must have been some sort of deputy placed by the king's *curia* to administer the holdings in the Greek-speaking areas of the escheated county.

Count Henry was, however, regarded as the ruling count in a charter of September 1170, also from Auletta, but in this he was called by his original Iberian name, as the transaction was authenticated in the time of their most pious lord, Count Rodrigo.[177] Two years later, in January 1172, Henry of Navarre ordered that a court be assembled in Eboli. Pagan the seneschal presided over this court, held in the church of St Lawrence in Eboli, on the orders of Count Henry (*per iussionem domini Comitis henrici*).[178] Cava appealed to the count's authority, on the grounds that it had received the mill from his predecessor, Count Nicholas of Principato, whose charter was presented before the court.

The count of Principato was attested again in the following year, in a donation made in July 1173 by Landulf the judge in the presence of Archbishop Romuald of Salerno to Pagan the seneschal, 'master of the land of Count Henry of Principato' (*magister terre Comitis Henrici Principatus*), as a reward for services rendered to the Salernitan church.[179] This Pagan the seneschal was the same Pagan who had held the court in Eboli in 1172 on the count's orders. His role as a 'master of the count's land' must have consisted, at least partially, of executing the count's instructions, and overseeing the judicial processes that fell within the comital authority.

Count Henry of Principato died at some point between 1173 and September 1177, since a charter issued in this latter month, probably in Auletta, was dated in the time of Countess Adelicia (ἐν τοῖς καιροῖς τῆς κωμϊτίσσας ἡμῶν ἀδίλαγϊα).[180] Although the connection between Adelicia and Henry of Navarre is not overtly stated, and there are no known surviving transactions conducted by the countess, it is safe to assume she was Henry's widow. Consequently, this Adelicia could also have been a member of the Sicilian royalty – the chronicle of Romuald of Salerno recorded that Henry of Navarre had married one of Roger II's daughters.[181] Countess Adelicia was attested again as the ruling countess in Auletta, in two private transactions conducted in 1179.[182] Henry's son William must have been a minor during this period; he is only attested as an acting count during Henry VI's reign. In April 1195, William as count of Principato and son and heir of Count Henry of Principato, issued a charter to Cava, confirming all the holdings that belonged to the church of St Blaise at Satriano.[183] It is unclear whether Count William, son of Henry, had become a count before William II's death, but he must have played only a marginal role during the convulsions of Tancred's reign, or he had changed sides adroitly, because he remained as count of Principato under the new Hohenstaufen dynasty.

Overlords in the Irpina and the so-called county of Sant'Angelo dei Lombardi

Although Philip of Balvano was recorded as a count in the *Quaternus magne expeditionis*, his activities are not subsequently documented until 1174. A royal court held in the abbey of the Holy Saviour at Goleto on 6 May 1174 to resolve a dispute between Abbess Marina and Bishop-elect John of Sant'Angelo dei Lombardi was attended by 'the very vigorous' (*strenuissimus*) Count Philip, Roger son of Turgisius of Crypta, Henry of Monticulo and Roger Frainella, lord of Oppido. Philip of Balvano and his sons Simon, Thomas and Geoffrey witnessed the judgement emanated from this court.[184] This same Geoffrey of Balvano subsequently became involved in the royal judicial administration on the peninsula, as, in 1184, he witnessed a judgement sanctioned by the king's master justiciars, counts Tancred of Lecce and Roger of Andria, calling himself son of the 'illustrious Count Philip of Balvano'.[185]

Although attested as a count, Philip of Balvano's role in this 1174 court lies on the margins between the king's justice and the comital domain. On the one hand, this was a provincial court summoned under royal authority; on the other, Count Philip subscribed the judgement using only his comital title, without claiming to hold any royal office. Furthermore, he held the court with his sons and people who appear to have been barons whose lordships neighboured Philip's own. As a count, Philip of Balvano would not have been in charge of the administration of the king's justice, but nonetheless his family must have been highly regarded by the royal *curia*, since Philip's uncle Gilbert of Balvano was a former royal official (a royal justiciar and *comestabulus*). This might have been one of the reasons why Count Philip was allowed to hold a royal *curia* within his uncle's *comestabulia*.[186] Of the local barons who accompanied Philip of Balvano, only Roger Frainella is recorded as one of his own vassals; according to the *Quaternus*, Roger of Oppido held an unnamed *feudum* of two *milites* from Philip of

Balvano.[187] Roger son of Turgisius, on the other hand, was a lord subordinated to Elias of Gesualdo.

Roger's father Turgisius of Crypta must have been the same Turgisius of Grottaminarda (*Grutta*) who was recorded in the *Quaternus* as an overlord of nine barons in the region of Philip of Balvano, but whose lordship was held *in servitio* of another overlord, Elias of Gesualdo.[188] Roger son of Turgisius must have accompanied Count Philip not simply as a lord of S. Giorgio, but in his condition as first-son and heir of the lord of Grottaminarda. Although Turgisius's presence is documented until 1183 (he was present when Count William of Caserta issued a confirmation to Cava in 1183), he must have been unable to attend this provincial royal court of 1174.[189] Elias of Gesualdo, although not holding comital rank, appears to have been a more economically powerful baron than Count Philip of Balvano, as his entry in the *Quaternus* reveals. Count Philip's demesne holdings comprised Sant'Angelo dei Lombardi, Calabritto, Caposele, *Viara*, and he was the lord of three other barons, for all of which he offered a total thirty-four knights (*milites*) and seventy-six foot soldiers (*servientes*) to the king's military levy. Elias of Gesualdo, meanwhile, held *in demanio* Gesualdo, Frigento, Aquapulida (modern Mirabella Eclano), Paternopoli, S. Magno sul Calore, Bonito, Lucera and *Sacntum Lupulum*. He was the lord of seven barons – one of them an overlord (Turgisius of Grottaminarda) – for these he offered a total of 142 knights (*milites*) and 414 foot soldiers (*servientes*) to the same *magna expeditio*.[190] However, it was Philip of Balvano who was recorded with the comital title, both in the *Quaternus* and in subsequent documents. Elias of Gesualdo was one of the few major overlords in the kingdom, excluding the Abruzzo, who held their lands directly from the crown and did not hold comital rank. Others included Richard son of Richard and William of S. Severino. Unsurprisingly, both Count Philip and Elias were involved in the kingdom's provincial administration.

According to Prignano's history, both Count Philip of Balvano and Elias of Gesualdo held a court in 1183 as 'royal constables and justiciars', in Fiorentino, which heard a dispute between Abbot Umfridus of *Terra Maggiore* (Torremaggiore) and Nicholas, son of Hector; the court resolved in favour of the abbot.[191] Just as had happened before, in 1174, the sons of these major barons attended the courts that their fathers held, not as lords but as officials of the crown. This example was, however, different, in that this court heard a controversy about an abbey that was not located in their own domains or directly related to their respective lordships, and it was held not in their region, Irpina, but in the Capitanata. Undoubtedly, Count Philip and Elias acted here, holding a court and summoning the local judges, as agents of the king's justice, and not as major barons exercising their seigniorial prerogatives. Elias of Gesualdo was again attested as a royal constable and justiciar (*regius comestabulus et iustitiarius*), in December 1186, when William son of Tristan granted Montevergine permission to use his demesne forest and lands for pasturage. This donation was subscribed by both Elias and his son Roger of Gesualdo.[192] This transaction must have been witnessed by Elias not because he was a royal official, but through his baronial authority, as the ultimate overlord of the grantor. Thus, William son of Tristan held his lordship from Turgisius of Grottaminarda, who in turn held it from Elias himself.[193] Nevertheless, it was not simply coincidental that the two overlords of this central region became royal officials.

The Balvano's growing influence and ties with the royal *curia* might have operated when Philip was granted Sant'Angelo dei Lombardi, together with other lordships and barons, and received the comital title. However, it must have been the economic and military influence that both Philip of Balvano and Elias of Gesualdo wielded as major landholders and overlords that pushed the Sicilian *curia* to employ them as officers of the king's justice. Unsurprisingly, in light of the military role the counts acquired during William II's reign, the title of royal *comestabulus* indicated that both Count Philip and Elias acted also as regional commanders of the royal armed forces.[194] In this way, while Elias of Gesualdo's rank was comparable to that of a count, Philip of Balvano's actual power base was smaller than that of almost all the other counts of the kingdom. The closest to Count Philip's domains was the county of Lesina, in that both counts acted as royal justiciars and both held relatively few *feuda* and dependent barons.

The last documented activity of Count Philip of Balvano took place in November 1186. According to a suspicious charter, edited by Ughelli, 'Count Philip of Balvano, lord of the *castellum* of Apice' made a donation to the library of the church of Benevento, subscribed by the count's sons Gilbert of Balvano and Lord Rao.[195] This document has been identified as a forgery, but Cuozzo argues that this was an altered extrapolation of a now lost original document, which he argues is demonstrated by the presence of his sons' names in the escathocol.[196] In other words, even if the details of the transaction might have been a fabrication, it seems to evoke a donation made by Count Philip, perhaps also in 1186.

The surviving evidence is scant for Count Philip of Balvano, but in none of that evidence is a county of Sant'Angelo dei Lombardi expressly attested. Hence, Philip of Balvano's county was not constituted in the same way as the rest, in that he held only a small cluster of lordships that lacked a dominant role even within his own region and that his lands do not seem to have operated as a unit for the exercise of comital authority. The Balvano family was certainly rewarded with the conferral of the comital rank on Philip and of those lordships in Irpina, but this became only one of the three major 'overlordships' present in this central region, which in the *Quaternus* were grouped together under the *comestabulia* of Gilbert of Balvano (d. 1156): Sant'Angelo dei Lombardi under Count Philip of Balvano, Gesualdo under Elias, and Conza. This did not necessarily imply that a county of Sant'Angelo dei Lombardi was formed and recognized as a territorial unit; instead, this county operated in the same way as the neighbouring lordship of Gesualdo. The key distinction here was the comital title, because although this might not have made Philip of Balvano the most prominent lord of the region, it certainly enhanced his family's status and domains, providing them with a foothold within the regional circumscription of which his father, Gilbert of Balvano, had previously been in charge. Perhaps if Elias of Gesualdo's relatives had been similarly influential, through having lordships in other regions of the mainland and previously serving the Sicilian crown, he too might have received the title of count. However, Elias's social leverage was limited to his own extensive lordship, which made him a royal judicial and military official, but no more than that.

The counties of Catanzaro and Squillace

In the province of Calabria, we hear nothing more of Count Hugh of Catanzaro for some years after he was 'spared' from being expelled by the royal *curia* during the takeover by the counts of Molise and Montescaglioso, although a papal letter (1171–81) recorded that his wife, Countess Clementia of Catanzaro (*C. comitissa Catacensis*), requested Alexander III to place the hospital of *Bonum Albergum*, built by Berard of Pietrabbodante in honour of St Thomas the Martyr, under apostolic protection.[197] In 1177, however, Count Hugh was one of the noblemen listed in the dower charter of William II's wife, Joan of England.[198] Unsurprisingly, there are no Calabrian charters that record Hugh Lupinus's activities as count – one should remember the paucity of surviving charters from Calabria. Count Hugh died before February 1195, in that it was in that month that his son by Countess Clementia, Hugh II Lupinus, is recorded for the first time as his successor, as count of Catanzaro.[199] Hugh II had become an important figure in the king's entourage even before he acquired his comital title. Hugh II Lupinus witnessed a March 1187 charter issued in Sicily by Qaid Richard, royal chamberlain and master of the royal dīwān, as 'royal seneschal' (*Lupinus domini Regis Senescalcus*); his brother Jordan subscribed this document as well, simply as Jordan Lupinus.[200]

A count of Squillace finally makes an appearance under William II. Count Alfonso of Squillace subscribed the king's dowry charter in 1177.[201] Nonetheless, as is the case with Catanzaro, the available documentary evidence from Calabria is practically non-existent for Squillace. It is not known when this Alfonso was appointed count, only that this must have occurred at some point between 1169 and the beginning of 1177. King Tancred ceded in May 1191 some holdings to the monastery of St Stephen del Bosco, which reportedly were taken from the sons of Alfonso, late count of Squillace and blood-relative of the king.[202] It is unclear how Count Alfonso was related to Tancred I: whether he was a member of the kin-group of the Hauteville royalty or a relative of Tancred's mother, from the family of the lords of Lecce. In any case, Count Alfonso of Squillace was already dead by 1191, and his sons did not appear to have been able to inherit his comital dignity.

7

Beyond the county

The counts' new military and political role

After the peninsular nobility and the Sicilian regime had overcome the turmoil and insurrections of the initial phases of the kingdom's settling, some of the counts began to play an additional and enhanced role in the kingdom's governance. From the royal *comestabuli* to the new comital royal functionaries, by the time of William II's reign a series of new mechanisms for military and political control had been instituted. These relied on both the development of the military administration that began with Roger II and mutated under William I, and the new type of consolidated counts revealed and explained in Chapter 5. The peninsular aristocracy and the comital rank thus provided key elements who strengthened William II's government, and this assistance went beyond the borders and the authority of their respective counties.

As the new period of stability inaugurated by William II opened up new opportunities for the counts to be involved in affairs beyond their counties, some of them occupied the highest positions among both the kingdom's nobility and the royal officials on the mainland. It is in this way that I explore and interpret here how a handful of counts acquired superior capacities as royal envoys, commanders of invading armies and judicial functionaries. It is not coincidental that this enhanced role played by the counts took place during the last decades of the 'Norman' dynasty; the chronological progression is justified, in that the extra-comital activities and tasks of these members of the nobility cannot be understood without the growth of the military administration on the mainland – in the midst of both invasions and rebellions – and the consolidation of the counties.

The counts and the kingdom's 'foreign relations' (1174–8)

The period between 1174 and 1178 was a milestone in the reign of William II. Four years had passed since his mother's regency and the turmoil of her relative's chancellorship. The reconfigured royal *curia* that followed the transient takeover that pushed Chancellor Stephen and Count Gilbert of Gravina out of the realm enacted a visibly distinctive policy. Archbishop Walter of Palermo, the king's former tutor, and the new royal *familiares* demonstrated a different attitude towards the continental nobility, which gave an implicit liberty to the kingdom's counts who for decades the Sicilian monarchy had either restricted or combatted; nevertheless, the years of internal division and insurrection were left in the past. Not only was the prominent count of Conversano and Loritello pardoned and restored back into his critical dual county, but some figures of the nobility were more involved in the kingdom's external policy. Several events of the years 1174–8 illustrate the fundamental role that some of the counts played in foreign affairs.

First, in July 1174, William II shifted his gaze eastward and launched his first foreign campaign. The king collected a large fleet, commanded by his cousin, for an attack on Egypt. The plan was for a two-front assault on Saladin in Egypt: one coming overland from Jerusalem, led by King Amalric and the other coming from Sicily, besieging Alexandria. Although the Sicilians were able to land and lay siege to Alexandria, Saladin was ready to deal with the Sicilian threat directly and caught them by surprise. The invading forces were forced to abandon the siege and sailed back to Sicily.[1] Given both Tancred's kinship with the king and the role he subsequently played as a military commander and great constable, he was without doubt the cousin whom William II sent as an admiral to Alexandria. Furthermore, the county of Lecce offered a strategic position in the Salento peninsula (the kingdom's easternmost point) and on the Adriatic southern coast, which must have facilitated Tancred's efforts to mobilize a fleet and gather knights and naval recruits from Apulia.

Two years later, in March 1176, King William II sent armed forces to the northern frontier of the kingdom to oppose the German army. The German archbishop of Mainz, Christian of Buch, was back in the Italian peninsula, and again he crossed the Alps not as a diplomat but as a military commander.[2] The *Annales Casinenses* recorded that, in 1176, Christian, chancellor of the emperor, besieged Carsoli and that Counts Roger of Andria and Tancred of Lecce, together with 'other counts' (*cum aliis comitibus*), marched there to oppose him.[3] The *Annales Ceccanenses* recorded another version of the same episode: the town of Carsoli was besieged by the imperial chancellor, and 'the counts of the king of Sicily' (*Comites regis Siciliae*) rose up against him with a vast army; however, on 10 March, the Germans were victorious and captured the city, and the Sicilians turned and took flight.[4] Although the latter account does not provide any specific names, it makes clear that the Sicilian army was defeated.

We do not know who exactly were those 'other counts' recorded in the chronicle of Ceccano; the writer might have used the term 'counts' in a rather generous and external way, without referring to the actual heads of the kingdom's counties. Spagnoletti, Cuozzo and Tescione have all suggested that the count of Caserta, Robert of Lauro, was one of the commanders sent by William II to face Christian of Buch.[5] Even if the Sicilian peninsular army sent to Carsoli included all or most of the counts, as leaders of their counties' contingents, the main reason behind the assumption of Robert of Caserta's participation is his title of 'great constable' (*magnus comestabulus*). Both Count Robert and Count Richard of Say were recorded as 'great constables' in 1172.[6] The count of Caserta bore this title from 1171 until his death in 1182. Conversely, Richard of Say, count of Gravina, is only once referred to as 'great constable', in a 1172 royal mandate, and he died before 1178. It would be striking, but not unlikely, if the counts of Caserta and Gravina co-commanded the army in Carsoli as *magni comestabuli* without being overtly mentioned by any of these sources. However, it seems more probable that, even if the Sicilian king mobilized a great army to face the Germans, he would not have sent all of his forces across the border, and instead would have left a contingent ready to face any possible threat of invasion. Tancred of Lecce and Roger of Andria must have then commanded an Apulian contingent that, after marching north and crossing the Abruzzo, ventured out of the realm to assist Pope Alexander III against the imperial threat. Meanwhile, Count Robert of Caserta may have led an army stationed in the Terra di Lavoro, in the eventuality that the Germans would have succeeded in central Italy and threatened to invade through papal Campania. However, despite Archbishop Christian's victory at Carsoli, the imperial campaign in Italy collapsed after Frederick Barbarossa's defeat in Legnano the following month, on 29 May.[7] Soon afterwards, in 1177, a peace treaty between the papacy and its allies, the north Italian city-states of the Lombard League, and Frederick Barbarossa was finally made: the treaty of Venice.

On the advice of Pope Alexander III, William II sent a delegation to take part in the negotiations and subscribe to the treaty of Venice, to secure peace with the German emperor. Romuald of Salerno, as one of the Sicilian delegates, provided a detailed account of the voyage, the negotiations and the aftermath. The archbishop of Salerno and Count Roger of Andria, 'great constable and master justiciar of all Apulia and the Terra di Lavoro', were sent by William II as his ambassadors to make peace in the name of the Sicilian crown. After the peace was negotiated, the royal ambassadors were received by Frederick Barbarossa, and obtained from him in August 1177 a *privilegium*, endorsed by the pope, by which the emperor and his son King Henry [VI] committed to uphold the peace for fifteen years. Pope Alexander, likewise, issued a sentence of excommunication against all those who would have disturbed or hampered this peace. Afterwards, the royal ambassadors were allowed to leave, and went back to Sicily, to meet the king in Palermo to deliver the *privilegium* of peace. Count Roger of Andria thereafter waited in vain for the arrival of the imperial ambassadors, until the king allowed him to return finally to Apulia on 22 February 1178.[8] Curiously, when Romuald of Salerno was in audience before the German emperor and the pope, he described the count of Andria as 'a truly discrete and prudent man, descendant of royal blood'. It is unclear what Romuald of Salerno truly meant here by calling him a descendant of royal blood. Count Roger of Andria was a cousin of Count Robert II of Civitate and member of a family of barons who were lords of Flumeri and Trevico, in Irpina, but does not appear to have been related in any way to the Sicilian royal family.[9] In any case, Count Roger of Andria had undoubtedly become a trustworthy and useful noble for the royal *curia*; he was one of the leaders of a mission that determined both the diplomatic and military course of the Italian peninsula for William's remaining years, paving the way for years of peace in the kingdom of Sicily and allowing William II to devote himself to foreign conquests in the east.

After the peace with the German emperor was reached, some tension remained in the March of Ancona, which was dealt with directly by the counts of Andria and Lecce in their conditions as royal officials. According to a letter sent by Alexander III to Frederick Barbarossa in 1179 (January–February), the pope turned to Count Roger of Andria and Count Tancred, the king's cousin (*regius consobrinus*), the 'master justiciars and great constables of Apulia and the Terra di Lavoro' (*magistri iusticiarii et magni comestabuli Apuliae et Terrae Laboris*), so that those mercenaries from the Sicilian realm would, 'under the penalty of their people and all their things' (*sub pena personarum et rerum omnium suarum*), stop assisting the Greeks (in Ancona), as they were invading the borders of both the (German) Empire and the papacy.[10] The pope, hence, was aware of who were the pertinent figures of authority in southern Italy able to deal with an issue of social control (i.e. military regulation and law enforcement). Interestingly enough, Alexander III did not have to address the Sicilian king, but was able to communicate directly with the king's top officials on the mainland.

The counts of Andria and Lecce, nevertheless, were not the only noblemen empowered to negotiate internationally on behalf of the king. After his engagement with Manuel Komnenos's daughter Maria had been broken off in 1172, William II sent, on the advice of the pope, a delegation to King Henry II of England to negotiate his betrothal to the latter's daughter. After the English king accepted the proposal, he sent his daughter Joan, together with a delegation of noblemen, to Saint-Gilles (southern France). William II, meanwhile, had sent his own corresponding delegation to meet the future queen consort of Sicily; this included Archbishop Alfanus of Capua, Bishop Richard of Syracuse and Count Robert of Caserta. The Sicilian delegation escorted Joan to Naples and then to Palermo, passing though Salerno and Calabria. After such a long voyage, Joan married William II of Sicily at Palermo cathedral, and was crowned queen of Sicily, on 13 February 1177. The dower given to the new queen comprised the 'county' (*comitatus*) of (Monte) Sant'Angelo, and the towns of Siponto and Vieste, together with many other *castella* and places.[11] The dower charter, given in Palermo on 10 February 1177 by the three royal *familiares* Archbishop Walter of Palermo, Bishop Richard of Syracuse and Vice-Chancellor Matthew of Aiello, was also witnessed by Count Robert of Caserta, Count Jocelyn of Loreto (*comes Lert.*), Count Alfonso of Squillace (*comes Scrullacensis*), Count Hugh of Catanzaro and Count Richard of Fondi.[12]

We know that the count of Caserta was by this time a *magnus comestabulus et magister iusticiarius*, so his presence here must have been mostly due to his role as high royal official – most likely for this same reason he was also included in the royal delegation that escorted Joan to Palermo. The count of Fondi must have been by this time Richard of Aquila, who as a 'gatekeeper' count of the Tyrrhenian border would have joined the escorting delegation. It is not clear why specifically the Abruzzese count of Loreto would have been present as a witness here, but it should be expected that at least one nobleman from the province of the Abruzzo would attend the king's wedding and subscribe his dowry; besides, Count Jocelyn was presumably trusted by the *curia* since the queen regent had made him a count ten years before.[13] The counts from Calabria, Hugh of Catanzaro and Alfonso of Squillace, likewise, may have been present as part of a Calabrese legation; Count Hugh of Catanzaro could have been the royal governor for Calabria as he had been during Stephen's chancellorship. However, it is also probable that they simply joined the royal delegation escorting Joan while they were travelling through the Calabrian peninsula.

Acerra and Lecce in the war against Constantinople

The *Annales Ceccanenses* recorded that in 1185 the king appointed Count Richard of Acerra (*comes Riccardus de Cerra*) as one of the two captains who led the army sent to invade the Eastern Roman Empire; the other captain was, we are told, a Count Aldwin (*comes Alduinus*). Meanwhile, Count Tancred (*comes Tancredus*) was sent as the admiral of the accompanying fleet.[14] In the confusion that followed the death of Manuel Komnenos (1180), William took the opportunity to attack the Eastern Empire and invade the Balkans, by intending to put on the throne of Constantinople Alexios Komnenos 'the cupbearer' (ἐπὶ τοῦ κεράσματος), a nephew of Emperor Manuel who had fled Constantinople in 1184.[15] The Sicilian king transported his land forces of mercenaries and knights to Illyria, where they captured its capital Dyrrachium on 24 June 1185. Meanwhile, the fleet sailed directly to Thessaloniki, seizing the provinces along the way as they capitulated. Eustace of Thessaloniki noted the Sicilians had more than 200 ships and a vast army of 80,000 soldiers (πεζῇ) and 5,000 knights (ἱππόται); similarly, Ibn Jubayr related that, while in Sicily, he saw an assembled fleet of 300 warships plus a hundred supply ships. The land forces lead by the count of Acerra surrounded Thessaloniki on 6 August 1185, and the navy commanded by the count of Lecce entered the city's harbour on 15 August 1185, besieged the city in concert and finally captured it on 24 August 1185.[16]

The two great constables at this time were Count Tancred and Count Roger of Andria, but the king instead sent Richard of Aquino, count of Acerra-Buonalbergo, who was Tancred's brother-in-law. This was not the first time that the *magnus comestabulus* for the mainland stayed on the mainland; it was sensible to keep a commander on the peninsula to maintain the internal military order. On the other hand, Richard of Aquino must have been considered a trustworthy noble thanks to his connection to Tancred of Lecce, but it was also sensible to send both brothers-in-law as commanders of the invading expedition, hoping perhaps that their operations could be thus coordinated better. Tancred's role as an admiral was expected here, in that this was not the first time he was placed in command of a fleet, and his lordships also had a strategic coastal position.[17]

Richard of Aquino hence must have been present in the capture of Dyrrachium and led the army that disembarked there and marched towards Thessaloniki. After the sack of Thessaloniki, the Sicilian invading army was halted in the battle of Demetritzes, where Alexios Branas launched a counteroffensive that routed the forces commanded by the count of Acerra, in the impetus given to the war by the new emperor, Isaac II Angelos, who replaced the usurper Andronikos Komnenos. We are told by Niketas Choniates that the two captains of the Sicilian army were captured; he too said that these were Count Richard of Acerra and 'Count Aldwin'. The Greek historian expands on the origins of this previously unattested Count Aldwin, as the latter was described as being 'not descended from a noble and prominent family, but instead was highly regarded by the king for his military skills; above all others at that time, he was bound with the dignity of generalship'.[18]

After waiting in vain to attack Constantinople in concert with the army of the count of Acerra and Aldwin, the Sicilian fleet returned to Sicily, *c*. November 1185, undisturbed but evacuating the recently captured islands as it withdrew. This retreat must have been led by the count of Lecce as the campaign's admiral. By contrast, the captive counts, Richard and Aldwin, were brought to the Greek emperor, Isaac II Angelos, as prisoners of war. According to Choniates, they rendered servile reverence and were questioned by the emperor himself. After a tense exchange between an arrogant Aldwin and the emperor, the two Sicilian commanders and counts were again placed under guard when they left.[19] Following Branas's decisive victory, the invading army was pushed back to Dyrrachium and ultimately back to the kingdom, ending abruptly the failed attempted Sicilian conquest of Constantinople.[20] At some point between the battle of Demetritzes and the loss of Dyrrachium, *c.* 1186, Count Richard of Acerra must have returned to his county in Italy.

Niketas Choniates placed Count Aldwin at the centre of his account, as a protagonist of the defeated Sicilian army, leaving Richard of Aquino in a marginal position. Eustathios of Thessaloniki, likewise, only makes an overt reference to Count Aldwin as commander of the 'Latin' invaders (i.e. the Sicilian army). First, Eustathios recalled having spoken to Count Aldwin (κόμης Ἀλδουίνος) about the disturbance caused by the invaders over the local Greek religious ceremonies, without having been able to accomplish anything, although in other respects the commander of the Sicilians seemed willing to accommodate the captured population.[21] Subsequently, the same Aldwin reportedly admitted the extensive number of deaths among the 'Latin' side, as he acknowledged that more than 3,000 of his men had died of disease.[22] Nonetheless, there is no evidence of any Count Aldwin in southern Italy, either before or after the capture of Thessaloniki. Even Choniates made this point when he described Aldwin as from a neither noble nor illustrious family. There is, however, an Aldwin of Candida, who subscribed as royal seneschal (*Aldwinus de Candida, domini regis senescallus*) the 1177 charter in which William II granted a dower to his wife Joan of England.[23] It is possible that the use of the title 'count' by the Greek witnesses was not an actual reflection of the sociopolitical arrangement of the Italian nobility, but instead their own cultural understanding of what a κόμης was supposed to be. The formal use of the term *comes* goes back to the time of the Roman Republic, when it was sometimes used to describe persons who accompanied those who went out to the provinces to act as governors. It was during the earlier Roman Empire that the comital title applied as a title of dignity to those who were in attendance to the emperor, particularly when he was travelling away from Rome; in the later Empire a range of specific functions and denoted high status came to be created using this title on elite military personnel.[24] In any case, western sources such as the *Annales Ceccanenses* may have used Eastern testimonies to inform the events surrounding the Sicilian invasion of the Eastern Empire. Consequently, the use of the title of 'count' for Aldwin indicated not his position among the kingdom's nobility but the role he played as a general during the Balkan campaign in 1185.

Judicial authority beyond the county

After having been involved in the trial against Richard of Mandra, count of Molise, Count Robert of Caserta must have returned to his lordship, keeping a low profile during the temporary takeover of Count Richard of Molise and Count Henry of Montescaglioso. However, he must have recovered his prominent status soon after Count Gilbert of Gravina left the realm. In June 1171, Count Robert presided over a court convened in Maddaloni, which heard a lawsuit between the bishops and the citizens of Teano and Sessa, as the former accused the latter of sneakily seizing their water stream. In all likelihood, this judicial role taken by Count Robert of Caserta was exercised not as a comital prerogative but as a task that belonged to the 'great constable and justiciar of Apulia and the Terra di Lavoro', as this is Robert's full title employed in the document that recorded this controversy (*D. Comes Robertus Caserte, Apulie et Terre Laboris magnus comestabulus et justitiarius*).[25] Although the town of Maddaloni is near Caserta, it was not part of the county of Caserta. According to the *Quaternus magne expeditionis*, four different barons held *feuda* in Maddaloni, three of whom were direct holders and only one held it *in servitio* from a lesser overlord, Walter de Molinis.[26] Likewise, Teano and Sessa were towns in the Terra di Lavoro that did not fall under the authority of any count, as indicated by the fact that the *feuda* located in these two places were held directly, *in demanio*, by lesser barons.[27] The judgement of 1171 was passed by the city judges of Capua, Aversa and Maddaloni, and the court that heard the controversy was not only presided over by the great constable and master justiciar, but on his instructions other local barons and Richard of Citro, royal constable, also sat in the court. The judges ultimately resolved the suit in favour of the people of Sessa. Under the advice of the local residents and of the royal constable and Count Robert, the judges refused the request of the Teano party to 'prove by combat' (*per pugnam se probare*) that the sworn testimony that Anneus of Rivomatrice and Lando Borell made in favour of Sessa was false, partially because 'this was a dispute between Lombards'.[28] The implication hence is not only that Anneus and Lando were Lombards but also that the use of judicial duels as a legal prerogative among Lombards was restricted by advice of royal functionaries (i.e. the master justiciar and constable). Besides presiding over what seems to have been a provincial judicial court,[29] and advising the local judges, Count Robert was also in charge of summoning the parties involved and relevant witnesses in this case.

In this same year, 1171, Count Robert of Caserta was present at the hearing of another legal dispute between a man called Tostaynus and the abbey of Cava, about some houses in Capua.[30] This Tostaynus was a son of Anneus of Rivomatrice, the same baron who had testified in Count Robert's court in Maddaloni in favour of the town of Sessa. In this instance, Robert was recorded also as both count and 'master constable and justiciar of all Apulia and the Terra di Lavoro' (*Casertanus comes et magister comestabulus et magister iusticiarius totius Apulie et Terre Laboris*). Although it is unclear where this court was held, its location was in all likelihood somewhere in the Terra di Lavoro; the city judge of Maddaloni was not present here, only the judges of Capua and Aversa. Additionally, two royal justiciars (*regis iusticiarii*) were present: Matthew of Avenabulo and John of Valle. This controversy recorded that a previous court held in Capua, and also presided over by Count Robert of Caserta as master justiciar and constable, and attended by John of Valle as royal justiciar, had resolved a controversy between Tostaynus and Anneus about the same Capuan houses. This resolution was subscribed by the judges of Sessa and Maddaloni.

In 1172, the count of Caserta received a mandate from William II, together with his colleague Count Richard of Say, in which both were addressed as 'great constables and master justiciars of all Apulia and the Terra di Lavoro' (*magni comestabuli et magistri justitiarii totius Apulie et Terre Laboris*). The transcription of this royal mandate survives in a September 1173 charter from Montecassino, which reportedly demonstrated, before the judges of Sora, that Roger II had restored some revenues and liberties to some of the churches of Sora. With a mandate dated 12 October 1172, William II had ordered his master justiciars to ascertain whether Roger II had given the monastery of St Dominic of Sora the annual fees of four churches and, if so, let the monastery have them.[31] It is unclear which of the two master justiciars actually conducted the judicial inquiry, but Richard of Say must have been by this time count of Gravina, not of Fondi.

Richard of Say was not attested further, but instead in November 1176 the new count of Montescaglioso-Lecce was described as master justiciar and great constable. The count of Gravina must therefore have died before then, leaving the office free for Tancred of Lecce to occupy it. This document of November 1176 was a record of a legal dispute between Egidius, abbot of the Most Holy Trinity of Venosa, and the men (*homines*) of S. Nicholas of Casa Vetere, over whom the abbot claimed to exercise lordship and jurisdiction. Here Tancred, as son of duke (Roger), count of Lecce and great constable and master justiciar of all Apulia and the Terra di Lavoro (*Ducis filius, dei et regia gratia Licii comes, magnus comestabulus et magister iusticiarius totius Apulie et Terre Laboris*) entrusted the judicial investigation on this matter to the bishop of Bitonto, the abbot of St Stephen in Monopoli, the royal justiciars Gentile of Comano and Bernard of Fontanella, the chamberlains of the Terra di Bari Teselgard and Rao, and some local barons.[32] Due to the location of all the actors involved in this dispute, it is evident that the pertinent master justiciar to administer this issue was the count of Lecce and not Robert of Caserta, as the former must have been much closer to the bishops, abbots and royal functionaries on the Adriatic coast. Had Count Richard of Gravina been alive, he would have equally been a pertinent authority for the dispute.

A now lost 1177 charter from Venosa recorded a dispute between the abbot of Cava and the men of the town of Casavena (*homines oppidi Casae veane*); the *incipit* suggests that Count Tancred of Lecce, as *magnus comestabulus et magister Justitiarius Apuliae et Terrae Laboris*, presided over the court that heard this case.[33] Since the document was reportedly part of the records of the abbey of Venosa, although the abbot of Cava was involved in the dispute, the town of Casavena must have been in the vicinity of Venosa's lands.

Back in the Terra di Bari, Tancred, son of the duke and count of Lecce, presided over a court, again as *comestabulus et magister iustitiarius totius Apulie et terre Laboris*, which heard a dispute between the church of St Nicholas of Bari and a local baron, Geoffrey Gentile. The church's delegates, Nicholas the *primicerius* and John the notary, presented a royal writ issued in Palermo in May 1180 by which Tancred of Lecce was ordered to investigate the alleged usurpation by Geoffrey Gentile of lands belonging to the church of St Peter of Sclavezulis, which was a dependency of St Nicholas of Bari. After hearing both parties, a resolution was issued on 21 February 1181 that established a fifteen-day deadline for an investigation into, and an assessment of, the damages to be conducted, which would allow the court to reach a final decision on the matter.[34] As one might expect, the court was attended by three judges of Bari (Amerutius, John Macciacotta and Petracca Buffus), who passed judgement, while

Tancred's role consisted of coordinating the entire judicial process, from receiving the king's orders and setting up the provincial court to commissioning the investigations and guaranteeing that justice was done.

Count Robert was recorded again, also in 1181, presiding over courts in Aversa and Capua. First, according to a now lost judgement made in Aversa, in the presence of Count Robert 'great constable and master justiciar of Apulia and the Terra di Lavoro' (*magnus comestabulus et magister justiciarius Apuliae et Terre Laboris*), the judges (of Aversa) John, Leon and Martin passed judgement on a controversy between Bishop Falco of Aversa and a certain Raynald son of Thomas, contravening thus an agreement contained in a charter (*instrumentum*) validated in the presence of the abbot of the Monastery of St Lawrence, Bishop Porfirio of Caserta and Bishop William of Avellino.[35]

Then, Robert of Caserta presided over another court in Capua, attended by the city judges, as well as by the bishops of Teano and Caserta. The bishop of Marsia brought to the court, held on 12 February 1181, a letter issued by King William II in Palermo, in which the royal curia ordered the constables to do justice (i.e. to investigate and resolve, but not necessarily to pass judgement themselves) concerning the alleged usurpation of the church of St Bartholomew of Avezzano by Gentile 'of Palearea' from the bishop of Marsia.[36] This letter was addressed to both great constables and justiciars on the mainland: Count Robert of Caserta and Count Tancred of Lecce. It is unclear, however, if the actual court held in Capua was presided over by both, or simply by Count Robert; the court's judgement survives only as a summary prepared by Di Meo.[37] Most probably, as in the legal case of 1171 discussed earlier, only the count of Caserta presided at this court, because the existence of two master justiciars must have allowed each one to be present and to exercise the royal judicial prerogative in different parts of the kingdom: the count of Caserta in the Terra di Lavoro, and the count of Lecce in southern and Adriatic Apulia. While the king might issue an order to both his top functionaries on the mainland, as they shared the same high office, in practice usually only one would execute the order in a provincial court.

Two letters sent by Count Robert of Caserta in 1182 shed light on his activities as a royal official, outside of both his own county and a provincial court. A letter, copied into a charter from Cava, was sent by Robert, as count of Caserta and great constable and master justiciar of all Apulia and the Terra di Lavoro (*Casertanus comes magnus comestabulus et magister iusticiarius tocius Apulie et Terre Laboris*) to William Buarumil, royal chamberlain (*regius camerarius*). By this letter, the count of Caserta ordered *ex regia parte* to not disturb the holdings and mill that the abbey held at Sarno.[38] Another letter, that survives in the chronicle-chartulary of Casauria, was sent by Count Robert to the abbey of St Clement in Casauria, and also attests the count of Caserta as master justiciar', although in this instance Count Robert did not describe himself as a constable (*Robertus Dei et Regis gratia Comes Casert. et Magister Justiciarius totius Apuliae et Terra-Laboris*).[39] In this letter, the count of Caserta exhorted *ex parte regia* the monks of St Clement to address any legal complaint either to Count Tancred of Lecce or to himself, as the abbey was in the hands of the king. This 'royal reminder' must have been sent to the abbey just after Abbot Leonas died, in 1182.[40] Although the title of 'constable' is omitted in this instance, this is most likely the result of the lack of a single and consistent labelling for the same office. Also, since the text of this mandate survives only as a copy, we cannot exclude scribal omission. In the previous 1171 judgement, Count Robert was recorded as 'great constable and justiciar', and not technically as 'master justiciar', which was a more common version of the title.[41] Nevertheless, at this stage, the great constables were ex officio master justiciars, although each title referred to a discrete administrative function; as constables, they were military commanders of the mainland forces and as justiciars, chief administrators of royal justice.

William II wrote from Capua on 19 January 1183 to Tancred, 'count of Lecce, master constable and master justiciar of Apulia and the Terra di Lavoro' (*comes Liccii, magnus comestabulus et magister iustitiarius Apulie et Terre Laboris*), explaining that the abbot of St Nicholas of Troia had complained that the citizens of Ascoli (Satriano) had invaded a property that the abbey used to hold, which had previously been confirmed to it by Roger II. Consequently, the king ordered Tancred to hear both parties and to reach the fairest and most reasonable resolution, to prevent any further complaint by the abbot. The dispute was eventually brought before a solemn court held in Barletta in November 1184, presided over by both great constables and master justiciars: Count Tancred of Lecce and Count Roger of Andria. Since Count Robert of Caserta was dead by then, the king must have appointed the count of Andria in his stead. The abbey's representatives presented as evidence both a royal charter and a donation made by the count of Loritello. In their defence, the representatives of Ascoli argued that the royal document did not confirm the specific holding in dispute and that the count of Loritello could not grant what was not his, and thus did not have the capacity to give that holding to the abbey. After having ordered an investigation on the actual boundaries of the comital dominions of Loritello, and having allowed each party to present fifteen witnesses, the court was unable to discern whose arguments were true. Thus, the court resorted to a judicial duel (*camfiones ad campum pervenerunt et sic factum nutu et voluntate divina*); the abbey's champion (*canfio monasterii pugnam optinuit*) defeated the one from Ascoli, and so the court validated the authenticity of the royal and comital charters presented by St Nicholas of Troia. Consequently, the counts of Lecce and Andria, as royal master justiciars, invested the abbey with the lands that were in dispute. The charter that recorded this judgement was drafted by Simon of Matera, the count of Lecce's own notary.[42]

Count Roger of Andria therefore became a central functionary for the royal *curia* soon after Count Robert of Caserta's death. Perhaps the unstable succession in the county of Caserta, or the fact that young William of Lauro was not as reliable, or experienced or as close to the royal entourage as his late father had been, forced the king's administration to select a more trustworthy count. Although one might have expected Count Robert's replacement also to be from the Terra di Lavoro, the other counts from this region had a record of dubious loyalty to the monarchy. Richard of Aquila, count of Fondi, and Count Richard of Carinola and Conza had been pardoned and had recovered their counties after having gone into exile as rebels. In addition, Richard of Aquila had been censured by the royal *curia* in 1179 for overstepping his judicial authority.[43] Roger son of Richard of Rupecanina, count of Alife, on the other hand, was a relative of the old lords of Caiazzo and Rupecanina who, until 1169, were enemies of the Sicilian kingdom.[44] As a result, the Sicilian king appointed a second Apulian count as master justiciar in 1183, which may explain why the court of Barletta was not presided over by just one count, as was the case in all previous instances under William II. From now on, and most likely until William II's death, the count of Andria shared the highest position of royal administration on the peninsula with the count of Lecce.

According to a January 1184 charter from Montevergine, Count Roger of Andria, as 'master constable and justiciar of Apulia and the Terra di Lavoro' (*magister comestabulus et iustiarius tocius Apulie et Terre Laboris*), issued an order to the judge of Mercogliano to investigate an alleged usurpation of land committed earlier by the late Count Roger of Avellino.[45] On 29 April the same year, a charter issued in S. Germano by the lords of Monte Millulo recorded that they were called before a court presided by Count Tancred, master justiciar, to answer charges brought by the abbot of Montecassino about a quarrel with the abbey's *homines* of St Peter of Avellana. To avoid the continuation of the litigation before the king's master justiciar, and no doubt the subsequent expense and delay, the lords of Monte Millulo agreed to accept the judgement of the abbatial court of Cassino.[46] This not only attests the continuing role played by the count of Lecce as a royal high official but also illustrates how a seigniorial legal process could develop on the mainland: beginning when a major landholder such as the abbot of Montecassino appealed to the king's jurisdiction, and unfolding as the master justiciar summoned the defendant to a provincial court of justice, opening up the possibility for the defendant to avoid the king's justice by submitting to the overlord's court.

Count Tancred and Count Roger were again recorded acting together as 'royal justiciars' (*Regis Iusticiariis*) in a judicial dispute in the county of Molise in May 1185, between Abbot William of St Sophia, Benevento and Roger Bozzardi, lord of Campolieto. The court, presided over by the count of Molise and composed of the judges of Boiano, ultimately passed judgement in favour of the abbey. However, Roger Bozzardi claimed that Count Tancred and Count Roger heard this dispute before as royal justiciars, and ruled in his favour, approving his right to exact *adiutorium*.[47] As discussed earlier, this instance illustrates the peculiar nature of the *adiutorium*, and the overlapping of the comital and royal authorities. It is however unclear when the master justiciars previously heard this case, or where they held the court that allegedly ruled in his favour, but this must have occurred at some point between 1183 and May 1185.

Tancred of Lecce was last attested as *egregius Comes Licii* and *magnus comestabulus et magnus justiciarius Apulie et Terre Laboris* in an April 1187 charter. This records a *concordia* by which Roger the monk, prior of the church of the Holy Sepulchre in Brindisi, renounced any claim over a piece of land in Calvignano, near Mesagne (15 kilometres southwest of Brindisi), located in royal land. This had been claimed by Abbess Scolastica of St Mary in Brindisi as land that lawfully belonged to her nunnery, but Prior Roger had expelled the peasants and driven them from their ploughs. The abbess filed a complaint to the count of Lecce, as the king's representative, and the master justiciar heard both parties, and summoned a court in which the abbess presented the donation that sustained her claim before the judges of the city of Brindisi and Eugenius, the *magister Regie Duane baronum*. Eventually, Prior Roger admitted his mistake and desisted from any action concerning the land in Calvignano.[48] As in every other such case, local judges were fundamental to the judicial process administered by the master justiciar, as it seems that the sole authority of counts or royal representatives was not sufficient to authenticate and legalize a transaction – in the same way judges were needed to pass judgement in civil disputes. They would, of course, contribute both their legal expertise, and local knowledge, to the court. Interestingly, in this case another important royal functionary, the master of the *duana baronum*, was also present.[49]

Overall, these accounts of legal and administrative processes illustrate the core duties that counts exercised as royal officials to coordinate the administration of justice. Great nobles, such as the counts of Caserta, Gravina, Lecce and Andria, must have enjoyed additional social and military leverage that would both have facilitated their roles as master justiciars in coordinating local judges and strengthened their authority as executors of judicial mandates. A situation that was avoided under Roger II's reign became increasingly common in the second half of the twelfth century: noblemen exercising both comital and royal authorities. The dual roles played by these 'enhanced counts' might well have been seen as a threat to Roger's government-in-the-making, but by the time of William II, this had become necessary to ensure the survival and continuity of the Sicilian royal authority on the continent and enforce proper conduct of local judicial processes. The counts who also held royal offices became the main guarantors of social control on the mainland, and as both heads of the nobility and representatives of the king's justice they could operate outside their own counties.

Conclusions

Following the thematic thread of county and nobility in Norman Italy, this book has made recourse to a wide range of material covering a period of more than sixty years. The study is neither an essay of general history nor a monograph of local histories. On the other hand, it traverses the distance in between the two and works as an instrument of questioning, based on a simple idea: the thorough examination of events, activities and particular relationships brings us closer to the understanding of general processes more than it takes us away. In presenting a rounded account of the comital class in the kingdom of Sicily, drawing on charters, chronicles, testimonies, records and other sources, a series of prosopographies and interpretations have uncovered a much clearer and nuanced picture of the nobility's own agency and its relationship with other agents of social control.

Navigating the imprecise vocabulary and documentary voids left by the numerous scattered sources is a reality which any scholar, regardless of approach, must accept. In analysing each source directly and cautiously, and contextualizing them with contemporary testimonies, one can assess the diplomatic and socio-historic relevance and value of the available material. The limited information the sources offer for periods of political turmoil and war create inconsistent and intermittent images of the different counties in the mainland provinces, which has forced this study to rely on a chronological progression to explore and analyse the growth and function of the county. Moreover, the collective agency of the nobility can only be understood when all the pieces of evidence are brought together, and the distinctions within the upper social echelon made explicit.

The counties in southern Italy were not only a product of the change and rearrangement caused by the installation of the Sicilian monarchy. They also became the endemic structure upon which the features of the territorial organization and the individual expectations and authority of the peninsular nobility were defined and preserved. For example, the scattered dominions within a single comital authority, which created the 'patchwork-like' arrangement of some of the county's territory, were usually the result of elevating lesser barons to the comital rank by granting them a core lordship elsewhere. Ancestral lordships were thus merged with clusters of tenant barons. This caused, for example, the county of Avellino to include lordships in the Terra di Lavoro, Buonalbergo to have another focus on Acerra and Caserta and Tricarico to hold dominions in Lauro and north of the former principality of Salerno. This would also explain why, at some point, the county of Andria included lordships in the Agri valley. This also justifies the presence of 'Sicilian counties', which were nothing but ancestral lordships that certain counts held alongside their mainland holdings: Count Sylvester of Marsico, lord of Ragusa; Count Simon, lord of Butera and Paternò;

and Geoffrey of Montescaglioso, lord of Caltanissetta, Noto and Sclàfani. However, in all these instances, tenant barons were actually clustered geographically; it was the *feuda* that the count held *in demanio* far from the *caput* that gave a toponymic reference to the comital title. The remaining 'spotted-like' counties were located in the modern region of Basilicata. This particular geographical area was a fluid region of scattered lordships assigned to the intertwined counties of Montescaglioso, Tricarico and Gravina.

The county did not begin as a fixed territorial demarcation, but it became a useful unit for organizing the powerful and loyal aristocracy and their tenure. As an agglomeration of lordships, the county under Roger II developed into a unit of power for manoeuvring with and against the upper strata of society. The created counties became protected and sanctioned spaces in which Norman rulers, local officials and pre-conquest aristocrats were merged together, allowing for both the legitimation of a new, royally sanctioned upper social rank and the continuation of pre-Norman customs and social groups. From then onwards, the bearers of the comital title can be identified much more precisely, and the clusters of comital authority began to acquire a clearer geographical delimitation. It is in this way that the comital aristocracy can begin to be identified as one of the bearers of historical continuity in southern Italy. Despite individual changes and episodes of conflict, the counts were able to reaffirm a discrete social status with political and military prerogatives that allowed the counties and their nobility to survive the Norman royal dynasty.

The original power of the peninsular nobility might have threatened the establishment of a successful kingdom, but it was only through this that the kingdom was able to survive as a unified political entity on both sides of the Straits of Messina. The legacy of Roger II's reign was a double-edged sword; although it explains the attempt by the monarchy to establish close control of the major barons in the peninsula, it eventually became the platform upon which the counts of the kingdom rebelled against the Palermitan regime and consolidated their position as an alternative centre of power.

The events of William I's reign gradually tested the limits of Roger II's legacy, serving to define the extent of both the counts' and the king's authorities. A single chief, the count, for all local lords: that was the political foundation on which a status community was bound in a single set, above the diversity of its components. Around the leaderships of the count of Loritello and Conversano, and then of the count of Gravina, the nobility acquired the protagonism and influence necessary to both oppose the effective operation of the Palermitan government and partially take control of the kingdom's political organization. The comital rank provided thus the status and common identity for the kingdom's overlords to stand against the king's admiral of admirals and master captains, to the point that Count Gilbert of Gravina even became chief royal commander. The comital authority must have acted, in the absence of the direct command of the royal *curia*, as a viable collection of social mechanisms for the control of the local population and the maintenance of economic and judicial activities. Furthermore, internal stability and peace in the continental provinces were reached by acknowledging the comital authority and allowing the nobility to be directly involved with royal structures of power.

We knew from the outset that major landholders and overlords were the dominant social force on the mainland, but as the complex dynamics between the royal and baronial forces became more evident, it has become clear that it is impossible to speak of a single and effective system of social control. Instead, we should discuss the fluid social hegemony exercised and defended by the counts. This hegemony was the result of individual profiles whose ties between relatives and allies crossed the limits of the different terms and fulfilled three functions: consolidating their authority over other members of the aristocracy; improving their influence over ecclesiastical, local and royal institutions; and embedding themselves in the upper strata of a new military order.

Some evidence has been provided for the very few officials the counts relied on to administer the county before William I's reign – most notably in the county of Avellino – but it was not until stability and peace were reached that functionaries acting as agents of comital power began to be broadly identified. The functionaries that served the count, and were neither royal nor public town officials, bore diverse titles, such as chamberlains, constables, seneschals and castellans. These comital functionaries could have acted either as part of the count's mobile entourage or as deputies responsible for the county's administration and the count's demesne holdings. The limited information the charters offer on the scope of the comital functionaries' responsibilities can be explained by the fact that each count provided a discrete and personal administrative arrangement, in pursuance perhaps of internally acknowledged local practices. It is clear that the counties of the kingdom's Norman period did not follow a general model of organization or common guidelines for their administrative personnel.

By William II's reign, the king's military control had to be merged with that of the counts, in that the counts were acknowledged not as mere overlords who owed military service to the monarchy but as royal generals in their condition as constables or *magni comestabuli*. The direct economic control the Sicilian king could have pretended to claim on the mainland through fiscal administration and confiscated overlordship was yielded when many exiled noblemen were allowed back to their dominions, keeping their rank as overlords. However, it was through the consolidation of the king's judicial supremacy that the monarchy was able to maintain a unified regime in all of the counties. The administration of justice was the area in which the Sicilian monarchy was able to openly circumscribe the nobility's practices, and effectively condition the political control of the counts. This is not only illustrated by the fact that some counts were enhanced by having become master justiciars but also by the judicial activity the counts exercised within their own counties. In the case of Count Richard of Fondi, where the count overstepped his authority, the superior prerogative of the king's justice was made clear.

On the eve of a new civil war and foreign intervention, William II's death opened up a new period of unrest. Tancred's election as the new king of Sicily, and the advent of the Hohenstaufen and Angevin dynasties, would administer a series of shocks to the south Italian nobility for the next century, but always on the basis of the sociopolitical roles established under the Norman dynasty. The changes made to the upper strata of the peninsular society after 1190 caused the expulsion of some counts, and the creation of new ones, but the comital positions and geographical spheres of authority were retained by the kingdom's ruling generations for centuries.[1] What once were Lombard dignities, Norman overlordships and then territorial clusters of tenants and contingents for the king's armed forces, became the political units upon which the nobility acquired its own identity, at the margins of the ever-present and ever-changing Sicilian royal government. After all, the German and French elites that would invade and infiltrate the kingdom in the following centuries did not speak of a Norman nobility but of an 'Italian' one.

The endurance and consolidation of the Italo-Norman aristocracy merits further discussion and deeper investigation. However, it is through the development of the county and the nobility's capacity to act on their own behalf that these issues can be best understood, without resorting to overarching conclusions or divorced regional case studies. The political agency of these counts, broadly, allowed the group to make its mark on the social, by allowing not only local lordships but also mechanisms of social control to perpetuate throughout the development of the Sicilian kingdom. Both the surviving members of the original kingless upper nobility and the new counts appointed by the monarch endured the convulsions of the kingdom's consolidation, and ensured that their lineages occupied a privileged position within the new social order. This was accomplished by ultimately accepting the king's authority, while simultaneously claiming their own individual roles in the kingdom's government. Hence, the counties of Norman Italy were the centres around which the extent of the royal power and the specific nature of local baronial authority were tested and defined. It is only through first considering the foundations laid by the counts and counties of the 'Norman' kingdom of Sicily that the changes and further development experienced by the nobility, under the constantly changing royal dynasties of following centuries, can be understood.

To conclude, the county became the social stage and political arena in which the upper aristocracy of the kingdom of Sicily was defined and consolidated. The counts that were confirmed, created and mutated during the kingdom's first decades outlived the first royal dynasty, and it was on the comital authority that the kingdom's nobility acted not only as lords but also as political leaders. The counts of Norman Italy reached the end of the twelfth century as neither Lombard nor Norman, but as the cornerstones of a new native south Italian territorial ruling class.

Appendix 1

A note on the *Duana Baronum*

There has been a long debate concerning the *duana baronum*. First, C.A. Garufi suggested that the *duana baronum* – which corresponded to the Greek bureau of the σεκρέτος τῶν ἀποκοπῶν – was an office developed under William II's reign to supervise 'feudal' concessions, as these related to the financial administration of royal holdings.[1] Evidence for the *duana baronum*'s equivalence to the Greek bureau can be found in a bilingual Latin-Greek privilege of January 1180, issued by Geoffrey of Moac. In this, Geoffrey styled himself as palatine chamberlain (*palatinus camerarius*) in charge (*magister*) of the *duana de secretis* and the *duana baronum*; in the Greek, he is attested as in charge (ὁ ἐπὶ) of τοῦ μεγάλου σεκρέτου and τοῦ σεκρέτου τῶν ἀποκοπῶν.[2] M. Caravale suggested that the *duana baronum* was different from the other royal fiscal bureaus in its administrative jurisdiction; the *duana baronum* allegedly had competence over only Apulia and the Terra di Lavoro.[3] Similarly, Takayama argued that the *duana baronum* was part of the administration of the peninsula under William II, as an office based in Salerno. Takayama's argument was then accepted by Johns and Oldfield.[4]

Takayama summarized the functions of the *duana baronum* as follows: granting of royal lands and holdings, communicating and issuing royal ordinances, granting permission for sale of lands, lending of monies, buying of houses and paying the sums owing, holding court, controlling officials and receiving indictments.[5] Although his argument of having the *duana baronum* as an established office in Salerno is not convincing – many documents regarding the bureau are unclear of its location – this list of tasks seems possible, as they are all limited to the financial and judicial administration of royal rights and holdings. The activities of the *duana baronum* are documented not only on the peninsula but also in Sicily. This is attested when Count William of Marsico sold his Palermitan houses to the royal *curia* in July 1176; he did so by conducting business with the *duana baronum* in Palermo.[6] This transaction is mentioned by Takayama, but he erroneously classifies the document's concerned area as Marsico. Count William's sale regarded only holdings in Palermo, and it was conducted in the presence of Qaid Mataracius, who was not only the *magister* of the *duana baronum* but also the chamberlain (*camerarius*) of the royal palace. The document was subscribed by Nicholas, the Greek-speaking *magister* of the *duana de secretis*, and by Raynald of Monte Forte, who was both the *magister iustitiarius* of the royal court (*regia magna curia*) and the Palermitan *comestabulus*.[7] Thus, the sale appears to have been conducted in Palermo.

Takayama suggests that the *duana baronum* was responsible for maintaining the *Quaternus magne expeditionis*, based on the assumption that this *duana* was an office dedicated exclusively to the administration of the peninsular dominions.[8] Since the *Quaternus* only dealt with peninsular lords, the geographical agreement is the basis of his suggestion. However, this is problematic, because the making and revision of the *Quaternus* was a gradual process from *c.* 1150 to 1168, whereas the earliest presence of someone in charge of the *duana baronum* was in March 1168 – Qaid Richard, bearing the new title ὁ ἐπὶ τοῦ σεκρέτου τῶν ἀποκοπῶν – and the earliest documented activity of the same bureau was not until September 1174.[9] Moreover, Takayama seems to have merged the administration of the king's finances and holdings on the one hand with the organization of military service on the mainland, and the supervision of the aristocracy's own prerogatives and holdings on the other. These last two functions do not accord with the competences of the *duana baronum* that Takayama had previously identified.

Finally, Takayama argues that one of the *duana baronum*'s main functions was to watch over and control the vassals and cities, and so the disappearance of baronial revolts was a result of its success. With this in mind, Takayama saw in the change of the head of the *duana baronum* from chamberlain (*camerarius*) to admiral (*stolii amiratus*) in 1178 – first under Walter of Moac and then Eugenius – a considerable transition 'from a more bureaucratic official to a more military-oriented administrative official'.[10] Even though one cannot argue against the military nature of a *stolii amiratus*, it is clear from all the documented cases presented here that the admirals as commanders of the fleet, at least during the Norman period, were never in charge of the mainland armed forces or the counts' military contingents. Except for Count William of Marsico's sale of his Palermitan holdings, none of the documented activities and tasks of the Italo-Norman counts related to or were affected by the *duana baronum*. As is explained in this chapter, the new role that the upper aristocracy, especially the counts, obtained was instrumental not only in reshaping the kingdom's military command but also in the administration of justice and the king's communication with other peninsular barons. If anything, the development of more sophisticated or specialized royal finance bureaus were the result of a new phase of internal social stability attained by the peninsular nobility and its involvement in the kingdom's governance, not the other way around.

To summarize, the *duana baronum* was a financial office that branched from the Palermitan royal bureaus, and oversaw the revenue, sales, transfers and disputes related to the king's conditional holdings and privileges – the traditionally called 'feudal concessions' – either on the island or on the peninsula. The *baronum* attached to its name seems to have been a reference to the baronial nature of these rights and holdings, which can be considered a type of 'partitioned' or 'detached' property or franchise, echoing thus the Greek name of the bureau – ἡ ἀποκοπή means 'something divided' or 'cut off'. By contrast, the *duana baronum* was not a royal office established to deal with the barons on the peninsula, much less a secretary for the kingdom's military administration.

Appendix 2

Figures

Figure 1 Funerary inscription of Matilda, daughter of Count Sylvester of Marsico.
Credit: Hervin Fernández-Aceves.

Figure 2 Tancred's triumphant entry into Palermo. Petrus de Ebulo, 'Liber ad honorem Augusti sive de rebus Siculis'. Bern, Burgerbibliothek, cod. 120.II [Nos 7–8], fol. 102r. *Credit:* Burgerbibliothek of Bern.

Figure 3 Address of Count Richard of Acerra and the archbishop of Salerno to the Neapolitans. Petrus de Ebulo, 'Liber ad honorem Augusti sive de rebus Siculis'. Bern, Burgerbibliothek, cod. 120.II [Nos 7–8], fol. 113r.
Credit: Burgerbibliothek of Bern.

Figure 4 Count Richard of Acerra and a band of *milites*. Bern, Burgerbibliothek, cod. 120. II [Nos 7–8], fol. 121r.
Credit: Burgerbibliothek of Bern.

Figure 5 Lead seal of Count Roger of Andria. Promis, Domenico, 'Notizia di una bolla di piombo del secolo XII', Atti della R. Accademia delle scienze di Torino, 4 (1869), 670-74. *Credit:* Public Domain.

Figure 6 Count Roger of Andria. Petrus de Ebulo, 'Liber ad honorem Augusti sive de rebus Siculis'. Bern, Burgerbibliothek, cod. 120.II [Nos 7–8], fols 99r and 104r.
Credit: Burgerbibliothek of Bern.

Appendix 3

Maps

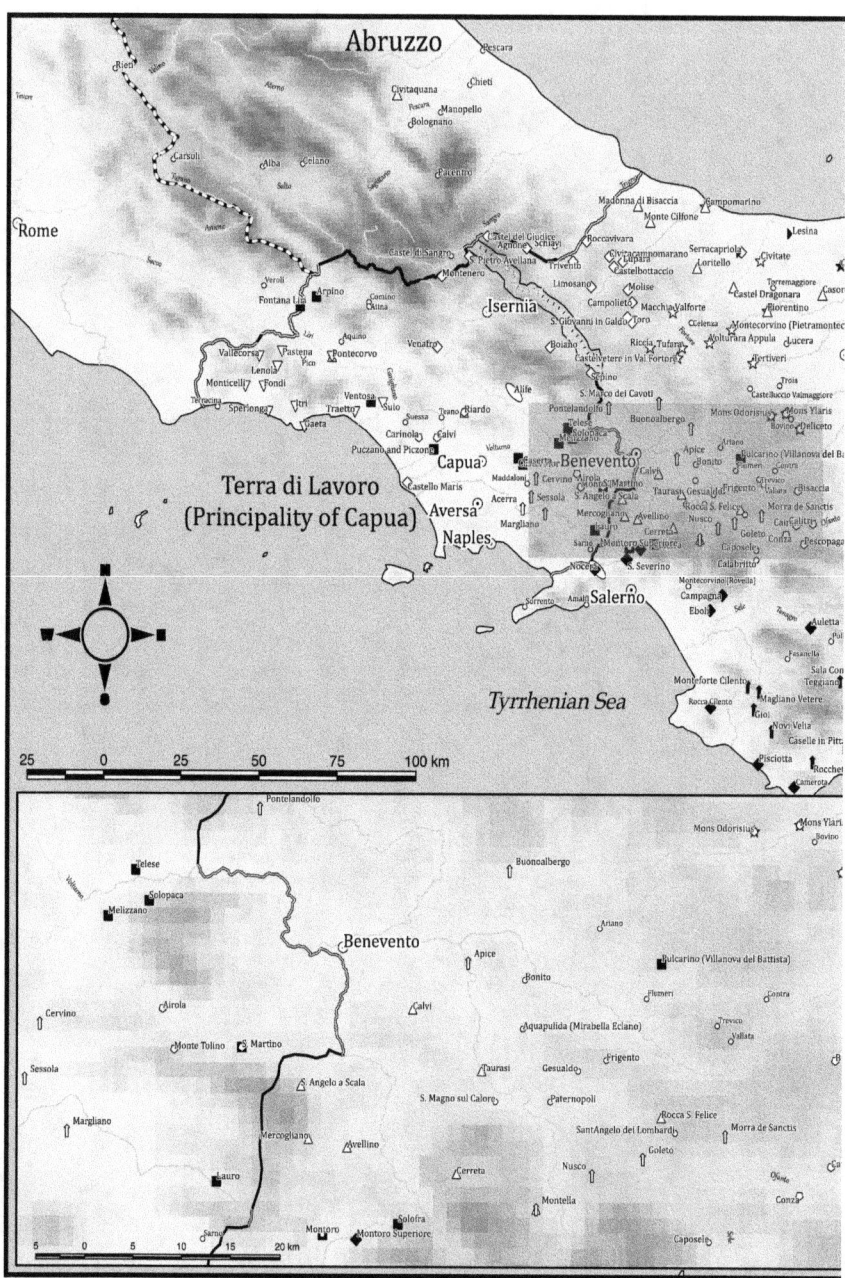

Map 1 The Norman kingdom of Sicily (1130–89).

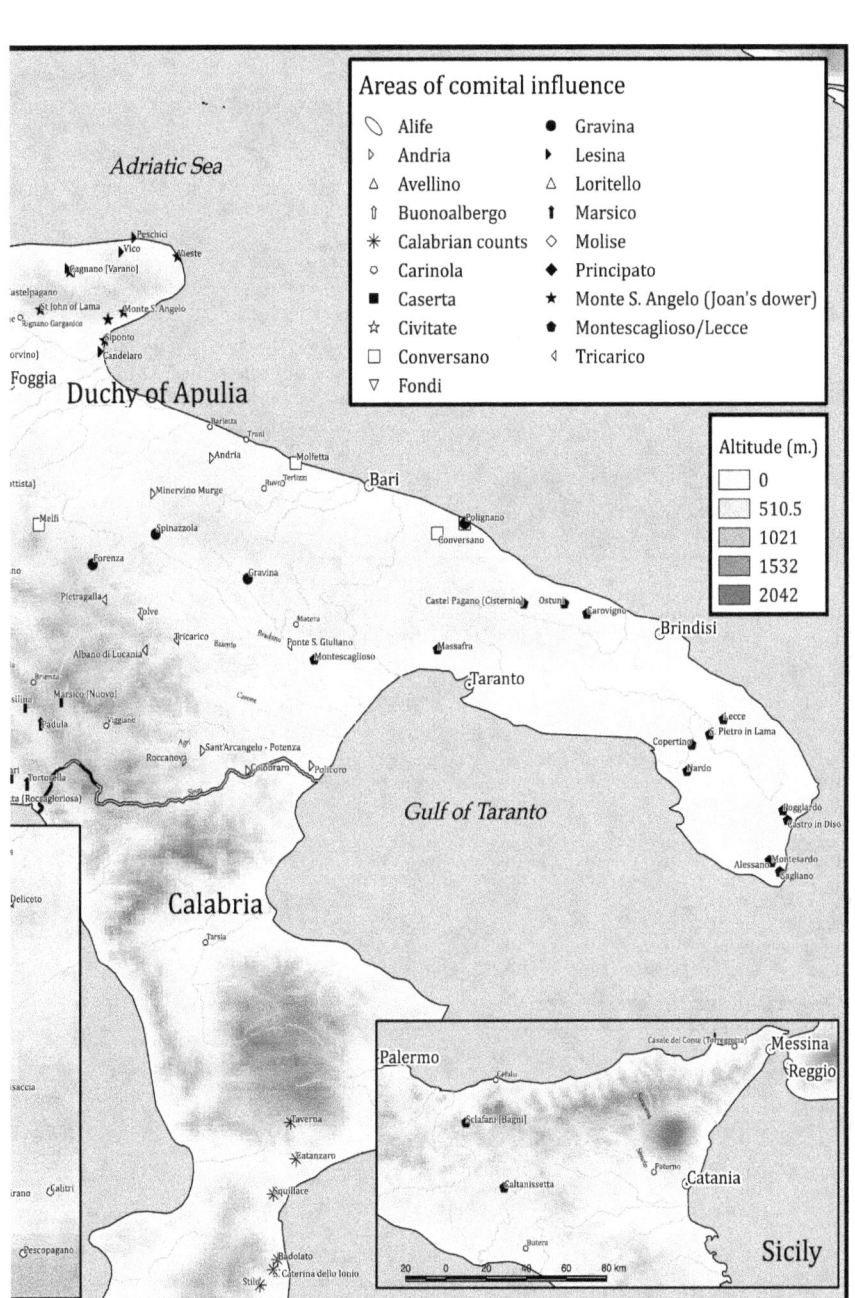

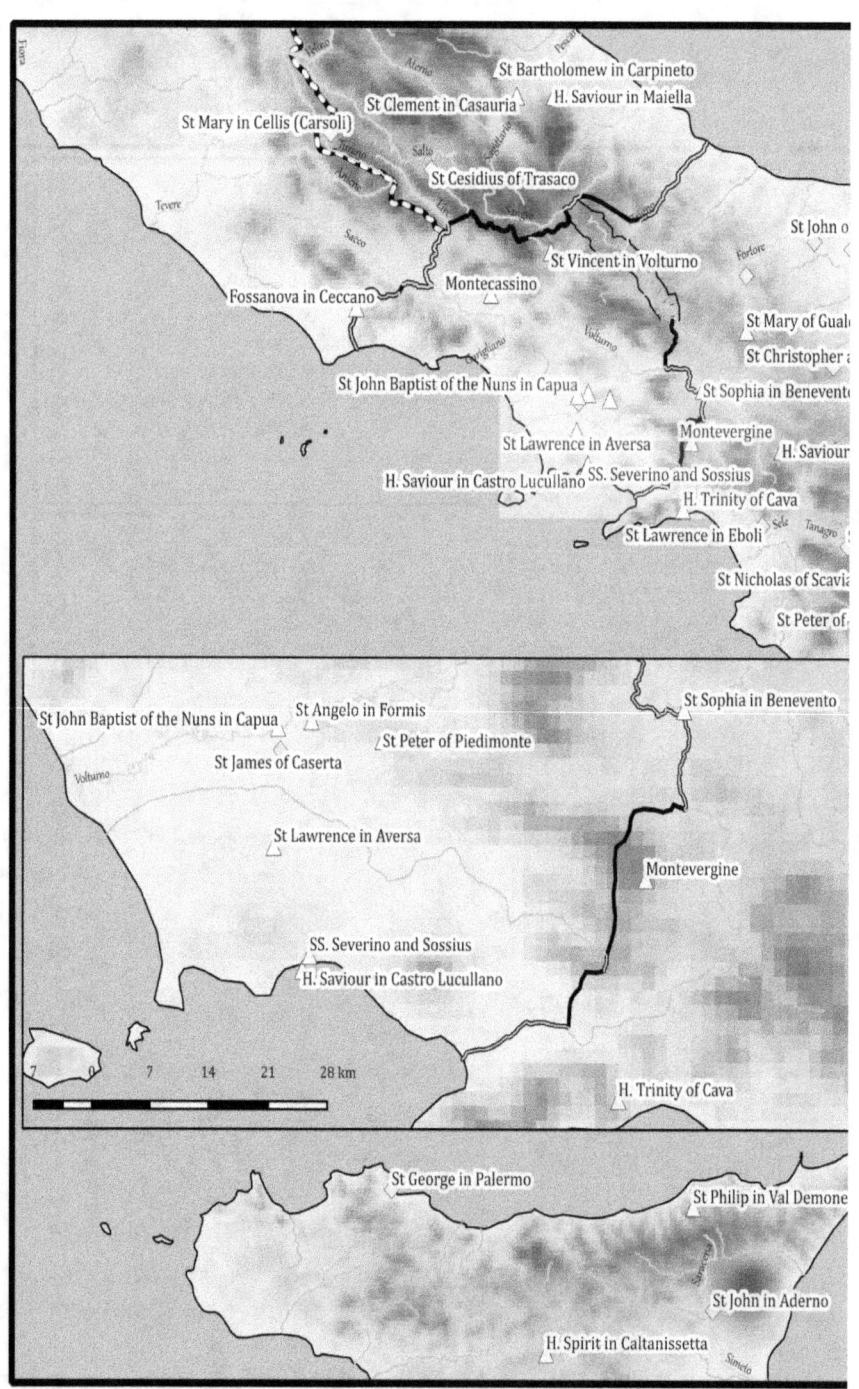

Map 2 Abbeys and churches involved in comital activities and transactions.

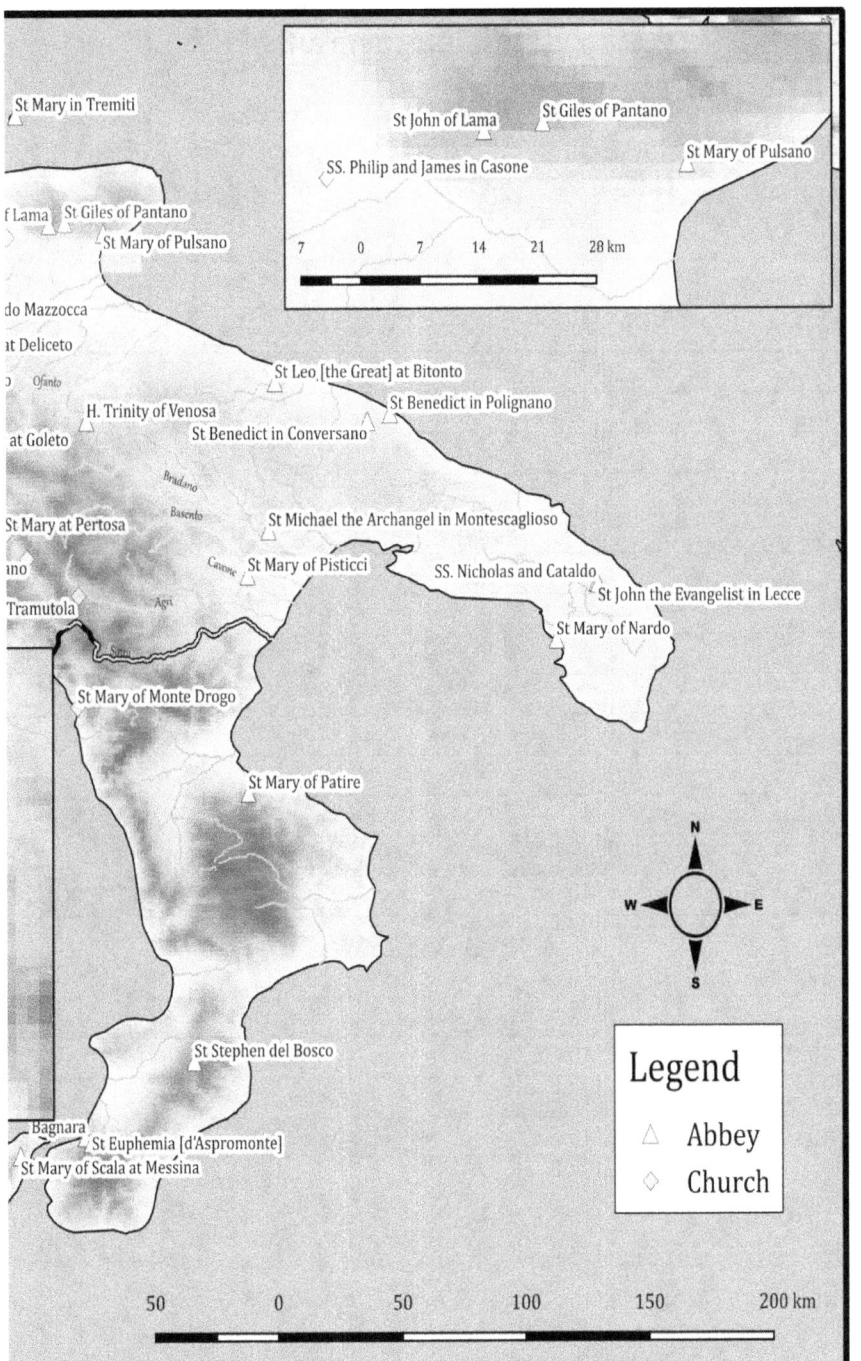

Appendix 4

Tables and diagrams

Chronological Table. The Counties of Apulia, Capua and Calabria (1130–89)

	Roger II
	1130 1131 1132 1133 1134 1135 1136 1137 1138 1139 1140 1141 1142 1143 1144 1145 1146 1147 1148 1149 1150 1151 1152 1153 1154 1155
Alife	
Andria	
Avellino	
Buonoalbergo/Acerra	
Carinola/Conza	
Caserta	
Catanzaro	
Civitate	
Conversano	
Fondi	
Gravina	
Lesina	
Loritello	
Marsico	
Molise	
Montescaglioso/Lecce	
Principato	
S. Angelo dei Lombardi	
Squillace	
Tricarico	

Uncertainty / Vacancy

| | Pre-kingdom count | | 1st appointed/succesor count | | 2nd | | 3rd | | 4th | | 5th |

| | William I | | William II |

Genealogical Network. Comital Kinship in the Norman Kingdom of Sicily (1137–89)

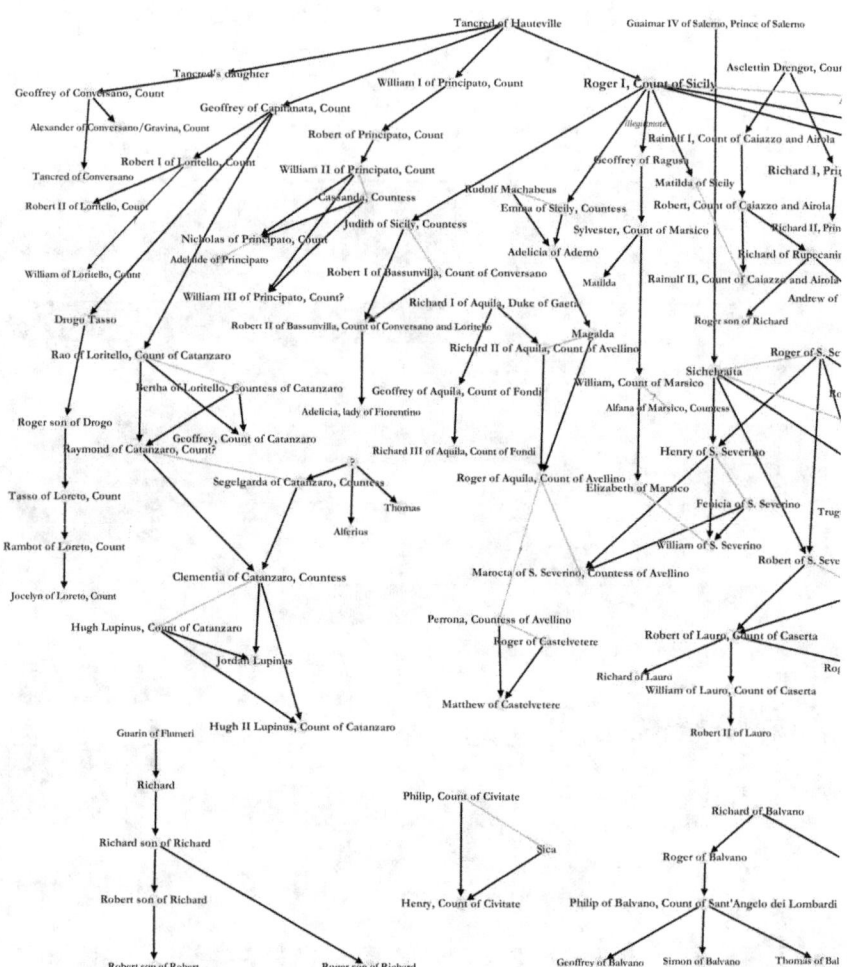

Type of Relationship
Lineage (Parent → Child)
Marriage/Concubinage
? Uncertain/Hypothesis
Otto/Tento of Savona
Manfred del Vasto
Adelaide del Vasto, Countess of Sicily
Boniface del Vasto, Marquis of Savona
Flandina
Manfred of Gravina, Marquis
Henry del Vasto, Lord of Paternò (Count?)
Philippa of Gravina, Marchioness
Simon of Policastro, Count
Sylvester of Gravina, Marquis
Jordan I, Prince of Capua
Roger II, King of Sicily
Hugh I of Molise, Count of Boiano
concubine
Robert I, Prince of Capua
illegitimate
Robert of Molise, Count of Boiano
Jordan II, Prince of Capua
Simon of Molise
Geoffrey II of Mortagne
Robert of Sorrento
Simon, Count of Mileto?
Juliana of Perche
Rupecanina, Count
Jonathan I, Count of Carinola
Gilbert of L'Aigle
Rotrou II of Perche
Berard of Alba, Count
Alfonso, Prince of Capua
Hugh II of Molise, Count of Boiano
Daughter of Berard
Margaret of L'Aigle
Stephen, Archbishop of Palermo
Bartholomew, Count of Carinola
William I, King of Sicily
Garcia Ramirez, King of Navarre
Peter of Celano, Count
Margaret of Navarre, Queen of Sicily
Richard, Count of Carinola, Duke of Gaeta
Roger III
Henry (Rodrigo), Count of Montescaglioso, Principato
Geoffrey of Medania, Lord of Acerra
Jonathan II, Count of Carinola and Conza
William II, King of Sicily
Stephanie, Countess
Adelicia, Countess of Principato
Bertram
Geoffrey
William, Count of Principato
Robert of Medania, Count of Buonoalbergo
concubine
Richard, Count of Carinola and Conza
Accardus, Lord of Lecce
Robert Capumaza
Judith
Raynald of Aquino
Emma II of Lecce, Abbess
Simon of Tivilla
Cecilia of Medania
Emma of Lecce
Roger of Acerra
Geoffrey of Lecce, Count of Montescaglioso
Roagia, Countess
Sibylla of Aquino
Alberada of Lucera
Roger II of Tricarico
Richard of Aquino, Count of Acerra
Tancred of Lecce, Count of Lecce
Sibylla, Countess
Gilbert
Bohemund of Tarsia, Count of Manopello
Stephanie, Countess
Bertram, Count of Andria
Carbonellus of Tarsia
Bohemund II of Tarsia
Richard of Mandra, Count of Molise
Henry of Ollia
Richard of Say, Count of Fondi, Gravina
Gilbert of Balvano
Gaitelgrima, Countess of Molise
Geoffrey of Ollia, Count of Lesina
Theodora, Countess of Gravina
Sibylla of Lesina, Countess
Tancred of Say, Count of Gravina
Roger, Count of Molise

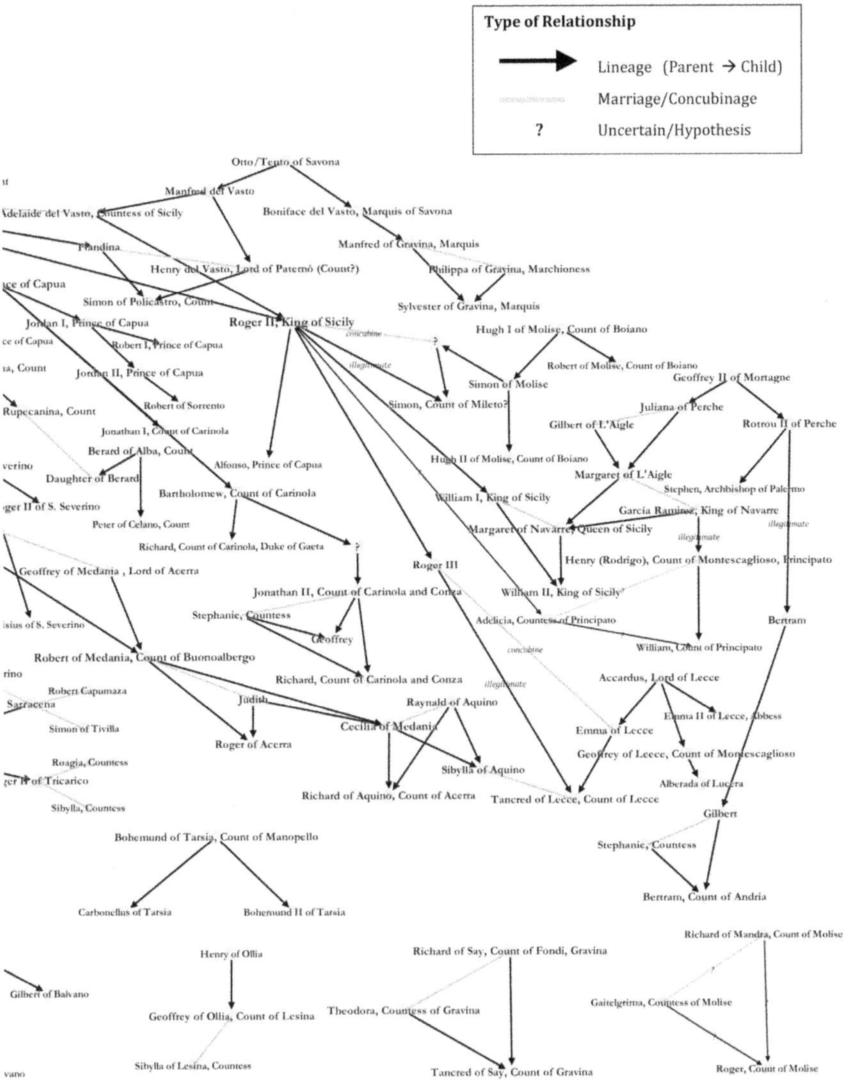

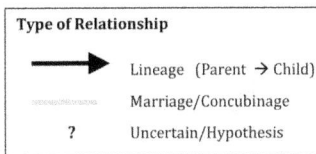

Notes

Introduction

1 Cuozzo, 'Montescaglioso', pp. 7–8.
2 Skinner, *Family Power in Southern Italy*; Drell, *Kinship & Conquest*; Metcalfe, *The Muslims of Medieval Italy*; Oldfield, *City and Community in Norman Italy*. It must also be noted, as a useful and early example of this trend, the work of Reynolds, who covered medieval Europe broadly, including the twelfth and thirteenth centuries. Reynolds, *Fiefs and Vassals*; Reynolds, *Kingdoms and Communities*.
3 Bloch, *La Société féodale*, pp. 266–70, 605–11; Cahen, *Le régime féodal de l'Italie normande*; Carocci, *Signorie di Mezzogiorno*.
4 On the structure of the Italo-Norman nobility and the unhelpfulness of 'feudal' concepts, see Loud, 'Le strutture del potere'.
5 For a parallel example of holdings being granted, taken back and re-granted, see the remarkable discussion about Saxony in the eleventh century by Leyser, 'The Crisis of Medieval Germany'.
6 This is one of the core critiques of 'feudalism' formulated by Elizabeth Brown and Susan Reynolds. Brown, 'The Tyranny of a Construct'; Reynolds, *Fiefs and Vassals*, pp. 48–52, 115–80, 181–2.
7 Jamison, 'Norman Administration'; Marongiu, 'A Model State in the Middle Ages'; Takayama, *The Administration*; Johns, *Arabic Administration in Norman Sicily*.
8 Jamison, 'Additional Work', p. 15; Cuozzo, 'Milites e testes', p. 150; Cuozzo, 'Prosopografia: i Balvano', pp. 79–81; Cuozzo, 'Montescaglioso', p. 29; Cuozzo, *Quei maledetti normanni*, pp. 105–13; Martin, *La Pouille*, pp. 770–95; Loud, 'Continuity and Change', pp. 333–7; Drell, *Kinship & Conquest*, pp. 44–5.
9 Takayama, *The Administration*.
10 Nef, *Conquérir et gouverner la Sicile islamique aux XIe et XIIe siècles*.
11 'Il manque à ce grand livre d'histoire une réflexion plus poussée en anthropologie et en sociologie'. Lejbowicz, 'Annliese Nef, Conquérir et gouverner la Sicile islamique aux XIe et XIIe siècles'.
12 This typology for the study of social control is based on the work of Michael Mann, who has presented an extensive theoretical and diachronic account of power in human history in his four-volume work on the sources of social power. In his corpus, Mann offers a historical sociology based upon a systematic insistence on the contingency and conjunctural character of history. This approach can be summed up in two premises that can be applied for the study of pre-modern political organizations: (1) societies are constituted of multiple overlapping and intersecting socio-spatial networks of power, and (2) a general account of societies, their structure and their history can best be given, independently of the existence of a fixed institutional framework, in terms of the interrelations of sources of power: ideological, economic, military and political relationships. Mann, *A History of Power from the Beginning to AD 1760*, pp. 1–34. See also Hall and Schroeder, *An Anatomy of Power*.

13 For a relevant discussion about Falco's chronicle, see Loud, 'The Genesis and Context'; Loud, *Creation of the Kingdom*, pp. 52-62. For the location of this and other abbeys relevant to this study, see Map 2.
14 *Romuald*, pp. 293-4.
15 Matthew, 'The Chronicle', pp. 267-71. Cf. Loud and Wiedemann, 'Introduction', pp. 52-3. The sources Romuald employed for the earlier entries of his universal chronicle must have included compilations of older authorities, including Isidore of Seville, Orosius and Paul the Deacon. He must have also used the *Annales Beneventani* (in their second or third year), the *Chronica Cavensis*, the chronicle of Lupus Protospatharius of Bari, the Troian *Annales*, and perhaps the Montecassino chronicle of Leo of Ostia and Peter the Deacon. Garufi's introduction in *Romuald*, pp. v-x.
16 Loud, 'Monastic Chronicles', pp. 106-26.
17 On the documents transcribed in the chronicle of Carpineto, see Holtzmann, 'Charters of Carpineto'.
18 Iannacci, 'Il Liber instrumentorum del monastero di San Salvatore a Maiella'.
19 It has been speculated, for example, that for the reign of Roger II the number of surviving documents might be no more than 10 per cent of the total of those issued. Brühl, *Urkunden und Kanzlei*, p. 34.
20 On the problem of the royal diplomatic evidence, see especially Loud, 'The Chancery and Charters'.
21 Rosenwein, *To Be the Neighbor of Saint Peter*; Barton, *Lordship in the County of Maine, c. 890-1160*, especially pp. 12-15; Davies and Fouracre, *The Settlement of Disputes*; Davies and Fouracre, *Property and Power*; Davies and Fouracre, *The Languages of Gift*.
22 Jamison, 'Foreword', I, pp. xv-xxiii.
23 Fernández-Aceves, 'Royal Comestabuli', pp. 5-12.

Chapter 1

1 *Roger II Diplomata*, no. 6, pp. 16-17.
2 George of Antioch is described by Alexander of Telese as the *magnus ammiratus* who commanded the maritime attack over Amalfi in 1131, a man 'most faithful to the king and most accomplished in secular matters'. *Al. Tel.*, bk II, chap. 8, p. 27. George of Antioch had previously been an official of the Zirid sultans of Ifriqiya, in Mahdia, who offered his services to the Sicilian ruler after he lost his favour with the new Zirid Sultan Yahya, c. 1108-13. By 1123, he had risen to second in command in Christodoulos's navy during the unsuccessful campaign to take Mahdia. It might have been around the year he is recorded in Montescaglioso that George of Antioch became Roger's principal minister, a position he kept until his death in 1151. See Ménager, *Amiratus*; Takayama, *The Administration*, pp. 66-7, 90-1; Johns, *Arabic Administration in Norman Sicily*, pp. 80-8; Metcalfe, *The Muslims of Medieval Italy*, pp. 124-8.
3 *Reg. Neap. Arch. Mon.*, V, no. 485, pp. 219-21; Balducci, *Regesto delle pergamene della curia arcivescovile di Chieti. 1006-1400*, pp. 94-6; *Cod. Dipl. Tremiti*, no. 90, pp. 262-4; Martin and others, *Registrum Petri Diaconi*, III, no 581, pp. 1579-88; Jahn, *Untersuchungen zur die normannischen Herrschaft in Süditalien (1040-1100)*, no. 16, pp. 400-1; *Chron. S. Sophiae*, pp. 736-8. Gattola's edition, although inferior to *Registrum Petri Diaconi: (Montecassino, Archivio dell'abbazia, reg. 3)*, provides in the

1113 transcribed charter a reproduction of the cruciform comital cypher that the 'count of counts' used as his *signum manus*. Gattola, *Accessiones*, I, pp. 716–17.
4 Jamison, 'Norman Administration', pp. 229–30.
5 Cuozzo, 'I comitati', p. 288.
6 Cuozzo, 'La contea normanna di Mottola e Castellaneta', especially pp. 7–8, and 34–9. On the extensively documented but controversial Richard the Seneschal, see Guerrieri, *Il conte normanno Riccardo Siniscalco*; Villani, 'Diplomi inediti di Riccardo Siniscalco e Costanza d'Altavilla'.
7 On the military nature of the comital dignity in Norman Italy, see Cuozzo, 'L'unificazione normanna'; Cuozzo, 'La contea normanna di Mottola e Castellaneta', pp. 7–8.
8 Loud, *The Age of Robert Guiscard*, pp. 246–52.
9 Martin, *La Pouille*, pp. 717–18, 725–7.
10 On this discussion, see Loud, *The Age of Robert Guiscard*, pp. 253–5.
11 Cuozzo, *La cavalleria*, p. 198.
12 Bachrach, *Early Carolingian Warfare*, pp. 213–17. The title of *comes* was not a Carolingian invention but a relatively old institution used in the late Roman Empire to honour elite military personnel who were accorded high status in the imperial army. The Merovingian rulers subsequently adopted the title, using it to honour notables who performed military and administrative functions. Alexander Murray has even suggested that this was the result of a direct institutional continuity between the Roman *comitatus* and the Frankish comital position. Jones, *The Later Roman Empire, 284–602*, I, pp. 104–7, 666; Frank, *Scholae Palatinae*, pp. 118–19, 226; Murray, 'From Roman to Frankish Gaul', pp. 56–60, 70–3, 90. Cf. Ian Wood, who instead argues that these titles were merely formal remnants of the Roman past, and did not convey specific administrative definitions that would differentiate them in practice. Wood, *The Merovingian Kingdoms 450–751*, pp. 261–3.
13 Ganshof, 'Charlemagne et les institutions de la monarchie franque', I, pp. 366–72; Costambeys, Innes and MacLean, *The Carolingian World*, pp. 179–83; Bachrach, 'Charlemagne', pp. 172–4, 187. For a discussion on the relationship between power and status of the Carolingian and post-Carolingian counts in northern France, see Reynolds, *Fiefs and Vassals*, pp. 111–14; Barton, *Lordship in the County of Maine, c. 890–1160*, pp. 77–81, 85–8.
14 *Al. Tel.*, bk 9, chap. 7, pp. 9–10.
15 Chalandon, *Histoire de la domination normande en Italie et en Sicile*, II.
16 Salvati, *Le Pergamene di Caiazzo*, nos 7, pp. 46–8; 13 pp. 57–9.
17 *Falco*, pp. 90–100.
18 *Pergamene di S. Nicola di Bari*, nos 67, pp. 115–16; 69 pp. 121–2. The October 1121 charter was originally dated 1122, indiction 15, but considering that the editor Nitti di Vito placed this document before a May 1122 charter, and that the notary most likely counted the indiction following the Constantinopolitan calendar (the Byzantine year began on 1 September), the correct year must be 1121. See also Martin, 'Les communautés', p. 83, n. 74.
19 *Al. Tel.*, bks 1, chap. 12, pp. 12–13; 2 chap. 38, pp. 41–2.
20 Jahn, *Untersuchungen zur die normannischen Herrschaft in Süditalien (1040–1100)*, pp. 262–5; Martin, *La Pouille*, pp. 737–40.
21 *Falco*, pp. 101–2.
22 *Al. Tel.*, bk 1, chap. 8, p. 10.
23 *Al. Tel.*, bk 1, chap. 18, pp. 16–17.

24 *Falco*, pp. 102–4.
25 *Falco*, pp. 66–70.
26 *Falco*, pp. 84–6.
27 *Chron. Cas.*, bk 4, chap. 93, p. 553. The year 1127 has been added in the margin by the editor. An 1148 charter subsequently records a dispute between Montecassino and '*dominus Pandulfus Aquini*'; Scandone, *Per la controversia*, p. 27 (quoting Codex Diplomaticus Aquinas, 1148, Cod. Ms. 640, p. 42).
28 *Chron. Cas.*, bk. 4, chap. 124, p. 600.
29 Mazzoleni, *Pergamene di Capua*, I, no. 11, pp. 26–31.
30 Bova, p. 247. Cf. Mazzoleni, who has dated the latter document 1114 instead; *Pergamene di Capua*, I, no. 12, pp. 31–3.
31 II, no. 290, pp. 196–8; Martin and others, *Registrum Petri Diaconi*, III, no. 577, pp. 1569–70.
32 Martin and others, *Registrum Petri Diaconi*, III, no. 603, pp. 1642–4.
33 *Cod. Dipl. Cajetanus*, II, no. 328, pp. 260–2.
34 The parentage between Bartholomew and Richard is attested in *Cod. Dipl. Cajetanus*, II, no. 262, pp. 142–3; *Cod. Dipl. Aversa*, no. 54, pp. 401–2.
35 Cava, *Arm. Mag.* F.37, ed. in Scandone, II, no. 113, p. 120.
36 Houben, *Die Abtei Venosa*, no. 89, pp. 322–3.
37 Cava, *Arm. Mag.* F.44. Abstract in Carlone, *Documenti per la storia di Eboli*, no. 110, pp. 52–3.
38 *Al. Tel.*, bk 2, chap. 48, pp. 46–7; chap. 68, p. 56; *Annales Casinenses*, p. 28.
39 *Chron. Cas.*, bk. 4, chap. 62, p. 525.
40 De Francesco, 'Origini e sviluppo dei Feudalismo nel Molise fino alla caduta della dominazione normanna' (1910 1909), 432–60, 640–71–98, 273–307; Jamison, *I conti di Molise e di Marsia nei secoli XII e XIII*.
41 *Chron. S. Sophiae*, pp. 772–8.
42 Martin and others, *Registrum Petri Diaconi*, III, no. 606, pp. 1648–9; Leccisotti, no. 2, pp. 89–90. See also Pontificio Ateneo di S. Anselmo, *Studia Benedictina: in memoriam gloriosi ante saecula XIV transitus S.P. Benedicti*, pp. 89–90; Hoffmann, 'Chronik und Urkunden', no. 606, p. 143; Dell'Omo, *Il Registrum di Pietro Diacono (Montecassino, Archivio dell'Abbazia, Reg. 3)*, p. 165.
43 *Chron. Cas.*, bk. 4, chap. 96, pp. 556–7. Cf. Gattola, *Accessiones*, I, p. 242.
44 Martin, *La Pouille*, p. 725.
45 *Chartes de Troia*, no. 44, pp. 171–2.
46 *Italia Sacra*, VI, cols 706–7.
47 *Cod. Dipl. Tremiti*, nos 99–100, pp. 284–6. See also Morlacchetti, *L'abbazia benedettina delle Isole Tremiti e i suoi documenti dall'XI al XIII secolo*, pp. 276–7.
48 See page 33.
49 *Cod. Dipl. Tremiti*, no. 94, pp. 267–9. Also, see Morlacchetti, *L'abbazia benedettina delle Isole Tremiti e i suoi documenti dall'XI al XIII secolo*, p. 269.
50 *Chron. Cas.*, bk. 4, chap. 82, p. 545.
51 *Chron. Cas.*, bk. 4, chap. 84, pp. 546–7.
52 Bachrach, 'Neo-Roman vs Feudal', pp. 4–6; Paul, 'Origo Consulum', pp. 147–8; King, *William of Malmesbury*, pp. 84–5; Barraclough, *The Charters of the Anglo-Norman Earls of Chester, c. 1071–1237*, no. 56, pp. 68–9; 81 93–4; 84 96–7; 90 103–4.
53 Paul, 'Origo Consulum', p. 148, n. 38.
54 Paul, 'Origo Consulum', p. 148. See also Haskins, *The Renaissance of the Twelfth Century*, pp. 127–52.

55 Cava, *Arm. Mag.* G.2, ed. in Garufi, 'I conti di Montescaglioso', no. 3, pp. 350–1.
56 *Castella* often refer to walled villages or fortifications, and not necessarily to 'castles'. Such fortified villages were the norm in Apulia and the Terra di Lavoro in the twelfth century, in contrast to the island of Sicily, where villages were usually open (*casalia*). Martin, *La Pouille*, pp. 267–89.
57 *Roger II Diplomata*, no. 6, pp. 16–17.
58 *William of Apulia*, p. 192.
59 Garufi, 'I conti di Montescaglioso', pp. 334–5; Antonucci, 'Goffredo conte di Lecce e di Montescaglioso', pp. 449–51. Umfridus is recorded as *comes Montis Scaviosi* in a 1085 donation by which he granted property to the monastery of St Michael the Archangel *in civitate vetera*, subscribed by *Gualterius, Goffredus filius domini Umfredus comes, domino Rao Machabeo, Asegatto*, among others. *Reg. Neap. Arch. Mon.*, VI, no. 6, p. 156.
60 Cuozzo, 'Montescaglioso', pp. 13–18.
61 Cuozzo, 'Montescaglioso', p. 26.
62 *Reg. Neap. Arch. Mon.*, VI, no. 20-3, pp. 184–93. See also Tansi, *Historia cronologica monasterii S. Michaelis Archangeli Montis Caveosi*, no. 13, pp. 149–52.
63 Cava, *Arm. Mag.* G.27, ed. in Garufi, 'I conti di Montescaglioso', no. 4, p. 352. Polla is a town located in the Diano valley, in eastern Cilento, near Salerno.
64 Jamison, *Catalogus Baronum*, ¶¶ 465, p. 87; 552-6, p. 102.
65 Jamison, 'Note e documenti', p. 456. For a brief discussion of the first Norman counts in Catanzaro, see Macchione, *Alle origini di Catanzaro*, pp. 44–6. On St. Stephen del Bosco, see below, note 120 (ch. 4).
66 '*Alexander Cupersanensis comes et Tanc Cupersani et Gauf Catenzarii comes et Robertus Gravini*'. *Roger II Diplomata*, no. 20, pp. 54–6.
67 Jamison, 'Note e documenti', p. 319; Cuozzo, 'I conti normanni di Catanzaro', pp. 110–14.
68 Montfaucon, *Palaeographia Graeca*, col. 396.
69 Feller, 'The Northern Frontier', pp. 47–8.
70 This is not to say that the memory of the Carolingian era had no effect on the legitimacy and status of the lords in the subsequent periods in lands where effective Carolingian rule is attested. For an example of a better documented case of post-Carolingian lordship, see the case of the county of Maine, in northern France, where the 'basis for the lordship of the tenth-century counts was possession of the same places, objects, and symbols of power that had been important during the Carolingian era'. Barton, *Lordship in the County of Maine, c. 890–1160*, pp. 70–1.
71 Feller, 'The Northern Frontier', pp. 59–61. See Genealogical Network. Also, see B. Pio's family tree. *Chron. de Carpineto*, Table 6.
72 *Roger II Diplomata*, no. 15, p. 43; *Cod. dipl. Molisano*, pp. 325–6.
73 Atto VII can be found as count of Teramo (*Aprutium*), 1101-1116. According to the chronicle of Casauria, c. 1099, Count Atto abandoned his own wife and brought another woman to live with him, namely Rogata, [Hugh] Mamouzet's widow. *Chron. Casauriense*, cols 874–75. Nonetheless, a November 1093 charter of Hugh Mamouzet suggests that Rogata was already dead (*pro anima Rogate Comitissa, qui fuit coniuge predicti Ugoni*). *Chron. de Carpineto*, no. 120, pp. 253–6, at p. 254. For a discussion of the Attonid's lineage and comital power, see Feller, *Les Abruzzes médiévales*, pp. 611–46, 685–97.
74 On the origins and development of the Borell family, see Rivera, 'Per la storia'; Jamison, 'Noce and Castiglione', I, pp. 54–6; Feller, 'The Northern Frontier', pp. 55–9.

75 *Chron. Casauriense*, col. 886.
76 In one of the chronicle's most striking passages, Count Richard of Manopello was struck down by St. Clement as punishment for his attacks on the abbey, and died mumbling 'Clement, do not persecute me' (*Clemens noli me percutere, noli Clemens*). *Chron. Casauriense*, cols 873–76, especially col. 874. Cf. Loud, *The Age of Robert Guiscard*, p. 144.
77 Loud, *The Age of Robert Guiscard*, p. 253, n. 58.
78 On the influence of Robert of Loritello in the region, and over the town of Chieti and its bishopric, see Feller, 'The Northern Frontier', pp. 61–4.
79 Ménager, 'Les fondations monastiques'; Cuozzo, 'Milites e testes', pp. 140–2, 158–60. Cf. Loud, 'The Abbey of Cava, Its Property and Benefactors in the Norman Era', pp. 157–9. See also Cava, *Arm. Mag.* F.44, and F.45.
80 Loud, 'Calendar'.
81 Landenolfus is attested as being in dispute with Montecassino over '*de alveo fluminis Gariliani*'. A date is not indicated here, although the chronicle records a donation by Geoffrey Ridellus of Gaeta, duke of Gaeta, made just after this episode, dated February 1075/1076. *Chron. Cas.*, bk 3, chap. 41, p. 419.
82 *Cod. Dipl. Cajetanus*, II, no. 262, pp. 142–3. Cf. G. Carelli, who assumes Bartholomew was Jonathan's son instead; Carelli, 'I conti Normanni di Calinulo (1062-1187)', p. 614. Also, cf. Loud, who suggests Count Richard of Carinola was the son of Jonathan as well, and not Bartholomew. Loud, 'Continuity and Change', pp. 332–3.
83 *Cod. Dipl. Aversa*, no. 54, pp. 94–5.
84 II, nos 290, pp. 196–8; 328 pp. 260–2.
85 See Skinner, *Family Power in Southern Italy*, pp. 158–60.
86 Geoffrey Malaterra records that '*Gaufridum de Conversano nepotem suis [Roberti ducis][…] filius […] sororis suae*'. Malaterra, bk. 2 chap. 39 p. 48. William of Apulia likewise stated that '*Robertus de Scabioso Monte comes dictus, Gosfredi frater, et ambo orti germana fuerant ducis*'. *William of Apulia*, p. 192. Interestingly enough, Orderic Vitalis agrees with the south Italian chroniclers, as he is correct in saying that Geoffrey of Conversano was *nepos* of Robert Guiscard, the first duke of Apulia, for his mother was probably the duke's sister. Chibnall, IV, bk 8 p. 33. For further discussion on the reception of the Italian chroniclers in the north of Europe, see Chibnall, *The World of Orderic Vitalis*, pp. 169–220, especially 213–14; Loud, 'Gens Normannorum'.
87 Martin, *La Pouille*, pp. 731–3; Loud, *The Age of Robert Guiscard*, p. 250. Cf. Jahn, *Untersuchungen zur die normannischen Herrschaft in Süditalien (1040–1100)*, pp. 203–5.
88 *Chartes de Troia*, no. 44, pp. 171–2.
89 *Romuald*, p. 183.
90 Caspar, 'Die Chronik von Tres Tabernae in Calabrien (Cronica Trium Tabernarum)', p. 41; Macchione, *Alle origini di Catanzaro*, p. 91. For a discussion on the nature and relevance of this source, the *Chronica trium tabernarum*, see the useful and recent study of Macchione, especially pp. 55–71.
91 Jamison, 'Note e documenti', p. 456.
92 As Cuozzo mentions, Rao's closeness to Roger Borsa can be attested in two charters in which the former subscribed donations made by the latter to the abbey of Cava; *Arm. Mag.* G.31, and G 36. Cuozzo, 'I conti normanni di Catanzaro', p. 110.
93 On Adam of Falloc, see Ménager, 'Inventaire', p. 273.
94 *Malaterra*, pp. 91–3. See also Cuozzo, 'I conti normanni di Catanzaro', pp. 110–11.
95 *Italia Sacra*, VII, cols 426–30.

96 Montfaucon, cols 396-97. See also Jamison, 'Note e documenti', pp. 455-6; Ménager, *Amiratus*, p. 175; Cuozzo, 'I conti normanni di Catanzaro', p. 111.
97 Ménager, 'Inventaire', pp. 330-6. On the origins of Count Hugh of Molise, see De Francesco, 'Feudalismo nel Molise', pp. 78-98; Jamison, *Molise e Marsia*, pp. 3-9. Cf. the latter with a previous, less extensive study that the author published two years before in English on the same topic; Jamison, 'County of Molise'.
98 Cava, *Arm. Mag.* F.37, ed. in Scandone, II, no. 63, p. 120.
99 Cava, *Arca* xx.27 (1114); *Arm. Mag.* E.30 (1115). The latter was edited in Scandone, *Avellino*, vol. 2, no. 50, pp. 113-14.
100 As attested in Cava, *Arca* xx.37 (1115). This document records the will of Count Richard, Count Henry's father, dated 1125. This Gaitelgrima was originally married to Drogo of Hauteville, then to Count Robert of Monte Sant'Angelo, and finally to Count Alfred. See also Loud, 'Continuity and Change', p. 327.

Chapter 2

1 *Al. Tel.*, p. 3.
2 Mazzarese Fardella, 'Problemi preliminari', p. 50.
3 *Falco*, p. 106; *Annales Casinenses*, p. 309. For an extended discussion on this papal schism and its relation to the Sicilian kingdom, see Deér, *Das Papsttum und die süditalienischen Normannenstaaten. 1053-1212*, pp. 212-15; Houben, *Roger II of Sicily*, pp. 50-3; Loud, 'Innocent II and the Kingdom of Sicily'.
4 Kehr, *Italia pontificia*, VIII, no. 35, pp. 36-7; Hoffmann, 'Langobarden, Normannen, Päpste. Zum Legitimationsproblem in Unteritalien', pp. 173-5.
5 Martin, *La Pouille*, pp. 734-6.
6 See page 67.
7 *Pergamene del Duomo di Bari*, no. 42, pp. 80-1. On Roger's possible consent, see Houben, *Roger II of Sicily*, p. 53.
8 *Al. Tel.*, bk 2, chap. 14, pp. 29-30; *Falco*, pp. 120-2.
9 Loud, *Creation of the Kingdom*, p. 31.
10 *Al. Tel.*, bk 2, chap. 18, p. 31.
11 *Falco*, pp. 122-4.
12 *Al. Tel.*, bk 2, chaps 19-21, pp. 31-2.
13 *Roger II Diplomata*, no. 20, pp. 54-6. It was considered degrading for kings to swear oaths in person, especially to their own subjects, a biblical concern based on Mt. 33.7.
14 *Al. Tel.*, bk 2, chaps 29-32, pp. 36-8; *Falco*, pp. 134-40.
15 *Al. Tel.*, bk 2, chaps 33-46, pp. 38-46.
16 *Falco*, pp. 150-2.
17 *Kinnamos*, pp. 36-7, 67, 139, 148-50, 170-4; *Gesta Frederici*, pp. 168-70, 178, 300; *Falcandus*, p. 154; *William of Tyre*, II, pp. 915, 927, 981-3; Hartmann, no. 18, pp. 29-30, 216 pp. 455-61, 233 pp. 497-9; Sudendorf, *Registrum oder merkwürdige Urkunden für die deutsche Geschichte*, II, no. 54, p. 132.
18 *Al. Tel.*, bk 2, chap. 48, pp. 46-7.
19 *Cod. Dipl. Verginiano*, III, no. 214, pp. 52-6.
20 *Al. Tel.*, bk 2, chaps 62-8, pp. 52-6. The term 'homage' is just as thorny as *feudum*. While this is discussed in note 73 (ch. 4), here it describes the performance of public acknowledgement of allegiance, and not necessarily a tenurial relationship.

21 Rivera, 'L'annessione'.
22 Jamison, 'Noce and Castiglione', I, pp. 59–60.
23 *Falco*, pp. 174–6; Caspar, *Roger II*, nos 108–10, pp. 528–9; *Roger II Diplomata*, no. 43, pp. 119–23. The three documents summarized by Caspar were originally issued in Greek, and the last two, issued in April and September respectively, survive only in subsequent witnesses. The 28 April charter survives only in later copies, while the 1 September document is today lost, only mentioned as a Latin translation in a March 1145 charter of the monastery of St Philip of Fragalà. See Loud, *Creation of the Kingdom*, p. 27, n. 81.
24 Caspar, *Roger II*, p. 180; Clementi, 'Historical Commentary', p. 335; Loud, *Creation of the Kingdom*, pp. 27–8.
25 Hugh had succeeded his uncle Robert, brother of his father, Count Simon, who died in 1117. See note 39 (ch. 1).
26 *Al. Tel.*, bk 2, chap. 68, p. 56.
27 *Castellum Maris*, though far from the lordship of Boiano, had long belonged to the Molise family. Hugh I of Molise granted in February 1097 fishing rights at *castello Maris* to the monastery of St Angelo in Formis. Inguanez, *S. Angelo in Formis*, no. 17, pp. 43–5.
28 Benevento, *Fondo S. Sofia*, vol. 2, no. 5. The reference to Abbot John shows that this must be 1121, which is also what the indiction number would suggest. The previous abbot of St Sophia, Bernard, died on 29 July 1120. Falco the notary mentioned must be Falco of Benevento, the only notary named Falco active in Benevento at this time. On the abbey of St Sophia in Benevento and its sources, see Loud, 'A Lombard Abbey'.
29 *Falco*, pp. 86–7. Robert's father, Richard, was in turn the son of Guarin of Frumari (Flumeri?), who was murdered by his own villeins; *Falco*, pp. 70–1. This Richard has been identified by J.-M. Martin in an 1120 Troian charter that records a donation made by count Robert of Loritello before other counts, the duke of Apulia and Pope Calixtus II. *Chartes de Troia*, no. 43, pp. 168–71.
30 '*Nomina autem baronum ducis, qui copti sunt et tenentur, hec sunt: comes R(ogerus) de Ariano, comes R. de Civitate et alii tales fere triginta*'. *Codex Uldarici*. Jaffé, *Monumenta Bambergensia*, pp. 442–4. Henry of Sant'Agata clearly refused here to acknowledge Roger's royal title, referring to him simply as *dux*.
31 Robert son of Richard was also remembered as a count in an undated royal charter of William I (1154–1166), which records the following: *In Apulia autem. in territorio catule. ecclesiam Sancte Marie cum omnibus pertinentiis et possessionibus suis. A Roberto comite filio Riccardi comitis. ecclesie vallis iosaphat largitam*. Garufi, *Documenti inediti*, no. 29, pp. 67–72. See also Cuozzo, 'Prosopografia: i Balvano', p. 79, n. 82. Fiorentino was a town in the Capitanata (modern ruins of Castel Fiorentino), between Lucera and San Severo; see Loud, *Creation of the Kingdom*, p. 174.
32 *Al. Tel.*, bk 3, chap. 6, pp. 62–3.
33 *Al. Tel.*, bk 3, chap. 32, p. 77.
34 *Al. Tel.*, bk 4, chap. 5, pp. 83–4.
35 *Falcandus*, pp. 60–2; Garufi, 'Gli Aleramici', nos 6–8, pp. 76–81.
36 On Henry's parentage, see Garufi, 'Gli Aleramici', pp. 49–50; Houben, *Roger II of Sicily*, pp. 22, 26.
37 Garufi, 'Paternò e i de Luci', pp. 160–3.
38 *William I Diplomata*, no. 16, p. 44. Count Simon was mistakenly remembered in another document as the brother of Adelicia, daughter of Rudolph Machabeus and

Countess Emma, which would have made Simon grandson of Roger I. *Sicilia Sacra*, I, p. 586.
39 *Roger II Diplomata*, no. 57, pp. 15–62, at p. 158; *William I Diplomata*, no. 16, p. 44; *Falcandus*, pp. 60–3, 84–5.
40 *Al. Tel.*, bk 1, chap. 1, p. 23.
41 Cuozzo, *Commentario*, pp. 694–5; Cuozzo, 'Prosopografia: i Balvano', p. 78. Cf. P. Skinner, who identified Jonathan as nephew of Richard instead; Skinner, *Family Power in Southern Italy*, p. 159.
42 This charter, dated 1123, records '*Riccardus Divina providente clementia Consul et Dux praefatae Civitatis olim Domini Bartholomei proles Capuane principi, et Calinulensi Comitibus piae recordationis filius*'. Cf. Skinner, who read this passage as if Richard bore the three titles: prince of Capua, count of Carinola and duke of Gaeta. Skinner, *Family Power in Southern Italy*, p. 159. The same lineage is recorded in a subsequent charter in 1127; *Cod. Dipl. Cajetanus*, II, no. 311, pp. 231–3. Also, see *Cod. Dipl. Cajetanus*, II, no. 326, pp. 256–7.
43 Fernández-Aceves, 'Civitate and Carinola', pp. 65–8.
44 *Romuald*, p. 265.
45 *Falco*, pp. 178–80. The *Annalista Saxo* confirms this, recording that the emperor sent Duke Conrad and part of his army to storm the fortress of Rignano, in the Gargano region, then to move to Monte Gargano to besiege the citadel until Lothar arrived with the rest of the army. The imperial army then marched over Troia, Canne, Barletta and Trani, before entering Bari. After four weeks there, Lothar returned to Trani and went to Melfi. *Annalista Saxo*, pp. 605–11.
46 *Annalista Saxo*, p. 606.
47 Fernández-Aceves, 'Civitate and Carinola', pp. 68–9.
48 *Falco*, p. 196.
49 *Falco*, pp. 206–30.
50 According to Alexander of Telese, the oath read '*ab ipsa hora et in antea justitiam et pacem teneret, et adiuvarent tenere*'. *Al. Tel.*, bk 1, chap. 21, pp. 18–19.
51 Mazzarese Fardella, 'Problemi preliminari', p. 50.
52 *Falco*, p. 230. Roger of Ariano was already out of prison, and most likely exiled from the kingdom, as he is recorded as present, together with the exiled prince of Capua, at the German royal court in April 1144, at Würzburg. Hausmann, *Conradi III. et Heinrici*, nos 99, pp. 176–7; 136 pp. 226–8.
53 *Catalogus Baronum*, ¶¶ 1008–12, pp. 181–2.
54 Scandone, *Per la controversia*, p. 24.
55 *Cod. Dipl. Verginiano*, III, no. 245, pp. 187–92.
56 Hausmann, *Conradi III. et Heinrici*, no. 136, pp. 226–8.
57 *Chron. de Ferraria*, p. 28.
58 Houben, *Roger II of Sicily*, p. 36. Cf. Jamison, *Molise e Marsia*, pp. 21–2.
59 Gattola, *Accessiones*, I, pp. 246–7. Trivento is a town in the region of Molise, northeast of Isernia and northwest of Campobasso, on the eastern bank of the River Trigno.
60 *Chron. Casauriense*, col. 891.
61 Loud, *Creation of the Kingdom*, pp. 45, 300, n. 10.
62 Rome, Biblioteca Apostolica Vaticana, Arch. Cap. S. Pietro Caps. LXXII, fasc. 53, no. 1 ('Liber instrumentorum monasterii Sancti Salvatoris de Maiella'), ff 9r [1144], 16rv [1142], 25v [1141]. Excerpts of these transactions can be found in an eighteenth-century monograph: 'Dissertatio', I, pp. XX–XXII. The 1144 mandate, fol. 9, can be also found in *Roger II Diplomata*, App. 3, no. 60, p. 308.

63 Garufi, 'I diplomi purpurei', pp. 26–8. The original documents are in Cava, *Arm. Mag.* G.19 and G.20; additionally, G.21 is a copy of G.20, and G.22 is a copy of G.19.
64 *Al. Tel.*, bks 3, chap. 28, pp. 74–5; chap. 33, pp. 77–8; 4 chaps 1–2, pp. 81–2; chap. 5, pp. 83–4.
65 This suggestion has been contested on the grounds that, judging by the date of his mother's marriage, Adam Avenel was in 1135 little more than fifteen years old, making him too young to have been a count and a commander. Jamison, 'Judex Tarentinus', pp. 342–4, n. 3.
66 Loud, *Creation of the Kingdom*, p. 116, n. 149.
67 *Pergamene di Conversano*, no. 81, pp. 180–1. On Count Robert's union with Judith of Sicily, see page 56. It is also noteworthy that the very problematic *Breve chronicon Northmannicum* also relates that Robert was created count of Conversano by Roger II, after Alexander of Conversano, the former holder of this comital seat, was defeated. Cuozzo, 'Il "Breve Chronicon Northmannicum"', p. 197. This *chronicon* is a short, anonymous Latin chronicle of the Norman conquest of southern Italy, probably written in Apulia in the early twelfth century. Its authenticity has nevertheless been called into question by André Jacob, who argued that it is an eighteenth-century forgery by Pietro Polidori. Jacob, 'Le Breve Chronicon Nortmannicum'.
68 '[…] *quam domimus Rob(ertus) Lisinensis comes, soccer domini Guidelmi eiusdem civitatis [Lesine] comitis'*. *Cod. Dipl. Tremiti*, no. 103, pp. 287–91, at p. 288.
69 De Francesco, *La badia benedettina*, p. 22.
70 The document also attests him as signatory of the agreement; '*Ego Guidelmus Lisinensi comes concedo et confirmo hanc kartulam et testis sum*'. *Cod. Dipl. Tremiti*, no. 103, pp. 287–91. A count Peter and a count Robert of Lesina are remembered in this transaction as former counts, and Robert of Lesina is also recorded as father-in-law (*socer*) of the current count William, but it is unclear who they were or when they ruled. A. De Francesco has identified Robert as the lord of Devia, recorded in 1104. De Francesco, *La badia benedettina*, p. 22. See also Morlacchetti, pp. 278–9.
71 *Falcandus*, pp. 84–6, 144–5, 154–5.
72 *Pergamene di Salerno*, no. 102, pp. 195–9.
73 *Pergamene di Salerno*, no. 103, pp. 199–201.
74 On the study of its condition as a forgery, see Carlone, *Rocchetta S. Antonio*, p. 74.
75 Cuozzo, 'Milites e testes', pp. 140–8.
76 Trinchera, no. 132, pp. 174–5. Original document found in Cava, *Perg. Greca*, p. 47.
77 Mattei-Ceresoli, 'Tramutola', no. 8, pp. 45–6.
78 Signatory as *Catenzarii comes* of a charter dated 22 June, relating to the city of Bari: '*Alexander Cupersanensis comes et Tanc Cupersani et Gauf Catenzarii comes et Robertus Gravini*'. *Roger II Diplomata*, no. 20, pp. 54–6.
79 *Roger II Diplomata*, no. 59, pp. 166–70, at 169.
80 Pratesi, *Carte dall'archivio Aldobrandini*, no. 14, pp. 41–2.
81 Montfaucon, *Palaeographia Graeca*, col. 396.
82 A Raymond is recorded in the 1112 Calabrian donation as Count Geoffrey's brother.
83 See pages 92 and 130.
84 See Chronological Table.
85 See *Catalogus Baronum*, pp. xv–xxii.
86 *Romuald*, p. 235.
87 Geoffrey of Medania, Robert's father, is attested in May 1118 as lord of Acerra and Sessola (*Gaufridus qui vocor de Medania, Suessolanorum et Acerranorum*). *Cod. Dipl. Aversa*, no. 117, pp. 25–7.

88 For an overview of the Abruzzese counts during the time of Roger II, see Feller, *Les Abruzzes médiévales*, pp. 765-7, 75-8.
89 The legal contention concerned the half of the church of St Mark in Agnone, the possession of which Montecassino disputed with Maynerius of Palena and Matthew of Pettorano; Count Hugh of Molise is recorded as having confirmed one half to Maynerius, ordering hence the other half to be restored to the church. The document, edited by Gattola, could not be found in the archive of Montecassino by Jamison in 1906, but C.H. Haskins saw it in May 1909 and July 1910. Haskins considered it an early copy rather than an original, and noted that there were no witnesses listed. Jamison, 'Norman Administration', p. 418. See also Haskins, 'England and Sicily', p. 643, n. 113; Gattola, *Accessiones*, I, pp. 246-7.
90 Jamison, 'Norman Administration', p. 334. Royal justiciars were initially dispatched from Sicily to the continent or appointed from regional lesser barons (such as Hugh Blancus, Roger of Barolo, Roger of Bisignano and Roger of Brahala) by the new monarchy *c.* 1140, as the king attempted to restore peace and order and involve himself in the local administration of justice. However, this 'office' was not new at this time, because it had long existed at the royal *curia* – *iusticiarius* in Latin corresponded to μὲγας κριτὴς in Greek. For a more detailed account of the origins and development of this office, see Takayama, *The Administration*, pp. 77-93.
91 Limosano, Lupara, Castelbotta and Civitacampomarano are towns in the west of the River Biferno, in modern Molise. Benevento, *Fondo S. Sofia*, vol. 28, no. 8, ed. in Jamison, *Molise e Marsia*, no. 1 pp. 81-3.
92 Benevento, *Fondo S. Sofia*, vol. 12, no. 41, ed. in Jamison, *Molise e Marsia*, no. 2, pp. 83-4. The document is a notarized copy of April 1270. This charter must be used carefully, for many of the St Sophia documents are known to be forgeries drafted in the thirteenth and fourteenth centuries. This document nonetheless records the usage of the older title of count of Boiano, rather than that of count of Molise, which would be unusual for a document made later when the county of Molise was well defined and widely known as such.
93 Venafro is on the western border of the region of Molise, east of S. Germano and west of the River Volturno, closer to the Tyrrhenian than to the Adriatic coast – a key location that surely connected the central region to the Terra di Lavoro and the road to Rome. See Map 1.
94 Benevento, *Fondo S. Sofia*, vol. 2, no. 4, ed. in Jamison, *Molise e Marsia*, no. 3, pp. 85-6. Both Toro and S. Giovanni in Galdo are small towns located E of Campobasso.
95 *Falcandus*, pp. 102-3.
96 Ménager, 'Inventaire', pp. 330-6; Cuozzo and Martin, *Pergamene di Sepino*, p. 45, n. 55.
97 Gattola, *Accessiones*, I, pp. 246-7.
98 Jamison, *Molise e Marsia*, nos 1, pp. 81-3, 3, pp. 85-6.
99 Jamison, *Molise e Marsia*, no. 2, pp. 83-4.
100 Jamison, 'County of Molise', pp. 535-6; Jamison, *Molise e Marsia*, pp. 11-13; *Catalogus Baronum*, p. 129 n. a; Jamison, 'Additional Work', p. 50.
101 Del Giudice, App. 1, no. 11, pp. 27-9.
102 Huillard-Bréholles and D'Albert de Luynes, IV, pp. 479-83, specifically 481. On the abbey in Pulsano and its order of hermits, see Mattei-Ceresoli, *La Congregazione*.
103 Martin, *Cartulaire de Sculgola*, II, no. 187, pp. 333-4. The document, a testimony originally dated July 1210, survives as a copy in the *registro* of St. Mary of Gualdo Mazzocca, a manuscript of the Biblioteca della SNSP. This chartulary contains the

charters of St Matthew of Sculgola, an obedience of St Mary of Gualdo, which was founded near the lost city of Dragonara in Capitanata, by William Borell *c.* 1177. Martin, 'Étude sur le Registro', p. 493. On St Mary of Gualdo, see Morrone, *Monastero di Sancta Maria de Gualdo Mazzocca*, 40–62.
104 Fernández-Aceves, 'Civitate and Carinola', p. 69.
105 Fernández-Aceves, 'Civitate and Carinola', pp. 69–71.
106 Trinchera, no. 133, pp. 175–6.
107 Brühl, *Roger II Diplomata*, no. 59, pp. 166–70.
108 *Roger II Diplomata*, nos 59–60, pp. 166–72.
109 Houben, *Die Abtei Venosa*, nos 121–2, pp. 355–7. Houben presents here the surviving summary from Prignano, 'Historia', fol. 96v. Cf. Crudo, *La SS. Trinità di Venosa*, pp. 243–4. See also Petrucci, 'Documenti di Bansuvilla', nos 1–2, p. 115; Ménager, 'Les fondations monastiques', nos 36–7, p. 109.
110 *Carte di Molfetta*, no. 16, pp. 30–1. The original document can be found in Cava, *Arm. Mag.* H.4.
111 Houben, *Die Abtei Venosa*, no. 130, p. 365. See also Crudo, *La SS. Trinità di Venosa*, pp. 244–5; Petrucci, 'Documenti di Bansuvilla', no. 4, pp. 115–16.
112 Houben, *Die Abtei Venosa*, no. 131, pp. 365–7. The original extract of the now lost document is found in Prignano, 'Historia', fols 96v–97r. Cf. Crudo, *La SS. Trinità di Venosa*, pp. 243–4. See Petrucci, 'Documenti di Bansuvilla', no. 5, p. 116; Ménager, 'Les fondations monastiques', no. 40, pp. 111–12.
113 Richard II of Aquila is recorded as brother of Geoffrey of Aquila, as count of Fondi and consequently as son of Richard I of Aquila. *Cod. Dipl. Cajetanus*, II, no. 323, pp. 250–1.
114 Brühl, *Roger II Diplomata*, no. 59, pp. 166–70.
115 Cava, *Arca*, xxv.106. Cf. Scandone, *L'alta valle del Calore*, II, no. 142, pp. 148–9.
116 The *stratigotus* can be identified as one of the typical Italo-Norman civil officers. Of obvious Byzantine origin, the *stratigoti* have been described as city magistrates with judicial prerogatives, active only in some major urban centres, including Messina, Naples and Amalfi. While they were originally provincial governors with military duties, the *stratigoti* of the Norman period were essentially restricted to a particular city as local administrators. On the *stratigoti*, see Garufi, 'Su la curia'; Falkenhausen, 'I ceti dirigenti prenormanni al tempo della costituzione degli stati normanni nell'Italia meridionale e in Sicilia', pp. 342–6; Martin, *La Pouille*, pp. 764–5; Oldfield, *City and Community in Norman Italy*, p. 26; Skinner, *Medieval Amalfi*, pp. 143–4.
117 Scandone, *L'alta valle del Calore*, II, no. 155, pp. 153–4. Cf. Gattola, *Accessiones*, I, pp. 256–7.
118 Prince Richard II of Capua granted and confirmed the town (*oppidum*) of Pontecorvo to Abbot Oderisius and Montecassino after having recovered it from the widow of the rebel *Gualguanus*, duke of Gaeta and lord of Pontecorvo (1092–1103). Martin and others, *Registrum Petri Diaconi*, III, no. 511, pp. 1399–401. See also Martin et al., *Registrum Petri Diaconi*, vol. 3, no. 630, pp. 1687–8.
119 'Exceptis castellis de foris cum pertinentiis illorum et feudum predicti Richardi de Aquila'. Martin and others, *Registrum Petri Diaconi*, III, no. 511, pp. 1399–401, especially p. 1400.
120 Martin and others, *Registrum Petri Diaconi*, III, no. 631, pp. 1688–9.
121 Martin and others, *Registrum Petri Diaconi*, III, no. 544, pp. 1497–8.
122 *Cod. Dipl. Verginiano*, IV, no. 306, pp. 24–6.
123 *Cod. Dipl. Verginiano*, IV, no. 307, pp. 28–30.

124 Garufi, *Necrologio di S. Matteo*, p. 142; *Catalogus Baronum*, ¶ 392, p. 70. This would confirm that Richard II of Aquila was recorded in the first royal *quaterniones*, c. 1150, as the original count of Avellino.
125 *Catalogus Baronum*, ¶ 155, p. 28. On Montescaglioso, see Cuozzo, 'Montescaglioso', pp. 7–24.
126 I.e. the descendants of Umfridus and Beatrix, such as Rudolph Machabeus, husband of Emma, Count Roger I's daughter.
127 '*Ego d(omi)na alb(erad)a goffridi licie filia divina favente clem(en)tia Luc(erie) civit(atis) do(omi)na*'. Cava *Arm. Mag.* H.11. An apparent contemporary copy and a later transcription of this transaction survive in H.12 and P.13 [a. 1365]. See also Cuozzo, *Commentario*, p. 194; Cuozzo, 'Montescaglioso', p. 30.
128 Garufi, 'I conti di Montescaglioso', pp. 326–8. Cf. Antonucci, p. 457; Poso, p. 57.
129 Antonucci, 'Goffredo conte di Lecce e di Montescaglioso', pp. 455–6; Poso, *Il Salento Normanno*, p. 67, n. 161.
130 *Falcandus*, pp. 70–3.
131 *Pergamene di Salerno*, no. 102, pp. 195–9.
132 On the study of its condition as a forgery, see Carlone, *Rocchetta S. Antonio*, p. 74. Cuozzo has already identified most of the individuals attested in this charter, who were local officials and barons allegedly established as members of the *entourage* of Count Nicholas. Cuozzo, 'Milites e testes', pp. 140–8.
133 Houben, *Die Abtei Venosa*, no. 128, pp. 361–2.
134 *Romuald*, p. 246.
135 Drell, *Kinship & Conquest*, p. 114. Drell employs a March 1135 charter, Cava's *Armaria Magna*, G.16, ed. in Carlone, *Falsificazioni e falsari*, no. 3, pp. 72–4. *Arm. Mag.* N.15 (1262) is a notarial copy of this charter. C. Carlone considered the document to be an extrapolation in the form of an original, though not an entirely made-up forgery.
136 *Roger II Diplomata*, nos 59, pp. 166–9, 60, pp. 170–2.
137 *Roger II Diplomata*, Documenta Ducis Rogerii, filii Rogerii II Regis, no. 1, pp. 237–8. Also, see Prologo, no. 37.
138 Deér, *Das Papsttum und die süditalienischen Normannenstaaten. 1053–1212*, no. 20.4, pp. 74–5.
139 Di Meo, *Annali Critico-Diplomatici del Regno di Napoli della Mezzana Età*, x, p. 206, n. 22. Di Meo uses as a source Gatta, p. 2. See also Cuozzo, *Commentario*, p. 32.
140 *Catalogus Baronum*, ¶ 100, pp. 18–19.
141 On the *comestabulia* of Tricarico, see Fernández-Aceves, 'Royal Comestabuli', pp. 20–1, 27–8.
142 *Romuald*, p. 244.
143 *Falcandus*, pp. 98–9.
144 *Falcandus*, pp. 260–1.
145 On the origins and activities of the early S. Severino family, see Portanova, 'I Sanseverino dalle origini'; Loud, 'Continuity and Change', pp. 326–33; Galante, 'Un esempio di diplomatica signorile'; Drell, *Kinship & Conquest*, pp. 185–90. Despite the considerable amount of documents that survive for the S. Severino family, one ought to use and analyse these charters carefully, as the authenticity of many of these Cava documents has been questioned; see Carlone, *Falsificazioni e falsari*; Carlone, *Documenti per la storia di Eboli*.
146 *Reg. Neap. Arch. Mon.*, v, no. 518, pp. 295–6.

147 Cava, *Arm. Mag.* F.36. Cf. Drell, who dated the document 1123. Drell, *Kinship & Conquest*, p. 128.
148 '*Robbertus filius cuiusdam Roggerii qui de Sancto Severino, qui sum domnus et habitator castelli qui dicitur Laure*'. Inguanez, *S. Angelo in Formis*, no. 59, pp. 159–61.
149 Portanova, 'I Sanseverino dal 1125', pp. 319–20.
150 Robert I of Lauro must have died, and his widow Sarracena remarried to Robert Capumaza before 1141. However, this was not the last time she remarried, because Sarracena is also recorded as widow of Simon of Tivilla. In 1159, Sarracena made a donation to Cava for the souls of her late husbands Robert Capumaza and Simon of Tivilla; apparently the memory of her first husband Robert of Lauro had ceased to be fresh in her mind by then. Cava. *Arm. Mag.* H.35.
151 '*Silvester Dei gratia Marsici comes, strenuissimi regis Rogerii salute ac nostri nostrorum que defunctorum parentum animarum redemptione*'. Ménager, 'Les fondations monastiques', no. 39, p. 111.
152 *Catalogus Baronum*, ¶ 597, p. 108.
153 Situated between the Alburni Mountains and the borders of the modern provinces of Campania and Basilicata, it is considered a geographical subregion of Cilento.
154 Mattei-Ceresoli, 'Tramutola', no. 14, pp. 108–11. Original document is found in Cava, *Arm. Mag.* H.17. The date recorded in the original charter is '*millesimo centesimo quinquagesimo quarto (1154), mense decembri, indictione secunda*'; but although the II indiction does correspond to the year 1154, the document's proem makes an explicit reference to the reign of King Roger II. Consequently, the document must have been issued before Roger II's death (1154) and after their reckoning of the New Year and indiction, which must have been on 25 December at the latest.
155 Cava, *Arm. Mag.* H.13, ed. in Mattei-Ceresoli, 'Tramutola', no. 15, pp. 111–12. The date recorded in the original charter is 1153, second indiction; but 1153 does not correspond to the second indiction, and the document's proem only refers to the reign of William I. The donation was made for the good memory of King Roger, clearly implying that Roger II was dead by then. Consequently, the correct year must be 1154.
156 Cava, *Arm. Mag.* H.19, ed. in Mattei-Ceresoli, 'Tramutola', no. 16, pp. 112–13.
157 *Catalogus Baronum*, ¶¶ 598–602, p. 109.
158 Cuozzo, 'Milites e testes', pp. 157, 160. This should not be confused with the hypothesis presented by Jamison, and seconded by Ménager, according to which the county of Principato was suppressed and dismembered *c*. 1166–8 in order to benefit and expand the counties of Marsico, Conza (a lordship of the count of Carinola), and Balvano (the county of Philip of Balvano, lord of Sant'Angelo dei Lombardi). Jamison, 'Norman Administration', p. 365; Ménager, 'Les fondations monastiques', p. 81.
159 Trinchera, *Syllabus Graecarum membranarum*, no. 145, pp. 192–3, 148, pp. 195–6, 160–4, pp. 204–16. Originals in Cava, *Perg. Greca*, 12, 52, 56, 58, 59, 60 and 61.
160 *Catalogus Baronum*, ¶¶ 659, 663, pp. 117–18.
161 *Catalogus Baronum*, ¶ 604, p. 110.
162 Trinchera, *Syllabus Graecarum membranarum*, no. 148, pp. 195–6.
163 Cf. Cuozzo, 'Milites e testes', pp. 159–60.
164 Jamison, 'Additional Work', p. 15; Cuozzo, 'Milites e testes', p. 150; Cuozzo, 'Prosopografia: i Balvano', pp. 79–81; Cuozzo, 'Montescaglioso', p. 29; Cuozzo, *Quei maledetti normanni*, pp. 105–13.
165 *Roger II Diplomata*, no. 148, pp. 53–4.

166 '*Cum apud Silvam Marcam cum Anfuso Neapolitanorum duce et Capuanorum principe, filio nostro, et comitibus nostris ceterisque baronibus et parte maxima populi regni nostri ad altercationes et iniusticias corrigendas congregaremur*'.
167 For an overview of the Germanic quadrille as a judicial concept in Italy, see Torelli, *Lezioni di storia del diritto italiano. Diritto privato. Le persone*, pp. 25–7.
168 Cuozzo, *Quei maledetti normanni*, pp. 106–7.
169 *Falco*, pp. 234–5; Loud, *Creation of the Kingdom*, pp. 244–5.
170 Jamison, 'Additional Work', pp. 15–17; Cuozzo, *Quei maledetti normanni*, p. 108.
171 E.g. Clementi, 'Definition of a Norman County', pp. 377–85; Martin, *La Pouille*, pp. 770–93; Feller, 'The Northern Frontier', p. 68; Carocci, *Signorie di Mezzogiorno*, pp. 142–3; Drell, *Kinship & Conquest*, pp. 44–5.
172 Martin, *La Pouille*, pp. 303–5, 770. Cf. Carocci, *Signorie di Mezzogiorno*, pp. 71–2, 142–3, 148, 233, 450–1. Although their approach rests on the supposed dichotomy between public and private authority, Martin and Carocci do not define what exactly they understand to be public in these instances. The concept of public authority could therefore range from a legalist definition derived from Roman law, to its equation with civic and even 'central' institutions. Strangely enough, 'public authority' remains one of the unclear conceptual bases on which the theory of feudal transformation stands. For a similar criticism, see Barton, *Lordship in the County of Maine, c. 890–1160*, pp. 126–7.
173 On this idea of *regalia*, see Cahen, *Le régime féodal de l'Italie normande*, pp. 111–15; Cuozzo, *La cavalleria*, pp. 143–6.
174 See Chronological Table.
175 On this question, see Martin, 'La frontière septentrionale', pp. 291–303; Feller, 'The Northern Frontier', pp. 64–6; Toomaspoeg, 'La frontière terrestre du Royaume de Sicile à l'époque normande', II, pp. 1205–24.
176 Amari and Schiaparelli, *L'Italia descritta nel 'Libro del re Ruggero' compilato da Edrisi [Al-Idrīsī]*, pp. 115–22.
177 *Catalogus Baronum*, ¶ 1020, p. 187.
178 *Falco*, pp. 232–5; Loud, *Creation of the Kingdom*, pp. 243–4.
179 Paris, Bibliothèque Nationale, *Lat.* 5411, fol. 246r, edited in *Roger II Diplomata*, no. 49, pp. 139–40. This royal privilege partially confirmed the dominions that St Clement had once held. The *castella* of Casale Plano and Colle Odoni were subsequently omitted among the *feuda* that abbot Oderisius of St Clement held in the counties of Manopello and *Aprutium*, according to the register for the Abruzzo. *Catalogus Baronum*, ¶ 1217, p. 252. On the territory that the abbey claimed to control, see Feller, *Les Abruzzes médiévales*, pp. 65–6.
180 *Chron. Casauriense*, cols 889–90; *Roger II Diplomata*, no. 50, pp. 141–3.
181 *Chron. Casauriense*, cols 891–92; *Roger II Diplomata*, no. 51, p. 144.
182 Rome, Biblioteca Apostolica Vaticana, Arch. Cap. S. Pietro Caps. LXXII, fasc. 53, no. 1 ('Liber instrumentorum monasterii Sancti Salvatoris de Maiella'), ff 9r.
183 Jamison, 'Norman Administration', App., no. 5, pp. 458–61. Cf. Feller, *Les Abruzzes médiévales*, pp. 768–72.
184 *Catalogus Baronum*, p. 183.
185 William I must have confirmed in 1156 to the papacy that the land north of the River Tronto, including part of the territory of the 'county' of Rieti, was outside of the kingdom's dominions, not only because the Abruzzese *quaternion* did not record these lands, but also it was at the treaty of Benevento (1156) that both Pope Adrian IV and the Sicilian monarchy agreed, although vaguely, on the extent of the

186 Feller, *Les Abruzzes médiévales*, pp. 783–4; Feller, 'The Northern Frontier', pp. 70–2.
187 Feller, *Les Abruzzes médiévales*, pp. 764, 768–70; Cuozzo, 'Il sistema difensivo', pp. 273–90.
188 Airola appears as a *feudum* of five *milites*, as part of the *demanio* of the count of Carinola. *Catalogus Baronum*, ¶ 995, pp. 178–9.
189 *Necrologio di S. Matteo*, p. 8.
190 *Catalogus Baronum*, ¶ 995, pp. 178–9. Although it could be argued that the Count Richard attested in the *Quaternus* was in fact his son, Richard II of Fondi, restored back to the county of Fondi after 1168, Count Richard I of Fondi is recorded as *[Gaiteae] Civitatis comes et miles streuissimus*, in a charter (*exemplar mutilum*) through which his mother Adelicia, *Gaieta Comitissa relicta quondam Domini Gaufridi*, and himself made a donation to the monastery of Cava, dated 1153 and issued in Gaeta. *Cod. Dipl. Cajetanus*, II, no. 363, pp. 280–1. Additionally, there is a Richard of Aquila likewise recorded in the *Quaternus* as an overlord of 14 barons in Calvi and Riardo, in the province of Capua, but these ancestral *feuda* must have fallen into the hands of the other branch of the Aquila family, as a subsequent charter (1174) reveals that Roger of Aquila, son of the Richard of Aquila who was the count of Avellino, was the ruling overlord in Calvi. *Catalogus Baronum*, ¶ 808, p. 148; *Cod. Dipl. Verginiano*, VI, no. 596, pp. 259–61.
191 *Catalogus Baronum*, ¶ 806–7, p. 148.
192 *Necrologio di S. Matteo*, p. 142.
193 *Falcandus*, p. 136.
194 *Catalogus Baronum*, ¶¶ 392–5, pp. 70–1.
195 He is recorded in a charter concerning delimitation of land as the overlord of Constantinus Aczarulus, as *domini comitis Rogerii de Medania*. *Cod. Dipl. Aversa*, no. 17, pp. 337–9.
196 He was part of the opposition to Maio of Bari, together with other nobles. *Falcandus*, pp. 60–2.
197 See note 90 (ch. 3).
198 Lingèvres (dép. Calvados, cant. Aunay-sur-Odon) is in fact a town 13 kilometres south of the city of Bayeux. Delisle, *Robert de Torigni*, p. 242, n. 2; Howlett, *Robert of Torigni*, p. 153. The use of the term *insula* here might indicate either a geographical mistake made by a northern chronicler unfamiliar with Italy's geography, who assumed Andria was an island in the Mediterranean, or a qualification made of the county as an administrative unit held in tenancy. Robert of Torigni also recorded that the county of Andria was recently captured by Roger II from the Emperor of Constantinople (*quam nuper idem rex super imperatorem Constantinopolitanum ceperat*), which evokes the unclear notion the chronicler had of the Norman attacks against the Byzantine rule in Apulia a century before. A new edition of Robert of Torigni's chronicle by Thomas Bisson is forthcoming. For a recent discussion about Robert of Torigni and his work, see Bates.
199 Delisle, *Robert de Torigni*, p. 295; Howlett, *Robert of Torigni*, p. 185.
200 Jamison, 'Norman Administration', p. 254.
201 Cuozzo, 'Prosopografia: i Balvano', p. 73.
202 On the origin and condition of Philip of Balvano's county, see pages 162–4.

kingdom's territories. This explains why it was recorded that Rieti was rebuilt in 1156 'with Roman assistance' (*reparatum cum adiutorio Romanorum*). Bethmann, *Annales Reatini*, p. 267; *William I Diplomata*, no. 12, pp. 32–5.

203 *Catalogus Baronum*, ¶ 433, p. 78. Cuozzo has already presented a well-documented study on the family of the lords of Balvano. See Cuozzo, 'Prosopografia: i Balvano'.
204 *Falcandus*, pp. 98–9.
205 Garufi, 'Gli Aleramici', p. 48.
206 *Cod. Dipl. Verginiano*, III, no. 285, pp. 348–50.
207 Drago Tedeschini, Fondo Opera Pia Sacro Monte dei Morti, no. 1, pp. 107–10.
208 Drago Tedeschini, Fondo Capitolare, no. 2, pp. 47–9.
209 Cava, *Arm. Mag.* H.21–6.
210 Cava, *Arm. Mag.* H.22.
211 *Catalogus Baronum*, ¶¶ 54–71, pp. 11–14.
212 Cava, *Arm. Mag.* F.36. See also Portanova, 'I Sanseverino dal 1125', pp. 326–7.
213 As attested in Cava, *Arm. Mag.* F.18.
214 On the mixed ancestry of the Medania, see Loud, 'Norman Traditions', pp. 50–1.
215 Garufi, 'Adelaide nipote di Bonifazio del Vasto e Goffredo figliolo del gran conte Ruggiero', IV, pp. 188–92; Mazzarese Fardella, *Feudi comitali*, p. 15. The familial tie between Sylvester and Geoffrey is recorded as such: '*Gaufridus bona memoria Comitis Rogerii filius, et Comes Silvester filius eiusdem Gaufridi ea Syracusana Ecclesia pia devotionis intuitu contulerunt*'. *Sicilia Sacra*, I, pp. 622–3.
216 Cava, *Arm. Mag.* H.17, ed. in Mattei-Ceresoli, 'Tramutola', no. 14, pp. 108–11.
217 Cava, *Arm. Mag.* H.13, ed. in Mattei-Ceresoli, 'Tramutola', no. 15, pp. 111–12.
218 Cava, *Arm. Mag.* H.19, ed. in Mattei-Ceresoli, 'Tramutola', no. 16, pp. 112–13.
219 Guerrieri, 'I conti di Lecce', no. 1, pp. 202–4, 3, pp. 208–90. For a summary of Geoffrey's ancestry, see Garufi, 'I conti di Montescaglioso', pp. 337–8; Cuozzo, 'Montescaglioso', p. 30.
220 Robert of Bassunvilla probably originated from the area of Caux, Normandy. Three charters of the monastery of Saint-Victor-en-Caux (dép. Seine-Maritime, cant. Luneray) refer to *Vassunvilla*: Archbishop Hugues of Rouen confirmed donations to Saint-Victor-en-Caux, including property *in Vassunvilla* (Vassonville, a town in the district of Tôtes), by charter dated 1137. Beaurepaire, *Recueil de chartes concernant l'abbaye de Saint-Victor-en-Caux*, p. 363.
221 Houben, *Roger II of Sicily*, p. 86. Also, see below, note 16 (ch. 3).
222 *Romuald*, p. 237.
223 *Kinnamos*, bk 4, chap. 2, p. 136; Delisle, *Robert de Torigni*, p. 295; Howlett, *Robert of Torigni*, p. 185.
224 On Hugh of Molise's sister, see *Chron. de Ferraria*, p. 28; Houben, *Roger II of Sicily*, p. 36. On Hugh of Molise having been married to King Roger's illegitimate daughter, see *Falcandus*, p. 102.
225 *Falcandus*, pp. 162–3.
226 Adelicia subscribed a donation made by her mother Emma in July 1119 (*Signum manus domine adelize predicte comitissa filie*). *Reg. Neap. Arch. Mon.*, VI, no. 23, pp. 191–3. Adelicia was also recorded in a very dubious entry, according to which she issued a charter in Sicily, in 1136, to the churches of St Elias of Adernò and St Andrew of Lentini, where she was remembered as the daughter of 'Rudolph Maniacis of Montescanusio' [corr. Machabeus of Montescaglioso], and sister of Count Simon (*ex dipl. Adelasiae Comitis Rodulphi Maniacis de Montecanusio* [corr. *Macabei de Montescaveosi*] *filae, ac Comitis Simonis sororis*). *Sicilia Sacra*, I, p. 586. Rudolph Machabeus, however, did not bear the comital title, and Count Simon was in fact the son of Henry of Paternò, Roger II's maternal uncle. The author of this entry had a vague idea of Adelicia's lineage, but was clearly confused about the details.

227 *Cod. Dipl. Verginiano*, v, no. 474, pp. 261–4, at 262.
228 Cf. Loud, 'William the Bad or William the Unlucky?' p. 105.

Chapter 3

1 See Chronological Table.
2 *Romuald*, p. 237. William I was crowned at Easter (18 April) 1151, becoming thus a co-ruler alongside his father King Roger. Chibnall, *H. Pontificalis*, p. 69. For an important discussion, see *Tyrants*, p. 221.
3 See page 56. Also, see Genealogical Network.
4 *Roger II Diplomata*, nos 59–60, pp. 166–72. On Robert I of Bassunvilla's death, see Trinchera, *Syllabus Graecarum membranarum*, no. 133, pp. 175–6.
5 Houben, *Die Abtei Venosa*, nos 121–2, pp. 355–7. Houben has presented here the surviving references and summaries that can be found in Prignano, 'Historia', fol. 96v. Cf. Crudo, pp. 243–4; Petrucci, 'Documenti di Bansuvilla', nos 1–2, p. 115; Ménager, 'Les fondations monastiques', nos 36–7, p. 109.
6 *Italia Sacra*, vi, cols 706–7.
7 *Cod. Dipl. Tremiti*, nos 99–100, pp. 284–6; *Annalista Saxo*, p. 606.
8 Jamison, 'Norman Administration', p. 254.
9 *Catalogus Baronum*, ¶ 291, p. 47.
10 Cuozzo, 'Ruggiero, conte d'Andria', pp. 129–33. See above, note 31 (ch. 2).
11 *Catalogus Baronum*, ¶¶ 357–63, pp. 61–3.
12 *Romuald*, p. 237. See also *Tyrants*, p. 221.
13 *Chron. Casauriense*, col. 895.
14 *Chron. de Carpineto*, bk 5, p. 78. Cf. Fuselli, *Il Chronicon di S. Bartolomeo di Carpineto*, p. 131.
15 Houben, *Die Abtei Venosa*, no. 131, pp. 365–7.
16 Chieti, Curia Arcivescovile, *Archivio storico*, perg. no 19. Summarized in *Italia Sacra*, vi, cols 706–7. The charter's left margin is partially damaged, and the year's last number is absent; however, the rest of the dating clause is legible: on the fourth year of King William, July, second indiction. Ughelli mistakenly dated it to 1157, because the fourth regal year of William I was 1154 – he was crowned at Easter 1151, and since then regarded co-ruler together with his father King Roger. Cf. Balducci, *Regesto delle pergamene della curia arcivescovile di Chieti. 1006–1400*, p. 7; Cuozzo, *Commentario*, p. 73.
17 *Falcandus*, pp. 64–5. See also *Tyrants*, pp. 63–4.
18 'οὗτος Ῥογερίον μὲν ἔτι περιόντος τὴν Ἰταλίας διεῖπεν ἀρχήν, ἐκίνου δὲ τετελευτηκότος ἐπὶ τὸν υἱόν τε Γιλιέλμον τῆς ἀρχῆς μετελθούσης, ἠνάγκαστο λοιπὸν ἐν ὑποστρατήγου λόγῳ διατελεῖν, ἑτέρου τὴν Ἰταλίαν διέποντος. καὶ δη τὴν ὕβριν οὐκ ἐνεγκὼν εἰς ἀποστασίαν εἶδε'. *Kinnamos*, bk. 4, chap. 2, p. 136.
19 William II's date of birth can be inferred from three references. First, Romuald of Salerno reported that young William II was twelve years old when he succeeded his father in the kingdom (*Romuald*, p. 254.); secondly, it has been recorded that William I died on 15 May 1166 (*Necrologio Cas.*, p. 67, fol. 290v; Garufi, *Necrologio di S. Matteo*, p. 70; *Annales Casinenses*, p. 312.); and finally we know that William II died in November 1189 at the age of 36 (*Annales Casinenses*, p. 314.). Although the *Annales Casinenses* record that William II was crowned in July, Garufi disagreed and

claimed that young William was in fact proclaimed king days after his father died, as Di Meo asserted that William II's rule lasted twenty-three years and six months. *Annales Casinenses*, p. 312; *Romuald*, p. 254, n. 2; Di Meo, *Annali Critico-Diplomatici del Regno di Napoli della Mezzana Età*, x, p. 293. In order to reconcile all these dates, William must have been born in 1153. Conversely, Loud follows the *Annales Casinenses* and suggests that a birthday in June 1153 would solve the discrepancies. *Tyrants*, p. 138, n. 132.
20 On this discussion, see Petrucci, 'Bassunvilla, Roberto', p. 186; *Chron. de Carpineto*, pp. 32–4.
21 'καὶ δὴ τὴν ὕβριν οὐκ ἐνεγκὼν εἰς ἀποστασίαν εἶδε. τοίνυν καὶ ἐπὶ Φρεδερίκον πέμψας Ἰταλίαν τε πᾶσαν καὶ Σικελίαν αὐτὴν ἐγχειριεῖν ἐπήγγελλε τούτῳ'. *Kinnamos*, bk. 4, chap. 2, p. 136.
22 *Chron. de Carpineto*, bk 5, p. 79.
23 Schmale, *Gesta Frederici*, bk 2, chaps 34–7, pp. 352–62; pp. 152–5. Additionally, Helmold of Bosau had provided in his *Chronica Slavorum* a contemporary testimony of the nobles' response to Frederick's intentions to march over Apulia: '*Diu est, ex quo fuimus in castris et desunt nobis stipendia, et tu dicis tibi Apuliam require et sic demum ad consecracionem veniri? Dura sunt haec et supra vires nostras. Quin pocius impleatur opus consecraciones, ut pateat nobis reditus patriae, respiremusque paululum de labore; postmodum magis expiditi redibimus expleturi quod nunc faciendum restat*'. Lappenberg and Schmeidler, *Helmoldi Presbyteri Bozoviensis Cronica Slavorum*, bk 1, chap. 81, p. 154. For an important discussion, see Loud, 'The German Emperors and Southern Italy during the Tenth and Eleventh Centuries', I, p. 604.
24 *Chron. de Carpineto*, bk 5, p. 79.
25 *Kinnamos*, bk. 4, chap. 2, pp. 136–7. Vieste is a maritime town located on the easternmost tip of the Gargano peninsula, 55 kilometres northeast of Monte Sant'Angelo. Interestingly enough, the Greek control of the Gargano peninsula was already confirmed in an October '1156' [corr. 1155] charter from the monastery of St Leonard of Siponto – a town 20 kilometres southwest of Monte Sant'Angelo – which was recorded as having been issued 'in the 1st ruling year [in Italy] of the most serene Roman emperor, Manuel Porphyrogennitos, our lord' (*serenisimo imperatore Romeon Porfirogeniton Maineli domino nostro .I. a. imperante*). Camobreco, *Regesto di S. Leonardo di Siponto*, no. 41, p. 26.
26 *Chron. Casauriense*, col. 895.
27 *Chron. Casauriense*, cols 895–6.
28 *Chron. Casauriense*, col. 896.
29 *Romuald*, p. 238.
30 *William of Tyre*, II, bk 18, chap. 2, p. 811; Babcock and Krey, eds., *A History of Deeds Done beyond the Sea*, II, p. 238.
31 Adrian IV was elected pope after the death of Pope Anastasius IV in December 1154. For additional information on Adrian IV's origins and career, see Bolton and Duggan.
32 *Romuald*, pp. 237–8.
33 *Falcandus*, pp. 60–3.
34 See pages 32–3.
35 *Falcandus*, pp. 62–5.
36 *Romuald*, p. 238.
37 *Falcandus*, pp. 66–7.
38 *Catalogus Baronum*, ¶¶ 89–99, pp. 17–18; 351–62, pp. 61–3.

39 *Falcandus*, pp. 70–1. The chronicle of Carpineto had recorded that a vast amount of money was seized from this Greek army after it was defeated and captured (*devictis Grecis eorumque copiosa quam attulerant accepta pecunia*). *Chron. de Carpineto*, bk 5, p. 79.
40 *Kinnamos*, bk 4, chap. 1, pp. 135–6; chap. 6, p. 148; chap. 7, p. 150.
41 Hartmann, *Das Briefbuch Abt Wibalds von Stablo und Corvey*, no. 216, p. 460; *Kinnamos*, bk 4, chap. 6, p. 148.
42 See note 17 (ch. 2).
43 *Obv.* Bust of St Catherine with nimbus and long hair, wearing a chlamys and a loros and holding (r. hand) a martyr's cross in front of her breast. Vertical inscription: H - ΑΓΙ - ΑЄΚ || ΤЄΡ - … [+] ἡ ἁγία Ἐκ(α)τερ[ίνα]. *Rev.* Inscription of three lines: | ALEXA. | ….OM.. | GRAVIN. [+] Alexa[nder c]ome[es] Gravin[e]. Jordanov, *Corpus of Byzantine Seals from Bulgaria*, II, no. 150, pp. 115–16.
44 See note 129 (ch. 2).
45 *Falcandus*, pp. 70–3.
46 *Falcandus*, pp. 74–7. On Roger's father, Richard son of Richard, lord of Contra, Flumeri, *S. Angelum*, Trevico and Vallata, see, *Catalogus Baronum*, ¶ 291, p. 47.
47 *Falcandus*, pp. 78–81.
48 *Romuald*, pp. 238–9.
49 *Annales Casinenses*, p. 311.
50 *Falcandus*, pp. 70–1. The appellation of Robert as 'of Sorrento', which was more commonly used after his defeat in the 1130s, comes from the fact that his mother was Gaitelgrima, a daughter of Duke Sergius of Sorrento.
51 *William of Tyre*, II, bk 18, chap. 2, p. 811.
52 Duchesne, *Liber Pontificalis*, II, pp. 393–4.
53 Monaco, *Sanctuarium Capuanum*, pp. 646–8.
54 *Chron. de Ferraria*, p. 29. Since Richard of Rupecanina was established before as brother of Rainulf, Andrew of Rupecanina must have been Richard's son.
55 Schmale, *Gesta Frederici*, bk 2, chap. 37, p. 362. Cf. Mierow, trans., *The Deeds of Frederick Barbarossa, by Otto of Freising and His Continuator Rahewin*, pp. 154–5.
56 *William of Tyre*, II, bk 18, chap. 2, p. 811; Babcock and Krey, eds., *A History of Deeds Done beyond the Sea*, II, p. 238.
57 *Annales Casinenses*, p. 311.
58 *Catalogus Baronum*, ¶ 835, p. 152. The paragraph breaks off without specifying the *feuda* held.
59 *Annales Ceccanenses*, p. 284.
60 Jamison, *Molise e Marsia*, p. 23.
61 Sepino is located 17 km. SE of Boiano. See Map 1.
62 Boglino, *Palermo e Santa Cristina*, p. 64. Cf. Gaetano, *Vitae Sanctorum Siculorum*, II, pp. 145–6, Animadversiones pp. 58–9. See also Cuozzo and Martin, *Pergamene di Sepino*, pp. 60–1.
63 *Necrologio Cas.*, p. 66, ff. 304v, 310r.
64 *Falcandus*, pp. 103–3.
65 *Romuald*, p. 239.
66 *Falcandus*, pp. 80–1.
67 Lupo Gentile, *Gli Annales Pisani di Bernardo Maragone*, pp. 15–16.
68 *Falcandus*, pp. 80–3; *Romuald*, p. 239; *Kinnamos*, bk 4, chap. 8, pp. 151–2; chaps 12–13, pp. 165–8.
69 *Annales Ceccanenses*, p. 284; *Annales Casinenses*, p. 311. The victory in Brindisi is recorded in a royal charter confirming the privileges of the archbishopric of Brindisi

in August 1156, the *arenga* of which describes in detail the appalling punishment inflicted on the people of the maritime town and the traitors. *William I Diplomata*, no. 15, pp. 42–4.
70 *Annales Casinenses*, p. 311.
71 *Chron. de Carpineto*, bk 5, pp. 79–80.
72 *William of Tyre*, II, bk 18, chap. 8, p. 820.
73 *Romuald*, p. 240.
74 *Falcandus*, pp. 84–5; *Annales Casinenses*, p. 311.
75 *Romuald*, p. 240.
76 *Catalogus Baronum*, ¶¶ 995–1007, pp. 179–81. Also, see Map 1 (comital area of Fondi).
77 The Via Appia had been one of the earliest and strategically most important roads since the time of the Roman Republic, connecting the central Tyrrhenian region to the southern Adriatic coast and stretching from Rome to Brindisi. For a general reference, see Cancik, Schneider and Salazar, XV, cols 368–69.
78 *Falcandus*, pp. 84–5; *Romuald*, p. 240.
79 *Falcandus*, pp. 84–5. See also *Tyrants*, pp. 74–5.
80 *Annales Casinenses*, p. 311.
81 *Catalogus Baronum*, ¶¶ 905, p. 162; 926, p. 165.
82 *Catalogus Baronum*, ¶¶ 932–46, pp. 166–8.
83 *Romuald*, p. 241.
84 *Falcandus*, pp. 80–5.
85 Garufi, 'I conti di Montescaglioso', pp. 339–40.
86 *Falcandus*, pp. 84–5.
87 See note 38 (ch. 2).
88 *Falcandus*, pp. 86–7.
89 Delisle, *Robert de Torigni*, p. 295; Howlett, *Robert of Torigni*, p. 185.
90 Kinnamos, bk 4, chap. 4, pp. 141–5. See also Brand, *Deeds of John and Manuel*, pp. 110–13; Jamison, 'Norman Administration', p. 286. By identifying Asclettin as a 'logothete', Kinnamos implies here that this Greek title was understood as an equivalent of the Sicilian 'chancellor', although as an external witness he would not have known precisely which term to use to reflect the sociopolitical realities of the Italo-Norman world.
91 *Falcandus*, pp. 84–5; *Chron. Casauriense*, col. 897.
92 *Cod. Dipl. Tremiti*, no. 107, pp. 297–9. Cf. Morlacchetti, *Tremiti e i suoi documenti*, 283. Henry of Ollia, son and heir of Lando of Ollia, ceded two fishermen of Varano (in the Gargano) to Cava before becoming royal justiciar, in October 1140. Cava, *Arm. Mag.* G.34.
93 *Cod. Dipl. Tremiti*, no. 108, pp. 300–3. Cf. Morlacchetti, *Tremiti e i suoi documenti*, pp. 284–5.
94 See note 140 (ch. 6).
95 *Chron. Casauriense*, cols 913–14.
96 Cava, *Arm. Mag.* H.32.
97 '*Domina quoque Comitisse et Rogerii filii eius Comitis precibus mediantibus*'. Cava, *Arm. Mag.* H.31, ed. in De Sivo, App., no. 2, pp. 338–40.
98 See note 32 (ch. 4).
99 See notes 10 (ch. 4) and 12 (ch. 4).
100 Cuozzo, 'Milites e testes', p. 161; Houben, *Roger II of Sicily*, p. 181.
101 Cuozzo, 'Milites e testes', p. 147.

102 On Lampus of Fasanella, see Fernández-Aceves, 'Royal Comestabuli', pp. 29–32.
103 *Pergamene di Salerno*, no. 103, pp. 190–201, especially 201.
104 *Falcandus*, pp. 86–7. See also *Tyrants*, p. 77.
105 *Catalogus Baronum*, ¶¶ 72–88, pp. 14–16.

Chapter 4

1 *Falcandus*, pp. 82–5.
2 *Italia Sacra*, VI, cols 706–7.
3 *Falcandus*, pp. 98–9.
4 Cava, *Arm. Mag.* H.28.
5 *Catalogus Baronum*, ¶ 71, p. 14.
6 *Falcandus*, pp. 98–9. See Genealogical Network. Also, see chart no II in *Tyrants*.
7 The name of Gilbert's father can be inferred from an 1131 document in which the presence of another grandson (*nepos*) of Count Rotrou is attested in the Ebro Valley, with the name 'Geoffrey Bertrandi'. Lacarra, ed., *Documentos para el estudio de la reconquista y repoblación del Valle del Ebro*, no. 210. Some support to this assumption is given by the fact that Gilbert of Gravina's son was named Bertram. See this discussion in Thompson, 'Family Tradition', p. 18, n. 55.
8 On the county of Perche, see Thompson, *Power and Border Lordship in Medieval France*; Thompson, 'The Lords of Laigle', pp. 183–4. For a summary of Rotrou's activities in the Iberian Peninsula, see Villegas-Aristizabal, 'Norman and Anglo-Norman Participation in the Iberian Reconquista c.1018–c.1248', pp. 109–11; Nelson, 'Rotrou of Perche and the Aragonese Reconquest'.
9 Scheffer-Boichorst, ed., *Chronica Albrici monachi Trium Fontium*, p. 794. The lordship of Tudela was the dowry of Margaret of L'Aigle, as confirmed by Roger of Hoveden when he described a dispute between the kings of Navarre and Castile in 1177. Stubbs, *Gesta Henrici II*, I, pp. 146–8.
10 *Romuald*, p. 244. According to the archbishop of Salerno, this conspiracy would have taken place by the time that Alexander III was elected pope.
11 *Falcandus*, pp. 98–9.
12 Di Meo, ed., *Annali Critico-Diplomatici del Regno di Napoli della Mezzana Età*, X, p. 206, n. 22. See also Gatta, *Memorie topografico-storiche della provincia di Lucania compresa al presente*, p. 2; Cuozzo, *Commentario*, p. 32.
13 *Chron. Casauriense*, col. 897.
14 *Catalogus Baronum*, ¶¶ 482, p. 91; 677, p. 120.
15 Cuozzo, *Commentario*, p. 291.
16 *Romuald*, pp. 244–5.
17 Situated at the southeastern slopes of the Aurunci, on the Via Appia, a few kilometres from the right bank of the Garigliano.
18 *Annales Ceccanenses*, p. 284.
19 *Kinnamos*, bk 4, chap. 14, pp. 170–1. The rank of protostrator originated as the title for the captain of the imperial stables. From the eleventh century, the position became more an honorific dignity for senior members of the court, than an actual office. In any case, Alexios Axouchos acted as a military commander in several campaigns during the middle reign of Emperor Manuel Komnenos. He was sent to

southern Italy in 1157, in an effort to retrieve the Byzantine position there following the defeat in 1156. Guilland, *Recherches sur les institutions byzantines*, I, pp. 478–97; Kazhdan, ed., *The Oxford Dictionary of Byzantium*, pp. 239, 1748–9.

20 *Annales Ceccanenses*, p. 284.
21 *Kinnamos*, bk 4, chap. 14, pp. 170–6.
22 *Annales Casinenses*, p. 311.
23 *Annales Casinenses*, p. 311.
24 *Falcandus*, pp. 98–9.
25 *Annales Casinenses*, p. 311.
26 *Italia Sacra*, VI, cols 810–11; Acocella, *Storia di Conza: Il gastaldato e la contea fino alla caduta della monarchia*, p. 131.
27 Cuozzo, 'Prosopografia: i Balvano', p. 82. Cf. Rinaldi, *Memoria pel comune di Pescopagano contro il comune di S. Menna*, pp. 37–9.
28 *Tyrants*, pp. 98–101.
29 *Roger II Diplomata*, App. 2, no. 3, pp. 265–6. The name Craon derives from the town in Mayenne, France, of the same name. Cf. Ménager, 'Inventaire', pp. 369–70.
30 *Roger II Diplomata*, no. 58, pp. 163–6.
31 Ménager, *Recueil des actes*, pp. 369–70.
32 Cava, *Arm. Mag.* H.13, ed. in Mattei-Ceresoli, 'Tramutola', no. 15, pp. 111–12.
33 *William I Diplomata*, no. 22, pp. 60–4, at 63.
34 These include Archbishop John of Bari, Bishop-elect Bernard of Catania, Bishop Gentile of Agrigento, Bishop Herbert of Tropea, Bishop-elect Gilbert of Patti, Bishop Robert of Messina, Bishop Tustinus de Mazara, Bishop-elect Richard of Syracuse, Bishop-elect Boso of Cefalù, Archbishop Roger of Reggio and Bishop Stephen of Mileto.
35 *Falcandus*, pp. 136–7. It could not be Count Simon 'of Policastro', as he was dead by this time. See above, page 72.
36 Jamison, *Molise e Marsia*, p. 17.
37 See above, page 35.
38 *Falcandus*, pp. 154–5.
39 See above, note 215 (ch. 2).
40 *Falcandus*, pp. 100–1.
41 *Falcandus*, pp. 88–9.
42 Jamison, 'Norman Administration', p. 287. Cf. Caravale, *Il regno normanno di Sicilia*, pp. 254–5.
43 Loud, 'New Evidence', no. 1, pp. 407–8. The original document (*Pergamene Aldobrandini*, Cartolario II, no. 13) was examined in the Biblioteca Apostolica Vaticana by Graham A. Loud before the collection was returned to the Aldobrandini family.
44 *Chron. Casauriense*, col. 903.
45 Jamison, 'Norman Administration', p. 288. Cf. Takayama, *The Administration*, pp. 105–8.
46 *Falcandus*, pp. 98–101.
47 *Romuald*, p. 245.
48 *Falcandus*, pp. 102–8.
49 *Falcandus*, pp. 126–9.
50 See above, page 56.
51 Houben, 'Le origini del principato', p. 17. Alfonso is last attested as prince of Capua in an 10 October 1144 charter from Aversa, and a March 1156 charter asserts in its

dating clause to have been made in the second year of William's princedom (*secundo anno principatus dimini Willelmi [...] Dei gratia principis Capuanorum et ducis Neapolitanorum*). *Cod. Dipl. Aversa*, nos 53–4, pp. 92–5.
52 *Falcandus*, pp. 136–7.
53 *Romuald*, p. 246.
54 *Falcandus*, pp. 144–5.
55 *Romuald*, p. 248.
56 The dignity of prince was limited in the kingdom of Sicily to the royal family, and its use was limited to the title of 'prince of Capua' – used either by the sons of the king or by the rebel Prince Robert of Capua, descendant of the Drengot princely family. After the kingdom's creation, and during the Norman dynasty, there was no direct relationship between the titles of prince and count.
57 *Kinnamos*, bk 4, chap. 6, p. 148. On the translation of the ethnonym Γερμανοί, see Brand, *Deeds of John and Manuel*, p. 115, App. 2.
58 Sudendorf, II, no. 54, p. 132.
59 *William of Tyre*, II, bks 20, chap. 4, p. 915; chap. 13, p. 927; 21, chap. 16, pp. 981–3.
60 *Kinnamos*, bk 4, chap. 15, p. 175.
61 *Falcandus*, pp. 162–3.
62 *Falcandus*, pp. 178–9. Cf. Portanova, 'I Sanseverino dal 1125', pp. 330–2. Cuozzo suggested that both Count Roger of Avellino and William of S. Severino went to the court of Frederick I after they were exiled. Cuozzo, 'A propos de la coexistence', pp. 50–1.
63 *Cod. Dipl. Verginiano*, V, no. 474, pp. 261–4.
64 *Falcandus*, pp. 162–3.
65 See above, page 85.
66 Garufi, *Tabulario di Monreale*, App. 1, no. 2, pp. 163–5. On the church of St Cataldo, see the recent survey in Di Liberto, 'Norman Palermo', pp. 153–6, 183–4.
67 See Figure 1.
68 'Of the illustrious Count Sylvester was born Matilda. Born on a Tuesday, on a Tuesday taken away. Being alive she had nine months, and she died surrendering her soul to heaven and her empty body to the ground, in this year of our lord 1161. Here she rested under the earth.' Cf. Morso, *Descrizione di Palermo antico*, pp. 239–40; Petrizzo, 'Kin Dynamics of the Hautevilles and Other Normans', p. 242.
69 Pio, *Guglielmo I d'Altavilla*, p. 81. Cf. Takayama, 'Familiares Regis', pp. 359–61.
70 *Falcandus*, pp. 164–71.
71 *Romuald*, p. 249; *Annales Ceccanenses*, p. 285.
72 *Falcandus*, pp. 172–3.
73 *Romuald*, p. 248. The usage here of the term *hominium* is rather illustrative. The notion of 'homage' was rarely employed in Italy, at least before the thirteenth century. The references to either *homagium* or *hominium* are scarce. The term *hominium* was employed before in the region, in a 1079–1090 complaint sent to Gregory VII about the bishop of Penne, in the Abruzzo. In this document the term *hominium* is used twice: first, it is stated that the deposed Bishop John of Penne was summoned to do homage to the newly appointed bishop (*Veni ante nostrum praesentiam coram omni multitudine huic nostro confratri hominium faci*); then, a 1079 charter appended to the complaint records that the same Bishop John had received those who had wrongly held the lands of his see into the fidelity of the holy church 'by means of homage and oath' (*omnes istos homines et alios per hominium et sacramentum recepi*

ad fidelitatem sancta ecclesiae). Hofmeister, *Libellus querulus de miseriis ecclesiae Pennensis*, pp. 1462–7, especially 1464 and 1467. Ganshof and Reynolds have already drawn attention to this evidence; Ganshof interpreted this homage as analogous to that done by tenants of subordinate property, whereas Reynolds also sees it as a sign of a more general submission or subjection. Ganshof, 'Note sur l'apparition du nom de l'hommage particulierement en France', pp. 31–2; Reynolds, *Kingdoms and Communities in Western Europe, 900–1300*, pp. 213–14. Cf. Cahen, *Le régime féodal de l'Italie normande*, pp. 42–7, 103–7.

74 *Annales Ceccanenses*, p. 285.
75 *Falcandus*, pp. 172–3.
76 Polignano is a coastal town in the Terra di Bari, 10 km. E of Conversano. See Map 1.
77 *Pergamene di Conversano*, no. 109, pp. 227–8. The original year recorded in the charter is 1163, tenth indiction, but Coniglio corrected this to 1162, assuming that the beginning of the indiction was reckoned in December and the new year started before December. Cf. Morea's edition, who suggests that the charter's original date (1163) is indeed correct, and that instead its indiction (tenth) was mistaken, and should have been eleventh, or even the twelfth, if the Greek reckoning were to be followed. Morea, *Chartularium di Conversano*, I, no. 106, pp. 205–6.
78 *Pergamene di Conversano*, no. 114, pp. 239–41.
79 *Falcandus*, pp. 172–5.
80 *Romuald*, p. 249.
81 *Annales Ceccanenses*, p. 285. The anonymous chronicle from Montecassino provides little detail, but, at least, recorded that in 1162 the king of Sicily went to Apulia and destroyed Taverna. *Annales Casinenses*, p. 312.
82 *Falcandus*, pp. 174–7.
83 *Romuald*, p. 251.
84 *Falcandus*, pp. 176–7.
85 *Annales Ceccanenses*, p. 285.
86 *Romuald*, p. 251, n. 4; Ménager, 'Inventaire', p. 344.
87 Pratesi, *Carte dall'archivio Aldobrandini*, no. 20, pp. 53–5. Carbonellus of Tarsia was the son of Bohemund I of Tarsia, the disgraced count of Manopello. However, the family of Bohemund of Tarsia was not completely disregarded, and his sons Carbonellus and Bohemund II remained active in Calabria as barons and judicial officers; the two were present in William II's court in Messina in 1167–1168. See below, note 115 (ch. 5).
88 *Falcandus*, pp. 178–9.
89 *Romuald*, p. 251.
90 *Annales Ceccanenses*, p. 285. Monte Arcano is located in the mountain range W of Fondi, upon which the sanctuary of the 'Madonna della Rocca' is found. See Map 1.
91 Tescione, *Caserta medievale*, p. 36. Cf. Siragusa, p. 216.
92 *Annales Ceccanenses*, p. 285.
93 *Kinnamos*, bk 4, chap. 15, pp. 172–6. Also, see *Falcandus*, pp. 88–9.
94 As attested in Cava, *Arm. Mag.* F.18.
95 Inguanez, *S. Angelo in Formis*, no. 60, pp. 161–3, at p. 162; Cava, Arca XXV.87. The document from Cava has been edited in Tescione, *Caserta medievale*, no. 1, p. 159. Also, see above, note 150 (ch. 2).
96 Tescione, *Caserta medievale*, p. 36, n. 148.

97 Inguanez, *S. Angelo in Formis*, no. 47, pp. 133–5. A reproduction of Count Robert's comital cruciform cypher survives in Gattola, *Accessiones*, I, p. 262.
98 Inguanez, *S. Angelo in Formis*, no. 50, pp. 140–3, at 141–2.
99 *Catalogus Baronum*, ¶¶ 964–70, pp. 172–3. See also Tescione, *Caserta medievale*, pp. 38–40.
100 *Falcandus*, pp. 178–9. See above, note 62 (ch. 4).
101 *Catalogus Baronum*, ¶¶ 959–60, pp. 170–1.
102 Salvati, *Le pergamene della SNSP II*, no. 1, pp. 29–30.
103 *Falcandus*, pp. 186–7.
104 *Falcandus*, pp. 196–7.
105 Scandone, *Montella II*, pp. 20, 28–9, 35–6.
106 See pages 143–5.
107 *Cod. Dipl. Verginiano*, v, no. 453, pp. 187–8.
108 *Catalogus Baronum*, ¶ 295, p. 48; Cuozzo, 'I conti normanni di Catanzaro', p. 67.
109 Cuozzo and Martin, *Pergamene di Sepino*, no. 1, pp. 75–6.
110 Cuozzo and Martin, *Pergamene di Sepino*, nos 2–3, pp. 76–80.
111 See above, note 10 (ch. 4).
112 *Cod. Dipl. Tremiti*, no. 108, pp. 300–3. Cf. Morlacchetti, *L'abbazia benedettina delle Isole Tremiti e i suoi documenti dall'XI al XIII secolo*, pp. 284–5.
113 *Chron. Casauriense*, cols 913–14.
114 *Chron. Casauriense*, cols 1010–11.
115 On the office of royal justiciar, its origins in the peninsula and its role, see above, note 90 (ch. 2).
116 See above, page 90.
117 *Falcandus*, pp. 182–3. On the reasons for the arrest of Henry Aristippus, see *Falcandus*, pp. 162–5.
118 *Falcandus*, pp. 186–7.
119 Cuozzo, 'I conti normanni di Catanzaro', p. 116.
120 Trinchera, *Syllabus Graecarum membranarum*, no. 167, pp. 219–21. This monastery was presumably St Stephen del Bosco (modern La certosa di Serra San Bruno e Santi Stefano), founded c. 1118. See Peters-Custot, *Bruno en Calabre*, pp. 122–3.
121 In addition to his partnership with the pope during Robert of Loritello's first rebellion (according to the *Liber Pontificalis*, pp. 393–4, he even swore fealty and paid homage to Pope Adrian IV), Andrew of Rupecanina was recorded to have been in Ancona in 1157, to have later been sent by the Greek commander (*protostrator*) Alexios Axouchos into southern Italy. The Greek source referred to Andrew as 'a count of an Italian city, valiant in might and well-supplied with bravery'. *Kinnamos*, bk 4, chap. 14, pp. 130–1. Also, Andrew of Rupecanina met with Frederick Barbarossa during the siege of Milan in 1158.
122 *Annales Ceccanenses*, p. 285.
123 *Annales Ceccanenses*, p. 285.
124 Pio, *Guglielmo I d'Altavilla*, pp. 43–64.
125 See above, note 107 (ch. 4).
126 *Annales Ceccanenses*, p. 285. Christian of Buch, archbishop of Mainz from 1165 until his death in 1183, served Emperor Frederick I for much of his pontificate as his imperial chancellor, and acted as a diplomat and general in Italy. Acht, III. Christian's role as a military leader is discussed in Arnold. On the political, legal, and ceremonial expressions of power of Archbishop Christian, and his relationship with the German Empire, see Burkhardt, *Mit Stab und Schwert*, pp. 163–6, 183–4, 228–32, 322–73, 403–40.

Chapter 5

1. See Chronological Table.
2. On William II's coronation, see note 19 (ch. 3).
3. *Romuald*, p. 254.
4. *Falcandus*, pp. 196–7.
5. *Falcandus*, pp. 206–7.
6. *Annales Ceccanenses*, p. 285.
7. *Chron. Casauriense*, p. 903.
8. Jamison, 'Norman Administration', pp. 290–1; Takayama, *The Administration*, pp. 106–9.
9. *Falcandus*, pp. 210–11.
10. *Falcandus*, pp. 210–11.
11. *Falcandus*, pp. 210–11.
12. See Figure 2.
13. *Falcandus*, pp. 210–13. Qaid Peter, a royal eunuch and naval commander, was one of the leading figures at the court of William I. For a discussion of Peter's identity and role, see Johns, *Arabic Administration in Norman Sicily*, pp. 222–8; Metcalfe, *The Muslims of Medieval Italy*, pp. 195–203.
14. *Falcandus*, pp. 212–15.
15. *Falcandus*, pp. 214–15; *Romuald*, p. 254.
16. *Annales Ceccanenses*, p. 285.
17. See pages 82–3.
18. *Annales Ceccanenses*, p. 285.
19. *William I Diplomata*, no. 12, pp. 32–5. On the relationship between the papacy and the kingdom of Sicily, see Cuozzo, *La monarchia bipolare*; Loud, *The Latin Church*, pp. 154–80.
20. *Kinnamos*, bk 4, chap. 14, pp. 170–1.
21. *Romuald*, p. 255; *Chron. de Ferraria*, p. 30; Schmale, *Italische Quellen über die Taten Kaiser Friedrichs I.*, pp. 196–7, 200. On Christian of Buch, see note 126 (ch. 4). On Frederick I's expedition in 1167, see more especially Freed, *Frederick Barbarossa*, pp. 334–48.
22. Appelt, *Friderici I. Diplomata*, nos 532, p. 475, 536, p. 483.
23. The local sources that recorded this retreat include *Annales Ceccanenses*, p. 286; *Romuald*, p. 256. Of course there are many other accounts in German and north Italian sources for this, such as the *Historia Welforum*, or Acerbus Morena's account in Güterbock, *Ottonis Morenae et Continuatorum Historia Frederici I*, pp. 205–7. Additionally, Freed argues this setback was the turning point of Emperor Frederick's reign. Freed, *Frederick Barbarossa*, pp. 343–5.
24. *Falcandus*, pp. 216–17.
25. See note 90 (ch. 3).
26. *Falcandus*, pp. 216–17.
27. *Falcandus*, pp. 226–9.
28. *Tyrants*, p. 157, n. 165.
29. See note 40 (ch. 6).
30. On Roger's relation with the Rupecanina, see page 139.
31. Cuozzo, *Commentario*, pp. 64–6, 322, 328–30; *Tyrants*, p. 157.
32. *Catalogus Baronum*, ¶ 1079, p. 205. See also Cuozzo, *Commentario*, p. 322.
33. *Catalogus Baronum*, ¶ 1095, p. 212. See page 23.

34 *Annales Ceccanenses*, p. 285.
35 Febonio, *Cat.*, pp. 23-4. Referenced in Kehr, *Italia pontificia*, IV, p. 245; Cuozzo, 'Ruggiero, conte d'Andria', p. 143, n. 43.
36 *Falcandus*, pp. 74-5.
37 *Catalogus Baronum*, ¶¶ 291-3, p. 47; 396, p. 71.
38 Campanile, *Notizie di nobiltà*, p. 344; Scandone, *Nusco*, p. 41, n. 21.
39 Scandone, *Montella II*, p. 37, n. 2; Scandone, *Nusco*, p. 41, n. 22. Also in *Italia Sacra*, VII, cols 535-6. The original document was found in the archive of *Real Casa Santa dell'Annunziata* (Naples), Inventario antico, no 213.
40 *Sicilia Sacra*, I, p. 624.
41 Ménager, 'Les fondations monastiques', no. 44, p. 112.
42 *Falcandus*, pp. 222-3.
43 See page 102.
44 *Falcandus*, pp. 228-9. Chancellor Stephen must have been a younger son of Count Rotrou II of Perche and his second wife, a 'sister of Count Patritius, an English lord' (*soror comitis Patricii, nobilis de Anglia*). Huygens, *William of Tyre*, II, bk. 14, chap. 1, pp. 632-3. This sister of Count Patritius was Hawise, daughter of Walter of Salisbury, sheriff of Wiltshire. Thompson, 'Family Tradition', p. 14. It seems that Count Rotrou named his son Stephen as a sign of goodwill towards his new ally, King Stephen of England. Thompson, *The County of Perche*, p. 80.
45 See pages 80-1, and note 7 (ch. 4).
46 *Falcandus*, 228-9.
47 *Romuald*, p. 255. Kathleen Thompson has suggested that Stephen of Perche, while young and destined for a career in the church, joined the cathedral chapter at Rouen but did not remain there long, because his colleagues later could not recall his name; the record of Stephen's contribution to the costs of the new chapterhouse describes him solely as 'the son of the count of Perche'. Thompson, 'Family Tradition', p. 17.
48 See Genealogical Network. Also, see chart no II in *Tyrants*.
49 *Italia Sacra*, X, col. 296; Di Meo, *Annali Critico-Diplomatici del Regno di Napoli della Mezzana Età*, X, pp. 299-300. Cf. Chalandon, *Histoire de la domination normande en Italie et en Sicile*, II, p. 231; 'The Image of the Tyrant', p. 161, n. 173.
50 *Pergamene di Salerno*, no. 145, pp. 337-40, especially 338.
51 Enzensberger, 'Il documento regio', p. 119; Enzensberger, 'Chanceries, Charters and Administration', p. 122.
52 Carlone, *Falsificazioni e falsari*, pp. 18-20.
53 *Tyrants*, pp. 161-2, nn. 174-5.
54 *Falcandus*, pp. 230-3, 242-3, 256-7.
55 *Romuald*, p. 255. She could have been in fact Countess Adelicia, who was recorded in a September 1177 charter from Auletta. See note 180 (ch. 6).
56 *Falcandus*, pp. 224-7.
57 *Falcandus*, pp. 244-5.
58 See Fernández-Aceves, 'Royal Comestabuli', pp. 21-2.
59 Roger of Tiron's grandfather Robert had witnessed Roger II's treaty with the count of Barcelona in 1128. *Roger II Diplomata*, no. 9, pp. 22-4. Additionally, a Robert son of Robert of Tiron (ρωπέρτος υιοῦ ρωπέρτου δὲ τεροῦν) made two donations to Calabrian churches in October 1154, and both transactions were subscribed by his son Roger; this donor must have been Roger of Tiron's father. Trinchera, ed., *Syllabus Graecarum membranarum*, nos 150-1, pp. 198-201.
60 *Falcandus*, pp. 250-1.

61 *Falcandus*, pp. 250–1. William of Gesualdo was the son of Elias of Gesualdo, a prominent overlord in the Irpina region who subsequently became a royal constable and justiciar. Cuozzo, *Commentario*, p. 194. Also, see pages 163–4.
62 See note 203 (ch. 2).
63 Houben, *Die Abtei Venosa*, no. 127, pp. 360–1. The record only survives in Prignano's 'Chron(ica) in Bergamena del Monist(ero) della Trin(ità) di Venosa'. Prignano, 'Historia', fol. 108v.
64 *Catalogus Baronum*, ¶ 694, p. 122.
65 *Falcandus*, pp. 250–7.
66 *Romuald*, p. 256.
67 Holtzmann, 'Papst-, Kaiser- und Normannenurkunden', no. 8, pp. 67–9.
68 *William II Diplomata*, no. 13, http://www.hist-hh.uni-bamberg.de/WilhelmII/pdf/D.W.II.013.pdf
69 Cf. Chalandon, who suggests that this Roger was the count of Geraci, in Sicily, but this seems even more unlikely because of the much richer documentation available for the island of Sicily and the fact that there were no counties in Norman Sicily. Chalandon, *Histoire de la domination normande en Italie et en Sicile*, II, p. 335.
70 *Falcandus*, pp. 260–1
71 See note 62 (ch. 4).
72 *Catalogus Baronum*, ¶ 438, pp. 79–80.
73 *Falcandus*, pp. 260–3.
74 Portanova, 'I Sanseverino dal 1125', pp. 321–8.
75 Cava, *Arm. Mag.* F.36.
76 Cava, *Arca* xxix.92.
77 On the possible intrigues behind the succession of Roger of S. Severino, see Portanova, 'I Sanseverino dal 1125', pp. 319–21.
78 *Falcandus*, pp. 260–3.
79 *Catalogus Baronum*, ¶ 294, p. 48.
80 *Catalogus Baronum*, ¶¶ 843, p. 153; 964, p. 172.
81 *Tyrants*, p. 183, n. 208.
82 *Falcandus*, pp. 264–5.
83 *Romuald*, p. 256.
84 *Falcandus*, pp. 266–71.
85 Houben, 'Le origini del principato', pp. 15–18. Cf. Jamison, 'Norman Administration', pp. 279–80. Also, see pages 152–3.
86 See pages 42–3.
87 *Falcandus*, pp. 270–7.
88 See note 91 (ch. 3).
89 *Falcandus*, pp. 278–81.
90 See page 119.
91 *Falcandus*, pp. 280–1.
92 On the composition of the royal *familiares* at this stage, see Takayama, '*Familiares Regis*', pp. 361–3; Takayama, *The Administration*, pp. 115–18.
93 *Catalogus Baronum*, ¶ 439, pp. 80–1.
94 On Florius of Camerota, see Fernández-Aceves, 'Royal Comestabuli', pp. 31–2.
95 *Falcandus*, pp. 280–1.
96 *Falcandus*, pp. 280–3.
97 *Romuald*, p. 256.
98 Brandileone, *Il diritto romano nelle leggi normanne e sveve del regno Sicilia*, pp. 103–4, 122–3; Monti, 'Il testo e la storia esterna delle assise normanne', I, p. 320.

99 Frier and others, *The Codex of Justinian*, III, p. 2376.
100 *Falcandus*, pp. 282–3.
101 *Catalogus Baronum*, ¶ 1105, p. 215.
102 *Falcandus*, pp. 282–3.
103 *Romuald*, p. 257.
104 *Falcandus*, pp. 282–3.
105 *Falcandus*, pp. 284–5.
106 *Romuald*, p. 257.
107 Holtzmann, 'Papst-, Kaiser- und Normannenurkunden', no. 7–8, pp. 70–2.
108 '*Casale quod dicitur Comitis et saracenice vocatur Rachal eimelum [Rahl el Melum] Rameth, situm in plano Milatii inter Montefortem et Ramet versus mare [...]*' Garufi, *Documenti inediti*, no. 44, pp. 101–2.
109 *Romuald*, p. 257.
110 *Falcandus*, pp. 302–5.
111 *Romuald*, p. 257.
112 *Falcandus*, pp. 304–7.
113 *Cod. Dipl. Verginiano*, 1982, vol. 5, no. 474, pp. 261–4.*Cod. Dipl. Verginiano*, 1982, vol. 5, no. 474, pp. 261–4.
114 *Falcandus*, pp. 308–11.
115 *Falcandus*, pp. 310–11.
116 *Falcandus*, pp. 314–17.
117 *William of Tyre*, II, bk 20, chap. 3, pp. 914–15.
118 *Romuald*, p. 257.
119 *Falcandus*, pp. 316–17.
120 *Romuald*, p. 257.
121 *Annales Casinenses*, p. 312.
122 *Falcandus*, pp. 316–17.
123 *Falcandus*, pp. 316–19.
124 *William of Tyre*, II, bk 20, chap. 3, pp. 914–15; Babcock and Krey, trans., *A History of Deeds Done beyond the Sea*, II, pp. 346–7.
125 *Falcandus*, pp. 318–19.
126 See page 92.
127 Garufi, *Documenti inediti*, no. 42, pp. 96–9.
128 See Fernández-Aceves, 'Civitate and Carinola', pp. 71–2.
129 Garufi, *Documenti inediti*, no. 42, pp. 96–9, at p. 98.
130 Jamison, 'Note e documenti', no. 2, pp. 465–70, especially p. 467.
131 Count Hugh of Catanzaro was subsequently remembered, by Pope Alexander III, as the spouse of Countess Clementia. Kehr, *Italia pontificia*, IX, p. 139.
132 Benevento, *Fondo S. Pietro*, vol. 6, no. 5. Partially ed. in Jamison, 'Bethlem', no. 10, p. 64.
133 See note 31 (ch. 7).
134 Hagemann, 'Kaiserurkunden aus Gravina', no. 3, pp. 196–7. Also, see note 110 (ch. 6).

Chapter 6

1 *Romuald*, p. 257.
2 See Chronological Table.
3 *Romuald*, p. 258.

4 *Annales Ceccanenses*, p. 286; *Annales Casinenses*, p. 312.
5 The original charter (*Pergamene dei Monasteri Soppressi* II. 156) was destroyed in 1943, together with all the other documents in its collection of the Archivio di Stato of Naples. Petrucci, 'Documenti di Bansuvilla', no. 7, p. 117.
6 On the identification of *Casalinovo*, see *Catalogus Baronum*, p. 65, n. 5. Also, see Map 1.
7 *Catalogus Baronum*, ¶ 368, p. 64.
8 See page 61.
9 *Pergamene di Barletta*, no. 119, pp. 164–5.
10 Petrucci, 'Documenti di Bansuvilla', no. 1, pp. 135–8.
11 Cava, *Arm. Mag.* I.14, ed. in *Carte di Molfetta*, no. 55, pp. 70–1.
12 *Chron. de Carpineto*, pp. 289–90; Petrucci, 'Documenti di Bansuvilla', no. 2, pp. 138–40.
13 *Cod. dipl. Molisano*, pp. 305–7, at 306.
14 *Catalogus Baronum*, ¶ 295 p. 48. Also, see Map 1.
15 *Italia Sacra*, VIII, cols 253–5.
16 Located in the vicinity of modern Bosco and Castel Dragonara, 20 kilometres southeast of Loritello. See Map 1.
17 Del Giudice, App. 1, no. 20, pp. xliii–xliv. These local fees, although sometimes regarded as public taxes, developed as baronial prerogatives in Apulia, and as such, fell within the count's authority. Martin, *La Pouille*, pp. 302–6.
18 '*Tempore domini nostri Roberti Dei et domini nostri regis Wi. Gratia palatinus comes Lorotelli*'. Martin, *Cartulaire de Sculgola*, I, no. 2, pp. 7–8.
19 Cava, *Arm. Mag.* I.26, ed. in *Carte di Molfetta*, no. 62, pp. 79–80.
20 Houben, *Die Abtei Venosa*, no. 162, pp. 386–7. Houben has presented here the surviving reference found in Prignano, 'Historia', fol. 109v. Cf. Ménager, 'Les fondations monastiques', no. 44, p. 114.
21 *Cod. dipl. Molisano*, pp. 239–41, at 240.
22 See page 33.
23 Gattola, *Accessiones*, I, pp. 265–6.
24 Jamison, 'Norman Administration', pp. 477–8.
25 Petrucci, 'Documenti di Bansuvilla', p. 118, n. 2.
26 *Chron. de Carpineto*, no. 137, pp. 289–90. The letter does not provide a year, but it is dated to the sixth indiction; the only possible year for this indiction is 1173, as 1158 is before William II's reign and 1188 is after Count Robert's death.
27 The town of Civitaquana is 25 kilometres west of Chieti. See Map 1.
28 '*existente camerario eius totius comitatus Lorotelli Roberto de Varo*'. *Chron. de Carpineto*, pp. 299–300.
29 Benevento, *Fondo S. Sofia*, vol. 2, no. 10.
30 *Pergamene di Conversano*, p. lii; Jamison, *Admiral Eugenius*, p. 88; Cuozzo, 'I conti normanni di Catanzaro', p. 118.
31 *Pergamene di Conversano*, no. 138, pp. 287–9. The charter was originally dated, following the Byzantine style, in September 1189, seventh indiction; therefore, the correct year must be 1188, not 1189. Cf. Morea, *Chartularium di Conversano*, I, no. 133, pp. 255–8.
32 Jamison, 'Norman Administration', p. 389, n. 3; Takayama, *The Administration*, p. 161, n. 114.
33 Naples, Biblioteca Nazionale, *Biblioteca Brancacciana* L.F.5, ff. 51r–232v (Camillo Tutini, 'Notationes desumptae ab Archiviis monasteriorum'), fol. 77v.

34 *Cod. Dipl. Verginiano*, VI, no. 533, pp. 124–9; Scandone, *Montella II*, no. 8, pp. 171–3.
35 Scandone, *S. Angelo dei Lombardi*, no. 11, p. 208.
36 *Cod. Dipl. Verginiano*, IX, no. 842, pp. 142–5.
37 *Italia Sacra*, I, cols 723–4.
38 Garufi, *Ryccardi de S. Germano*, pp. 9–10.
39 Thanks to Richard of Acerra's participation in this subsequent episode, depictions of this count survive in the illuminated account of Peter of Eboli. Count Richard was portrayed, among some other instances, as an authority figure holding a sword, together with the archbishop of Salerno, addressing the Neapolitans; see Figure 3. In another illustration, Count Richard was depicted as a commander of a band of *milites*; see Figure 4.
40 Del Giudice, App. 1, no. 14, pp. xxxi–xxxii.
41 Cuozzo, *Commentario*, p. 266; Loud and Wiedemann, 'Introduction', p. 26. See Genealogical Network.
42 Mazzoleni, *Pergamene di Capua*, no. 9, pp. 40–2; Ambrosio, *Le pergamene di S. Maria della Grotta di Vitulano (BN) (secc. XI-XII)*, no. 13, pp. 23–4.
43 Salvati, *Le pergamene della SNSP II*, no. 1, pp. 29–30.
44 Benevento, *Fondo S. Pietro*, vol. 6, no. 5, ed. in Jamison, 'Bethlem', no. 10, p. 64; Cuozzo, 'Ruggiero, conte d'Andria', p. 165.
45 Prignano, 'Historia', fol. 60r. Referenced in Cuozzo, 'Ruggiero, conte d'Andria', p. 166.
46 Promis, 'Notizia di una bolla di piombo del secolo XII', p. 670. Also, see Figure 5. Interestingly enough, the subsequent portrayals made by Peter of Eboli depict Count Roger of Andria with a long and white beard. See Figure 6.
47 Cuozzo, 'Ruggiero, conte d'Andria', p. 166.
48 See pages 169 and 176.
49 *Cod. Dipl. Verginiano*, VI, no. 569, pp. 359–65.
50 *Catalogus Baronum*, ¶ 808, p. 148.
51 For a description of the early foundations of the Order in Sicily, see Toomaspoeg, 'La frontière terrestre du Royaume de Sicile à l'époque normande', pp. 41–51.
52 *Sicilia Sacra*, I, p. 934.
53 *Cod. Dipl. Verginiano*, VII, no. 614, pp. 54–7.
54 Grimoald's actual title is not clear; in the document's original form, that section is illegible, and the editor has proposed the following reading: *Gri[maldus filius [...] qui magister iustiti]e est in Terra Laboris*. However, the peninsular master justiciars are only documented as high officials in charge of all Apulia and the Terra di Lavoro, and under William II's reign, this positon was occupied only by counts. As a lesser baron, and if he was in fact in charge of the *iustitie* in the Terra di Lavoro, he must have been simply a provincial justiciar, or perhaps a deputy acting for the master justiciar. On the noblemen who acted as master justiciars on the mainland, see pages 172–8.
55 *Cod. Dipl. Verginiano*, VII, no. 681, pp. 286–9.
56 *Cod. Dipl. Verginiano*, VII, nos 686, pp. 302–3, 688, pp. 308–10.
57 *Cod. Dipl. Verginiano*, VIII, no. 733, pp. 117–20.
58 '*Perrona olim comitissa Avellini et Matheus Castelli Veteris eius filius dei gratia domini Taurassi*'. *Cod. Dipl. Verginiano*, X, no. 997, pp. 318–22.
59 Scandone, *L'alta valle del Calore*, II, pp. 60–7.
60 *Cod. Dipl. Verginiano*, XI, no. 1091, pp. 319–22. Also, se Genealogical Network.
61 *Falcandus*, pp. 178–9.
62 See above, note 26 (ch. 4).

63 The town of Calitri is located 12 kilometres northeast of Conza, along the banks of the River Ofanto. See Map 1.
64 Rome, Archivio Segreto Vaticano, *Arch. Boncompagni-Ludovisi* prot. 270, no. 9 [A].
65 The ruins of a medieval castle, identified as *Castrum Monticuli*, can be found in the zone of Gli Sgarroni, which appears to have been a residence for a Norman baron in the twelfth and thirteenth centuries. Licinio, *Castelli medievali*, p. 191.
66 *Catalogus Baronum*, ¶ 699, p. 124.
67 Palanza, 'Per un conte normanno di Avellino', pp. 127–30.
68 See page 40.
69 Garufi, *Documenti inediti*, no. 42, pp. 96–9. Also, see page 130.
70 Jamison, *Admiral Eugenius*, p. 101. Cf. Cuozzo, who estimates that the letter was written after 25 June 1175, when the canons of Cefalù were given royal dispensation to elect Guido their bishop, and before 1193; the Italian scholar did not consider that Guido would have been referred to as *electus* before his confirmation, as it was the contemporary customary practice, and that Count Richard could not have been able to issue a confirmation after his removal and imprisonment. Cuozzo, 'Prosopografia: i Balvano', p. 84.
71 Prignano, 'Historia', fol. 109r. This document was found in the donation register of the now lost archive of S. Annunziata of Naples, caps. 387, no. 24.
72 Houben, *Die Abtei Venosa*, no. 156, p. 383.
73 *Cod. Dipl. Verginiano*, VIII, no. 757, pp. 193–7.
74 Rome, Biblioteca Apostolica Vaticana, *Vat. Lat.* 8222, ff. 49r–63r ('Privilegia Ecclesie Monasterii S. Trinitatis de Venusio'), fol. 57v.
75 Caetani, *Regesta chartarum*, I, p. 13. On the Amalfitan tarì, see Skinner, *Medieval Amalfi*, p. 16.
76 Pescatore, 'Le piu antiche pergamene dell'Archivio arcivescovile di Capua (1144–1250)', pp. 31–3. Reproduced in Tescione, *Caserta medievale*, no. 4, pp. 164–5.
77 See above, note 97 (ch. 4).
78 Caetani, *Regesta chartarum*, I, p. 14.
79 Cava, *Arm. Mag.* I.21, ed. in Graziani, pp. 18–20. One should not assume that these *homines censiles* were vassals in the traditional sense of the word – as with any other term of classic 'feudalism'. It is common to see these terms such as *homines*, *censiles*, *servi* or *villani* translated as 'vassals', even though there is no clear relationship of submission, much less of homage or allegiance. In the south Italian context, at least in the Salernitan region up to the thirteenth century, these words reflected a social condition with regard to peasant labour obligations: these men were settlers or villagers who acted as tenant-farmers in certain places or hamlets. Nevertheless, *censiles* were clearly not free men, and were bound to pay rent to their lord. This charter is indeed a good example both of this social condition and of the lack of clear definitions of attachment, as the abbey required a confirmation from the donor's heir that the *censiles* who had previously been granted with the land, and their descendants, would not work for the donor's heir, but for the abbey instead. See Loud, 'The Monastic Economy', pp. 150–61.
80 Cava, *Arm. Mag.* H.35, H.39. The former was edited in Graziani, pp. 15–16. Cf. Scandone, who confused Sarracena's Cava documents. Scandone, *Montella II*, p. 23 n. 1.
81 On Sarracena's dower and holdings, see Scandone, *Montella II*, pp. 22–4; Tescione, *Caserta medievale*, p. 43.

82 Cava, *Arca* xxxvi.38, ed. in Tescione, *Caserta medievale*, no. 5, pp. 165-7. The notary of this charter, Peter, must have been the same Peter who drafted the other 1178 transaction (Cava, *Arm. Mag.* I.21).

83 Caetani, *Regesta chartarum*, I, pp. 14-16; Jaffé, *Regesta*, II, no. 13094, p. 324. Another papal bull was issued to Bishop Porfirio on the same day, 14 August 1178. It placed the church of Caserta under papal protection as well. Tescione, 'Il privilegio de 1178'.

84 *Italia Sacra*, VI, col. 480. According to Ughelli, the church was dedicated to two more saints besides James: St Nicholas and St Basil. On the church's possible holdings and large size, see Tescione, *Caserta medievale*, p. 43.

85 Caetani, *Regesta chartarum*, I, p. 16.

86 His death is recorded only as part of the scattered obituaries, without providing a specific month or year. *Necrologio di S. Matteo*, p. 208.

87 Cava, *Arm. Mag.* L.4, ed. in Tescione, *Caserta medievale*, no. 6, pp. 167-8.

88 The name of this bishop is not legible in the document's current form (*domino [...] esino episcopo*), but Kamp has suggested this could be the bishop of Telese (*[Tel]esino*). Kamp, *Kirche und Monarchie*, p. 292, n. 8.

89 *Necrologio di S. Matteo*, p. 42. See also Abignente, 'Le Chartulae fraternitatis ed il Libro de' confratres della chiesa Salernitana', p. 457; Tescione, *Caserta medievale*, p. 45.

90 Cava, *Arm. Mag.* L.15, ed. in Tescione, *Caserta medievale*, no. 7, pp. 168-70.

91 Cava, *Arca* xl.100, ed. In Tescione, *Caserta medievale*, no. 8, pp. 170-1.

92 See note 82 (ch. 6).

93 Tescione, *Caserta medievale*, no. 9, pp. 172-4.

94 Cava, *Arm. Mag.* L.23, ed. In Graziani, *Purdgavine*, pp. 20-2. On tenant-farmers, see note 79 (ch. 4).

95 These tenant-farmers of Solofra must have been the same men and their descendants of those that Sarracena granted to the abbey in 1159, and that her son Count Robert of Caserta confirmed in 1178. See page 146.

96 Cava, *Amr. Mag.*, L.30.

97 Cava, *Arca* xliii.110, ed. in Tescione, *Caserta medievale*, no. 10, pp. 174-5.

98 'Ecclesia s. Thomae mart. a Roberto comite de Caserta in territorio Montorio aedificata'. Kehr, *Italia pontificia*, VIII, p. 236. See also Tescione, *Caserta medievale*, p. 41, n. 179.

99 See pages 118-9.

100 Cuozzo, *Commentario*, p. 31. Cuozzo cites here a record in a sixteenth-century manuscript (*Visitatio illustrissimi, et reverendissimi domini Joannis Baptistae Santonio, episcopi Tricaricensis. Anno 1588*), which to this day can be found in the Archivio storico diocesano di Tricarico, *Fondo Curia vescovile, Serie Visite pastorali*, Busta 1. On this manuscript, see Biscaglia and Ginetti, 'Le visite pastorali della diocesi di Tricarico (1588-1959)', p. 306.

101 Cava, *Arm. Mag.* L.16, ed. in *Actes de Gargano*, no. 55, pp. 152-4. Copy in *Arm. Mag.* L.14. This concession was confirmed in November 1219 by Count Gentile of Lesina, master justiciar of Apulia and the Terra di Lavoro. *Arm Mag.* M.13, ed. in *Actes de Gargano*, no. 64, pp. 169-71.

102 See note 94 (ch. 6).

103 Cava, *Arm. Mag.* L.27.

104 *Catalogus Baronum*, ¶ 295, pp. 48-9.

105 *Cod. Dipl. Verginiano*, VII, no. 623, pp. 90-4. Volturara Appula is around 50 kilometres southwest of Civitate (modern San Paolo di Civitate); on the other hand,

Celenza Valforte is northwest of Volturara, near the River Fortore, and around 45 kilometres southwest of Civitate. See Map 1.
106 Naples, Biblioteca della Società Napoletana di Storia Patria, *Compre e vendite* 2 AA III.17, ed. in Ambrosio, *Le pergamene di S. Maria della Grotta di Vitulano (BN) (secc. XI-XII)*, no. 32, pp. 53-4. The charter's original date clause provides the year 1180, but given that it was dated in the twelfth indiction, the year must be corrected. Cf. De Blasiis and Parisio, 'Elenco delle pergamene già appartenenti alla famiglia Fusco ed ora acquisite dalla Società Napoletana di Storia Patria' (no. 44, p. 783); Cuozzo, *Commentario*, p. 67.
107 The original charter (*Pergamene dei Monasteri Soppressi*, III. 226) was destroyed in 1943, together with all the other documents in its collection of the Archivio di Stato of Naples. Jamison, 'Norman Administration', pp. 356, n. 3, 364; Cuozzo, *Commentario*, pp. 67-8.
108 On this monastery, see above, note 103 (ch. 2).
109 Garufi, *Ryccardi de S. Germano*, p. 21.
110 Cava, *Arm. Mag.* I.20.
111 Houben, *Die Abtei Venosa*, no. 168, pp. 390-1.
112 An authenticated donation that was transcribed into a *diploma* issued by King Charles II of Anjou on 17 November 1304. Del Giudice, *Codice diplomatico del regno di Carlo I. e II. d'Angiò*, no. 15 pp. xxxii–xxxvii, at pp. xxxv–xxxvi.
113 See page 114.
114 Hagemann, 'Kaiserurkunden aus Gravina', no. 3, pp. 196-7.
115 See note 31 (ch. 7).
116 See chapter 7.
117 Rome, Archivio Segreto Vaticano, *AA Arm.* I.xviii.118.
118 See note 12 (ch. 7).
119 *Italia Sacra*, I, cols 723-4.
120 *Italia Sacra*, I, col. 725.
121 Subiaco, Biblioteca S. Scolastica, *Archivio Colonna* III, BB xxix.20.
122 Count Marinus of Traetto had granted a quarter of this *castellum* to Montecassino in 1058, and Abbot Desiderius had granted a privilege to the inhabitants in 1061. *Cod. Dipl. Cajetanus*, II, nos 204, pp. 17-20; 213, pp. 37-9. See also Loud, *Church and Society*, p. 42.
123 *Catalogus Baronum*, ¶ 155, p. 28.
124 *Catalogus Baronum*, ¶¶ 108, p. 20; 125, p. 22; 131-6, pp. 24-5; 153-4, pp. 27-8.
125 Cf. Jamison, 'Additional Work', pp. 53-5; Houben, 'Le origini del principato', pp. 19-21.
126 See page 161.
127 Palumbo, *Tancredi conte di Lecce e re di Sicilia e il tramonto dell'età normanna*, pp. 86-7.
128 *Choniates*, I, p. 359; Stubbs, II, p. 141; *Annales Casinenses*, p. 314.
129 Palumbo, *Tancredi conte di Lecce e re di Sicilia e il tramonto dell'età normanna*, pp. 57-110.
130 Pastore, *Le pergamene di S. Giovanni Evangelista in Lecce*, no. 8 pp. 19-21; for Anacletus' concession, see no. 2 pp. 4-7.
131 Pastore, *Le pergamene di S. Giovanni Evangelista in Lecce*, no. 11, pp. 27-8.
132 Palumbo, *Tancredi conte di Lecce e re di Sicilia e il tramonto dell'età normanna*, pp. 248-9.
133 de Leo, ed., *Le carte del monastero dei Santi Niccolò e Cataldo in Lecce*, no. 3, pp. 7-13.

134 *Italia Sacra*, IX, col. 77; de Leo, ed., *Le carte del monastero dei Santi Niccolò e Cataldo in Lecce*, pp. 209–10.
135 de Leo, ed., *Le carte del monastero dei Santi Niccolò e Cataldo in Lecce*, nos 6, pp. 21–4; 10, pp. 30–1; 19, pp. 34–6.
136 Pepe, Add., no. 3, pp. 197–9.
137 See note 42 (ch. 7).
138 Fortunato, no. 5, pp. 38–42. Referred in Prignano, 'Historia', fol. 109r.
139 Morea, *Chartularium di Conversano*, I, no. 133, pp. 255–8.
140 Cava, *Arm. Mag.* I.7. A copy of this charter is *Arca* xxxiv.62, ed. in *Actes de Gargano*, no. 46, pp. 135–7. The count's father, Henry of Ollia, had previously ceded these fishermen in October 1140. Cava, *Arm. Mag.* G.34.
141 *Cod. Dipl. Tremiti*, no. 117, pp. 324–6.
142 *Chron. Casauriense*, cols 1012–13.
143 Cuozzo, *Commentario*, p. 95. Taken from a register, which Cuozzo consulted in 1974 from the curial archive of the bishopric of S. Severo, and that is now unavailable. The record is *Inventarium omnium bonorum stabilim Venerabili Monasterii Sancti Johannis in Plano, et Sancate Trinitatis de Sancto Severo*, fol. 7v. St John in Piano is 9 kilometres south of Lesina. See Map 1.
144 Ménager, *Recueil des actes*, pp. 35, 181–6; *Cod. Dipl. Tremiti*, nos 54, pp. 168–70; 81, pp. 282–4; Loud, *The Age of Robert Guiscard*, pp. 249, 256.
145 Cava, *Arm. Mag.* I.39 (Copied in I.38), ed. in *Actes de Gargano*, no. 52, pp. 146–9.
146 See note 12 (ch. 7). On Siponto and Vieste, see note 25 (ch. 3).
147 See pages 32–3.
148 Stubbs, *Gesta Henrici II*, I, p. 170.
149 See note 42 (ch. 7).
150 Palumbo, *Tancredi conte di Lecce e re di Sicilia e il tramonto dell'età normanna*, pp. 130–3.
151 Garufi, *Tabulario di Monreale*, App., no. 2, pp. 163–5. On the *duana baronum*, see Appendix.
152 *Sicilia Sacra*, I, pp. 433–5; *William II Diplomata*, no. 89, http://www.hist-hh.uni-ba mberg.de/WilhelmII/pdf/D.W.II.089.pdf.
153 Houben, *Die Abtei Venosa*, nos 147–9, pp. 377–9; 153–4, pp. 381–2.
154 Cava, *Arca* xl.96 (To appear in Graham A. Loud's forthcoming edition of 'Selected Charters of the Abbey of Cava, 1097–1200').
155 Portanova, 'I Sanseverino dal 1125', pp. 333–5.
156 Cava, *Arm. Mag.* L.34, ed. in Mattei-Ceresoli, 'Tramutola', no. 20, pp. 117–18.
157 *Catalogus Baronum*, ¶ 597, p. 108.
158 Gattola, *Ad historiam abbatiae Cassinensis accessiones*, p. 243. Dated in 1169, but given it was issued in the fourth indiction and in William II's fourth regnal year, it should be 1170. Original in Montecassino, *Archivio*, caps. 102 fasc. 2 no. 3.
159 See note 167 (ch. 6).
160 *Pergamene di Terlizzi*, nos 101, pp. 128–9; 110, pp. 136–7.
161 Cf. Jamison, 'County of Molise', pp. 547–8.
162 Garufi, *Documenti inediti*, nos 47–8, pp.109–12; Pratesi, *Carte dall'archivio Aldobrandini*, no. 23, pp. 60–2. See also Takayama, *The Administration*, pp. 119–21.
163 Loud, 'A Lombard Abbey', no. 5, pp. 302–3. Jamison has pointed out that there is indication that Richard of Mandra visited for two days the hermit John of Tufara, in Serracapriola (in the Capitanata), to hear his words with great devotion. Jamison, *Molise e Marsia*, p. 27.

164 Garufi, *Documenti inediti*, no. 54, pp. 124–6.
165 See Jamison, 'County of Molise', pp. 536–41.
166 Cf. Jamison, 'County of Molise', p. 543.
167 Benevento, *Fondo S. Sofia*, vol. 8, no. 37, ed. in Jamison, *Molise e Marsia*, pp. 159–61.
168 Also witnessed the 1170 charter that Richard of Mandra issued as count of Molise, while at the baths of Pozzuoli. See note 163 (ch. 6).
169 The *adiutorium* was equivalent to the Norman *collecta*, according to the peace treaty Count Alexander of Conversano, Tancred of Conversano, Count Geoffrey of Catanzaro and Robert of Gravina had sworn to the city of Bari in 1132 in the name of the king (*adiutorium, quod ex nostre gentis [Normannorum] consuetudine collecta vocatur. Roger II Diplomata*, no. 20, pp. 54–6, at 56.) This consisted of some sort of extraordinary contribution levied by overlords from their holders *in demanio* or villains. Cahen, *Le régime féodal de l'Italie normande*, pp. 75–7; Martin, *La Pouille*, p. 823; Carocci, *Signorie di Mezzogiorno*, p. 182.
170 '*maxime cum debitum adjutorium conveniens et moderatum valent ab ipsis / maxime cum debitum adiutorium et moderatum et conveniens volent ab ipsis*'. Brandileone, *Il diritto romano nelle leggi normanne e sveve del regno Sicilia*, pp. 97, 120; Monti, 'Il testo e la storia esterna delle assise normanne', I, p. 132.
171 Jamison, 'County of Molise', p. 532.
172 The term *augmentum* was seldom employed in other contemporary texts, but it is attested in the late eleventh century, in a document from the abbey of St Sophia in Benevento (June 1076–September 1091), relative to Fiorentino: *Vat. Lat.* 13491, no. 9. Matera; Martin, *Chartes de Troia*, p. 759, n. 508. On this collection of documents from St Sophia in the Vatican, see Massa, 'L'archivio dell'abbazia di Santa Sofia di Benevento', pp. 464–5.
173 *Catalogus Baronum*, ¶ 798, p. 146.
174 *Cartulaire de Sculgola*, I, no. 23, pp. 42–3; *Cod. dipl. Molisano*, pp. 336–7.
175 Rivelli, *Memorie storiche della città di Campagna*, pp. 96–7. Cited in Cuozzo, 'Milites e testes', p. 162.
176 'στρατιγός ὀλέττας ἀτταβιανό ὁ υἱός νικολάου βιτζιούσος καὶ δεσκώμης πέτρος γίτζος'. Trinchera, *Syllabus Graecarum membranarum*, no. 172, pp. 227–8.
177 'ἐν τοῖς καιροῖς τοῦ εὐλαβεστάτου ἡμῶν κώμης ὀρρήκος'. Trinchera, *Syllabus Graecarum membranarum*, no. 177, pp. 232–3.
178 Cava, *Arca* xxxiv.15. Lucas Guarna was attested again as royal justiciar in August 1189, when he made a donation to Cava in August 1189. Cava, *Arca* xlii.35.
179 Ménager, 'Les fondations monastiques', no. 41, pp. 112–13.
180 Trinchera, *Syllabus Graecarum membranarum*, no. 191, pp. 251–2. Original in Cava, *Pergamene Greca*, no. 68.
181 See note 55 (ch. 5).
182 'ἐν τοῖς καιροῖς τῆς κωμτίσσης ἡμῶν ἀδιλάγια'. Trinchera, *Syllabus Graecarum membranarum*, no. 195, pp. 256–7. 'ἐν τοῖς καιροῖς τῆς κωμϊθίσσης ἡμῶν ἀ[δι]λάγια'. *Cod. Dipl. Verginiano*, VII, no. 620, pp. 75–9.
183 Cava, *Arm. Mag.* L.38, ed. in Clementi, 'Some Unnoticed Aspects', App., no. 1, pp. 355–6.
184 De Blasiis and Parisio, 'Elenco delle pergamene già appartenenti alla famiglia Fusco ed ora acquisite dalla Società Napoletana di Storia Patria', no. 29, p. 779; Scandone, *S. Angelo dei Lombardi*, no. 10, p. 208.
185 *Chartes de Troia*, no. 102, pp. 302–8, at 308.

186 Cuozzo, 'Prosopografia: i Balvano', pp. 63–6. On Gilbert of Balvano's role as royal constable, see Fernández-Aceves, 'Royal Comestabuli', pp. 17–19.
187 *Catalogus Baronum*, ¶ 703, p. 125.
188 *Catalogus Baronum*, ¶¶ 708–18, pp. 126–8.
189 On Turgisius' activities and sons, see Cuozzo, *Commentario*, pp. 202–3. Also, see note 87 (ch. 6).
190 *Catalogus Baronum*, ¶¶ 702–24, pp. 124–9.
191 Prignano, 'Historia', fol. 18v.
192 *Cod. Dipl. Verginiano*, VIII, no. 780, pp. 279–82.
193 *Catalogus Baronum*, ¶ 709, p. 126.
194 For a discussion on the *royal comestabuli*, see Fernández-Aceves, 'Royal Comestabuli', pp. 12–29.
195 *Italia Sacra*, VIII, cols 131–2.
196 Cuozzo, 'Prosopografia: i Balvano', p. 74.
197 Kehr, *Italia pontificia*, IX, p. 139.
198 See note 12 (ch. 7).
199 Stumpf-Brentano, p. 448; Jamison, *Admiral Eugenius*, p. 159, n. 4; Clementi, 'Calendar', no. 55, n. 8.
200 Garufi, *Documenti inediti*, no. 88, pp. 214–16.
201 See note 12 (ch. 7).
202 Zielinski, *Tancredi et Willelmi III. Regum Diplomata, Codex Diplomaticus Regni Siciliae*, 5, no. 12, p. 30. On St Stephen del Bosco, see note 225 (ch. 4).

Chapter 7

1 Ibn al-Athir described the Sicilian army as a massive contingent of 200 warships, 36 ships carrying horses, 6 ships full of siege engines, 40 supply ships, and transporting 1,500 knights, 50,000 foot soldiers and 500 archers; William of Tyre recorded a fleet of 200 Sicilian ships sailing towards Alexandria, whereas the *Annales Pisani* said that it comprised 150 galleys and 50 transport ships. *William of Tyre*, II, bk 21, chap. 3, p. 963; Amari, *Biblioteca arabo-sicula*, I, pp. 493–6; Richards, *The Chronicle of Ibn Al-Athīr for the Crusading Period from al-Kāmil Fī'l-Ta'rīkh*, II, pp. 229–30; *Chron. de Ferraria*, p. 31; *Annales Casinenses*, p. 312; Lupo Gentile, *Gli Annales Pisani di Bernardo Maragone*, p. 43. Cf. Amari, *Storia dei Musulmani di Sicilia*, III, pp. 507–9; Chalandon, *Histoire de la domination normande en Italie et en Sicile*, II, pp. 395–7. For an important discussion of this episode, see Stanton, *Norman Naval Operations in the Mediterranean*, pp. 146–8.
2 On Christian of Buch, see note 126 (ch. 4).
3 *Annales Casinenses*, p. 312. Carsoli is located 65 kilometres east of Rome, within the modern province of L'Aquila, in the Abruzzo; by the twelfth century, however, it was beyond the kingdom's northern borders. The toponym *Cellis* has only remained to name the church of St Mary in Carsoli.
4 *Annales Ceccanenses*, p. 286.
5 Spagnoletti, *Ruggiero, ultimo conte normanno di Andria*, p. 27; Cuozzo, *Commentario*, p. 274; Tescione, *Caserta medievale*, p. 38. Tescione also uses as a reference for this premise an eighteenth-century work: Testa, *De vita et rebus gestis Guilielmi II*, pp. 216–7.

6   See note 31 (ch. 7).
7   *Romuald*, pp. 266-7.
8   *Romuald*, pp. 269-93.
9   See pages 112-3.
10 Weiland, *Friderici I. Constitutiones*, no. 409, pp. 584-5. Recorded in Jaffé, *Regesta*, II, no. 13019, p. 319; Kehr, *Italia pontificia*, VIII, p. 54. The letter must have been issued in response to the landing of a Greek mercenary army in the Marches, at the end of 1178. Georgi, *Friedrich Barbarossa und die auswärtigen Mächte*, pp. 335-8. Cf. Chalandon, *Histoire de la domination normande en Italie et en Sicile*, II, pp. 384-5.
11 *Romuald*, pp. 268-9; Stubbs, *Radulfus de Diceto*, I, pp. 413-14; Stubbs, *Gesta Henrici II*, I, pp. 157-8.
12 Stubbs, *Gesta Henrici II*, I, pp. 169-72. On the newly created honour of Monte Sant'Angelo, see page 155.
13 *Falcandus*, pp. 226-9.
14 *Annales Ceccanenses*, p. 287.
15 This Alexios Komnenos must have been the son of Alexander Komnenos Batatzes, who was the son of Manuel's sister Eudoxia by Theodore Batatzes. Varzos, *Η Γενεαλογία των Κομνηνών*, II, pp. 390-1. Cf. Brand, *Byzantium Confronts the West*, p. 54.
16 *Choniates*, I, p. 297; Kyriakidis, *Eustazio*, pp. 58-69, 94-5, 104-5, 149-53; Amari, *Biblioteca arabo-sicula*, I, p. 169.
17 See page 154.
18 'ὁ Ἀλδουΐνος κόντος, γένους μὲν οὐ φὺς εὐγενοῦς καὶ λαμπροῦ, διὰ δὲ τὴν κατὰ πόλεμον δεξιότητα αἰδέσιμος ὢν τῷ ῥηγὶ καὶ τότε ὑπὲρ πάντας τὸ τῆς στροττηγίας ὑπ ἐζωσμένος σέμνωμα'. *Choniates*, I, p. 359.
19 *Choniates*, I, pp. 362-7.
20 For a discussion about this military campaign, see Stanton, *Norman Naval Operations in the Mediterranean*, pp. 151-6.
21 Kyriakidis, *Eustazio*, p. 126.
22 Kyriakidis, *Eustazio*, p. 148.
23 See note 12 (ch. 7).
24 Jones, *The Later Roman Empire, 284-602*, I, pp. 104-7. Also, see note 12 (ch. 1).
25 The original document is now lost, and survives only as a transcription. Pellegrino, *Historia principum Langobardorum*, III, pp. 273-6; *Italia Sacra*, VI, cols 552-4. Referenced in Di Meo, *Annali Critico-Diplomatici del Regno di Napoli della Mezzana Età*, X, p. 347; Tescione, *Caserta medievale*, p. 37; Jamison, 'Norman Administration', Calendar, no. 35, p. 431. Cf. Takayama, who appears to have mistaken Jamison's sources, and duplicated this single witness as if there were two different instances for Count Robert of Caserta in 1171. Takayama, *Administration of the Kingdom*, pp. 144, 217-18.
26 *Catalogus Baronum*, ¶¶ 897, p. 160; 916-17, pp. 163-4; 932, p. 166.
27 *Catalogus Baronum*, ¶¶ 905, p. 162; 926, p. 165; 932-9, pp. 166-7.
28 '[P]ugnan in hoc casu locum non habere, tum quia inter Longobardos erat quaestio, tum quia de his, quae non viderant Theanenses, pugnare non debebant'. Pellegrino, *Historia principum Langobardorum*, III, pp. 275-6; *Italia Sacra*, VI, col. 553. Judicial duels appear to have survived as a practice in southern Italy at least until the thirteenth century, as Frederick II included in his legislation (1231) an explicit clause forbidding the practice, which aimed to be implemented in all cases and among both 'Franks' (i.e. Normans) and Lombards. Huillard-Bréholles and D'Albert de Luynes, *Historia*

diplomatica Friderica Secundi, IV, pp. 105–6; Stürner, *Die Konstitutionen Friedrichs II. für das Königreich Sizilien*, pp. 338–9. For a discussion on judicial duels in southern Italy, see Leicht, 'Territori longobardi e territori romanici', p. 119.
29 On the development of these courts of justice, see Pescione, *Corti di giustizia nell'Italia meridionale*, pp. 88–91.
30 Cava, *Arca* xxxiii.91, ed. in Tescione, *Caserta medievale*, no. 2, pp. 160–3.
31 Tescione, *Caserta medievale*, no. 3, pp. 162–4.
32 Houben, *Die Abtei Venosa*, no. 146, pp. 376–7. Cf. Palumbo, *Tancredi conte di Lecce e re di Sicilia e il tramonto dell'età normanna*, p. 246.
33 *Italia Sacra*, VII, col. 687. Summarized in Ménager, 'Les fondations monastiques', p. 113; Palumbo, *Tancredi conte di Lecce e re di Sicilia e il tramonto dell'età normanna*, pp. 247–8.
34 *Pergamene di S. Nicola di Bari*, no. 145, pp. 249–51.
35 Tescione, *Caserta medievale*, pp. 43–4. The document was transcribed by Del Giudice in an unpublished dissertation on the counts of Caserta; this work survives in the collection of texts and notes Del Giudice, *Codice diplomatico del regno di Carlo I. e II. d'Angiò*, vol. 4, of the SNSP.
36 Di Meo, *Annali Critico-Diplomatici del Regno di Napoli della Mezzana Età*, x, p. 413.
37 Palumbo, *Tancredi conte di Lecce e re di Sicilia e il tramonto dell'età normanna*, p. 255.
38 Cava, *Arca* xxxviii.34, partially ed. in Haskins, 'England and Sicily', p. 455 (Edited in Loud's forthcoming Selected Charters). Referenced in Palumbo, *Tancredi conte di Lecce e re di Sicilia e il tramonto dell'età normanna*, p. 255.
39 *Chron. Casauriense*, col. 916.
40 *Chron. Casauriense*, col. 915.
41 Cf. Takayama, *The Administration*, pp. 143–5.
42 *Chartes de Troia*, no. 102, pp. 302–8.
43 See note 121 (ch. 6).
44 See page 139.
45 *Cod. Dipl. Verginiano*, VIII, no. 733, pp. 117–20.
46 Gattola, *Accessiones*, I, p. 266. Referenced in Palumbo, *Tancredi conte di Lecce e re di Sicilia e il tramonto dell'età normanna*, p. 258.
47 See note 167 (ch. 6).
48 Monti, *Codice diplomatico brindisino: 492–1200*, no. 23, pp. 44–6.
49 On the *duana baronum*, see Appendix.

Conclusions

1 For further discussion, see Martin, 'L'ancienne et la nouvelle aristocratie féodale'; Martin, 'L'aristocratie féodale et les villes'; Loud, 'Le strutture del potere'.

Appendix 1

1 Garufi, 'Sull'ordinamento amministrativo', pp. 240–5. Garufi's proposal was accepted by Caspar and Chalandon, only with slight modifications. Caspar, *Roger II*, pp. 315–18; Chalandon, *Histoire de la domination normande en Italie et en Sicile*, II, pp. 648–53. See also Takayama, *The Administration*, pp. 14–15.

2 Cusa, *I diplomi greci ed arabi di Sicilia pubblicati nel testo originale*, I, no. 136, pp.489–90. No Arabic title for this office has survived, but M. Amari noted a possible connection between the Greek name of the office σεκρέτος τῶν ἀποκοπῶν and the the dīwān al-iqṭāʿāt (bureau of 'fiefs'), since both ἀποκοπή and iqṭāʿ are derived from roots signifying 'partition', 'detachment' and 'division', and an original Arabic name was possibly translated into Greek. Amari, *Storia dei Musulmani di Sicilia*, pp. 87–8; Johns, *Arabic Administration in Norman Sicily*, p. 206.
3 Caravale, 'Gli uffici', pp. 177–223. Also, see Kamp, 'Von Kammerer zum Sekreten', p. 52.
4 Johns, *Arabic Administration in Norman Sicily*, pp. 206–7; Oldfield, *City and Community in Norman Italy*, pp. 84–5, 90.
5 Takayama, *The Administration*, pp. 145–55, especially p. 152.
6 Garufi, *Tabulario di Monreale*, App. 1, no. 2, pp. 163–5.
7 Garufi, *Tabulario di Monreale*, App. 1, no. 2, pp. 163–5. The Palermitan *comestabulus* acted as the constable of the royal household or stables, and not as a military official for the mainland.
8 Takayama, *The Administration*, p. 156. Cf. Caravale, 'Gli uffici', pp. 206, 216.
9 Kehr, *Die Urkunden der normannisch-sicilischen Könige*, no. 19, pp. 438–9; Perla, 'Una charta iudicati dei tempi normanni', pp. 346–7. J. Johns, accepting Takayama's opinion, stated that 'the *quaterniones* of the *duana baronum* seem to have been registers of feudal holdings in the duchy of Apulia and the principality of Capua, and these are presumed to have been the records from which the *quaternus magne expeditionis* was – the register of military service levied from those provinces in 1150–68.' This is even more problematic, as he implies that the *duana baronum* was already producing *quaterniones* in the peninsula by 1150. Johns, *Arabic Administration in Norman Sicily*, p. 174.
10 Takayama, *The Administration*, p. 157. The first admiral attested as *magister* of the *duana baronum* is Walter of Moac, who was recorded in a May 1178 charter as '*regii fortunati stolii amiratus et magister regie duane de secretis et duane baronum*'. Cava, Arca xxxvi.26.

Bibliography

Manuscript sources

[Most of the unedited documents courtesy of Graham A. Loud]

Benevento, Museo del Sannio.
Fondo S. Pietro, vol. 6, no 5.
Fondo S. Sofia, vols 2, nos 4–5, 10; 8 no. 37; 28 no. 8; 41 no. 2.

Bern, Burgerbibliothek.
Cod. 120.II [Nr. 7–8] (Petrus de Ebulo, 'Liber ad honorem Augusti sive de rebus Siculis')

Cava de' Tirreni, Archivio della Abbazia di S. Trinità.
Armaria Magna C.7; D.6; E.30; F.18–20, 36–7, 43–5; G.2, 13, 19–27, 31, 34, 36; H.4, 11, 13, 17, 19, 21–6, 28, 31–2, 35, 39; I.7, 14, 20–1, 26, 38–9; L.4, 14–16, 20, 23, 27, 34, 38; N.15.
Arcae xx.27, 37; xxv.3, 38, 40, 87, 106; xxvi.45; xxvii.117; xxviii.37; xxix.92; xxxiii.91; xxxiv.15, 91; xxxvi.36, 38; xxxviii.34; xl.96, 100; xlii.35; xliii.110.

Chieti, Curia Arcivescovile.
Archivio storico perg. no 19.

Naples, Biblioteca della Società Napoletana di Storia Patria.
Compre e vendite 2 AA III.17.

Naples, Biblioteca Nazionale.
Biblioteca Brancacciana L.F.5, ff. 51r-232v. (Tutini, Camillo. 'Notationes desumptae ab Archiviis monasteriorum')

Paris, Bibliothèque Nationale.
Lat. 5411.

Rome, Biblioteca Angelica.
Cod. 276-7 (Prignano, Giovan B., 'Historia delle famiglie di Salerno normande')

Subiaco, Biblioteca S. Scolastica.
Archivio Colonna III BB xxix.20.

Vatican City, Archivio Segreto Vaticano.
Archivum Arcis (AA) Armaria I.xviii.118.
Archivium Boncompagni-Ludovisi prot. 270, no. 9 [A].

Vatican City, Biblioteca Apostolica Vaticana.
Arch. Cap. S. Pietro caps. LXXII, fasc. 53, no. 1. ('Liber instrumentorum monasterii Sancti Salvatoris de Maiella')
Vat. Lat. 8222, ff. 49r-63r. ('Privilegia Ecclesie Monasterii S. Trinitatis de Venusio')

Printed primary sources

Amari, Michele, ed., *Biblioteca arabo-sicula*, 2 vols (Turin/Rome: Ermanno Loescher, 1880), i.
Amari, Michele, and Celestino Schiaparelli, eds., *L'Italia descritta nel 'Libro del re Ruggero' compilato da Edrisi [Al-Idrīsī]* (Rome: Coi tipi del Salviucci, 1883).
Ambrosio, Antonella, ed., *Le pergamene di S. Maria della Grotta di Vitulano (BN) (secc. XI-XII)* (Battipaglia: Laveglia & Carlone, 2013).
Appelt, Heinrich, ed., *Friderici I. Diplomata*, MGH DD, F I.2 (Hanover: Hahn, 1979).
Balducci, Antonio, ed., *Regesto delle pergamene della curia arcivescovile di Chieti*. 1006–1400 (Casalbordino: N. De Arcangeli, 1926).
Barraclough, Geoffrey, ed., *The Charters of the Anglo-Norman Earls of Chester, c. 1071–1237*, The Record Society of Lancashire and Cheshire, 126 (Gloucester: Alan Sutton, 1988).
Beaurepaire, Charles de, ed., *Recueil de chartes concernant l'abbaye de Saint-Victor-en-Caux*, Mélanges publiés per la Société de l'histoire di Normandie, 5 (Rouen-Paris: Société de l'Historie de Normandie, 1898).
Bethmann, Ludwig C., ed., *Annales Reatini*, MGH SS, 19 (Hanover: Hahn, 1866).
Bova, Giancarlo, ed., *Le pergamene normanne della Mater Ecclesia Capuana: 1091–1197* (Naples: Edizioni Scientifiche Italiane, 1996).
Brühl, Carlrichard, ed., *Rogerii II. Regis Diplomata Latina*, Codex Diplomaticus Regni Siciliae, 2 (Cologne: Böhlau, 1987).
Caetani, Gelasio, ed., *Regesta chartarum: regesto delle pergamene dell'Archivio Caetani*, 6 vols (Perugia: F. lli Stianti, 1922), i.
Camobreco, Fortunato, ed., *Regesto di S. Leonardo di Siponto*, Regesta Chartarum Italiae, 10 (Rome: E. Loescher & Co., 1913).
Carabellese, Francesco, ed., *Le carte di Molfetta* (1076–1309), Cod. Dipl. Barese, 7 (Bari: Levante, 1912).
Carabellese, Francesco, ed., *Le pergamene della Cattedrale di Terlizzi* (971–1300), Cod. Dipl. Barese, 3 (Bari: Commisione provinciale di archeologia e storia patria, 1899).
Carlone, Carmine, *Documenti cavensi per la storia di Rocchetta S. Antonio* (Altavilla Silentina: Edizioni Studi Storici Meridionali, 1987).
Carlone, Carmine, *Documenti per la storia di Eboli* (Salerno: Carlone Editore, 1998).
Caspar, Erich, ed., 'Die Chronik von Tres Tabernae in Calabrien (Cronica Trium Tabernarum)', *QFIAB*, 10 (1907), 1–56.
Chibnall, Marjorie, ed., *The Ecclesiastical History of Orderic Vitalis*, 6 vols (Oxford: Clarendon Press, 1973), iv.
Chibnall, Marjorie, ed., *The Historia Pontificalis of John of Salisbury* (Oxford: Clarendon Press, 1956).
Clementi, Dione R., 'Calendar of the Diplomas of the Hohenstaufen Emperor Henry VI Concerning the Kingdom of Sicily', *QFIAB*, 25 (1955), 86–225.
Codex Diplomaticus Cajetanus, 2 vols (Montecassino: Abbey of Montecassino, 1891), ii.
Coniglio, Giuseppe, ed., *Le pergamene di Conversano* (901–1265), Cod. Dipl. Pugliese, 20 (Bari: Società di storia patria per la Puglia, 1975).
Cuozzo, Errico, ed., 'Il "Breve Chronicon Northmannicum"', *Bullettino dell'Istituto Storico Italiano per il Medio Evo e Archivio Muratoriano*, 83 (1971), 131–232.
Cuozzo, Errico, and Jean M. Martin, eds., *Le pergamene di S. Cristina di Sepino* (1143–1463) (Rome: École française de Rome, 1998).

Cusa, Salvatore, ed., *I diplomi greci ed arabi di Sicilia pubblicati nel testo originale*, 2 vols (Palermo: Stabilimento tip. Lao, 1868), i.

D'Angelo, Edoardo, ed., *Pseudo Ugo Falcando. De rebus circa regni Siciliae curiam gestis Epistola ad Petrum de desolatione Siciliae* (Florence: Sismel, 2014) [also published as (Roma: Istituto storico italiano per il Medio Evo, 2014)]; [translated as] *The History of the Tyrants of Sicily by 'Hugo Falcandus', 1154–69*, trans. by Graham A. Loud and Thomas Wiedemann (Manchester: Manchester University Press, 1998).

D'Angelo, Edoardo, ed., *Falcone di Benevento. Chronicon Beneventanum: città e feudi nell'Italia dei normanni* (Florence: Edizioni del Galluzzo, 1998).

De Nava, Ludovica, ed., *Alexandri Telesini abbatis Ystoria Rogerii regis Sicilie, Calabrie atque Apulie*, FSI, 112 (Rome: Istituto storico italiano per il Medio Evo, 1991).

Del Giudice, Giuseppe, ed., *Codice diplomatico del regno di Carlo I. e II. d'Angiò* (Naples: Stamperia della Regia Università, 1869).

Delisle, Léopold, ed., *Chronique de Robert de Torigni, abbé du Mont-Saint-Michel* (Rouen: A. Le Brument, 1872).

Di Meo, Alessandro, ed., *Annali Critico-Diplomatici del Regno di Napoli della Mezzana Età*, 12 vols (Naples: Stamperia Simoniana, 1805), x.

van Dieten, Jan L., ed., *Nicetae Choniatae Historia*, Corpus fontium historiae Byzantinae, 11, 2 vols (Berlin: Walter de Gruyter, 1975), i.

Drago Tedeschini, Corinna, ed., *Le pergamene dell'archivio diocesano di Gravina (secc. XI-XIV)*, Cod. Dipl. Pugliese, 37 (Bari: Società di storia patria per la Puglia, 2013).

Duchesne, Louis M., ed., *Liber Pontificalis*, 2 vols (Paris: Ernest Thorin, 1892), ii.

Enzensberger, Horst, ed., *Guillelmi I. Regis Diplomata*, Codex Diplomaticus Regni Siciliae, 3 (Cologne: Böhlau, 1996).

Enzensberger, Horst, ed., *Guillelmi II. Regis Siciliae Diplomata* 1166–1189, 2016, http://www.hist-hh.uni-bamberg.de/WilhelmII/index.html (accessed 1 August 2016).

Febonio, Munzio, *Historiae Marsorum libri tres, una cum eorundem episcoporum catalogo* (Naples: M. Monaco, 1678).

Figliuolo, Bruno, and Rosaria Pilone, eds., *Codice diplomatico molisano (964–1349)* (Campobasso: Palladino, 2013).

Frier, Bruce W., Serena Connolly, Simon Corcoran, Michael Crawford, John N. Dillon, Dennis P. Kehoe, and others, eds., *The Codex of Justinian*, trans. by Fred H. Blume, 3 vols (Cambridge: Cambridge University Press, 2016), iii.

Fuselli, Enrico, ed., *Il Chronicon di S. Bartolomeo di Carpineto* (L'Aquila: Libreria Colacchi, 1996).

Gallo, Alfonso, ed., *Codice diplomatico normanno di Aversa* (Naples: Luigi Lubrano editore, 1926).

Garufi, Carlo A, ed., *Catalogo illustrato del tabulario di S. Maria Nuova in Monreale*, Documenti per servire alla storia di Sicilia: Diplomatica, 19 (Palermo: Era nova, 1902).

Garufi, Carlo A, ed., *I documenti inediti dell'epoca normanna in Sicilia*, Documenti per servire alla storia di Sicilia, I.18 (Palermo: Lo Statuto, 1899).

Garufi, Carlo A, ed., *Necrologio del Liber confratrum di S. Matteo di Salerno*, FSI, 56 (Rome: Istituto storico italiano per il Medio Evo, 1922).

Garufi, Carlo A, ed., *Romualdi Salernitani Chronicon*, RIS, 7, 2nd edn (Città di Castello: S. Lapi, 1935).

Garufi, Carlo A, ed., *Ryccardi de Sancto Germano Notarii Chronicon*, RIS, 18, 2nd edn (Bologna: N. Zanichelli, 1938).

Giordano, Anna, ed., *Le pergamene dell'archivio diocesano di Salerno (841–1193)* (Salerno: Laveglia & Carlone, 2015).

Güterbock, Ferdinand, ed., *Ottonis Morenae et Continuatorum Historia Frederici I.*, MGH SS rer. Germ., 7 (Berlin: Weidmann, 1930); [also translated as] *The Deeds of Frederick Barbarossa, by Otto of Freising and His Continuator Rahewin*, trans. by Charles C. Mierow, Records of Western civilization, 49 (New York: Columbia University Press, 1953).

Hartmann, Martina, ed., *Das Briefbuch Abt Wibalds von Stablo und Corvey*, MGH Briefe d. dt. Kaiserzeit, 9 (Hanover: Hahn, 2012).

Hausmann, Friedrich, ed., *Conradi III. et filii eius Heinrici Diplomata*, MGH DD, K III (Vienna: Böhlau, 1969).

Hoffmann, Hartmut, ed., *Chronica Monasterii Casinensis*, MGH SS, 34 (Hanover: Hahn, 1980).

Hofmeister, Adolf, ed., *Libellus querulus de miseriis ecclesiae Pennensis*, MGH SS, 30.2 (Leipzig: K.W. Hiersemann, 1934).

Howlett, Richard, ed., *The Chronicle of Robert of Torigni*, Chronicles of the Reign of Stephen, Henry II and Richard I, 4 (London: Eyre and Spottiswoode, 1889).

Huillard-Bréholles, Jean L., and Honoré D'Albert de Luynes, eds., *Historia diplomatica Friderica Secundi*, 6 vols (Paris: Plot Fratres, 1855), i.

Huygens, Robert B., ed., *Willelmi Tyrensis Archiepiscopi Chronicon*, Corpus christianorum, 63, 2 vols (Turnhout: Brepols, 1986), ii; [translated as] *A History of Deeds Done beyond the Sea, by William of Tyre*, trans. by Emily A. Babcock and August C. Krey, 2 vols (New York: Columbia University Press, 1943), ii .

Inguanez, Mauro, ed., *I Necrologi Cassinesi. I Il Necrologio del Cod. Cassinese 47*, FSI, 83 (Roma: Istituto storico italiano per il Medio Evo, 1941).

Inguanez, Mauro, ed., *Regesto di S. Angelo in Formis* (Montecassino: Camastro & figli, 1925).

Jaffé, Philipp, ed., *Monumenta Bambergensia* (Berlin: Weidmann, 1869).

Jaffé, Philipp, ed., *Regesta pontificum romanorum ab condita ecclesia ad annum post Christum natum 1198*, 2nd edn, 2 vols (Leipzig: Veit et comp., 1888), ii.

Jahn, Wolfgang, *Untersuchungen zur die normannischen Herrschaft in Süditalien (1040–1100)* (Frankfurt: P. Lang, 1989).

Jamison, Evelyn M., ed., *Catalogus Baronum*, FSI, 11 (Rome: Istituto storico italiano per il Medio Evo, 1972).

Jordanov, Ivan, ed., *Corpus of Byzantine Seals from Bulgaria*, 3 vols (Sofia: Agato Publishers, 2006), ii.

Kehr, Paul F., ed., *Italia pontificia. Regnum Normannorum, Campania*, 10 vols (Berlin: Weidmann, 1935), viii.

Kehr, Paul F., ed., *Italia pontificia. Samnium, Apulia, Lucania*, 10 vols (Berlin: Weidmann, 1962), ix.

Kehr, Paul F., ed., *Italia pontificia. Umbria, Picenum, Marsia*, 10 vols (Berlin: Weidmann, 1909), iv.

King, Edmund, ed., *William of Malmesbury*: Historia Novella, trans. by K. R. Potter, 2nd edn (Oxford: Clarendon Press, 1998).

Kyriakidis, Stilpon, ed., *La espugnazione di Tessalonica [di] Eustazio di Tessalonica* (Palermo: Istituto Siciliano di Studi Bizantini e Neoellenici, 1961).

Lacarra, José María, ed., *Documentos para el estudio de la reconquista y repoblación del Valle del Ebro* (Zaragoza: Anubar, 1985).

Lappenberg, Johann M., and Bernhard Schmeidler, eds., *Helmoldi Presbyteri Bozoviensis Cronica Slavorum*, MGH SS rer. Germ., 32 (Hanover: Hahn, 1937).

Leccisotti, Tommaso, 'Antiche prepositure cassinesi nei pressi del Fortore e del Saccione', *Benedictina*, 1 (1947), 83–133.
de Leo, Pietro, ed., *Le carte del monastero dei Santi Niccolò e Cataldo in Lecce: (secc. XI–XVII)* (Lecce: Centro di Studi Salentini, 1978).
Leyser, Karl, 'The Crisis of Medieval Germany', in *Proceedings of the British Academy*, 69 (Oxford: Oxford University Press, 1984).
Licinio, Raffaele, *Castelli medievali: Puglia e Basilicata, dai Normanni a Federico II e Carlo I D'Angiò* (Bari: Dedalo, 1994).
Loud, Graham A., 'A Calendar of the Diplomas of the Norman Princes of Capua', *PBSR*, 49 (1981), 99–143.
Lupo Gentile, Michele, ed., *Gli Annales Pisani di Bernardo Maragone* (Bologna: N. Zanichelli, 1936).
Martin, Jean M., ed., *Chronicon Sanctae Sophiae: cod. Vat. Lat. 4939* (Rome: Istituto storico italiano per il Medio Evo, 2000).
Martin, Jean M., ed., *Le cartulaire de S. Matteo di Sculgola en Capitanate (Registro d'instrumenti di S. Maria del Gualdo 1177–1239)*, Cod. Dipl. Pugliese, 30, 2 vols (Bari: Società di storia patria per la Puglia, 1987), ii.
Martin, Jean M., ed., *Le cartulaire de S. Matteo di Sculgola en Capitanate (Registro d'instrumenti di S. Maria del Gualdo 1177–1239)*, Cod. Dipl. Pugliese, 30, 2 vols (Bari: Società di storia patria per la Puglia, 1987), i.
Martin, Jean M., ed., *Les actes de l'Abbaye de Cava concernant le Gargano (1086–1370)*, Cod. Dipl. Pugliese, 32 (Bari: Società di storia patria per la Puglia, 1994).
Martin, Jean M., ed., *Les chartes de Troia. Édition et étude critique des plus anciens documents conservés à l'Archivio Capitolare. I (1024–1266)*, Cod. Dipl. Pugliese, 21 (Bari: Società di storia patria per la Puglia, 1976).
Martin, Jean M., Pierre Chastang, Errico Cuozzo, Laurent Feller, Giulia Orofino, Aurélie Thomas, and others, eds., *Registrum Petri Diaconi (Montecassino, Archivio dell'abbazia, reg. 3)*, 4 vols (Roma: École française de Rome, 2015), iii.
Mathieu, Marguerite, ed., *Guillaume de Pouille. La Geste de Robert Guiscard* (Palermo: Istituto Siciliano di Studi Bizantini e Neoellenici, 1961).
Mazzoleni, Jole, ed., *Le pergamene della Società Napoletana di Storia Patria. Parte I. Il fondo pergamenaceo del monastero di S. Maria della Grotta* (Naples: L'arte tipografica, 1966).
Mazzoleni, Jole, ed., *Le pergamene di Capua*, 3 vols (Naples: Università degli Studi di Napoli, 1957), i.
Meineke, Augustus, ed., *Joannis Cinnami [Kinnamoi] epitome rerum ab Ioanne et Alexio Comnenis gestarum*, Corpus Scriptorum Historiae Byzantinae, 26 (Bonn: Weber, 1836); [translated as] *The Deeds of John and Manuel Comnenus*, by John Kinnamos, trans. by Charles M. Brand (New York: Columbia University Press, 1953).
Ménager, Léon R., ed., *Recueil des actes des ducs normands d'Italie (1046–1127). I: Les premiers ducs (1046–1087)* (Bari: Grafica Bigiemme, 1980).
Montfaucon, Bernard de, ed., *Palaeographia Graeca* (Paris: L. Guerin, 1708).
Monti, Gennaro M., ed., *Codice diplomatico brindisino: 492–1200* (Brindisi: V. Vecchi, 1940).
Monti, Gennaro M., 'Il testo e la storia esterna delle assise normanne', in *Studi di storia e di diretto in onore di Carlo Calisse*, 3 vols (Milan, 1940), i, 295–348.
Morea, Domenico, ed., *Il chartularium del monastero di S. Benedetto di Conversano* (Montecassino: A. Forni, 1892), i.

Muratori, Lodovico A., ed., *Chronicon Casauriense, auctore Iohanne Berardi*, RIS, 2 (Milan: Societas Palatina, 1726).
Nass, Klaus, ed., *Die Reichschronik des Annalista Saxo*, MGH SS, 37 (Hanover: Hahn, 2006).
Nitti di Vito, Francesco, ed., *Le pergamene del Duomo di Bari* (952–1264), Cod. Dipl. Barese, 1 (Trani: V. Vecchi, 1897).
Nitti di Vito, Francesco, ed., *Le pergamene di Barletta, archivio capitolare* (897–1285), Cod. Dipl. Barese, 8 (Trani: V. Vecchi, 1914).
Nitti di Vito, Francesco, ed., *Le pergamene di S. Nicola di Bari. Periodo normanno* (1075–1194), Cod. Dipl. Barese, 5 (Bari: V. Vecchi, 1900).
Pastore, Michela, ed., *Le pergamene di S. Giovanni Evangelista in Lecce* (Lecce: Centro di studi salentini, 1970).
Pepe, Ludovico, ed., *Il libro rosso della città di Ostuni. Codice diplomatico compilato nel MDCIX da Pietro Vincenti* (Valle di Pompei: Bartolo Longo, 1888).
Pertz, Georg H., ed., *Annales Casinenses*, MGH SS, 19 (Hanover: Hahn, 1866).
Pertz, Georg H., ed., *Annales Ceccanenses*, MGH SS, 19 (Hanover: Hahn, 1866).
Pertz, Georg H., and Augusto Gaudenzi, eds., *Ignoti Monachi Cisterciensis S. Mariae de Ferraria Chronica et Ryccardi de Sancto Germano Chronica priora* (Naples: F. Giannini, 1888).
Petrucci, Armando, ed., *Codice diplomatico del Monastero Benedettino di S. Maria di Tremiti*: 1005–1237, FSI, 98 (Rome: Istituto storico italiano per il Medio Evo, 1960).
Pio, Berardo, ed., *Alexandri Monachi Chronicorum liber Monasterii Sancti Bartholomei de Carpineto* (Rome: Istituto storico italiano per il Medio Evo, 2001).
Pirri, Rocco, ed., *Sicilia sacra disquisitionibus, et notitiis illustrata*, 3rd edn, 2 vols (Palermo: Haeredes Petri Coppulae, 1733), i.
Pontieri, Ernesto, ed., *De rebus gestis Rogerii Calabriae et Siciliae comitis et Roberti Guiscardi ducis fratris eius, auctore Gaufredo Malaterra*, RIS, 5.1 (Bologna: N. Zanichelli, 1928).
Pratesi, Alessandro, ed., *Carte latine di abbazie calabresi provenienti dall'archivio Aldobrandini* (Vatican City: Bibliotheca Apostolica Vaticana, 1958).
Prignano, Giovan B., 'Historia delle famiglie di Salerno normande' (Cod. 276-77, Biblioteca Angelica, Rome).
Prologo, Arcangelo di Gioacchino, ed., *Le carte che si conservano nella archivio del capitolo metropolitano della città di Trani: dal IX secolo fino all'Anno 1266* (Barletta: V. Vecchi, 1877).
Regii Neapolitam Archivii Monumenta, 6 vols (Naples: Equitis G. Nobile, 1861), vi.
Richards, Donald S., tran., *The Chronicle of Ibn Al-Athīr for the Crusading Period from al-Kāmil Fī 'l-Ta 'rīkh*, 3 vols (Aldershot: Ashgate, 2006), ii.
Salvati, Catello, ed., *Le pergamene della Società Napoletana di Storia Patria. Parte II. Note di diplomatica sigli Atti giudiziari* (Naples: Arte Tipografica, 1966).
Salvati, Catello, ed., *Le pergamene dell'archivio vescovile di Caiazzo* (1007–1265) (Caserta: Società di storia patria di Terra di Lavoro, 1983).
Scheffer-Boichorst, Paul, ed., *Chronica Albrici monachi Trium Fontium*, MGH SS, 23 (Hanover: Hahn, 1874).
Schmale, Franz J., ed., *Italische Quellen über die Taten Kaiser Friedrichs I.*, Ausgewählte Quellen zur deutschen Geschichte des Mittelalters. Freiherr vom Stein-Gedächtnisausgabe, 17a (Darmstadt: Wissenschaftliche Buchgesellschaft, 1986).
Schmale, Franz J., ed., *Ottonis Episcopi Frisingensis et Rahewini Gesta Frederici seu rectius Cronica*, trans. by Adolf Schmidt (Darmstadt: Wissenschaftliche Buchgesellschaft, 1965).

Stubbs, William, ed., *Gesta Regis Henrici Secundi Benedicti Abbatis*, Rerum Britannicarum Medii Aevi Scriptores, 49, 2 vols (Cambridge: Cambridge University Press, 1867), i.
Stubbs, William, ed., *Gesta Regis Henrici Secundi Benedicti Abbatis*, Rerum Britannicarum Medii Aevi Scriptores, 49, 2 vols (Cambridge: Cambridge University Press, 1867), ii.
Stubbs, William, ed., *Radulfi de Diceto decani Lundoniensis opera historica*, Rerum Britannicarum medii aevi scriptores, 68, 2 vols (London: Longman & Company, 1876), i.
Stürner, Wolfgang, ed., *Die Konstitutionen Friedrichs II. für das Königreich Sizilien*, MGH Const., 2 Suppl. (Hanover: Hahn, 1996).
Sudendorf, Hans F., ed., *Registrum oder merkwürdige Urkunden für die deutsche Geschichte*, 3 vols (Berlin: Franz Duncker, 1951), ii.
Trinchera, Francisco, ed., *Syllabus Graecarum membranarum* (Naples: J. Cataneo, 1865).
Tropeano, Placido M., ed., *Codice diplomatico verginiano*. 13 vols (Montevergine: Edizioni Padri Benedettini, 1977–2000), ii, iii, iv, v, vi, vii, viii, ix, x, xi.
Ughelli, Ferdinando, and Nicolò Coleti, eds., *Italia sacra sive de Episcopis Italiae*, 2nd edn, 10 vols (Venice: S. Coleti, 1717–1722), i, vi, vii, viii, ix, x.
Weiland, Ludwig, ed., *Friderici I. Constitutiones*, MGH Const., 1 (Hanover: Hahn, 1893).
Zielinski, Herbert, ed., *Tancredi et Willelmi III. Regum Diplomata*, Codex Diplomaticus Regni Siciliae, 5 (Cologne: Böhlau, 1982).

Secondary sources

[Items starred thus * also contain editions of source material]

Abignente, Giovanni, 'Le Chartulae fraternitatis ed il Libro de' confratres della chiesa Salernitana', *ASPN*, 13 (1888), 449–83.
Acht, Peter, 'Christian I', in *Neue Deutsche Biographie*, 26 vols (Berlin: Duncker & Humblot, 1957), iii, 226–7.
Acocella, Vito, *Storia di Conza: Il gastaldato e la contea fino alla caduta della monarchia sveva* (Benevento: Istituto Maschile V. E. III, 1928) [extracted from *Atti della Società Storica del Sannio*, 1927].
Amari, Michele, *Storia dei Musulmani di Sicilia*, ed. by Carlo A. Nallino, 2nd edn, 3 vols (Catania: R. Prampolini, 1939), iii.
Amari, Michele, *Studi medievistici*, ed. by Francesco Giunta (Palermo: S.F. Flaccovio, 1970).
*Antonucci, Goffredo, 'Goffredo conte di Lecce e di Montescaglioso', *Archivio Storico per la Calabria e la Lucania*, 3 (1933), 449–59.
Arnold, Benjamin, 'German Bishops and Their Military Retinues in the Medieval Empire', *German History*, 7 (1989), 161–83.
Bachrach, Bernard S., 'Charlemagne and Carolingian Military Administration', in *Empires and Bureaucracy in World History: From Late Antiquity to the Twentieth Century*, ed. by Peter Crooks and Timothy H. Parsons (Cambridge: Cambridge University Press, 2016), pp. 170–96.
Bachrach, Bernard S., *Early Carolingian Warfare: Prelude to Empire* (Philadelphia: University of Pennsylvania Press, 2000).
Bachrach, Bernard S., 'Neo-Roman vs Feudal: The Heuristic Value of a Construct for the Reign of Fulk Nerra, Count of the Angevins (987–1040)', *Cithara*, 30 (1990), 3–32.
Barton, Richard E., *Lordship in the County of Maine, c. 890–1160* (Woodbridge: Boydell Press, 2004).

Bates, David, 'Robert of Torigni and the *Historia Anglorum*', in *The English and Their Legacy, 900-1200: Essays in Honour of Ann Williams*, ed. by David Roffe (Woodbridge: Boydell and Brewer, 2012), pp. 175-84.
Biscaglia, Carmela, and Michela Ginetti, 'Le visite pastorali della diocesi di Tricarico (1588-1959)', *Bollettino storico della Basilicata*, 27 (2011), 291-364.
Bloch, Marc, *La Société féodale* (Paris: Albin Michel, 1982).
Boglino, Luigi, *Palermo e Santa Cristina* (Palermo: Tip. delle Letture Domenicali, 1881).
Bolton, Brenda, and Anne J. Duggan, eds., *Adrian IV, the English Pope, 1154-1159: Studies and Texts* (Aldershot: Ashgate, 2003).
Brand, Charles M., *Byzantium Confronts the West, 1180-1204* (Cambridge, USA: Harvard University Press, 1968).
*Brandileone, Francesco, *Il diritto romano nelle leggi normanne e sveve del regno Sicilia* (Turin: Fratelli Bocca, 1884).
Brown, Elizabeth A., 'The Tyranny of a Construct: Feudalism and Historians of Medieval Europe', *The American Historical Review*, 79.4 (1974), 1063-88.
Brühl, Carlrichard, *Urkunden und Kanzlei König Rogers II. von Sizilien* (Cologne: Böhlau, 1978).
Burkhardt, Stefan, *Mit Stab und Schwert: Bilder, Träger und Funktionen erzbischöflicher Herrschaft zur Zeit Kaiser Friedrich Barbarossas: Die Erzbistümer Köln und Mainz im Vergleich* (Ostfildern: Thorbecke, 2008).
Cahen, Claude, *Le régime féodal de l'Italie normande* (Paris: Geuthner, 1940).
Campanile, Giuseppe, *Notizie di nobiltà* (Naples: Luc'Antonio de Fuseo, 1672).
Cancik, Hubert, Helmuth Schneider, and Christine F. Salazar, eds., *Brill's New Pauly: Encyclopaedia of the Ancient World. Antiquity*, 22 vols (Brill: Leiden, 2010), xv.
Caravale, Mario, 'Gli uffici finanziari nel Regno di Sicilia durante il periodo normanno', *Annali di storia del diritto. Rassegna internazionale*, 8 (1964), 177-23.
Caravale, Mario, *Il regno normanno di Sicilia* (Rome: Giuffrè, 1966).
Carelli, Guido, 'I conti Normanni di Calinulo (1062-1187): Note storiche', *Rivista araldica*, 11 (1913), 609-16.
Carlone, Carmine, *Falsificazioni e falsari cavensi e verginiani del secolo XIII* (Altavilla Silentina: Edizioni studi storici meridionali, 1984).
Carocci, Sandro, *Signorie di Mezzogiorno: società rurali, poteri aristocratici e monarchia (XII-XIII secolo)* (Rome: Viella, 2014).
Caspar, Erich, *Roger II (1101-1154) und die Gründung der normannisch-sicilischen Monarchie* (Innsbruck: Wagner, 1904).
Chalandon, Ferdinand, *Histoire de la domination normande en Italie et en Sicile*, 2 vols (Paris: A. Picard et fils, 1907), ii.
Chibnall, Marjorie, *The World of Orderic Vitalis: Norman Monks and Norman Knights* (Rochester: Boydell & Brewer, 1996).
Clementi, Dione R, 'Definition of a Norman County in Apulia and Capua', in *Catalogus Baronum. Commentario*, ed. by Errico Cuozzo, FSI, 101.2 (Rome: Istituto storico italiano per il Medio Evo, 1984), pp. 377-84.
Clementi, Dione R, 'Historical Commentary on the Libellus of Alessandro di Telese', in De Nava, Ludovica, ed., *Alexandri Telesini abbatis Ystoria Rogerii regis Sicilie, Calabrie atque Apulie*, FSI, 112 (Rome: Istituto storico italiano per il Medio Evo, 1991), pp. 175-336.
*Clementi, Dione R, 'Some Unnoticed Aspects of the Emperor Henry VI's Conquest of the Norman Kingdom of Sicily', *Bulletin of the John Rylands Library*, 36 (1954), 328-59.

Costambeys, Marios, Matthew Innes, and Simon MacLean, *The Carolingian World* (Cambridge: Cambridge University Press, 2011).

*Crudo, Giuseppe, *La SS. Trinità di Venosa: memorie storiche, diplomatiche, archeologiche* (Trani: V. Vecchi, 1899).

Cuozzo, Errico, 'A propos de la coexistence entre Normands et Lombards dans le Royaume de Sicile. La révolte féodale de 1160–1162', in *Peuples du Moyen Âge. Problèmes d'identification. Séminaire sociétés, idéologies et croyances au Moyen Âge*, ed. by Claude Carozzi and Huguette Taviani-Carozzi (Aix-en-Provence: Publications de l'Université de Provence, 1996), pp. 45–56.

Cuozzo, Errico, *Catalogus Baronum: Commentario*, FSI, 101.2 (Rome: Istituto storico italiano per il Medio Evo, 1984).

*Cuozzo, Errico, 'I conti normanni di Catanzaro', *Miscellanea di Studi / Università degli studi della Calabria*, 2 (1982), 109–27.

Cuozzo, Errico, 'Il sistema difensivo del regno normanno di Sicilia e la frontiera abruzzese nord-occidentale', in *Une region frontalière au Moyen Âge* (Rome: École française de Rome, 2000), pp. 273–90.

Cuozzo, Errico, *La cavalleria nel Regno normanno di Sicilia* (Atripalda: Mephite, 2002).

Cuozzo, Errico, 'La contea di Montescaglioso nei secoli XI–XIII', *ASPN*, 103 (1985), 7–37.

Cuozzo, Errico, 'La contea normanna di Mottola e Castellaneta', *ASPN*, 110 (1992), 7–46.

Cuozzo, Errico, *La monarchia bipolare: il regno normanno di Sicilia* (Pratola Serra: Elio Sellino, 2000).

Cuozzo, Errico, 'Le istituzioni politico-amministrative legate alla conquista. Le ripartizioni territoriali: i comitati', in *I caratteri originali della conquista normanna. diversità e identità nel Mezzogiorno (1030–1130)*, ed. by F. Violante and R. Licinio, Atti del Centro di Studi Normanno-Svevi, 16 (Bari: Dedalo, 2006), pp. 287–304.

Cuozzo, Errico, 'L'unificazione normanna e il regno normanno-svevo', in *Storia del Mezzogiorno II. Il Medieovo* (Naples: Del Sole, 1989), pp. 593–825.

Cuozzo, Errico, '"Milites" e "testes" nella contea normanna di Principato', *Bullettino dell'Istituto Storico Italiano per il Medio Evo e Archivio Muratoriano*, 88 (1979), 121–64.

Cuozzo, Errico, 'Prosopografia di una famiglia feudale normanna: i Balvano', *ASPN*, 98 (1980), 61–80.

Cuozzo, Errico, *'Quei maledetti normanni': cavalieri e organizzazione militare nel mezzogiorno normanno* (Naples: Guida, 1989).

*Cuozzo, Errico, 'Ruggiero, conte d'Andria: ricerche sulla nozione di regalità al tramonto della monarchia normanna', *ASPN*, 20 (1981), 129–68.

Davies, Wendy, and Paul Fouracre, eds., *Property and Power in the Early Middle Ages* (Cambridge: Cambridge University Press, 2002).

Davies, Wendy, and Paul Fouracre, eds., *The Languages of Gift in the Early Middle Ages* (Cambridge: Cambridge University Press, 2010).

Davies, Wendy, and Paul Fouracre, eds., *The Settlement of Disputes in Early Medieval Europe* (Cambridge: Cambridge University Press, 1992).

De Blasiis, Giuseppe, and Nicola Parisio, 'Elenco delle pergamene già appartenenti alla famiglia Fusco ed ora acquisite dalla Società Napoletana di Storia Patria', *ASPN*, 8 (1883), 153–61, 332–8, 775–87.

De Francesco, Armando, *La badia benedettina di Tremiti e il Chartularium tremitense* (Catanzaro: Gaetano Silipo, 1910).

De Francesco, Armando, 'Origini e sviluppo dei Feudalismo nel Molise fino alla caduta della dominazione normanna', *ASPN*, 34–5 (1909), 432–60, 640–71; 70–98, 273–307.

*De Sivo, Giacinto, *Storia di Galazia Campana e di Maddaloni* (Naples, 1865).

Deér, Jozsef, ed., *Das Papsttum und die süditalienischen Normannenstaaten*. 1053–1212, Historische Texte: Mittelalter, 12 (Göttingen: Vandenhoeck u. Ruprecht, 1969).

Dell'Omo, Mariano, *Il Registrum di Pietro Diacono (Montecassino, Archivio dell'Abbazia, Reg. 3). Commentario codicologico, paleografico, diplomatico* (Montecassino: Publicazioni Cassinesi, 2000).

Di Liberto, Rosi, 'Norman Palermo: Architecture between the 11th and 12th Century', in *A Companion to Medieval Palermo: The History of a Mediterranean City from 600 to 1500*, ed. by Annliese Nef, trans. by Martin Thom (Leiden: Brill, 2013), pp. 139–94.

*'Dissertatio de antiquitate, ditione, juribus variaque fortuna Abbatiae S. Salvatoris ad Montem Magellae', in *Collectio Bullarum Sacrosanctae Basilicae Vaticanae* (Rome: Giovanni Maria Salvioni, 1747), i.

Drell, Joanna H., *Kinship & Conquest: Family Strategies in the Principality of Salerno during the Norman Period*, 1077–1194 (Ithaca, USA: Cornell University Press, 2002).

Enzensberger, Horst, 'Chanceries, Charters and Administration in Norman Italy', in *The Society of Norman Italy*, ed. by Alex Metcalfe and Graham A. Loud (Leiden: Brill, 2002), pp. 117–50.

Enzensberger, Horst, 'Il documento regio come strumento del potere', in *Potere, società e popolo nell'età dei due Guglielmi*, Atti del Centro di Studi Normanno-Svevi, 4 (Bari: Dedalo, 1981), pp. 103–38.

Falkenhausen, Vera von, 'I ceti dirigenti prenormanni al tempo della costituzione degli stati normanni nell'Italia meridionale e in Sicilia', in *Forme di potere e struttura sociale in Italia nel Medioevo*, ed. by Gabriella Rossetti Pepe, Istituzioni e società nella storia d'Italia, 1 (Bologna: Il mulino, 1977).

Feller, Laurent, *Les Abruzzes médiévales: territoire, économie et société en Italie centrale du IXe au XIIe siècle* (Paris: École française de Rome, 1998).

Feller, Laurent, 'The Northern Frontier of Norman Italy, 1060–1140', in *The Society of Norman Italy*, ed. by Alex Metcalfe and Graham A. Loud (Leiden: Brill, 2002), pp. 47–73.

Fernández-Aceves, Hervin, 'Political Manoeuvring in the Norman Kingdom of Sicily: Civitate and Carinola in the Development of the South-Italian County', *White Rose College of the Arts & Humanities Journal*, 2 (2016), 63–73.

Fernández-Aceves, Hervin, 'Royal Comestabuli and Military Control in the Sicilian Kingdom: A Prosopographical Contribution to the Study of Italo-Norman Aristocracy', *Medieval Prosopography*, 34 (2019), 1–40.

*Fortunato, Giustino, *Santa Maria di Vitalba* (Trani: V. Vecchi, 1898).

Frank, R. I., *Scholae Palatinae: The Palace Guards of the Later Roman Empire* (Rome: American Academy, 1969).

Freed, John, *Frederick Barbarossa: The Prince and the Myth* (New Haven: Yale University Press, 2016).

*Gaetano, Ottavio, *Vitae Sanctorum Siculorum*, 2 vols (Palermo: Cirilli, 1657), ii.

*Galante, Maria, 'Un esempio di diplomatica signorile: i documenti dei Sanseverino', in *Civiltà del Mezzogiorno d'Italia: libro, scrittura, documento in età normanno-sveva*, ed. by Filippo D'Oria (Cava dei Tirreni: Carlone Editore, 1994), pp. 279–331.

Ganshof, François L., 'Charlemagne et les institutions de la monarchie franque', in *Karl der Grosse. Lebenswerk und Nachleben*, ed. by Wolfgang Braunfels, 5 vols (Düsseldorf: L. Schwann, 1965), i, 349–93.

Ganshof, François L., 'Note sur l'apparition du nom de l'hommage particulièrement en France', in *Aus Mittelalter und Neuzeit. [Festschrift] Gerhard Kallen zum 70*, ed. by J. Engel and H. Klinkenberg (Bonn: P. Hanstein, 1957), pp. 29–42.

Garufi, Carlo A., 'Adelaide nipote di Bonifazio del Vasto e Goffredo figliolo del gran conte Ruggiero. Per la critica di Goffredo Malaterra e per la diplomatica dei primi tempi Normanni in Sicilia', *Rendiconti e memorie della Real Accademia di scienze, lettere* ed arti dei Zelanti di Acireale 3 (1905), iv, 185–216.

Garufi, Carlo A., 'Gli Aleramici e i Normanni in Sicilia e nelle Puglie', in *Centenario della nascita di Michele Amari* (Palermo: Virzì, 1910), pp. 47–83.

*Garufi, Carlo A., 'I diplomi purpurei della cancelleria normanna ed Elvira prima moglie di re Ruggero (1117? - febbraio 1135)', *Atti della Reale Accademia di Scienze Lettere e Arti di Palermo*, 7 (1904), 3–31.

*Garufi, Carlo A., 'Per la storia dei sec. XI e XII. Miscellanea diplomatica. II. I conti di Montescaglioso', *Archivio Storico per la Sicilia Orientale*, 9 (1912), 324–66.

*Garufi, Carlo A., 'Per la storia dei sec. XI e XII. Miscellanea diplomatica. III. La contea di Paternò e i de Luci', *Archivio Storico per la Sicilia Orientale*, 10 (1913), 160–80.

Garufi, Carlo A., 'Su la curia stratigoziale di Messina nel tempo normanno-svevo. Studi storico-diplomatici', Archivio Storico Messinese, 5 (1904), 1–49.

Garufi, Carlo A., 'Sull'ordinamento amministrativo normanno in sicilia Exhiquier o Diwan? Studi storico-diplomatici', *Archivio Storico Italiano*, 27 (1901), 225–63.

*Gatta, Costantino, *Memorie topografico-storiche della provincia di Lucania compresa al presente* (Naples: Presso Gennaro Muzio, 1732).

*Gattola, Erasmo, *Ad historiam abbatiae Cassinensis accessiones*, 2 vols (Venice: S. Coleti, 1734), i.

*Gattola, Erasmo, *Historia abbatiae Cassinensis per saeculorum seriem* (Venice: S. Coleti, 1733).

Georgi, Wolfgang, *Friedrich Barbarossa und die auswärtigen Mächte: Studien zur Aussenpolitik* 1159–1180 (Frankfurt am Main: P. Lang, 1990).

*Graziani, Antonioe, *Purdgavine* (Avellino: G. laccheo, 1883).

Guerrieri, Giovanni, 'I conti normanni di Lecce nel secolo XII', *ASPN*, 25 (1900), 196–217.

*Guerrieri, Giovanni, *Il conte normanno Riccardo Siniscalco, 1081–1115, e i monasteri Benedettini Cavesi in terra d'Otranto* (Trani: V. Vecchi, 1899).

Guilland, Rodolphe, *Recherches sur les institutions byzantines*, 2 vols (Berlin: Akademie-Verlag, 1967), i.

Hagemann, Wolfgang, 'Kaiserurkunden aus Gravina', QFIAB, 40 (1960), 188–200.

Hall, John A., and Ralph Schroeder, eds., *An Anatomy of Power: The Social Theory of Michael Mann* (Cambridge: Cambridge University Press, 2006).

*Haskins, Charles H., 'England and Sicily in the Twelfth Century', *The English Historical Review*, 26.103–4 (1911), 433–47, 641–65.

Haskins, Charles H., *The Renaissance of the Twelfth Century* (Cambridge, USA: Harvard University Press, 1927).

Hoffmann, Hartmut, 'Chronik und Urkunden in Montecassino', QFIAB, 51 (1971), 93–206.

*Hoffmann, Hartmut, 'Langobarden, Normannen, Päpste. Zum Legitimationsproblem in Unteritalien', QFIAB, 58 (1978), 137–80.

*Holtzmann, Walther, 'Papst-, Kaiser- und Normannenurkunden aus Unteritalien I', QFIAB, 35 (1945), 46–85.

Holtzmann, Walther, 'The Norman Royal Charters of S. Bartolomeo di Carpineto', *PBSR*, xxiv (1956), 94–100.

*Houben, Hubert, *Die Abtei Venosa und das Mönchtum im normannisch-staufischen Süditalien* (Tübingen: Niemeyer, 1995).

Houben, Hubert, 'Le origini del principato di Taranto', Archivio Storico Pugliese, 61.I-IV (2008), 7-24.
Houben, Hubert, *Roger II of Sicily: A Ruler between East and West*, trans. by Graham A. Loud (Cambridge: Cambridge University Press, 2002).
Iannacci, Lorenza, 'Il Liber instrumentorum del monastero di San Salvatore a Maiella', *Studi Medievali*, III.53 (2012), 717-69.
Jacob, André, 'Le Breve Chronicon Nortmannicum: un véritable faux de Pietro Polidori', *QFIAB*, 66 (1986), 378-92.
Jamison, Evelyn M., 'Additional Work on the Catalogus Baronum', *Bullettino dell'Istituto storico italiano per il Medio Evo* ed Archivio Muratoriano 83 (1971), 1-63.
Jamison, Evelyn M., *Admiral Eugenius of Sicily: His Life and Work and the Authorship of the Epistola Ad Petrum and the Historia Hugonis Falcandi Siculi* (London: Oxford University Press, 1957).
Jamison, Evelyn M., 'Foreword', in *Catalogus Baronum*, FSI, 11 (Istituto storico italiano per il Medio Evo, 1972), i.
*Jamison, Evelyn M., *I conti di Molise e di Marsia nei secoli XII e XIII* (Casalbordino: Nicola de Arcangelis, 1932).
Jamison, Evelyn M., 'Judex Tarentinus', *Proceedings of the British Academy*, 53 (1967), 289-344.
*Jamison, Evelyn M., 'Note e documenti per la storia dei Conti Normanni di Catanzaro', *Archivio storico per la Calabria e la Lucania*, 1 (1931), 451-70.
*Jamison, Evelyn M., 'The Abbess Bethlem of S. Maria di Porta Somma and the Barons of the Terra Beneventana', in *Oxford Essays in Medieval History, presented to Herbert Edward Salter* (Oxford: Clarendon Press, 1934), pp. 33-67.
*Jamison, Evelyn M., 'The Administration of the County of Molise in the Twelfth and Thirteenth Centuries', *English Historical Review*, 45.177 (1930), 1-34.
*Jamison, Evelyn M., 'The Norman Administration of Apulia and Capua: More Especially Under Roger II and William I, 1127-1166', *PBSR*, 6 (1913), 211-481.
*Jamison, Evelyn M., 'The Significance of the Earlier Medieval Documents from S. Maria della Noce and S. Salvatore di Castiglione', in *Studi in onore di Riccardo Filangieri*, 3 vols (Naples: Arte tipografica, 1959), i, 51-80.
*Johns, Jeremy, *Arabic Administration in Norman Sicily: The Royal Dīwān* (Cambridge: Cambridge University Press, 2002).
Jones, A. H. M., *The Later Roman Empire, 284-602: A Social, Economic, and Administrative Survey*, 3 vols (Oxford: Basil Blackwell, 1964), i.
Jones, Arnold H., *The Later Roman Empire, 284-602: A Social, Economic, and Administrative Survey*, 2 vols (Oxford: Basil Blackwell, 1964), i.
Kamp, Norbert, *Kirche und Monarchie im staufischen Königreich Sizilien. I: Prosopographische Grundlegung. Bistümer und Bischöfe des Königreichs* 1194-1266. *2: Apulien und Kalabrien* (Munich: W. Fink, 1975).
*Kamp, Norbert, 'Von Kammerer zum Sekreten: Wirtschaftsreformen und Finanzverwaltung im staufischen Konigreich Sizilien', in *Probleme um Friedrich II.*, ed. by J. Fleckenstein, Vorträge und Forschungen 16 (Sigmaringen: Jan Thorbecke Verlag, 1974), pp. 43-92.
Kazhdan, Alexander P., ed., *The Oxford Dictionary of Byzantium* (New York: Oxford University Press, 1991).
*Kehr, Karl A., *Die Urkunden der normannisch-sicilischen Könige* (Innsbruck: Wagner, 1902).
*Leccisotti, Tommaso, 'Antiche prepositure cassinesi nei pressi del Fortore e del Saccione', *Benedictina*, 1 (1947), 83-133.

Leicht, Pier S., 'Territori longobardi e territori romanici', in *Atti del I Congresso internazionale di Studi Longobardi* (Spoleto: L'Accademia spoletina, 1952).

Lejbowicz, Max, 'Annliese Nef, Conquérir et gouverner la Sicile islamique aux XIe et XIIe siècles', *Cahiers de recherches médiévales et humanistes*, 2012, http://crm.revues.org/12719 (accessed 27 August 2017).

*Loud, Graham A., 'A Lombard Abbey in a Norman World: St Sophia. Benevento, 1050–1200', in *Anglo-Norman Studies, XIX: Proceedings of the Battle Conference 1996*, ed. by Christopher Harper-Bill (Woodbridge: Boydell Press, 1997), pp. 273–306.

Loud, Graham A., *Church and Society in the Norman Principality of Capua: 1058–1197* (Oxford: Clarendon Press, 1985).

Loud, Graham A., 'Continuity and Change in Norman Italy: The Campania during the Eleventh and Twelfth Centuries', *Journal of Medieval History*, 22.4 (1996), 313–43.

Loud, Graham A., 'Innocent II and the Kingdom of Sicily', in *Pope Innocent II (1130-43): The World vs the City*, ed. by John Doran and Damian J. Smith, Church, Faith and Culture in the Medieval West (London: Routledge, 2016), pp. 172–80.

Loud, Graham A., 'Le strutture del potere: la feudalità', in *Il Mezzogiorno normanno-svevo fra storia e storiografia*, Atti del Centro di Studi Normanno-Svevi, 20 (Bari: Dedalo, 2014), pp. 147–68.

Loud, Graham A., 'Monastic Chronicles in the Twelfth-Century Abruzzi', in *Anglo-Norman Studies, XXVII: Proceedings of the Battle Conference 2004*, ed. by John Gillingham (Woodbridge: Boydell & Brewer, 2005), pp. 101–31.

*Loud, Graham A., 'New Evidence for the Workings of the Royal Administration in Mainland Southern Italy in the later Twelfth Century', in *Puer Apuliae: Mélanges offerts à Jean-Marie Martin*, ed. by Errico Cuozzo, Vincent Déroche, Annick Peters-Custot, and Vivien Prigent, Monographies, 30 (Paris: Association des amis du centre d'histoire et civilisation de Byzance, 2008), pp. 395–417.

Loud, Graham A., 'Norman Traditions in Southern Italy', in *Norman Tradition and Transcultural Heritage: Exchange of Cultures in the 'Norman' Peripheries of Medieval Europe*, ed. by Stefan Burkhardt and Thomas Foerster (Farnham: Ashgate, 2013), pp. 35–56.

*Loud, Graham A., *Roger II and the Creation of the Kingdom of Sicily* (Manchester: Manchester University Press, 2012).

Loud, Graham A., 'The Abbey of Cava, Its Property and Benefactors in the Norman Era', in *Anglo-Norman Studies, IX: Proceedings of the Battle Conference 1986*, ed. by R. Allen Brown (Woodbridge: Boydell & Brewer, 1987), pp. 143–77.

Loud, Graham A., *The Age of Robert Guiscard: Southern Italy and the Norman Conquest* (Harlow: Longman, 2000).

Loud, Graham A., 'The Chancery and Charters of the Kings of Sicily (1130–1212)', *The English Historical Review*, 124 (2009), 779–810.

Loud, Graham A., 'The Genesis and Context of the Chronicle of Falco of Benevento', in *Anglo-Norman Studies, XV: Proceedings of the Battle Conference 1992* (Woodbridge: Boydell & Brewer, 1993), pp. 177–98.

Loud, Graham A., 'The Gens Normannorum: Myth or Reality?' in *Proceedings of the Battle Conference on Anglo Norman Studies IV*, ed. by R. Allen Brown (Woodbridge: Boydell Press, 1981), pp. 104–16.

Loud, Graham A., 'The German Emperors and Southern Italy during the Tenth and Eleventh Centuries', in *'Quei maledetti Normanni': Studi offerti a Errico Cuozzo per suoi settent'anni da Collegui, Allievi, Amici*, ed. by Jean M. Martin and Rosanna Alaggio, 2 vols (Ariano Irpino: Tipografia Villanova, 2016), i, 583–606.

Loud, Graham A., 'The Image of the Tyrant in the Work of "Hugo Falcandus"', *Nottingham Medieval Studies*, 57 (2013), 1-20.
Loud, Graham A., *The Latin Church in Norman Italy* (Cambridge: Cambridge University Press, 2007).
Loud, Graham A., 'The Monastic Economy in the Principality of Salerno during the Eleventh and Twelfth Centuries', *PBSR*, 71 (2003), 141-79.
Loud, Graham A., 'William the Bad or William the Unlucky? Kingship in Sicily 1154-1166', *Haskins Society Journal*, 8 (1999), 99-113.
Loud, Graham A., and Thomas Wiedemann, 'Introduction', in *The History of the Tyrants of Sicily by 'Hugo Falcandus', 1154-69*, trans. by Graham A. Loud and Thomas Wiedemann (Manchester: Manchester University Press, 1998), pp. 1-53.
*Macchione, Antonio, *Alle origini di Catanzaro: la Chronica trium tabernarum* (Bari: Mario Adda editore, 2012).
Mann, Michael, *A History of Power from the Beginning to AD 1760. The Sources of Social Power 1*, 2nd edn (New York: Cambridge University Press, 2012).
Marongiu, Antonio, 'A Model State in the Middle Ages: The Norman and Swabian Kingdom of Sicily', *Comparative Studies in Society and History*, 6.3 (1964), 307-20.
Martin, Jean M., 'Étude sur le Registro d'istrumenti di S. Maria del Galdo suivie d'un catalogue des actes', *Mélanges de l'Ecole française de Rome. Moyen Age*, 92.2 (1980), 441-510.
Martin, Jean M., 'La frontière septentrionale du royaume de Sicile à la fin du XIIIe siècle', in *Une région frontalière au Moyen Âge. Les vallées du Turano et du Salto entre Sabine et Abruzzes*, ed. by Étienne Hubert (Rome: École française de Rome, 2000), pp. 291-303.
Martin, Jean M., *La Pouille du VIe au XIIe siècle*, Collection de l'École française de Rome, 179 (Rome: École française de Rome, 1993).
Martin, Jean M., 'L'ancienne et la nouvelle aristocratie féodale', in *Le eredità normanno-sveve nell'età angioina: persistenze e mutamenti nel Mezzogiorno*, Atti del Centro di Studi Normanno-Svevi, 15 (Bari: Dedalo, 2004), pp. 101-36.
Martin, Jean M., 'L'aristocratie féodale et les villes', in *Eclisse di un regno: l'ultima età sveva*, Atti del Centro di Studi Normanno-Svevi, 19 (Bari: Dedalo, 2012), pp. 119-62.
Martin, Jean M., 'Les communautés d'habitants de la Pouille et leurs rapports avec Roger II', in *Società, potere e popolo nell'età di Ruggero II*, Atti del Centro di Studi Normanno-Svevi, 3 (Bari: Dedalo, 1979), pp. 73-98.
Massa, Paola, 'L'archivio dell'abbazia di Santa Sofia di Benevento', *Archiv für Diplomatik, Schriftgeschichte, Siegel- und Wappenkunde*, 61 (2016), 433-66.
Matera, Enzo, 'Le più antiche carte del monastero di S. Sofia di Benevento. Codice Vaticano latino 13491 (aa. 784-1330). Saggio di edizione' (unpublished PhD, Università degli Studi di Roma 'La Sapienza', 1985).
Mattei-Ceresoli, Leone, *La Congregazione Benedettina Degli Eremiti Pulsanesi: Cenni Storici* (Bagnacavallo: Società Tipografiaca editrice, 1938).
*Mattei-Ceresoli, Leone, 'Tramutola', *Archivio Storico per la Calabria e la Lucania*, 13 (1943), 32-46, 91-118.
Matthew, Donald J., 'The Chronicle of Romuald of Salerno', in *The Writing of History in the Middle Ages. Essays Presented to Richard William Southern*, ed. by R. H. C. Davis and J. M. Wallace-Hadrill (Oxford: Clarendon Press, 1981), pp. 239-74.
Mazzarese Fardella, Enrico, *I feudi comitali di Sicilia dai Normanni agli Aragonesi* (Milan: A. Giuffrè, 1974).
Mazzarese Fardella, Enrico, 'Problemi preliminari allo studio del ruolo delle contee nel regno di Sicilia', in *Società, potere e popolo nell'età di Ruggero II*, Atti del Centro di Studi Normanno-Svevi, 3 (Bari: Dedalo, 1979), pp. 41-54.

Ménager, Léon R., *Amiratus- Ἀμηρᾶς, l'émirat et les origines de l'amirauté (XIe-XIIIe siècles)* (Paris: S.E.V.P.E.N., 1960).

Ménager, Léon R., 'Inventaire des familles normandes et franques emigrées en Italie méridionale et en Sicile (XIe-XIIIe siècles)', in *Roberto il Guiscardo e il suo tempo*, Atti del Centro di Studi Normanno-Svevi, 1 (Bari: Dedalo, 1975), pp. 259-390.

*Ménager, Léon R., 'Les fondations monastiques de Robert Guiscard, duc de Pouille et de Calabre', *QFIAB*, 39 (1959), 1-116.

Metcalfe, Alex, *The Muslims of Medieval Italy* (Edinburgh: Edinburgh University Press, 2009).

*Monaco, Michele, *Sanctuarium Capuanum* (Naples: Octavium Beltranum, 1630).

Morlacchetti, Erica, *L'abbazia benedettina delle Isole Tremiti e i suoi documenti dall'XI al XIII secolo*, Studi Vulturnensi, 4 (Cerro al Volturno: Volturnia, 2014).

Morrone, Fiorangelo, *Monastero di Sancta Maria de Gualdo Mazzocca: Badia-Baronia di S. Bartolomeo in Galdo* (Naples: Arte Tipografica, 1998).

Morso, Salvadore, *Descrizione di Palermo antico* (Palermo: Presso Lorenzo Dato, 1827).

Murray, Alexander C., 'From Roman to Frankish Gaul: "Centenarii" and "Centenae" in the Administration of the Merovingian Kingdom', *Traditio*, 44 (1988), 59-100.

Nef, Annliese, *Conquérir et gouverner la Sicile islamique aux XIe et XIIe siècles* (École française de Rome, 2011).

Nelson, Lynn H., 'Rotrou of Perche and the Aragonese Reconquest', *Traditio*, 26 (1970), 113-33.

Oldfield, Paul, *City and Community in Norman Italy* (Cambridge: Cambridge University Press, 2011).

Palanza, Albina, 'Per un conte normanno di Avellino', *ASPN*, 41-2 (1917), 124-37, 516-28, 68-78.

Palumbo, Pier F., *Tancredi conte di Lecce e re di Sicilia e il tramonto dell'età normanna*. (Lecce: Edizioni del Lavoro, 1991).

Paul, Nicholas L., 'Origo Consulum: Rumours of Murder, a Crisis of Lordship, and the Legendary Origins of the Counts of Anjou', *French History*, 29.2 (2015), 139-60.

*Pellegrino, Camillo, *Historia principum Langobardorum*, ed. by Francesco M. Pratillo, 2nd edn, 4 vols (Naples: Johannes de Simone, 1751), iii.

*Perla, R., 'Una charta iudicati dei tempi normanni', *ASPN*, 9 (1884), 342-7.

*Pescatore, Luigi, 'Le piu antiche pergamene dell'Archivio arcivescovile di Capua (1144-1250)', *Campania sacra: rivista di storia sociale e religiosa del mezzogiorno*, 2 (1971), 22-98.

Pescione, Raffaele, *Corti di giustizia nell'Italia meridionale: dal periodo normanno all'epoca moderna* (Milan: Societa editrice Dante Alighieri, 1924).

Peters-Custot, Annick, *Bruno en Calabre. Histoire d'une fondation monastique dans l'Italie normande: S. Maria de Turri e S. Stefano del Bosco* (Rome: École française de Rome, 2014).

Petrizzo, Francesca, 'Kin Dynamics of the Hautevilles and Other Normans' (University of Leeds, 2018).

Petrucci, Armando, 'Bassunvilla', Roberto, in *Dizionario biografico degli Italiani*, ed. by Alberto M. Ghisalberti (Rome: Istituto della Enciclopedia italiana, 1960).

*Petrucci, Armando, 'Note di diplomatica normanna. I. I documenti di Roberto di "Bansuvilla", II conte di Conversano e III conte di Loretello', *Bullettino dell'Istituto storico italiano per il Medio Evo* ed Archivio Muratoriano 71 (1959), 113-40.

Pio, Berardo, *Guglielmo I d'Altavilla: gestione del potere e lotta politica nell'Italia normanna: 1154-1169*, Il mondo medievale, 24 (Bologna: Pàtron, 1996).

Pontificio Ateneo di S. Anselmo, ed., *Studia Benedictina: in memoriam gloriosi ante saecula XIV transitus S.P. Benedicti* (Vatican City: Libreria Vaticana, 1947).

Portanova, Gregorio, 'I Sanseverino dal 1125 allo stermino del 1246', *Benedictina*, 23 (1976), 319–63.
Portanova, Gregorio, 'I Sanseverino dalle origini al 1125', *Benedictina*, 23 (1976), 105–49.
*Poso, Cosimo D., *Il Salento Normanno. Territorio, istituzioni, società* (Galatina: Congedo, 1988).
*Promis, Domenico, 'Notizia di una bolla di piombo del secolo XII', *Atti della R. Accademia delle scienze di Torino*, 4 (1869), 670–4.
Reynolds, Susan, *Fiefs and Vassals: The Medieval Evidence Reinterpreted* (Oxford: Oxford University Press, 1996).
Reynolds, Susan, *Kingdoms and Communities in Western Europe, 900–1300*, 2nd edn (Oxford: Oxford University Press, 1997).
Rinaldi, Antonio, *Memoria pel comune di Pescopagano contro il comune di S. Menna* (Potenza: A. Pomarici, 1889).
*Rivelli, Antonino V., *Memorie storiche della città di Campagna* (Salerno: A. Volpe, 1895).
Rivera, Cesare, 'L'annessione delle Terre d'Abruzzo al regno di Sicilia', *Archivio Storico Italiano*, 7.6 (1926), 199–309.
Rivera, Cesare, 'Per la storia delle origini dei Borrelli conti di Sangro', *ASPN*, 44 (1919), 48–92.
Rosenwein, Barbara H., *To Be the Neighbor of Saint Peter: The Social Meaning of Cluny's Property, 909–1049* (Ithaca, NY: Cornell University Press, 1989).
*Scandone, Francesco, *L'alta valle del Calore. II. Il feudo e il municipio di Montella dal dominio dei Normanni a quello della Casa d'Aragona* (Palermo: A. Trimarchi, 1916).
*Scandone, Francesco, *L'alta valle del Calore. VII. La cittá di Nusco. Parte prima.* (Naples: Tip. Laurenziana, 1970).
*Scandone, Francesco, *L'alta valle dell'Ofanto. I. Città di S. Angelo dei Lombardi dalle origini al sec. XIX* (Avellino: Tip. Pergola, 1957).
Scandone, Francesco, *Per la controversia sul luogo di nascita di S. Tommaso d'Aquino: Esame critico di aclune pubblicazioni recenti a pro'di Roccasecca (Caserta) e di Belcastro (Catanzaro)* (Naples: Stabilimento tipografico M. d'Auria, 1903).
*Scandone, Francesco, Storia di Avellino: Abellinum *feudale*. Avellino durante la dominazione de' *normanni* (1077–1195), 2 vols (Naples: Armanni, 1948), ii.
Siragusa, Giovanni B., *Il regno di Guglielmo I in Sicilia*, 2nd edn (Palermo: Sandron, 1929).
Skinner, Patricia, *Family Power in Southern Italy: The Duchy of Gaeta and Its Neighbours, 850–1139* (Cambridge: Cambridge University Press, 1995).
Skinner, Patricia, *Medieval Amalfi and Its Diaspora, 800–1250* (Oxford: Oxford University Press, 2013).
Spagnoletti, Riccardo O., *Ruggiero, ultimo conte normanno di Andria* (Trani: V. Vecchi, 1890).
Stanton, Charles D., *Norman Naval Operations in the Mediterranean*, Warfare in History (Woodbridge: Boydell Press, 2011).
Stumpf-Brentano, Karl F., *Die Reichskanzler, vornehmlich des X., XI. und XII. Jahrhunderts* (Innsbruck: Wagner, 1865).
Takayama, Hiroshi, 'Notes and Documents: *Familiares Regis* and the Royal Inner Council in Twelfth-Century Sicily', *The English Historical Review*, 104.411 (1989), 357–72; [reprinted in] Takayama, Hiroshi, *Sicily and the* Mediterranean *in the* Middle Ages, Variorum Reprint (London: Routledge, 2019), pp. 33–51].
Takayama, Hiroshi, *The Administration of the Norman Kingdom of Sicily* (Leiden: E.J. Brill, 1993).

*Tansi, Serafini, *Historia cronologica monasterii S. Michaelis Archangeli Montis Caveosi* (Naples: Typografia Abbatiana, 1746).

*Tescione, Giuseppe, *Caserta medievale e i suoi conti e signori: lineamenti e ricerche*, 3rd edn (Caserta: Libreria G.D.C., 1990).

Tescione, Giuseppe, 'Il privilegio de 1178 di Alessandro III per la Chiesa Casertana', in *Studi in onore di* Mons. Luigi *Diligenza* (Aversa: Libreria G.D.C., 1989), pp. 247–56.

Thompson, Kathleen, 'Family Tradition and the Crusading Impulse: The Rotrou Counts of the Perche', *Medieval Prosopography*, 19 (1998), 1–33.

Thompson, Kathleen, *Power and Border Lordship in Medieval France: The County of the Perche, 1000–1226* (Boydell & Brewer, 2002).

Thompson, Kathleen, 'The Lords of Laigle: Ambition and Insecurity on the Borders of Normandy', in *Anglo-Norman Studies*, XVIII: *Proceedings of the Battle Conference 1995*, ed. by Christopher Harper-Bill (Woodbridge: Boydell & Brewer, 1996), pp. 177–99.

Toomaspoeg, Kristjan, 'La frontière terrestre du Royaume de Sicile à l'époque normande: questions ouvertes et hypothèses', in *'Quei maledetti Normanni': Studi offerti a Errico Cuozzo per suoi settent'anni da Collegui*, Allievi, Amici, ed. by Jean M. Martin and Rosanna Alaggio, 2 vols (Ariano Irpino: Tipografia Villanova, 2016), ii, 1205–24.

Toomaspoeg, Kristjan, 'L'insediamento dei grandi ordini militari cavallereschi in Sicilia, 1145–1220', in *La presenza dei Cavalieri di San Giovanni in Sicilia* (Rome: Gran Magistero del Sovrano Militare Ordine di Malta, 2001), pp. 41–51.

Torelli, Pietro, *Lezioni di storia del diritto italiano. Diritto privato. Le persone* (Milan: A. Giuffrè, 1949).

Varzos, Konstantinos, *Η Γενεαλογία των Κομνηνών*, 2 vols (Thessaloniki: Centre for Byzantine Reserach - AUT, 1984), ii.

*Villani, Matteo, 'Diplomi inediti di Riccardo Siniscalco e Costanza d'Altavilla. Per la storia della diocesi di Castellaneta e dell'insediamento cavense in Puglia', *ASPN*, 106 (1988), 7–31.

Villegas-Aristizabal, Lucas, 'Norman and Anglo-Norman Participation in the Iberian Reconquista c.1018 - c.1248' (unpublished PhD, University of Nottingham, 2007).

Wood, Ian, *The Merovingian Kingdoms 450–751* (London: Routledge, 1994).

Index

'Abd al Mu'min, caliph   108
Abdenago, son of Hannibal   122, 130
Abruzzo   9, 22–4, 33–5, 38, 49–52, 63–7, 70, 74, 75, 77, 79, 81, 92–3, 98, 101, 111–13, 124, 129, 131, 136, 137, 169
Absalom, abbot of Tremiti   135
Accardus, lord of Lecce and Ostuni   42, 55
Acerenza   29
Acerra   38
   counts (*see* Buonalbergo, counts; Richard of Aquino; Roger of Medania)
   county   137–8 (*see also* Buonalbergo, county)
   lordship   52, 81, 113, 179
Acquabella   17
Adam, count of Conversano   36
Adam, lord of Catanzaro and Rocca Falluca   25
Adam Avenel   36, *see also* Adam, count of Conversano
Adelaide, countess of Principato   37, 43, 46
Adelaide del Vasto, countess of Sicily   25, 32, 54
Adelicia, countess of Principato   162
Adelicia, lady of Fiorentino   137
Adelicia of Adernò   56, 87, 89, 141
Adelicia of Bassunvilla   40
Adernò   141
   St Elias, church   217 n.226 (ch. 2)
   St John, church   141
administration   3, 48–9, 51, 66, 82, 98–100, 103, 106, 151, 159, 163, 178, 181, 184-4
   justice   16, 47, 50, 93, 122–4, 141–2, 149, 152, 158–60, 162, 172–8, 181
Adrian IV, pope   64, 65, 68, 70–1, 109, 219 n.31 (ch. 3)
Agnes, countess of Caserta   146
Agnes, wife of Henry of Sarno   19

Agnone, *see* Borell [IV], lord of Agnone
Agnone, church of St Mark in   211 n.89 (ch. 2)
Agri, river   43, 45, 46, 116, 179
Agrigento bishopric   85
Agromonte   82
Airola, lordship   17, 52, 69, 145, *see also* Rainulf [II] of Caiazzo
Alan, bishop of Chieti   79
Alba county   111, 112, *see also* Berard, count of Alba
Albano di Lucania   44
Alberada, lady of Lucera   42
Albert del Vasto, 'count' of Gravina   80
Aldwin, count   171, 172
Aldwin of Candida   172, *see also* Aldwin, count
Aleramici, family   32, 53, 80
Alexander, count of Conversano, count of Gravina   17, 18, 22, 28, 30, 67, 89
Alexander, monk and chronicler of Carpineto   6, 61–2
Alexander, prior of Maiella   35
Alexander III, pope   103–4, 109, 114, 146, 153, 165, 169, 170
Alexander Komnenos Batatzes   239 n.15 (ch. 7)
Alexander of Alife   148
Alexander of Telese   5
Alexander of Troia   136
Alexander the monk   88–9, *see* Alexander, count of Conversano and Gravina
Alexandria   168
Alexios Axouchos, protostrator   83, 89, 109
Alexios Branas   171, 172
Alexios Komnenos, son of Nikephoros Bryennios   67, 93
Alexios Komnenos 'the cupbearer'   171
Alexios son of John *Coliander*   41
Alfana, countess of Marsico   157

Alfanus, archbishop of Capua 83, 170
Alfanus of Camerota, archbishop of
    Capua 114
Alfonso, count of Squillace 165, 170
Alfonso, king of Aragón and Navarre 81,
    115
Alfonso, prince of Capua 32, 47, 49
Alfred, count 25, 207 n.100 (ch. 1)
Alife 17, 83
    castrum 139
    counts 37, 105 (*see also* Malgerius,
        count of Alife; Roger son of Richard
        [of Rupecanina])
    county 69, 95, 96, 111, 139
    lordhsip 69, 95
Almaric, king 168
Amalfi 70
amiratus stolii 184
Anacletus II, pope 27, 28, 153
Anastasius IV, pope 219 n.31 (ch. 3)
anathema 17, 41, 169
Ancona 83, 89
    march 169–70
Andrew of Rupecanina, count 68–71,
    73, 82–4, 93–5, 102, 108, 109, 114,
    139, 145
    count of Comino 101, 112
Andria 41, 44, 73, 74
    counts 25, 53, 73, 77, 132, 178 (*see
        also* Bertram of Perche; Geoffrey,
        count of Andria; Peter, count of
        Andria; Richard of Lingèvres;
        Roger son of Richard)
    county 53, 98, 110, 139–40, 179
Andronikos Komnenos 171
Angevin, dynasty 181
Anglona, church of St Lawrence in 157
Anjou, comital dinasty 20, 21
Anna Komnene 67
Anne, mother of Richard of Carinola 18
Apice, *castellum* 164
Aprutium 22, 50–1
    bishopric 50
Apulia 9, 17, 28, 30, 62, 66, 67, 69, 83,
    86, 91, 92, 96, 99, 100, 105, 106,
    109, 112, 113, 117–20, 125, 128,
    140, 145, 168, 183
    Adriatic 10, 15, 17, 20, 25, 29, 37,
        39, 41, 49, 60, 63, 64, 72, 73, 76, 77,
        92–3, 98, 110, 128, 131, 140, 156,
        158, 174, 175
    dukes 13, 14, 16, 18, 22, 24, 25, 27,
        35, 43, 44, 120, 206 n.86 (ch. 1)
Aquapulida 163
Aquila, family 52, 56, 141, 143, 150
Aquilonia, *see* Carbonara
Aquino 82–3
    counts 26, 35 (*see also* Lando of
        Aquino; Pandulf of Aquino)
    lords 35
Aquinus of Moac 92, 103, 104
Arce 69
Ariano 48
    assizes 6 (*see also* legislation)
    counts 52, 67 (*see also* Jordan, count
        of Ariano; Roger count of Ariano)
armies 16, 28, 29, 34, 49–50, 50
    count of Andria 76
    German 33, 63–4, 109, 144, 168–70
    Greek 64, 67, 69, 70, 73, 75, 76, 82,
        110
    Greek, 'French' contingent 89
    Greek (mercenary) 239 n.10 (ch. 7)
    king's 32, 53, 66, 77, 83, 84, 86, 92–5,
        100, 101, 103–4, 107, 108, 112, 114,
        120, 128, 163, 168, 171
    papal 68, 109
    Sicilian 238 n.1 (ch. 7)
Asclettin Drengot 24
Asclettin of Catania, chancellor 66, 70,
    86
Ascoli (Satriano) 176
assemblies 48
    Melfi 34
    Silva Marca 3, 47–8
Aternum 136, 137
Atina 82
Attonids 23, 24
augustalis 140
Auletta 37, 46, 161–7
Avellana, abbey of St Peter 38, 177
Avellino 34, 41, 141
    castellum 42, 90, 126
    counts 20, 41 (*see also* Perrona,
        countess of Avellino; Richard of
        Aquila [II]; Roger of Aquila)
    county 53, 75, 140–3, 158, 179, 181
    jurisdiction 143

St Basil, church 126
Aversa 32, 36, 175
  bishopric 7
  judges 173, 175
  St Lawrence, abbey 45, 175

Badolato 25, 99–100, 175
Bagnara, church of St Mary of 134
baiuli, magistri
  Avellino 141-2
  Molise 158
Balvano, family 53, 164
banishment and exiles 29, 30, 63, 67,
    68, 71, 75, 79, 88, 96, 105, 209 n.52
    (ch. 2)
Barano, church of St Angelo of 136
Bari 15, 22, 28, 29, 33, 41, 60, 70, 73, 98,
    110, 174
  archbishopric 7
  judges 174
  princes 16 (*see also* Grimoald,
    'prince' of Bari)
  St Nicholas, church 174
Barletta 154, 176
  lordship 17, 33
Bartholomew, count of Carinola 24, 33
Bartholomew of Garsiliato 68
Bartholomew of Parisio, sister of 114
Bartholomew of Perche 92
Basento, river 43, 44
Basil, judge of Caserta 146
Basilicata 154
Basilicata, region 9
Beatrix, sister of Robert Guiscard 21
Bella 82
Belmonte 23
Benedict, prior of St Peter of Scafati 94
Benevento 15, 23, 30, 34, 52, 65, 66, 68,
    70, 71, 140
  libary (church) 164
  St Mary of Porta Somma,
    nunnery 132
  St Sophia, abbey 38, 86, 137, 158,
    159, 160, 177
  treaty (1156) 109, 215 n.185 (ch. 2)
Benincasa, abbot of Cava 147, 148, 157
Berard, count of Alba 38, 101, 112
Berard of Pietrabbodante 165
Berengarius of Gisay 116

Bernard, abbot of St Sophia,
    Benevento 208 n.28 (ch. 2)
Bernard, bishop-elect of Catania 223
    n.34 (ch. 4)
Bersentium 156
Bertha of Loritello, countess 22, 25, 37
Bertram of Perche, count of Andria 76,
    81, 92, 110, 111, 113–14, 127, 139
Biferno, river 31
Bitonto
  bishopric 174
  monastery of St Leo [the Great] at 54
Bohemund of Taranto 25
Bohemund of Tarsia, count of
    Manopello 35, 49–51, 57, 64, 66,
    74, 75, 82, 101, 121
Bohemund [II], count of Manopello 81,
    82, 91, 117–18, 120, 122, 124, 129,
    131, 137
Bohemund [II] of Tarsia 121, 126
Boiano 38, 39, 108, 158
  bishopric 157 (*see also* Robert,
    bishop of Boiano)
  counts 20, 38, 56, 63, 63 (*see also*
    Molise, counts; Hugh II of Molise;
    Robert of Molise, count of Boiano;
    Simon of Molise, count of Boiano
    (d. 1117))
  county 63 (*see also* Molise, couty)
  judges 159, 177
Bolognano, *castellum* 50
Boniface del Vasto, marquis of Savona and
    Western Liguria 32, 53–4, 80
boni homines 45–6, 140, 147, 151, 154
Bonito 163
Bonum Albergum, hospital of St Thomas
    the Martyr of 165
Borell [IV], lord of Agnone 30
Borells 23, 30, *see* Borell [IV], lord of
    Agnone; Oderisius [II], count of
    Sangro; Theodinus, count of Sangro
Bosco, abbey of St Stephen del 22, 165
Boso, bishop-elect of Cefalù 223 n.34
    (ch. 4)
Bovino
  bishopric 135
  lordship 135, 137
Bradano, river 44
Brienza 21, 22

Brindisi 29, 64, 67, 70, 89
   Holy Sepulchre, church of 177
   judges 177
   lordship 17
   St Mary, abbey 177
Bryennios, Nikephoros 67
Buonalbergo
   counts 57, 81 (*see also* Acerra, counts; Richard of Aquino; Robert of Medania; Roger of Medania)
   county 52, 55, 75, 113, 137–8, 179
Butera 32, 70, 72, 92
   castellum 68
   lordship 65, 120, 179
Byzantine empire, *see* Eastern empire

Caccamo 88, 91, 93
Cagnano 156
Caiazzo
   counts 67, 94–5, 101, 111, 139 (*see also* Rainulf I of Caiazzo (d. 1088); Rainulf [II] of Caiazzo)
   lordship 69
Calabria 9, 13, 22, 24, 28, 34, 37, 38, 53, 56, 57, 76, 86, 91, 92, 93, 99–100, 114, 118, 121, 130, 131, 144, 165, 170
Calabritto 163
Calitri, *see* Castellum Caletri
Calixtus II, pope 208 n.29 (ch. 2)
Caltanissetta 42, 67
   lordship 120–1, 180
Calvi 140
   lordship 141
Calvignano 177
camerarii 97, 99–100, 107, 184
   Bari 174
   comital 74, 95, 135, 139, 145, 149, 154
      Montescaglioso 154 (*see also* Montescaglioso, honour)
   palatine (royal) 99, 106, 156, 183 (*see also* Peter, qaid)
   royal 46, 47, 72, 121, 122, 137, 165, 175 (*see also* Richard, qaid)
   St Michael the Archangel, abbey 21
Campagna, *castellum* 161–6
Campania, papal 95, 103, 109, 114, 169
Campolieto, lordship 159, 160, 177
Campomarino 97
   lordship 135, 137
Campuri 82
Candelaro 156
Canne 33
Capitanata 15, 20, 23, 31, 32, 36, 52, 63, 98, 137, 163
capitanei, magistri 59, 86, 87, 92, 105, 106, 110, 122, 124, 127, 128, 129, 138
capitaneus, title 114
Caposele 163
Capua 34, 40, 41, 43–4, 66, 147–8, 175
   archbishopric 17, 83, 114, 170
   judges 173, 175
   nunnery of St John the Baptist 68
   princes 15, 16, 18, 24, 32, 101, 120
   principality 9, 15, 17, 20, 24, 28, 29, 30, 34, 41, 68, 72–3, 79, 82, 83, 92, 95 (*see also* Terra di Lavoro)
   St John Baptist, nunnery 94, 146
Carbonara 144
Carbone, abbey of St Anastasius of 14
Carbonellus of Tarsia 126
Carinola
   counts 24, 38, 57, 83, 130 (*see also* Bartholomew, count of Carinola; Jonathan [I], count of Carinola; Jonathan [II], count of Carinola; Richard, count of Carinola; Richard [II], count of Carinola and Conza)
   county 40, 52, 96, 143–5
   St Mary outside, church 18
Carolingian roots 16, 22, 23, 51, 203 nn.12–13, 205 n.70 (ch. 1)
Carovigno 152
Carpineto, abbey of St Bartholomew of 6, 136, 137
Carsoli 168
   St Mary, church 238 n.3 (ch. 7)
Casale Plano, *castellum* 50
Casalinovo, *masseria*, *see* Casone
Casauria, abbey of St Clement in 6, 23, 50, 64, 74, 82, 98, 154, 175
Casavena 174
Caselle in Pittari 46
Caserta 32, 146
   bishopric 74, 175

counts 37, 94–5, 178 (*see also* Agnes, countess of Caserta; Robert [II] of Lauro; William of Lauro)
county 94, 96, 105, 119, 145–9, 179
lordship 94
St James, church 146
Casone lordship 134, 137
Cassandra, countess of Principato 19
Castel di Sangro, *see* Sangro, *castellum*
Castel Fiorentino (ruins), *see* Fiorentino, 208 n.31 (ch. 2)
castellan, comital 134, 138
Castello a Mare 126
Castellum Caletri 144
Castellum Maris, see Castel Volturno
Castel Pagano 156
Castelvecchio 38
Castel Volturno 31
Castrum Monticuli 233 n.65 (ch. 6)
Catalogus Baronum, see Quaternus magne expeditonis
Catania, St Mary, church 141
Catanzaro 25, 86–7
counts 16, 22, 37, 38, 57, 92 (*see also* Bertha of Loritello, countess; Clementia, countess of Catanzaro; Geoffrey, count of Catanzaro; Hugh Lupinus; Hugh [II] Lupinus; Rao of Loritello; Raymund, count of Catanzaro; Segelgarda, countess of Catanzaro)
county 99–100, 131, 165
Caux, abbey of Saint-Victor-en 217 n.220 (ch. 2)
Cava, abbey of the Most Holy Trinity of 7, 8, 14, 19, 21, 25, 36, 37, 41, 45, 55, 74, 80, 119, 134, 136, 146–50, 154, 155, 157, 161, 162, 173–5
Ceccano 108–9, *see also* Fossanova in Ceccano, abbey
Cecilia of Medania 138
Cefalù, cathedral 144
Celano, *see* Rambot, count of Celano
Celenza, church of the Holy Spirit 149–50
Cephalicchia 156
ceremony, comital appointment 108
Cerentia 31
Cerreta 141
Cervaro, valley 84, 145

Cervino 74
chamberlain, *see camerarii*
chancellorship 59, 61, 62, 66, 115–16, 221 n.90 (ch. 3), *see also* Asclettin, chancellor; Maio of Bari; Robert of Selby; Stephen of Perche
chaplain, comital, *see* Pagan, chaplain
Chieti 22–4, 49, 50
bishopric 20, 35, 60, 61, 79
Christian of Buch 103, 109, 168, 226 n.126 (ch. 4)
Christodoulos 13, 25
Cilento 21, 22, 43, 45, 46, 94, 110
Civitaquana 136
Civitate 74, 135
bishopric 135
counts 57, 63, 130 (*see also* Henry, count of Civitate; Jonathan [II], count of Carinola; Philip, count of Civitate; Robert [II] son of Robert; Robert son of Richard; Sica, countess of Civitate)
county 40, 76, 96–8, 135, 149–50
lordship 31, 33
Clementia, countess of Catanzaro 37, 86–7, 92, 99–100, 130, 131, 165
Cociano, church of St Dominic at 149
Colle Odoni, *castellum* 50
comes comitum 14, 20
comestabuli 47, 79, 107, 162
comital 88, 135, 157, 159 (*see also* Richard of Mandra)
king's military entourage 107, 116, 183
royal 44, 59, 75, 93, 96, 117, 128, 154, 163, 164, 167, 173 (*see also* Elias of Gesualdo; Gilbert of Balvano; Lampus of Fasanella; Richard of balvano; Robert of Quallecta; Roger [II] of Lauro, count of Tricarico)
comestabuli, magistri 98, 103, 104, 114, 116, 124, 128, 132, 142
of all Calabria 130–1 (*see also* Hugh Lupinus; Richard of Say)
comestabuli, magni 106, 107, 146, 151, 168–77, 181
comestabulia 47, 51, 96, 112, 117, 162, 164
justitia (*see* Manopello, justiciarate)
Comino 82, 83, 101

Conchile, church of St Apollinarius
    Martyr in   25
Conrad, duke   209 n.45 (ch. 2)
Conrad III, king of Germnay   35, 48, 67
constable, *see comestabuli*
Constantine Aczarulus   74
Constantine Otto   83
Constantinople   89, 93, 171
constitutions, of the kingdom, *see* legislation
consul, title   16, 20
Contra   60
Contra, county   112
Conversano   28, 36, 74
    counts   25, 56 (*see also* Adam, count of Conversano; Alexander, count of Conversano; Geoffrey, count of Conversano; Robert of Bassunvilla; Robert of Bassunvilla [II])
    county   63, 76, 98, 124, 133–7, 180
    St Benedict, abbey   137, 154
Conza, cathedral of St Mary   84
    counts   84 (*see also* Jonathan [II], count of Carinola; Richard [II], count of Carinola and Conza; Stephanie, countess of Conza)
    county   143–5
    lordhsip   38, 40, 81, 96, 117, 164
Corato   17
coronations   27, 56, 61, 63–4, 66, 218 n.19 (ch. 3)
court (judicial)
    at Ariano (royal)   48
    at Aversa (royal)   175
    at Barletta (royal)   154, 156, 176–7
    at Boiano (comital)   159
    at Capua (royal)   86, 175
    at Eboli (comital)   161–70
    at Fiorentino (royal)   163
    at Foggia (royal)   106
    at Goleto (royal)   162
    at Isernia (royal)   157
    itinerant   47
    at Maddaloni (royal)   173
    at Melfi (royal)   117
    at Montecassino (abbatial)   177
    at Palermo (royal)   151–2
    at Serracapriola (comital)   160
court, royal, *see* curia regis

curia regis   5, 9, 38, 40, 42, 43–4, 53, 57, 60, 71–2, 74–5, 82, 85, 86, 90–2, 98–100, 102, 104, 105–8, 110, 111, 113–19, 122, 124, 126–30, 132, 134, 136–7, 140, 144, 149, 151, 152, 154, 156, 157, 160–4, 167, 169, 175, 176, 180
currency
    ducat   48
    scyphate   29
    solidi   20
    tarì, Amalfitan   146
    tarì, Palermitan   156

Dalmatia   29, 30
Deliceto   130
    church of St Christopher at   130, 144
    countess (*see* Segelgarda, countess of Catanzaro)
    lordship   145
demesne
    comital (Loritello)   134
    comital (Molise)   158
    comital (Sant'Angelo dei Lombardi)   163
    royal   35, 53, 60
Demetritzes, battle   171, 172
Desiderius, abbot of Montecassino   235 n.122 (ch. 6)
dīwān, *magister* of the royal   165, *see also* Richard, qaid
Dorostolon (modern Silistra)   67
Doukas, John   93
Dragonara   135, 212 n.103 (ch. 2)
Drengot, family   70, 83, 224 n.56 (ch. 4)
Drengots   24, 33
Drogo of Hauteville   54, 207 n.100 (ch. 1)
Drogo 'the Badger'   23, 112
duana baronum   90, 156, 177–8, 183–4
duana de secretis   183
    duana de secretis, magister (Greek)   156
duel, judicial   173, 176, 239 n.28 (ch. 7)
Durantus, judge of S. Martino   145
Dyrrachium   171, 172

Eastern empire   6, 64, 67, 70, 94, 95, 102, 138, 160, 171
Egidius, abbot of Venosa   174
Egypt   168

Elce, abbey of St Mary in 144
Elias of Gesualdo 163, 164
Elizabeth of Marsico 157
Elvira of Castile 35
Emma, abbess of St John the Evangelist in Lecce 153
Emma of Lecce 43, 57, 87
Emma of Sicily 13, 21, 36, 56
England 4, 20
Eremburga of Mortain 32
Eudoxia Komnenos 239 n.15 (ch. 7)
Eugenius, admiral 177–8, 184
Everard, count of Squillace 53, 65, 68, 72, 100
exiles, *see* banishment and exiles

Falco, bishop of Aversa 175
Falco of Benevento 5, 31
familiares regis 90, 99, 105–8, 110, 121, 122, 127, 151, 157, 158, 167, 170
fees and taxes 48
    adiutorium 135, 159–60, 177, 237 n.169 (ch. 6)
    collectors (ἀπέτιται) 99–100
    exportation 125
    forisfactura 135
    glandaticum 46
    incultum 15, 48
    platea 135, 137 (*see also plateaticum*)
    plateaticum 15, 48, 98, 125, 159
    portaticum 15, 125
    redemption 96, 105
    tenure, annual 121
    terraticum 159
Fenicia of S. Severino 89–90, 118
Ferraria, abbey of S. Maria of 5
feuda 9, 22, 40, 41, 44, 45, 46, 48–52, 54, 60, 61, 63, 66, 69, 71–3, 76, 80, 82, 85, 95, 97, 112, 118–19, 130, 131, 134, 135, 140, 144, 152, 157, 160, 162, 164, 173, 180
feudalism, criticism 2–3, 48, 141, 224 n.73 (ch. 4), 233 n.79 (ch. 6), 215 n.172 (ch. 2)
Fiorentino 39–40, 135, 163, 208 n.31 (ch. 2), 31
    lordship 137
Flandina, daughter of Roger I 32
fleet, Sicilian 168, 238 n.1 (ch. 7)

Florius of Camerota 122, 229 n.94 (ch. 5)
Flumeri 60
    castrum 140
    lordhsip 112, 140, 169
Foggia 106
Fondi
    bishopric 151
    counts 20, 21, 40, 57, 83, 132 (*see also* Geoffrey of Aquila; Richard of Aquila [III], count of Fondi; Richard of Say)
    county 9, 52, 71, 82, 83, 93, 96, 108–9, 114, 150–2
Forca, *castella* 20
Forenza 80
    lordship 54
forgeries and fabrications 36–7, 40, 43–4, 85, 115, 136, 164, 210 n.67 (ch. 2)
Formis, church of St Angelo in 45, 94, 146
Fossanova in Ceccano, abbey 5, 82
Fountain, church of St Mary of the 156
France 20, 21
franci homines 153
Frederick [I] Barbarossa, emperor 63, 64, 66, 71, 83, 95, 103–4, 109, 110, 169
Frederick II, emperor 39
Frigento 163
frontiers 22, 23, 24, 30, 31, 38–9, 49–52, 63, 65, 101, 108–9, 169–70, 215 n.185 (ch. 2)
Gaeta 25, 31, 33, 40, 52
    dukes and consuls 16, 19, 25, 40, 41 (*see also* Geoffrey Ridellus, duke of Gaeta; Gualguanus, duke of Gaeta and lord of Pontecorvo; Jonathan [II], count of Carinola; Richard, count of Carinola)
Gaitelgrima, countess of Molise 160–1
Gaitelgrima, daughter of Guaimar of Salerno 26
Gaitelgrima of Sorrento 220 n.50 (ch. 3)
galleys, armed 127
García Ramírez, king of Navarre 81, 116
Gargano 64, 92–3, 154
Garigliano, river 71, 83, 84, 109, 155, 206 n.81 (ch. 1)
Geneisos the notary 100

Genestrella   20
Gentile, bishop of Agrigento   223 n.34 (ch. 4)
Geoffrey, count of Andria   17, 18, 29, 30
Geoffrey, count of Catanzaro   22, 25, 37, 40, 144
Geoffrey, count of Conversano   17, 25
Geoffrey, count of Tricarico   43
Geoffrey [II], count of Mortagne   81
Geoffrey of Aquila, count of Fondi   52, 71
Geoffrey of Balvano   162
Geoffrey of Capitanata   37
Geoffrey of Conza   84
Geoffrey of Lecce, count of Montescaglioso   42, 55, 57, 67, 68, 72, 81, 96, 112, 113, 116, 120, 152, 180
Geoffrey of Medania, lord of Acerra   38, 55
Geoffrey of Moac   183
Geoffrey of Ollia, count of Lesina   36, 74, 76, 98, 154–5, 156
Geoffrey of Ragusa   55
Geoffrey of Say   93
Geoffrey Ridellus, duke of Gaeta   206 n.81 (ch. 1)
George of Antioch   13
Gerace, *see* Roger, count of Gerace
Geraci, counts   229 n.69 (ch. 5)
German empire, *see* Western empire
German invasion   30, 33, 34
Gesualdo   163, 164
Gilbert, bishop-elect of Patti   223 n.34 (ch. 4)
Gilbert of Balvano   96, 117, 162, 164
Gilbert of L'Aigle   81
Gilbert of Perche, count of Gravina   53, 80, 81, 91, 92, 98, 103, 104, 105–10, 115, 118, 120, 121, 129, 131
   count of Loritello   124, 127, 128–9
Gioi   46
Giso, bishop of Fiorentino   135
glandes, *see* pasturage rights
Gli Sgarroni, *see* Castrum Monticuli
Goleto   138
Goleto, abbey of the Holy Saviour at (modern S. Guglielmo al Goleto)   113, 138, 144, 162
Gonzolinus, count   103

governor, royal   106, 110, 114, 130–1, 138, *see also gubernatore totius regni* Calabria (*see comestabuli, magistri, totius Calabrie*)
Gravina   67
  bishopric   54
  castellum   54
  church   150–1
  counts   28, 79, 132, 178 (*see also* Albert del Vasto; Alexander, count of Conversano and Gravina; Gilbert of Perche; Richard of Say; Stephanie, countess of Gravina; Tancred of Say; Theodora, countess of Gravina)
  county   53, 80, 105, 180
  marquises   53–5 (*see also* Manfred, marquis of Gravina; Philippa, marchioness of Gravina)
great constable, *see comestabuli, magni*
Greek empire, *see* Eastern empire
Gregory VII, pope   224 n.73 (ch. 4)
Grimoald, 'prince' of Bari   17, 28
Grottaminarda   163
Grottole   17
Guaimar [IV], prince of Salerno   24, 26, 94
Gualdo Mazzoca, abbey of St Mary of   135, 150
Gualguanus, duke of Gaeta and lord of Pontecorvo   212 n.118 (ch. 2)
Guarmundus son of Walter   97
gubernatore totius regni   106
Guido, bishop of Cefalù   144
Guido, prior of St Egidius   154, 155
Guimund of Montellari   112

Hannibal, count of Celano   124
Hauteville   22, 25
  Loritello branch   22–5, 37, 51, 64–5, 130
  royal family   55–7, 59–60, 62, 85, 165
Henry, bishop of Sant'Agata   31
Henry, count of Civitate   149–50
Henry, count of Sarno   18, 19, 25, 30, 34–5
Henry II, king of England   170
Henry VI, emperor   143, 144, 169
Henry Aristippus   90

Henry del Vasto   32, 33, 120
Henry [Rodrigo] of Navarre   123, 125, 128
   count of Montescaglioso   116–21, 127, 131
   count of Principato   153, 161–2
Henry of Ollia   74, 98, 154
Henry of S. Severino   45, 55, 118–19
herbae, *see* pasturage rights
Herbert, bishop of Tropea   223 n.34 (ch. 4)
Hermits of Driene, monastery   40
Hodegetria, monastery of Magna   25
Hohenstaufen, dynasty   11, 143, 162, 181
Holy Roman empire, *see* Western empire
Holy Saviour in 'Castro Lucullano', abbey   138
homage and fealty   30, 31, 35, 91, 103, 207 n.20 (ch. 2), 224 n.73 (ch. 4), 226 n.121 (ch. 4)
homagium, *see* homage and fealty
homines censiles, *see* tenant-farmers
hominium, *see* homage and fealty
Honorius II, pope   17, 18, 27
Hugh [I] of Molise   25, 70
Hugh [II] of Molise, count of Boiano   19, 20, 25, 30, 31, 33, 35, 38–40, 56, 60, 69, 97, 157
Hugh Lupinus, count of Catanzaro   129–31, 165, 170
Hugh [II] Lupinus
   count of Catanzaro   165
   count of Conversano   137
Hugh of Capua, archbishop of Palermo   69–70, 85
Hugh of Molise, lord of Sepino   97
Hugh of Rochefort   111
Hugo Falcandus, *see* Pseudo-Falcandus
Hugues, archbishop of Rouen   217 n.220 (ch. 2)

Al-Idrisi   6, 49
Ifriqiya   202 n.2 (ch. 1)
Illyria   171–2
Innocent II, pope   27, 31, 44
Innocent III, pope   151
Irpina, region   9, 17, 28, 38, 117, 119, 138, 162–4
Isaac II Angelos, emperor   171

Ischia (Isclia Maior)   85
Isernia   19, 157, 158
Isernia, bishopric   157, *see also* Raynald, bishop of Isernia
Itri   108–9
iustitiarii   35, 107
   comital   157, 158
   Melfi (royal)   154 (*see also* Melfi, justiciarate)
   Monte Sant'Angelo, honour (royal)   156
   Montescaglioso (royal)   154 (*see also* Montescaglioso, honour)
   royal   38, 50, 74, 75, 93, 98, 117, 154, 162, 163, 173, 174, 177, 211 n.90 (ch. 2)
   Terra di Lavoro   142
iustitiarii, magistri   9, 62, 122, 130–2, 136–7, 146, 151, 156, 160, 170, 181, 183
   for all Apulia and the Terra di Lavoro   138, 142, 159, 169, 173–7

James, count of Tricarico   148
Jerusalem   29, 127
   kingdom   88, 89, 126, 127, 168
   pilgrimage   144
   St Mary de Latina   125
   Temple Mount (*Templum Domini*)   127
Joan of England, queen of Sicily   151, 155, 156, 170
Jocelyn, count of Loreto   111, 112, 170
Joetta of Caserta   147
John, abbot of Montevergine   141
John, abbot of St Sophia, Benevento   208 n.28 (ch. 2)
John, archbishop of Bari   223 n.34 (ch. 4)
John, bishop-elect of Sant'Angelo dei Lombardi   162
John, bishop of Aversa   37, 40, 94
John, bishop of Fondi   151
John, bishop of Malta   126
John, bishop of Penne   224 n.73 (ch. 4)
John, emir   32
John, prior of St Leonard   20
John Berard, monk and chronicler of Casauria   6, 61–2
John Doukas   67
John Kinnamos   6

John of Tufara, hermit   236 n.163 (ch. 6)
John of Venafro, master judge of the county of Molise   159
Jonathan [I], count of Carinola   24
Jonathan [II], count of Carinola   33, 40, 69, 84, 143–4
  count of Civitate   39–40
  count of Conza   81, 93
  duke of Gaeta   33, 40
Jordan, count of Ariano   18, 31
Jordan [I], prince of Capua   24
Jordan Lupinus   165
judicial supremacy   47, 93, 122, 136–7, 141, 152, 173, 174–5, 176, 177–8, 181
Judith d'Évreux   32
Judith of Sicily   36, 56, 59
Judith of Sicily, countess   74
Juliana of Perche   81
justice, *see* administration, justice
justiciar, *see* iustitiarius

kinship   15, 22–4, 32, 33, 45, 53–4, 55–7, 94, 101, 119, 138, 157
knights, *see* milites

Lama, abbey of St John of   156
Lampus of Fasanella   75, 222 n.102 (ch. 3), 47
Landenolfus of Carinola   24
Lando of Aquino, count   18
Landulf of Salerno   94
Larino, church of   136
Lastignano   20
Latin East   4
Lauro
  castellum   147
  castrum   45
  counts   94 (*see also* Robert [II] of Lauro, count of Caserta)
  lordhsip   94, 119, 146–8, 179
Lazio   71
Lecce   152, 153
  bishopric   153
  counts   178 (*see also* Montescaglioso, counts; Tancred of Lecce)
  county   152–4

lordship   42–3, 55 (*see also* Accardus, lord of Lecce and Ostuni; Geoffrey of Lecce, count of Montescaglioso)
SS. Nicholas and Cataldo, abbey   153
St John the Evangelist, nunnery   47, 153
legislation   6, 123–4, 159–60
Lentini, church of St Andrew   217 n.226 (ch. 2)
Leo, consul of Fondi   20
Leonas, abbot of Casauria   175
Lesina   41, 74
  counts   36, 57 (*see also* Geoffrey of Ollia; Peter, count of Lesina (d. 1092); Peter [II], count of Lesina; Rao, count of Lesina; Robert, count of Lesina; Sibylla, countess of Lesina; William, count of Lesina)
  county   98, 105, 154–6
lignamina ad incidendum, see timber rights
Limosano   38
Lippary, abbey   93
logothete   73
Lombard League   169
Lombard roots   15, 18, 20, 23, 24, 26, 30, 41, 48, 51, 55, 173, 182
Loritello   63, 74
  counts   15, 23, 24, 34, 49 (*see also* Robert [I] of Hauteville, count of Loritello; Robert [II] of Hauteville, count of Loritello; Robert of Bassunvilla (II))
  county   61, 76, 79, 98, 124, 133–7, 176, 180
Lothar, emperor   18, 20, 31, 33, 49, 60
Lucera   163
Lucius III, pope   136, 173

Maddaloni   74
Magalda [of Adernò]   56, 60, 141
magister militum (Naples)   16, 30, 34, *see also* Sergius [VII] Naples
magister terre Comitis Principatus, see Pagan the seneschal
Magliano Vetere   46
magna expeditio   6, *see also* army, king's
Mahdia   202 n.2 (ch. 1)

Maiella, abbey of the Holy Saviour at M.   6, 30, 35, 50
Maiella, mountain range   49
Mainz, archbishop   168, *see also* Christian of Buch
Maio of Bari   53, 61–2, 65, 67, 68, 70, 72, 79, 81–5, 87, 90, 106
Maiore, river   150
Malgerius, count of Alife   95, 96, 139
Malgerius of Altavilla (Salentina)   22
Mandra   119, 121
manescalcus, comital   135, *see also* Philip the maschal
Manfred, marquis of Gravina   54
Manfred del Vasto   32
Manopello   52, 74
   counts   57, 64–5, 77 (*see also* Bohemund of Tarsia, count of Manopello; Bohemund [II], count of Manopello; Richard of Manopello, count (d. after 1103); Robert of Manopello, count)
   county   23, 24, 35, 50, 98
   justiciarate   38, 50–1, 101, 131
   lordship   49
Manuel Komnenos, emperor   35, 48, 64, 89, 94, 170
Margaret of L'Aigle   81, 115
Margaret of Navarre, queen of Sicily   81, 92, 105, 111, 115, 118, 122, 125–6, 129
Margliano   38
Mari, church of St Andrew in   47
Maria, wife of William of Principato   24
Maria Komnenos   170
Marina, abbess of Goleto   162
Marinus, abbot of Cava   46
Marinus of Traetto, count   235 n.122 (ch. 6)
Marius Borell   69, 86
Marocta of S. Severino   89–90, 95, 96, 143
marquio, *see* marquis, title
marquis, title   54, 80, *see also* Gravina, marquises
marshal, *see manescalcus*
Marsia   22, 23, 50–1, 112
   bishopric   175

Marsico
   counts   43, 105 (*see also* Alfana, countess of Marsico; Sylvester, count of Marsico; William, count of Marsico)
   county   45–6, 55, 75, 76, 114, 156–7
Marsico Nuovo   45
Martin, qaid   122
master captain, *see capitanei, magistri*
master justiciar, *see iustitiarii, magistri*
Mataracius, qaid   156, 183
Matera
   castrum   29
   lordship   67
Mathew, marquis   33
Matilda, infant daughter of Count Sylvester   90, 99, 185
Matilda, sister of Roger II of Sicily   17, 28
Matthew Bonellus   39, 70, 83, 87, 88, 91
Matthew of Aiello, *see* Matthew the notary
Matthew of Castelvetere   143
Matthew the notary   85, 87, 99, 109, 122, 126, 170
Medania, family   55, 113
Melfi   34, 70
   justiciarate   154 (*see also* Richard of Balvano)
   lordship   41
Mercogliano   142
   castellum   126
   judges   177
   jurisdiction   143
Messina   13, 92, 97, 118, 127, 136
   bishopric   85
   court at   118–25
   St Mary of Scala, nunnery   125
Michael Palaiologos   64, 67
Mignano, treaty (1139)   44
Milan   83
Mileto   85
military mobilisation   15, 16, 47, 51, 66, 76–7, 93, 98, 103, 107, 128, 131, 135, 160, 168, 184
milites   15, 25, 32, 49–50, 53, 60, 61, 66, 70, 72, 73, 76, 83, 84, 86, 93, 95, 104, 106, 116, 118–21, 128, 131, 134, 135, 141, 144, 147, 152, 154, 157, 160, 162, 163, 168, 171, 188
   salaried   107

Minervino 17
Minturno, *see* Traetto
Mirabella Eclano, *see* Aquapulida
Mocava, church of St Nazarius de la 19
Molfetta
   lordship 40–1, 60, 61, 134, 136, 137
Molise
   counts (*see* Boiano, counts; Gaitelgrima, countess of Molise; Richard of Mandra; Roger, count of Molise)
   county 39, 96, 97, 108, 112, 117, 157–61, 177 (*see also* Boiano, county)
   family 97
   jurisdiction 158
Monopoli, abbey of St Stephen in Monopoli 174
Monte Arcano 93
Montecassino 5, 34, 38, 41–2, 50, 82–3, 93, 132, 136, 152, 157, 174
Montecorvino
   castrum 115
   lordship 150
Monte Drogo, church of St Mary of 139
Monte Drogo (della Grotta), church of St Mary of 111
Monteforte Cilento 46
Montella 138
   lordship 96
Monte Millulo 177
Montepeloso 29
Monte Porzio, battle 109
Monte Sant'Angelo in Gargano
   counts 33, 32 (*see also* Simon, count of Monte Sant'Angelo in Gargano)
   county 170
   honour 155–6
Montescaglioso
   counts 21, 42, 55, 125, 152 (*see also* Geoffrey of Lecce; Henry [Rodrigo] of Navarre; Robert, count of Montescaglioso (d. before 1099); Tancred of Lecce)
   county 55, 67–8, 76, 96, 120, 152–4, 180
   honour 154 (*see also* Richard of Balvano)
   lordship 13, 21, 22 (*see also* Robert [II], lord of Montescaglioso; William, lord of Montescaglioso)
Montevergine, abbey of St Mary of 30, 35, 119, 138, 140–2, 145, 149, 163, 177
Monticchio Sgarroni, *see Monticulum*
Monticulum 144
Montoro 45, 148–9
   lordship 94, 118–19
   St Thomas, church 148
Muro Lucano 82
Muwahids, king of, *see* ʿAbd al Mu'min, caliph

Naples 30–2, 70, 138, 170, 187
   dukes (*see magister militum* (Naples), Alfonso, prince of Capua)
   SS. Severino and Sossius, abbey 148
   St Mary a Capella, church 40
Nardò, abbey of St Mary of 115
Navarre 81
Nicholas, archbishop of Salerno 187
Nicholas, count of Principato 18, 19, 24, 30, 36–7
Nicholas Frascenellus 94
Nicholas son of Qaid Peter 156
Nicholas the *primicerius* 174
Niketas Choniates 6
Nocera, battle 29
Normandy 4, 20, 21, 25, 39, 53, 115, 217 n.220 (ch. 2)
notary, comital 135, *see* Griffus of Molfetta
Noto 43, 67
   lordship 120–1, 180
Novi Velia 46
Nusco 96, 113, 138

oath swearing 41–2, 31, 63, 64, 71, 91, 209 n.50 (ch. 2)
Octaiano and Fellino 71–2
Oddo, abbot of Montecassino 41–2
Oderisius, abbot of Montecassino 212 n.118 (ch. 2)
Oderisius [II], count of Sangro 23, 30
Oderisius of Marsia, count 23
Ofanto, valley 84
Olecino, church of St Mary of 135
Oliver, abbot of Carpineto 136

Oppido   162
Orgeolo   91
Ostuni   42–3, 152, 153
Otto of Freising   6

Pacentro   49
Padula   46
Pagan, chaplain   144
Pagan the seneschal   161
palatine count   20, 33, *see also* William, count of Loritello
palatine county   133–7
palatinus, title   136
Palermo   13, 27, 28, 66, 68, 69–70, 72, 74, 75, 79, 83, 85, 87–92, 99, 108, 110, 112–15, 125–7, 151, 157, 158, 160–3, 169, 170, 183, 186
   archbishopric   65, 116 (*see also* Hugh of Capua, archbishop of Palermo; Stephen of Perche; Walter Ophamil)
   cathedral   72
   St Cataldo, church   90
   St George, church   156
Palmerius of Auriconta   148
Pandulf, count of Marsia   23
Pandulf of Aquino, count   18, 35
papal schism   27
Pascal III, anti-pope   103–4
pascua utenda, *see* pasturage rights
Pastena   108–9
pasturage rights   46, 113, 137, 151
Paternò   32
   lordship   120, 179
Paternopoli   163
Patire, abbey of St Mary of   25
Patritius, (English) count   228 n.44 (ch. 5)
Penne   22, 23, 50–1
Perche, county   115
Peregrinus of Giso   116
Perno, church of St Mary of   154
Perrona, countess of Avellino   143
Pertecara   116
Pescara   48, 49
   bishopric   82
Pescara, river   20, 24, 33
Peschici   154, 156
Petazati, church of St Paul of   20
Peter, count of Andria   25

Peter, count of Celano   112
Peter, count of Lesina (d. 1092)   154–5
Peter, Qaid   99, 105–8, 110, 121, 123
Peter, son of Leo of Fondi   20
Peter [II], count of Lesina   24
Peter of Capua   146
Peter the Deacon, register of   19
Petrarch of Taranto   134–5
Philip, count of Civitate   149, 150
Philip, count of Sangro   81, 131
Philip of Balvano, count   53, 117, 162–4
Philippa, marchioness of Gravina   54, 80
Philip the marschal   135
Piano, abbey of St John in   74, 154
Pico   108–9
   castellum   42
Piczone   146
Piedimonti, abbey of St Peter of   145–6
Pietragalla   44
Pietramontecorvino, *see* Montecorvino
Pisa   109
Pisticci, abbey of St Mary of   14, 21
Polido de Thora   95
Polignano   92
Polla   22
   St Peter the Apostle, church   22
Pontecorvo   41–2
Porfirio, bishop of Caserta   146, 147, 175
Posta   82
Potenza   44
Pozzuoli   158
Prignano, Giovan Battista   7, 136, 144, 163
prince, title   87–8, 120, 224 n.56 (ch. 4)
Principato
   counts   46, 57 (*see also* Adelaide, countess of Principato; Adelicia, countess of Principato; Cassandra, countess of Principato; Henry [Rodrigo] of Navarre; Nicholas, count of Principato; William [I], count of Principato; William [II], count of Principato; William [III], count of Principato; William [IV], count of Principato)
   county   75, 76, 161–2
protostrator   222 n.19 (ch. 4), *see also* Alexios [Axouchos]
Pseudo-Falcandus   5

publicum [*dominium*]   41, 54, 126
Pulcarino   119
Pulsano, abbey of St Mary of   39, 156
Quaternus magne expeditonis   9, 19, 30, 37, 39, 42, 44–8, 51, 53, 54, 60, 61, 66, 71, 76, 80, 94, 95, 97, 110–13, 116–19, 121, 130, 131, 134, 135, 138, 141, 144, 152, 160, 162–4, 173, 184
   Abruzzo *quaternion*   49, 50–1, 81, 111, 112, 131

Ragusa   46, 85, 99, 157
   lordship   55, 57, 114, 179
Rainald, chancellor   109
Rainulf, abbot of Montecassino   83
Rainulf, bishop of Chieti   24
Rainulf, count of Aversa   24
Rainulf, count of Celano   124
Rainulf [I] of Caiazzo (d. 1088)   24
Rainulf [II] of Caiazzo   17, 18, 24, 28–31, 34, 35, 52, 83, 95, 102
Rambot, count of Celano   38
Rambot, count of Loreto   112
Ranulf II, earl of Chester   20
Rao, bishop of Trivento   157
Rao, bishop of Volturara Appula   149–50
Rao, count of Lesina   20
Rao of Loritello, count of Catanzaro   22, 25, 130
Raymond, son of Rao of Loritello   25
Raymund, count of Catanzaro, *see* Rao of Loritello, count of Catanzaro
Raynald, bishop of Isernia   157
Raynald of Aquino   138
Raynald of Monte Forte   183
Raynald of Pietrabbondante   160
Raynald of Troia   136
Reggio Calabria   120, 125
Riardo, lordship   141
Richard, bishop-elect of Syracuse   90, 99, 108, 122, 126, 170, 223 n.34 (ch. 4)
Richard, count of Carinola   18–20, 24, 25, 33
   duke of Gaeta   19, 25, 33
Richard, count of Manopello (d. after 1103)   23
Richard, count of Sarno   25
Richard, qaid   126, 165, 184

Richard [II], count of Carinola and Conza   84, 143–5, 176
Richard of Aquila [I]   41, 52
Richard of Aquila [II], count of Avellino (d. 1152)   40, 41–2, 53, 56, 74
Richard of Aquila [III], count of Fondi   52, 71, 72, 75–6, 81–2, 93, 102, 108–10, 150, 151–2, 170, 176, 181
Richard of Aquino, count of Acerra (and Buonalbergo)   137–8, 153, 170–1, 172, 187, 188
Richard of Balvano   117, 154
Richard of Lauro   147, 148
Richard of Lingèvres, count of Andria   53, 73, 75, 76, 98, 110
Richard of Mandra, count of Molise   79, 88, 107–8, 110, 111, 113, 115–18, 121–4, 127–9, 131, 157–60
Richard of Rupecanina, count   34
Richard of Say   93, 103, 104, 111, 151
   count of Fondi   114, 127–8, 131, 132, 150
   count of Gravina   132, 150–1, 168, 173–4
Richard Pygnardus   20
Richard son of Guarin of Flumeri   60
Richard son of Richard   60, 112–13, 163
Richard the Seneschal   14
Ricigliano   50–1, 82, 215 n.185 (ch. 2)
Rignano (Garganico)   33, 34
   castellum   134
Rimini   109
Roagia, countess of Tricarico   149
Robert, bishop of Boiano   157
Robert, bishop of Catanzaro   130
Robert, bishop of Civitate   135
Robert, bishop of Messina   223 n.34 (ch. 4)
Robert, count of *Aprutium*   38, 50
Robert, count of Lesina   36, 210 n.70 (ch. 2)
Robert, count of Manopello   23, 24
Robert, count of Monte Sant'Angelo   207 n.100 (ch. 1)
Robert, count of Montescaglioso (d. before 1099)   21
Robert, earl of Gloucester   20
Robert I, prince of Capua   24
Robert II, prince of Capua   17, 18, 28, 30, 35, 63, 68–9, 71, 75–6

Robert Capumaza 45, 94
Robert Guiscard 13, 54
Robert of Bassunvilla [I], count of
    Conversano 36, 40, 56
Robert of Bassunvilla [II]
    count of Conversano 40–1, 56, 59, 60
    count of Loritello and
        Conversano 59–65, 67, 68, 70–3,
        75, 79, 81, 83, 86, 91–3, 101, 103,
        107, 133–7
Robert of Bova 88
Robert [I] of Hauteville, count of
    Loritello 20, 23, 25, 60
Robert [II], lord of Montescaglioso 22
Robert [II] of Hauteville, count of
    Loritello 14, 20, 25, 53, 60, 102
Robert of Lauro [I] 45, 94
Robert of Lauro [II], count of
    Caserta 93, 94, 96–8, 102, 118,
    119, 121, 122, 129, 132, 145–7, 151,
    168–70, 172–6
Robert of Lauro [III] 147
Robert of Medania, count of
    Buonalbergo 38, 52, 53, 55, 60, 81
Robert of Molise 97
Robert of Molise, count of Boiano 19
Robert of Quallecta 47
Robert of Selby, chancellor 35, 66, 117
Robert son of Richard, count of
    Civitate 31, 32, 39, 40, 53, 60–1,
    113
Robert [II] son of Robert, count of
    Civitate 53, 73–4, 96–7, 113, 149,
    169
Rocca Cilento 45
Rocca Cilento, lordship 94, 118–19
Rocca Fallucca 25
Rocca of Craon 85
Rocca S. Felice 143
Rocchetta, *castellum* 157
Rodrigo of Navarre 116
Roger, abbot of Elce 144
Roger, archbishop of Reggio 223 n.34
    (ch. 4)
Roger, count of Ariano 17, 18, 28, 31,
    33, 35
Roger, count of Molise 159–61, 177
Roger I, count of Sicily 25, 32, 54, 57,
    85, 93

Roger [I], count of Tricarico 44, 75,
    81–2, 97
Roger II, king of Sicily 13, 14, 17, 18,
    21–3, 27–35, 40, 47, 49–51, 53, 59,
    62, 174, 176, 180
Roger [II], count of Caserta 4–45
Roger III, duke of Apulia 43, 44, 49, 87
Roger Borsa, duke of Apulia 25
Roger Bozzardi 159, 160, 177
Roger Machabeus 21, 22
Roger of Aquila, count of Avellino 53,
    56, 57, 60, 74, 87–9, 95, 96, 103,
    111, 113, 118, 120, 122, 126, 129,
    140–3, 177
Roger of Baro 154
Roger of Castelvetere 143
Roger of Craon 84–5
Roger of Gerace, count 118, 122, 126,
    127, 129
Roger [II] of Lauro, count of
    Tricarico 44–5, 97, 118, 122, 147
Roger of Martorano 86–7, 92
Roger of Medania, count of Buonalbergo
    and Acerra 53, 74, 81, 93, 96, 111,
    113, 137
Roger of S. Severino 45
Roger of Tiron 116–17, 122
Roger of Yscla, 'count' 85
Roger Sclavus 89, 91, 92
Roger son of Richard 159
    count of Alba 67, 111, 113, 127–9,
    131
    count of Andria 132, 138–40, 142,
    151, 168, 169, 171, 176–7, 189, 190
Roger son of Richard [of Rupecanina],
    count of Alife 111, 139, 176
Roger son of Turgisius 163
Roger son of Turgisius of Crypta 162
Roger the monk, prior of the Holy
    Sepulchre in Brindisi 177
Roman law 124
Rome 7, 27, 63–5, 71, 102, 109, 172
    papacy 27, 65, 102, 109, 151, 153,
    170, 227 n.19 (ch. 5)
Romuald [II], archbishop of Salerno 5,
    6, 116, 126, 161–73
Romuald Guarna, *see* Romuald II,
    archbishop of Salerno
Rotrou II, count of Perche 81, 115

royal family, *see* Hauteville, royal family
Rudolph Machabeus   13, 21, 36, 56
Rusticus, bishop of Chieti   20

Sacntum Lupulum   163
S. Angelum   60
sacramenta, see oath swearing
sacrilege   123
St Andrew, church   35
St Benedict in Polignano, nunnery   92, *see also* Scolastica, abbess of St Benedict in Polignano
St Casideus   20
St Catherine   220 n.43 (ch. 3)
    translatio   69–70
St Ephrem, church   130
St Erasmus, church   161–5
Saint-Gilles   170
St Pamfilus, church of   20
St Thomas Apostle, cathedral   61, *see also* Chieti, bishopric
Sala Consilina   45, 157
Saladin, sultan   168
Salento, peninsula   14, 43, 152
Salento peninsula   168
Salerno   18, 28, 30, 34, 40, 43–4, 65, 70, 86, 91, 99, 147, 170, 183
    archbishopric   5, 7, 43 (*see also* Romuald II, archbishop of Salerno; William, archbishop of Salerno)
    former principality   9, 24, 29, 37, 45, 68, 75, 76, 92, 94, 119, 131, 145–7
Salpi, lake   92–3
Sanctum Julianum   44
Sanctus Angelus in Vico, abbey   39
Sangro   23
    castellum   49, 112
    counts   69 (*see also* Oderisius [II], count of Sangro; Philip, count of Sangro; Simon, count of Sangro; Theodinus, count of Sangro)
    river   23, 24, 49
Santa Maria della Noce, sanctuary of   23
Sant'Angelo dei Lombardi   163
    county   53, 162–4
Sarconem   116
Sarno, counts   30, 41, 67, 175, *see also* Henry, count of Sarno; Richard, count of Sarno

Sarracena   94, 146, 214 n.150 (ch. 2)
Satriano, church of St Blaise at   162
Scafati, abbey of St Peter of, *see* Benedict, prior of St Peter of Scafati
S. Caterina dello Ionio   100
Scaviano, church of St Nicholas of   157
Schiavi di Abruzzo   101
Sclàfani   67
    lordship   43, 120–1, 180
Sclavezulis, church of St Peter   174
Scolastica, abbess of St Benedict in Polignano   92
Scolastica, abbess of St Mary in Brindisi   177
Sculcula   20
Sculgola, abbey of St Matthew of   212 n.103 (ch. 2)
seals   67, 140, 157, 189, 220 n.43 (ch. 3)
sebastos, see Michael Palaiologos
Segelgarda, countess of Catanzaro   37, 92, 99–100, 130
Sele, river   19
senescalci
    Gravina   92
    Marsico   157
    Principato   161
    royal   86, 87, 106, 165, 172
    Tricarico   149
seneschal, *see senescalci*
Sepino   158
    castrum   69–70
    lordhsip (*see* Hugh of Molise, lord of Sepino)
    St Cristina, church   97
Sergius, duke of Sorrento   220 n.50 (ch. 3)
Sergius [VII], duke of Naples   30, 31, 34
Serracapriola   156
Serracapriola, *castellum*   160
Serra San Bruno e Santi Stefano, La certosa di, *see* Bosco, abbey of St Stephen del
Serre, *castrum*   19
Sessa   173
Sessola   38
S. Fele   82
S. Germano   68, 83, 177
S. Giovanni in Galdo   38
Sibylla, countess of Lesina   155, 156
Sibylla, countess of Tricarico   149

Sibylla of Aquino 153
Sibylla of Burgundy 35
Sica, countess of Civitate 149–50
Sichelgaita of Salerno 55, 94
Sicily 9, 13, 14, 29, 31, 32, 38, 42, 46, 56, 57, 63, 68, 76, 85, 87, 88, 91, 93, 99, 100, 115, 117, 118, 120, 125, 142, 156, 157, 165, 179–80, 183–4
Sika, *see* Sichelgaita of Salerno
Sila, forest 121
Silva Marca 47
Simon [of Policastro], count 179
Simon, count of Monte Sant'Angelo in Gargano 32, *see also* Simon of Policastro
Simon, count of Sangro 30, 67, 81, 111–12, 118, 122, 124, 129
Simon, prince, son of Roger II 85, 87–9
Simon, prince of Capua 35
   mother of 35
Simon del Vasto, *see* Simon of Policastro
Simon of Balvano 162
Simon of Matera 176
Simon of Mileto, 'count' 85, 88
Simon of Molise 160–1
Simon of Molise, count of Boiano (d. 1117) 19, 25
Simon of Policastro, count 32, 63, 65, 68, 70, 72, 89, 120
Simon of Tivilla 214 n.150 (ch. 2)
Simon the seneschal 86, 87, 106
Sini, river 43
Siponto, St Leonard, abbey 33, 135, 155, 170
S. Lorenzo, castrum 103
S. Magno sul Calore 163
S. Martino 145
Solofra 146
Solopaca 94
sons of Amicus, family 24, 25, 41, 51, 64–5, 155
sons of Borell, *see* Borells
Sora
   judges 174
   St Dominic, abbey 174
Spinazzola 54
Spoleto, duchy 22, 23, 51, 52
Squillace 53
   bishopric 25

counts 38, 100, 118 (*see also* Alfonso, count of Squillace; Everard, count of Squillace)
county 165
S. Quirico 156
S. Salvarore, *casale* 137
SS. Elias and Anastasius in Val Sinni, monastery of 118
S. Severino 45
   castrum 90, 119
   family 44–5, 55, 94–5, 118, 121, 147, 157, 213 n.145 (ch. 2)
   lordship 94, 118–19
S. Severo, bishopric 236 n.143 (ch. 6)
Stephanie, countess of Conza 84
Stephanie, countess of Gravina 92
Stephen, admiral 85
Stephen, bishop of Mileto 223 n.34 (ch. 4)
Stephen, king of England 228 n.44 (ch. 5)
Stephen of Perche 114, 115, 119–22, 125–7, 129, 130
Stephen the admiral (emir) 86
Stilo 100
   region 117
strategos/stratigotus 41, 42, 75, 100, 141–2, 161, 212 n.116 (ch. 2)
   Auletta 46
   Avellino 141–2
   S. Caterina dello Ionio 100
   Stilo 100
Suessa 71–2
Sylvester, count of Marsico 43, 45, 55, 57, 60, 74–5, 84, 85, 87, 90, 91, 98–9, 102, 110, 156, 179, 185
Sylvester, marquis of Gravina 80
Syria 126–7, 128

Tanagro, river 46
Tancred of Conversano 17, 22, 28–30
Tancred of Lecce 72, 87–9, 159, 165, 169
   admiral of the fleet 168, 171
   count of Lecce (and Montescaglioso) 151–4, 161, 174–6
   king of Sicily 137, 138, 156, 181, 186, 188, 190
Tancred of Say, count of Gravina 150–1
Tancred of S. Fele 82
Taormina 123, 125
   castellum 125

Taranto   29, 91–3
   gulf   21, 43, 68–9, 73, 154
   principality   87–8, 120, 152–3
Tarentinus the judge   122, 130
Tarsia   35, 82
Taurasi   143
   lordship (*see* Matthew of Castelvetere; Roger of Castelvetere)
Taverna   25, 92
Tavoliere delle Puglie, *see* Capitanata
Teano   71–2, 173
   bishopric   173, 175
Teggiano   45
Telese   94
   bishops   147
tenant-farmers   15, 146, 233 n.79 (ch. 6)
tenure, *see also feuda*
   a domino Rege   112, 120, 160
   in demanio   40, 44, 45, 51, 54, 60, 66, 71, 76, 94, 95, 104, 152, 155, 157, 163, 173, 180
   in servitio   44–6, 49, 51, 69, 71, 76, 95, 104, 122, 156, 163
Terlizzi   158
   St Nicholas, church   40–1
Termini [Imerese]   88
Terracina   88
Terra Barese, *see* Bari
Terra di Lavoro   9, 17, 20, 32, 34, 37, 39, 62, 68, 69, 86, 91–3, 95, 96, 100, 101, 105, 106, 108–9, 113, 114, 120, 131, 138, 139, 141, 142, 145, 148, 169, 173, 175, 176, 183, *see also* Capua; principality
Terra Maggiore, abbey   39
Terrae Sancti Benedicti, *see* Montecassino, abbey
Terra d'Abruzzo *see* Abruzzo
Theodinus, count of Sangro   23, 30, 38, 112
Theodora, countess of Gravina   132, 150–1
Theodora, daughter of Alfanus of Camerota   114
Theodore Batatzes   239 n.15 (ch. 7)
Thessaloniki, capture   171
Thiron-Gardais   117
Thomas, marquis   33
Thomas of Balvano   162
Thomas of Carbonara   144

Thomas of Catanzaro   92
Thomas of Frassineto   137
Thomas Sarracenus   81
timber rights   113, 151, 156
title interchangeability   20, 21
Tolve   44
Toro   38
Torremaggiore, *see* Terra Maggiore
Tortorella   46
Traetto   82, 108–9, 151
Tramutola, abbey of St Peter of   45–6, 157
Trani   33, 44, 73, 76
Trasaco, church of St Cesidius of   112
treaties
   Benevento (1156) (*see* Benevento, treaty)
   Mignano (1139) (*see* Mignano, treaty)
   Venice (1177) (*see* Venice, treaty)
   w. Constantinople (1156)   83, 89, 93–4
   w. Count of Barcelona (1128)   228 n.59 (ch. 5)
   w. Robert [II] Bassunvilla (c. 1169) 134
Tremiti, abbey of Santa Maria a Mare in   20, 60, 74, 98, 154
Trevico, lordship   60, 67, 112, 140, 169
Tricarico   44
   counts   57, 105 (*see also* Geoffrey, count of Tricarico; James, count of Tricarico; Roger [I], count of Tricarico; Roger [II] of Lauro; Sibylla, countess of Tricarico)
   county   44, 75, 76, 96, 148–9, 179, 180
Trigno, river   23, 24
Tripoli   53
Trivento   35, 38, 158
   bishopric   157 (*see also* Rao, bishop of Trivento)
Troia   30, 33–5, 70, 121
   St Nicholas, abbey   176
Trugisius of S. Severino   45
Tudela, lordship   81, 115, 222 n.9 (ch. 4)
Turgisius of Crypta, *see* Turgisius of Grottaminarda (Grutta)
Turgisius of Grottaminarda (Grutta)   162–3
Turi   137

Tusciano   19
Tustinus, bishop of Mazara   223 n.34 (ch. 4)
Tyrilla   18
Tyrrhenian front   29, 63, 93, 102

Umfridus, abbot of *Terra Maggiore*   39, 163
Umfridus, 'count' of Calvi   24
Umfridus of Montescaglioso   21
Ursus, bishop-elect of Gravina   54

Val Demone, monastery of St Philip in   118
Valione, river   150
Vallata   60, 112, 140
Vallesurda, church of St Nicholas in   157
Vallo di Diano   45, 46, 157
Valva   22, 23
Varano   154, 156
  river   155
Vassunvilla   217 n.220 (ch. 2)
Venafro   38, 108, 158, 160
Venice, treaty   169
Venosa, abbey of the Most Holy Trinity of   14, 40-1, 43, 61, 144-5, 156, 174
Ventosa, *casale*   146
Veroli   103
Via Appia   71, 109, 221 n.77 (ch. 3)
Viara   163
Vice-chancellor, *see* Matthew the notary; Walter Ophamil
vice comes   142
Vico   156
vicus   146
Vieste   64, 155, 170
Viggiano   116
Villanova del Battista, *see* Pulcarino
Vizzini   117
Volturno, abbey of St Vincent on   23, 101
Volturno, river   31

Walter, abbot of St Lawrence of Aversa   37, 40
Walter, archbishop of Palermo, vice-chancellor   142-3, 167, 170

Walter of Moac   184
Walter of Salisbury, sheriff of Wiltshire   228 n.44 (ch. 5)
Walter Ophamil, archbishop of Palermo   167, 170
Walter son of Amicus, count of Lesina   155
Welforum, *Historia*   227 n.23 (ch. 5)
Western empire   6, 52, 67, 102
Wibald of Corvey   6
William, abbot of Piedimonti   145-6
William, abbot of St Sophia in Benevento   159, 177
William, archbishop of Salerno   36, 54
William, bishop of Avellino   175
William, count of Lesina   36, 74, 75, 88-9
William, count of Loritello   20, 33, 35, 49, 60
William, count of Marsico   99, 111, 114, 156-7, 183
William, duke of Apulia   13, 18, 19
William, lord of Montescaglioso   21
William I, king of Sicily   32, 37, 59, 61, 64, 65, 72, 76, 80-3, 88, 94, 96, 97, 99, 100, 103, 114, 180
William [I], count of Principato   24
William II, king of Sicily   62, 105, 115, 118, 125-6, 129, 132, 156, 167, 169, 170, 175, 177, 181, 183
William [II], count of Principato   19
William [III], count of Principato   43, 46, 75, 88
William [IV], count of Principato   162
William Englisus, daughters   160
William of Craon   85
William of Gesualdo   117
William of Hauteville, lord of Biccari   20
William of Lauro, count of Caserta   138, 147, 176
William of S. Severino   89, 95, 118-19, 122, 126, 157, 163
William of Tyre   6

Yahya, sultan (Zirid)   202 n.2 (ch. 1)
Ylaria Cervus   160

www.ingramcontent.com/pod-product-compliance
Lightning Source LLC
Chambersburg PA
CBHW072127290426
44111CB00012B/1810